A Five-Year Study of the First Edition of the Core-Plus Mathematics Curriculum

a volume in
Research in Mathematics Education

Series Editor:
Barbara J. Dougherty, *Iowa State University*

Research in Mathematics Education

Barbara J. Dougherty, Series Editor

A Five-Year Study of the First Edition of the Core-Plus Mathematics Curriculum (2010)
by Harold L. Schoen, Steven W. Ziebarth, Christian R. Hirsch, and Allison BrckaLorenz

The Classification of Quadrilaterals: A Study in Definition (2008)
by Zalman Usiskin

A Decade of Middle School Mathematics Curriculum Implementation: Lessons Learned from the Show-Me Project (2008)
edited by Margaret R. Meyer and Cynthia W. Langrall

The History of the Geometry Curriculum in the United States (2008)
by Nathalie Sinclair

Mathematics Curriculum in Pacific Rim Countries—China, Japan, Korea, and Singapore: Proceedings of a Conference (2008)
edited by Zalman Usiskin and Edwin Willmore

The Intended Mathematics Curriculum as Represented in State-Level Curriculum Standards (2006)
edited by Barbara Reys

A Five-Year Study of the First Edition of the Core-Plus Mathematics Curriculum

by

Harold L. Schoen
University of Iowa

Steven W. Ziebarth
Western Michigan University

Christian R. Hirsch
Western Michigan University

and

Allison BrckaLorenz
Indiana University

Contributing Authors

Christopher S. Hlas
University of Wisconsin Eau Claire

Kristin Cebulla Thompson
University of Iowa

IAP

Information Age Publishing, Inc.
Charlotte, North Carolina • www.infoagepub.com

Library of Congress Cataloging-in-Publication Data

A five-year study of the first edition of the Core-Plus Mathematics curriculum
/edited by Harold L. Schoen, Steven W. Ziebarth, Christian R. Hirsh, and Allison BrckaLorenz.
p. cm.—(Research in mathematics education)
Includes bibliographical references.
ISBN 978-1-60752-414-4 (hardcover)—ISBN 978-1-60752-413-7 (pbk.)—
ISBN 978-1-60752-415-1 (e-book)
1. Mathematics—Study and teaching (Secondary)—United States—Evaluation.
2. Curriculum evaluation—United States. I. Schoen, Harold L. II. Ziebarth Steven W.
III. Hirsh, Christian R. IV. BrckaLorenz, Allison. V. Title: A five-year study of the first edition of the Core-Plus Mathematics curriculum.
QA13.F54 2010
510.71'273—dc22

2009053955

This volume is based on work supported in part by the National Science Foundation (NSF) under grants no. MDR-9255257, ESI-9618193, and ESI-0137718. Any opinions, findings, and conclusions or recommendations expressed in this material are those of the authors and do not necessarily reflect the views of the NSF.

Printed and bound by CPI Group (UK) Ltd, Croydon, CR0 4YY

CONTENTS

PREFACE

The longitudinal study reported in this volume adds to the body of scholarly work that focuses on the efficacy of *Standards*-based mathematics curricula, in this case, the Core-Plus Mathematics curriculum. Most other reported evaluations of this curriculum have studied the impact of unpublished field-test versions. Not only was the curriculum still under development at the time of those studies, but students and teachers were also relative novices at the use of a *Standards*-based curriculum. Those earlier studies were mainly 1 year or less in duration, although some field-test studies examined data collected over 3 years or more. Some schools in those studies used the Core-Plus Mathematics curriculum with all students as it was intended, but students in the comparisons were typically from schools that used two mathematics curricula, Core-Plus Mathematics and a conventional curriculum. Academic tracking may be a confounding variable in comparative studies of this type. (See Chapter 14 for a discussion of this difficulty that draws on results from the present study.)

At the beginning of the present study (Fall 1997), the three participating schools were just completing their fourth year of involvement in the Core-Plus Mathematics field test. Many of the teachers had participated in professional development programs that specifically prepared them to teach the curriculum. Many also had 1 to 3 years of prior experience teaching the curriculum. Virtually all high school students in each school used the Core-Plus Mathematics curriculum, and the feeder middle schools used a *Standards*-based curriculum as well. Except for those who transferred in or out of these schools during Grades 6 through 12, students in the study's sample had completed up to 7 years of *Standards*-based mathematics coursework by the end of their senior year. Some students in the study who were accelerated also completed AP Statistics and/or AP Calculus. Thus this may be the first study with all of the following characteristics:

- The study focused on fairly stable implementations of a published first edition of a high school *Standards*-based curriculum that was used by all students in each school in the study.
- Nearly all students in the study experienced up to 7 years of *Standards*-based mathematics curricula in middle school and high school.
- The study monitored students' mathematical achievement, beliefs, and attitudes for 4 years of high school and 1 year after.

This volume is divided into four main parts: Background; Yearly Patterns in Student Achievement; Attitudes, Beliefs, and Conceptions of Students; and Post-High School Survey, Individual Cases, and Perspectives. The four chapters (Chapters 1–4) in the Background section provide, respectively, a description of the curriculum and the process used to develop it, a review of related scholarly literature to set a research context for the study, a description of the method and procedures used in the study, and, finally, the beliefs and implementation practices of the teachers of the *Standards*-based curriculum in the three participating schools.

In the second section, Yearly Patterns in Student Achievement (Chapters 5–8), one chapter each is dedicated to describing student achievement in the 4 high school years of the study. The focus of the achievement measures varied from year to year. In the first year, students completed a standardized test of quantitative thinking at the beginning, as a baseline achievement measure, and in equivalent form at the end of the year. Students also completed a researcher-developed posttest of objectives across the four content strands of the curriculum, and selected students were interviewed using problems from across the strands. In the second year, both the written test and the interview problems focused on algebra and functions. Mathematical literacy was the focus in the third year. The fourth-year focus was advanced mathematics and reasoning and proof. In order to enrich the description each year, statistical comparisons were made and interpreted between schools, gender groups, and groups defined by level of entering mathematical achievement. Some comparisons between the achievement of students in this study and outside groups of students were also provided when appropriate data were available.

The third section of the volume, Attitudes, Beliefs, and Conceptions of Students, contains two chapters (9 and 10). Specific attitudes of students about Courses 1 and 2 are described in the first of these chapters. The second chapter describes students' more general beliefs about mathematics and their conceptions of mathematics. The affective survey instrument used in the third and fourth years of the study measures the extent to which students' conceptions of mathematics and how it is learned agree with the conceptions that underlie a *Standards*-based curriculum. The instrument includes such conceptions as the connected structure of mathematics, its usefulness, its changing nature, the importance of conceptual understanding and problem solving, and the extent to which students can monitor their own work. Again, statistical analyses in these two chapters included comparisons by school, gender, and entering mathematical achievement level.

The fourth section, Post-High School Survey, Individual Cases, and Perspectives, extends and adds texture to the portrait of achievement and affective patterns reported in previous chapters. The section's first chapter, Chapter 11, describes the results of a post-high school survey administered to target students during their first year after high school. The results focus mainly on the mathematics courses that students took in college and the grades that they earned. In addition, students' reflections, after their first college semester, on the strengths and weaknesses of their high school mathematics program are discussed. Chapter 12 details the experiences of 3 students, 1 from each school, across the 5 years of the study as examples of individual student variability over time within the summary group results presented in the previous chapters. During the study, a local controversy about the use of a *Standards*-based curriculum developed in one school and is elaborated in Chapter 13. While some resistance may be expected when any nonconventional curriculum materials or teaching approaches are adopted, this controversy and its impact on teachers and students appears to be exacerbated by the current, Internet-aided "math wars." The final chapter (14) begins with a summary and discussion from a longitudinal perspective of the information and insights provided by the results of the study. Further interpretations are discussed concerning the gender results, teacher differences and the related issues of academic tracking, the effect of local controversy about *Standards*-based curricula, and the implications of this study for the second edition of the curriculum.

Readers should be aware that this longitudinal study was conducted by members of the Core-Plus Mathematics Project from 1997 through 2002 with the guidance of an outside advisory group. The evaluation was under the codirection of the first and second authors with the assistance of the fourth author. The third author is the principal investigator of the Core-Plus Mathematics Project. Beginning in 2002, the second author directed the formative evaluation of the second edition of the curriculum, copyrighted 2008, 2009, and 2010, which the results of the reported study helped to inform in ways that are discussed in the last chapter of this volume.

As a development and research endeavor, the Core-Plus Mathematics Project was committed to developing a 4-year, *Standards*-based high school mathematics curriculum for all students, documenting its effectiveness for stakeholders who mainly define effectiveness in terms of student achievement when compared to conventional curricula, and ensuring that the curriculum was used widely enough to have a significant impact in the nation's schools. For the project evaluators, these pressing concerns necessarily took precedence over conducting knowledge-building research, although in some cases project members encouraged or mentored the conduct of such studies by others. In fact, the urgent press of other project work delayed the publication of this book, but we believe it will still be useful and informative to the mathematics education professionals and practitioners.

In this volume, the main results are presented and discussed in the body of the chapters. To make the reading less daunting, more extensive data tables and statistical tests are relegated to chapter appendices. Item data and all unpublished testing instruments are available for reference online (http://www.wmich.edu/cpmp/evaluation.html) as a baseline of instruments and data for future curriculum evaluators or users who may wish to compare results of new groups of students to those in this study on common tests or surveys. Taken together, this volume, the supplement at the project website, and the first edition *Core-Plus Mathematics* materials serve as a fairly complete description of the nature and impact of an exemplar of first edition *Standards*-based high school mathematics curricula as it existed and was implemented with all students in three schools around the turn of the twenty-first century.

ACKNOWLEDGMENTS

The longitudinal study of the efficacy of the first edition of Core-Plus Mathematics was funded through a grant from the National Science Foundation (NSF). We express our appreciation to NSF and, in particular, to our program officer, John Bradley, for his commitment to the importance of curriculum evaluation and for his ongoing support and input.

The authors would also like to thank the members of the longitudinal study advisory group, Diana Lambdin, of Indiana University, Ed Silver, of the University of Michigan, and Norman Webb, of the University of Wisconsin, for their valuable advice as this study unfolded. Diana, Ed, and Norm advised the project at each step—the design and planning, choice of instruments, analysis, and reporting. Their reactions to our annual progress reports during the study stimulated our thinking and helped us make valuable adjustments in our procedures for the following year. Their continued support of our efforts was an invaluable motivation throughout the project.

We are also greatly indebted to the teachers, administrators, and students of the three schools in this study. Their agreement to participate in this study was essential. Their exceptionally high level of cooperation and openness throughout the study enriched the quality of the data and the knowledge that the study generated.

Our research assistants during the project also deserve our sincere thanks for all that they did to make the study a reality—making phone calls to follow up on written surveys, gathering and verifying demographic data, transcribing mountains of interviews and observations, helping to make sense of the various sets of data, drafting sections of chapters, and responding to later chapter drafts, to name a few of the invaluable tasks these assistants performed. At the University of Iowa, in addition to coauthor Allison BrckaLorenz, Christopher Hlas and Kristin Cebulla Thompson were particularly helpful in the manuscript preparation process. The other assistants at the University included Kathy Rueter, Christine Sprecher, Cos Fi, Kelly Finn, and Bettie Truitt. At Western Michigan University, the assistants on the project were Sheila Eisenhauer, Anna Kruizenga, Kelly MacLean, Marcia Weinhold, Canace Rauh, and Ashley Wiersma.

A special thanks is extended to Hope Smith. Her help in preparing the final manuscript of this volume was invaluable and greatly appreciated.

We would also like to thank Cathy Kern, Kathy Wright, and Angie Reiter for their diligent work on the rather daunting clerical demands of the study, including the large and sometimes rushed copying and mailing tasks required to get the various instruments to the schools in a timely fashion, the processing and organizing of the completed instruments when they were returned, following up with lead teachers at the schools as needed to be sure all data were returned, ordering office supplies, and the list goes on and on. Finally, we would like to acknowledge Teri Ziebarth for overseeing the budget of the project and making all travel arrangements at Western Michigan University.

PART I

BACKGROUND

CHAPTER 1

THE CORE-PLUS MATHEMATICS CURRICULUM DESIGN AND DEVELOPMENT

The Core-Plus Mathematics Project (CPMP) was funded by the National Science Foundation (NSF) in 1992 to develop and evaluate a comprehensive 3-year high school mathematics curriculum reflecting content, instruction, and assessment recommendations in the *Curriculum and Evaluation Standards for School Mathematics* (National Council of Teachers of Mathematics [NCTM], 1989). As part of the 5-year award (MDR-9255257), CPMP also developed four prototype units for a fourth-year course that would serve as a transition to college mathematics. In 1997, the NSF awarded a second 5-year grant (ESI-9618193) to CPMP to develop and evaluate a complete fourth-year course to continue the preparation of students for college mathematics and to conduct a longitudinal summative evaluation of the complete first edition of the 4-year curriculum published by Everyday Learning and subsequently by Glencoe/McGraw-Hill. The published 4-year curriculum was titled *Contemporary Mathematics in Context: A Unified Approach* (Coxford et al., 1997, 1998, 1999; Coxford et al., 2001).

This chapter provides an overview of the goals and research-based design and development of the first edition of the Core-Plus Mathematics curriculum. The chapter draws substantially on a chapter by Fey and

A Five-Year Study of the First Edition of the Core-Plus Mathematics Curriculum, pp. 3–21

Hirsch (2007) in *Perspectives on the Design and Development of School Mathematics Curricula* (Hirsch, 2007). The second chapter summarizes the body of research on *Standards*-based curricula conducted over the last 15 years with emphasis on prior studies of the field-test version of the Core-Plus Mathematics curriculum. The remainder of the volume describes the methodology, tools, findings, and implications of a 5-year longitudinal study of students who completed an NSF-funded *Standards*-based middle school mathematics program, 3 or 4 years of the first edition of the Core-Plus Mathematics program, and, in some cases, Advanced Placement Calculus and/or Advanced Placement Statistics.

In the last chapter of this volume (Chapter 14), the study's results are summarized and its implications are discussed. In that chapter, design and development issues from Chapter 1 are revisited from the perspective of the second edition of the Core-Plus Mathematics curriculum, funded by the NSF in 2002 (ESI-0137718). The focus in that discussion is on how the second edition's design and development were informed by the findings of the present study and on the major changes from the first to the second edition.

PROJECT GOALS

From the outset, the goals of the CPMP development team were to create a high school curriculum that would enable schools to successfully negotiate many of the difficult challenges of curricular reform outlined in *Everybody Counts* (National Research Council, 1989), particularly

- expanding the traditional vision of school mathematics that offered minimal mathematics for the majority and advanced mathematics for a few in order to provide a significant core of important mathematics for all students;
- retaining the goal of offering a strong preparation for future studies in mathematics and its applications, but increasing attention to mathematical topics that are relevant to students' present and future needs;
- transforming the perception of mathematics as a fixed body of arbitrary rules to an active science of patterns;
- shifting the instructional emphasis on paper-and-pencil calculations and manipulations to full use of calculators and computers.

By way of addressing these broad goals, the CPMP team committed to developing and evaluating a four-course curriculum beginning with a 3-

year core sequence of broadly useful mathematics for all students. The goal of the core courses was to prepare students for success in college, in careers, and in daily life in contemporary society. Recognizing the importance of the enrollment of college-bound students in a mathematics course during their senior year and the increasing quantitative demands of undergraduate programs outside of mathematics, the physical sciences, and engineering, the development team also committed to developing a flexible fourth-year course that builds on the 3-year core program and continues the preparation of students for success in college. The remainder of this chapter is a description of the design principles and development process that led to the product of the development team's efforts, the first edition of the Core-Plus Mathematics curriculum.

DESIGN PRINCIPLES

The creation of the Core-Plus Mathematics curriculum and instructional materials was guided by design principles derived from the shared understanding of the development team and their advisors about high school mathematics and effective approaches to its teaching and learning. There are at least five dimensions of the design.

Mathematical Content

The development of the Core-Plus Mathematics curriculum began with the belief that the essence of mathematics is its concepts and reasoning methods for making sense of observations and experiences in the real world involving data, change, shape, enumeration, and chance. Concepts like similarity, expressions and equations, distributions, networks, and algorithms help to describe and analyze visual, numeric, and stochastic patterns. Operators like transformations, functions, logical inference rules, and matrices help to extend patterns and solve problems. This view of mathematics as a broadly useful subject led to several important design principles that shaped the scope and sequence of mathematical topics in the Core-Plus Mathematics curriculum:

- The curriculum should include major content strands that develop concepts and skills in algebra and functions, statistics and probability, geometry and trigonometry, and discrete mathematics.
- In addition to learning specific facts, principles, and procedures associated with the core content strands, the curriculum should pay explicit attention to developing students' mathematical habits of

mind (Cuoco, Goldenberg, & Mark, 1996), such as visualizing, searching for and explaining patterns, thinking recursively, making and testing conjectures, justifying and proving, and optimizing.

- The curriculum should explicitly develop students' understanding and skill in the use of mathematical modeling, including the processes of data collection, representation, interpretation, prediction, and simulation.

To the extent feasible within educational policy constraints in typical school settings, these principles guided the development of the mathematical content in the 4-year curriculum.

Curriculum Sequence and Organization

Choosing the mathematical concepts and skills to be developed was an important first step in mapping the curriculum framework. Grade placement and ordering of the mathematical topics posed another challenge. The development team's work in this regard was guided by the following principles:

- The curriculum should include significant and broadly useful topics from each content strand in each year of the program.
- Topics from the separate content strands should be developed in coherent, focused units that exploit useful connections to the other strands.
- The mathematical content in each year of the curriculum should reflect judgments of what would be most important for students to know if that was to be their last formal experience in school mathematics.

Commitment to these curriculum sequence and organization principles led to a program that treats and connects each main content strand in each year. Furthermore, in a departure from long-standing curricular traditions, topics are placed where they seem most natural and important rather than where they have "always been." For instance, formal algebraic symbol manipulation is gradually built up over all 4 years of the curriculum instead of being concentrated in the first and third high school years. More complex manipulative skills are delayed to a point later in the curriculum when they can be studied intensively by students who will need them in future mathematical work. Formal logical inference and geometric proof developed "semilocally" occur somewhat later than tradition would dictate, although informal reasoning and the justification of results occur earlier and in more pervasive ways than in conventional U.S. curricula. Similarly, topics such as data analysis, recursion, geometric transformations (including coordinate representations), matrices, and simulation (Monte Carlo) methods occur earlier and more pervasively than in more traditional curricula.

The Role of Technology

Two of the underlying assumptions of the NCTM standards for Grades 9–12 were (1) graphing calculators would be available to all students at all times, and (2) a computer would be available in every classroom for demonstration purposes and all students would have access to computers for individual work (NCTM, 1989, p. 124). At the outset of the development of the Core-Plus Mathematics curriculum, field-test teachers cautioned against making strong assumptions about access to computers. Thus the first edition of the curriculum was designed with an assumption that students would have ready access only to graphing calculators. However, the incorporation of graphing calculators in the curriculum materials enabled multiple representations of mathematical ideas and supported a variety of robust strategies for mathematical thinking and quantitative problem solving.

To some extent, judgments about the reasonable impact of calculator and computer tools were influenced by the time frame for intended implementation of the curriculum. The first edition curriculum design and development did not assume ready access to emerging interactive geometry tools or computer algebra systems. However, in the revision of the Core-Plus Mathematics curriculum begun with support from NSF in 2002 and described in Chapter 14, a more significant commitment was made to the use of interactive geometry software, spreadsheets, computer algebra systems, data analysis and simulation software, and tools for exploratory work in graph theory. Since the second edition is designed for use in schools beginning in 2008, about 10 years after the first edition made its appearance, more robust assumptions about technology seemed warranted.

Instructional Design

Traditional conceptions of mathematics education assign to textbooks the responsibility for clear and concise explanations of mathematical ideas and procedures, with illustrative examples with solutions to guide students' work on subsequent practice exercises. Of course, this model for curriculum materials is based on a conception of direct instruction that assigns the same role to teachers. Imaginative teachers have always enhanced textbook presentations by designing lessons that engage students more actively in exploration and discovery of mathematical principles—believing that students learn and remember best those ideas that they have made sense of for themselves.

Design and development of the Core-Plus Mathematics curriculum materials were based on an explicit intention to support problem-based, student-centered classroom activity shaped by current theory and research on teaching and learning available at the time, that is, in the early to mid-1990s. More up-to-date related references are provided in later chapters, especially in Chapter 2. In the development of materials for individual units and lessons, the aim was to implement the following instructional principles:

- School mathematics is best learned and understood as an active science of patterns involving quantity and change, shape and motion, data and chance, and enumeration and algorithms (Steen, 1990).
- Any introduction of new mathematics will be most effective if the ideas and techniques appear in problem contexts that students find engaging and that connect to their prior knowledge. Authentic applied problems are especially useful contexts for learning, but significant pure mathematical problems are often useful also (Hiebert et al., 1996).
- Effective mathematics instruction frequently engages students in collaborative small-group investigations of problem situations that encourage student-to-student dialogue, followed by teacher-led whole-group summarizing activities that lead to analysis, abstraction, and further application of underlying mathematical ideas (Cobb, 1995; Davidson & Kroll, 1991). There is also evidence that small-group collaborative learning encourages a range of social skills conducive to the learning styles of student groups who are currently underrepresented in mathematics (Oakes, 1990).
- Students should be regularly involved in mathematical activities like searching for and explaining patterns, making and verifying conjectures, generalizing, applying, proving, and reflecting on the process (Freudenthal, 1983; Gravemeijer, 1990).

Commitment to these instructional design principles led to the development of curriculum materials that are intended to support a modified *launch–explore–summarize* model. For each lesson, an introductory problem situation provides a context for the class investigation, and it is used for initial discussion and informal assessment involving the teacher and the whole class. Then students collaborate in small groups to solve short sequences of selected problems and to summarize their findings in response to several post-investigation questions that are discussed with the teacher and the whole class. Homework tasks following the lessons are designed to engage students in applying, organizing, reflecting on, and extending their evolving mathematical understanding.

The instructional model for which Core-Plus Mathematics materials are written has led to the creation of student text material that is a thoughtfully constructed and empirically tested sequence of problems, not an archive of results and illustrative, worked examples. The investigations often involve hands-on experiments, data analysis and modeling, and technology-based exploration of patterns. In order to accommodate the learning needs of all students, especially in Courses 1 through 3, most investigations and sequences of investigations are constructed so that the entry point is familiar and concrete to students—usually more verbal than symbolic. Development of robust concept images (Tall, 1991) precede formal definitions that often appear at the end of an investigation or lesson. Similarly, use of symbols is delayed and developed gradually, with the symbols and symbolic operations drawing meaning from the earlier, more concrete settings. All students, therefore, learn from the same curriculum materials. Of course, not all students reach the same level of formal mathematical sophistication, with some students and classes going more deeply into the content via extension problems and optional investigations or lessons.

The following examples may provide a feel for the content and instructional approach. An introductory lesson on the geometry of three-dimensional shapes begins with an experiment in which students test the load-bearing capacity of columns with bases of constant perimeter but varying shapes. After collecting and organizing experimental data, students look for a numerical pattern relating the number of sides in the polygonal base to column load-bearing capacity. The lesson makes the important point that geometric form and function are closely related, and it also connects geometric properties to algebraic representations and numerical patterns.

In another early unit, students conduct experiments that simulate bungee jumping and analyze patterns in the relation between jumper weight and bungee cord stretch as a prelude to the study of algebraic expressions and equations. In another investigation, they explore patterns in gender distribution of juries and multi-child families as an introductory context for the concepts and techniques of probability and statistics. In a Course 2 unit, they study patterns in computer graphic images and then the related ideas of coordinate geometry, transformations, congruence, and similarity. An analysis of patterns in transportation and communication networks in Course 2 leads to important concepts in graph theory that are widely used in computer and management sciences.

Introductory investigations like those described above are always accompanied by opportunities for students to analyze and abstract underlying mathematical structures that can be applied in other contexts and that, themselves, often are the subject of further investigations. Later investigations in the same or related content strands go on to develop the mathematical ideas in more formal and symbolic directions. The intent is for the materials and instructional approach to provide students with both access and challenge. All students become engaged in significant mathematical ideas and methods that are developed in ways that are inquiry-oriented and initially both concrete and flexible enough to allow access to students with minimal mathematical interest and aptitude and ultimately rich and formal enough to challenge students with high levels of mathematical aptitude. The extent to which this goal is met in practice is an important focus of the longitudinal study reported in this volume.

Assessment Principles

Assessing what students know and are able to do is an integral part of the curriculum's instructional model. There are opportunities for assessment in each phase of the instructional cycle. First, Think About This Situation questions in the lesson launch allow teachers to assess the prior knowledge that students bring to investigation of the new topic. Next, while students collaborate in small groups to explore new ideas and solve problems, teachers are able to monitor the group work and see where students are gaining insights or experiencing difficulties. An end-of-investigation Checkpoint provides explicit questions designed to guide a whole-class summary of investigation results and offers opportunity to further check student progress and to formalize class agreement on important mathematical ideas and methods. The summarizing questions are followed by On Your Own problems that provide individual students feedback on their understanding of the new material.

Since the student text is not a reference book of complete results (there are no answers in the student text for investigation or homework problems), students are prompted in several ways to construct their own summaries of important ideas and to record them in a mathematical toolkit journal that evolves over time. This record of students' thinking and understanding supplies them and their teachers with another useful tool to monitor the progress of their learning.

In addition to support for continual monitoring of students' progress during instruction, materials are provided in print and electronic formats for teachers to use or adapt as quizzes, unit examinations, project and take-home assessments, and midterm and final assessments. These assessment materials are designed to measure the mathematical content, processes, and habits of mind that are valued in the curriculum. In addition, extra symbolic skill practice and preparation for high stakes standardized tests are provided as supplements to the curriculum and assessment materials.

DEVELOPMENT PROCESS AND PRODUCT

The Core-Plus Mathematics curriculum was developed in consultation with an international advisory board, mathematicians, instructional specialists with expertise in equity and access issues, and classroom teachers. The overall scheme of curriculum development was similar in many respects to the iterative process outlined in the literature of design research (Design-Based Research Collective, 2003), design experiments (Brown, 1992; Collins, 1992), developmental research (Gravemeijer, 1994), and engineering research (Burkhardt & Schoenfeld, 2003). Each course was the product of a 4-year research, development, and evaluation process. After a year of initial development with local trials, the pilot version of each course was tested in 19 Michigan high schools. During this pilot year, CPMP teachers in those schools provided extensive feedback to the authors by noting what worked and what was in need of revision. In addition, students in the Core-Plus Mathematics classes were pretested at the beginning of Course 1 and posttested at the end of Course 1 and at the end of each course thereafter. The needed revisions identified by pilot teachers' annotated units and focus group meeting comments and by students' assessment results were made promptly so that a revised, field-test version was ready for trials during the following school year.

The third year of development was the beginning of the national field test, conducted over 4 years in 36 schools in 11 states—Alaska, California, Colorado, Georgia, Idaho, Iowa, Kentucky, Michigan, Ohio, South Carolina, and Texas. A broad cross-section of students from urban, suburban, and rural communities with ethnic and cultural diversity was represented. Field-test schools were encouraged to include students in each course with a wide range of achievement and interest in mathematics and, where possible, to group students heterogeneously. Limitations at each site did not always make this possible. Evaluative data, including evaluators' field notes, teacher annotated units, and input from focus group meetings with field-test teachers, were used by the authors to make further revisions in the materials before they were finally published for wide use. The

Table 1.1. Timetable for the Development and Evaluation of the First Edition of the Core-Plus Mathematics Curriculum

	Course 1	*Course 2*	*Course 3*	*Course 4*	*Post-High School*
1992–1993	R & D				
1993–1994	Pilot Test	R & D			
1994–1995	Field Test	Pilot Test	R & D		
1995–1996	Refinement	Field Test	Pilot Test	R & D	
1996–1997	Published	Refinement	Field Test	R & D	
1997–1998	Longitudinal Study	Published	Refinement	Pilot Test	
1998–1999		Longitudinal Study	Published	Field Test	
1999–2000			Longitudinal Study	Refinement	
2000–2001				Published; Longitudinal Study	
2001–2002					Longitudinal Study

timetable for the cycle of development, formative evaluation, and revision of the curriculum is given in Table 1.1 above. The "longitudinal study" listed in the table is the focus of the present volume.

The First Edition of the Curriculum

To briefly synthesize some of the earlier description, in each year of the curriculum, mathematics is organized along interwoven strands of algebra and functions, geometry and trigonometry, statistics and probability, and discrete mathematics. Each of these strands is developed in focused units connected by common topics such as symmetry, functions, matrices, and data analysis and curve fitting. The strands also are connected across units by mathematical habits of mind such as visual thinking, recursive thinking, searching for and explaining patterns, making and checking conjectures, reasoning with multiple representations, and providing convincing arguments and proofs.

The choice of curriculum organization was influenced by the importance of connections among related concepts and procedures in developing deep understanding of mathematics (Skemp, 1987). This curriculum organization breaks down the artificial compartmentalization of traditional "layer cake" curricula in the United States and addresses weaknesses identified in the 1995 TIMSS (Third International Mathematics and Science Study) findings (Schmidt, McKnight, Cogan, Jakwerth, & Houang, 1999). In addition, developing mathematics each year along multiple strands capitalizes on the different interests and talents of students and helps students develop diverse mathematical insights (Hirsch & Coxford, 1997).

The following two tables provide an overview of the scope and sequence of the first edition of the 4-year Core-Plus Mathematics curriculum. Table 1.2 provides an overview of the scope and sequence of units in the first three courses. These courses are intended as core mathematics for all students.

Table 1.2. Unit Titles of the First Edition of the Core-Plus Mathematics Curriculum: Courses 1–3

Unit	*Course 1*		*Course 2*		*Course 3*
1	Patterns in Data		Matrix Models		Multiple-Variable Models
2	Patterns of Change		Patterns of Location, Shape, and Size		Modeling Public Opinion
3	Linear Models		Patterns of Association		Symbol Sense and Algebraic Reasoning
4	Graph Models		Power Models		Shapes and Geometric Reasoning
5	Patterns in Space and Visualization		Network Optimization		Patterns in Variation
6	Exponential Models		Geometric Form and Its Function		Families of Functions
7	Simulation Models		Patterns in Chance		Discrete Models of Change
Capstone	Planning a Benefits Carnival	**Capstone**	Forests, the Environment, and Mathematics	**Capstone**	Making the Best of It: Optimal Forms and Strategies

Table 1.3. Unit Titles of the First Edition of the Core-Plus Mathematics Curriculum: Course 4

Core Units	*Additional Units for Students Intending to Pursue Programs in:* *Mathematical, Physical, and Biological Sciences or Engineering*	*Social, Management, and Health Sciences or Humanities*
1 Rates of Change	6 Polynomial and Rational Functions	5 Binomial Distributions and Statistical Inference
2 Modeling Motion	7 Functions and Symbolic Reasoning	9 Informatics
3 Logarithmic Functions and Data Models	8 Space Geometry	10 Problem Solving with Algorithms and Spreadsheets
4 Counting Models		

Recognizing the need for college-bound students to enroll in a mathematics course during their senior year and the increasing quantitative demands of many undergraduate programs, the development team designed a flexible fourth-year course that builds on the 3-year core program and continues the preparation of students for success in college. Course 4 consists of a core of four units for all college-bound students, plus additional units. This course design enables teachers to organize classes that support further mathematical preparation for either calculus-based or non-calculus-based undergraduate programs (see Table 1.3 above). Descriptions of the key mathematical ideas by units in first-edition Courses 1–4 are provided in the Chapter 1 Appendix. Samples of the instructional materials themselves may be found at http://www.wmich.edu/cpmp/1stEdCurriculumMaterials.html

CHAPTER SUMMARY AND DISCUSSION

This chapter describes the goals, design principles, and development process used to produce the first edition of the Core-Plus Mathematics program. These goals, principles, and processes underlie the intended, written curriculum. In practice, most teachers interpret and adapt a written curriculum to suit their own style, values, and perceptions of their students' needs (cf. Remillard, Herbel-Eisenmann, & Lloyd, 2009). The ways in which individual teachers interpreted and transformed the intent of the Core-Plus Mathematics curriculum during this study are discussed in Chapter 4.

Since the late 1990s, many research studies of *Standards*-based curricula have been conducted. Reports of these are summarized in Chapter 2 with particular emphasis on studies that focused on the Core-Plus Mathematics curriculum. With few exceptions, students in these studies used an unpublished, field-test version of the curriculum. In Chapter 3, the methods and procedures used in this study are described. The study results are presented and interpreted in the remainder of this volume.

ACKNOWLEDGMENTS

The principal and coprincipal investigators of the Core-Plus Mathematics Project are Christian Hirsch (Western Michigan University), Arthur Coxford (University of Michigan), James Fey (University of Maryland), and Harold Schoen (University of Iowa). Collaborators included Gail Burrill (University of Wisconsin), Eric Hart (Maharishi University of Management), Brin Keller (Michigan State University), Beth Ritsema (Western Michigan University), Rebecca Walker (Grand Valley State University), Ann Watkins (California Sate University, Northridge), and Steven Ziebarth (Western Michigan University).

APPENDIX

1st Edition Units and Topics

CPMP Course 1 Units	
Unit 1	**Patterns in Data** develops student ability to make sense out of real-world data through use of graphical displays and summary statistics. *Topics include* distributions of data and their shapes, as displayed in number line plots, histograms, box plots, and stem-and-leaf plots; scatterplots and association; plots over time and trends; measures of center including mean, median, mode, and their properties; measures of variation including percentiles, interquartile range, mean absolute deviation, and their properties; transformations of data.
Unit 2	**Patterns of Change** develops student ability to recognize important patterns of change among variables and to represent those patterns using tables of numerical data, coordinate graphs, verbal descriptions, and symbolic rules. *Topics include* coordinate graphs, tables, algebraic formulas (rules), relationships between variables, linear functions, nonlinear functions, and *NOW-NEXT* recurrence relations.
Unit 3	**Linear Models** develops student confidence and skill in using linear functions to model and solve problems in situations that exhibit constant (or nearly constant) rate of change or slope. *Topics include* linear functions, slope of a line, rate of change, intercepts, the distributive property, linear equations (including $y = a + bx$ and *NOW-NEXT* forms), solving linear equations and inequalities, using linear equations to model given data, and determining best-fit lines for scatterplot data.

Appendix continues on next page.

APPENDIX CONTINUED

CPMP Course 1 Units	
Unit 4	**Graph Models** develops student ability to use vertex-edge graphs to represent and analyze real-world situations involving relationships among a finite number of elements, including scheduling, managing conflicts, and finding efficient routes. *Topics include* vertex-edge graph models, optimization, algorithmic problem solving, Euler circuits and paths, matrix representation of graphs, graph coloring, chromatic number, digraphs, and critical path analysis.
Unit 5	**Patterns in Space and Visualization** develops student visualization skills and an understanding of the properties of space-shapes including symmetry, area, and volume. *Topics include* two- and three-dimensional shapes, spatial visualization, perimeter, area, surface area, volume, the Pythagorean Theorem, polygons and their properties, symmetry, isometric transformations (reflections, rotations, translations, glide reflections), one-dimensional strip patterns, tilings of the plane, and the regular (Platonic) solids.
Unit 6	**Exponential Models** develops student ability to use exponential functions to model and solve problems in situations that exhibit exponential growth or decay. *Topics include* exponential growth, exponential functions, fractals, exponential decay, recursion, half-life, compound growth, finding equations to fit exponential patterns in data, and properties of exponents.
Unit 7	**Simulation Models** develops student confidence and skill in using simulation methods (particularly those involving the use of random numbers) to make sense of real-world situations involving chance. *Topics include* simulation, frequency tables and their histograms, random digit tables and random number generators, independent events, the Law of Large Numbers, and expected number of successes in a series of binomial trials.
Capstone	**Planning a Benefits Carnival**

CPMP Course 2 Units	
Unit 1	**Matrix Models** extends student ability to use matrices and matrix operations to represent and solve problems from a variety of real-world settings while connecting important mathematical ideas from several strands. *Topics include* matrix models in such areas as inventory control, social relations, archeology, recidivism, ecosystems, sports, tournament rankings, and Markov processes; matrix operations, including row sums, matrix addition, scalar multiplication, matrix multiplication, and matrix powers; properties of matrices; and matrix methods for solving systems of linear equations.
Unit 2	**Patterns of Location, Shape, and Size** develops student understanding of coordinate methods for representing and analyzing relations among geometric shapes, and for describing geometric change.

Appendix continues on next page.

Topics include modeling situations with coordinates, including computer-generated graphics; distance in the coordinate plane, midpoint of a segment, and slope; designing and programming algorithms; methods for solving systems of equations; coordinate and matrix models of isometric transformations (reflections, rotations, and translations) and of size transformations; and similarity.

Unit 3 **Patterns of Association** develops student understanding of the strength of association between two variables, how to measure the degree of the relation, and how to use this measure as a tool to create and interpret prediction lines for paired data.

Topics include rank correlation, Pearson's correlation coefficient, cause and effect related to correlation, impact of outliers on correlation, least squares linear models, the relation of correlation to linear models, and variability in prediction.

Unit 4 **Power Models** develops student ability to recognize data patterns that involve direct or inverse power variation, to construct and analyze those models and combinations such as quadratic models, and to apply those models to a variety of problems.

Topics include basic power models with rules of the form $y = ax^b$ and combinations of power models with other simple models; analysis of quadratic models and equations from tabular, graphic, and symbolic viewpoints; square root and cube root relations, and fractional power and radical expressions.

Unit 5 **Network Optimization** extends student ability to use vertex-edge graphs to represent and analyze real-world situations involving network optimization, including optimal spanning networks and shortest routes.

Topics include vertex-edge graph models, optimization, algorithmic problem solving, matrices, trees, minimal spanning trees, shortest paths, Hamiltonian circuits and paths, and Traveling Salesperson problems.

Unit 6 **Geometric Form and Its Function** develops student ability to model and analyze physical phenomena with triangles, quadrilaterals, and circles and to use these shapes to investigate trigonometric functions, angular velocity, and periodic change.

Topics include parallelogram linkages, pantographs, similarity, triangular linkages (with one side that can change length); sine, cosine, and tangent ratios, indirect measurement; angular velocity, transmission factor, linear velocity; periodic change, radian measure, period, amplitude, and graphs of trigonometric models of the form $y = A \sin (Bx)$ or $y = A \cos (Bx)$.

Unit 7 **Patterns in Chance** develops student ability to understand and visualize situations involving chance by using simulation and mathematical analysis to construct probability distributions.

Topics include probability distributions and their graphs, Multiplication Rule for Independent Events, waiting-time (or geometric) distributions, expected value, rare events, summation notation, and an introduction to the binomial distribution.

Capstone **Forests, the Environment, and Mathematics**

Appendix continues on next page.

APPENDIX CONTINUED

CPMP Course 3 Units	
Unit 1	**Multiple-Variable Models** develops student ability to construct and reason with linked quantitative variables and relations involving several variables and several constraints. *Topics include* formulas, including the Law of Sines and the Law of Cosines, relating several variables by a single equation; systems of equations with several dependent variables or constraints; patterns of change in one or more variables in response to changes in others; solution of systems of equations and inequalities; and linear programming.
Unit 2	**Modeling Public Opinion** develops student understanding of how public opinion can be measured. The situations analyzed include elections (where there are more than two choices) and sample surveys, including political polling. *Topics include* preferential voting, vote-analysis methods, Arrow's theorem, fairness in social decision making; surveys, sampling, sampling distributions, relationship between a sample and a population, confidence intervals, margin of error; and critical analysis of elections and surveys.
Unit 3	**Symbol Sense and Algebraic Reasoning** develops student ability to represent and draw inferences about algebraic relations and functions using symbolic expressions and manipulations. *Topics include* formalization of function concept, notation, domain, and range; use of polynomial, exponential, and rational expressions to model relations among quantitative variables; field properties of real numbers and their application to expression of algebraic relations in equivalent forms and to solution of equations and inequalities by methods including factoring and the quadratic formula, and algebraic proof.
Unit 4	**Shapes and Geometric Reasoning** introduces students to formal reasoning and deduction in geometric settings. *Topics include* inductive and deductive reasoning, counterexamples, the role of assumptions in proof; conclusions concerning supplementary and vertical angles and the angles formed by parallel lines and transversals; conditions insuring similarity and congruence of triangles and their application to quadrilaterals and other shapes; and necessary and sufficient conditions for parallelograms.
Unit 5	**Patterns in Variation** extends student understanding of the measurement of variation, develops student ability to use the normal distribution as a model of variation, and introduces students to the probability and statistical inference involved in the control charts used in industry for statistical process control. *Topics include* standard deviation and its properties, normal distribution and its relation to standard deviation, statistical process control, control charts, control limits, mutually exclusive events, and the Addition Rule of Probability.
Unit 6	**Families of Functions** reviews and extends student ability to recognize different function patterns in numerical and graphical data and to interpret and construct appropriate symbolic representations modeling those data patterns.

Appendix continues on next page.

Topics include review of linear, polynomial, exponential, rational, and trigonometric functions (including effects of parameters on numeric and graphic patterns) and construction of function rules for function tables and graphs that are transformations of basic types (translation, reflection, stretch).

Unit 7 **Discrete Models of Change** extends student ability to represent, analyze, and solve problems in situations involving sequential and recursive change.

Topics include iteration and recursion as tools to model and analyze sequential change in real-world contexts; arithmetic, geometric, and other sequences; arithmetic and geometric series; finite differences; linear and nonlinear recurrence relations; and function iteration, including graphical iteration and fixed points.

Capstone **Making the Best of It: Optimal Forms and Strategies**

The mathematical content and sequence of units in Course 4 allows considerable flexibility in tailoring a course to best prepare students for various undergraduate programs. For students intending to pursue programs in the *mathematical, physical, and biological sciences or engineering,* we recommend the following sequence of units:

Unit 1 → Unit 2 → Unit 3 → Unit 4 → Unit 6 → Unit 7 → Unit 8 → Unit 5, 9, or 10

For students intending to pursue programs in the social, management, and some of the health sciences or humanities, the following sequence of units is recommended:

Unit 1 → Unit 2 (reduced) → Unit 3 → Unit 4 (reduced) → Unit 5 → Unit 9 → Unit 10

The accompanying *Teacher's Guide* provides suggestions on how particular lessons in selected units can be omitted or streamlined without loss of continuity. Depending on time available, additional units of study can be selected based on student performance and interests.

CPMP Course 4 Units

Unit 1 **Rates of Change** develops student understanding of the fundamental concepts underlying calculus and their applications.

Topics include average and instantaneous rates of change, derivative at a point and derivative functions, accumulation of continuously varying quantities by estimation, the definite integral, and intuitive development of the fundamental theorem of calculus.

Unit 2 **Modeling Motion** develops student understanding of two-dimensional vectors and their use in modeling linear, circular, and other nonlinear motion.

Topics include concept of vector as a mathematical object used to model situations defined by magnitude and direction; equality of vectors, scalar multiples, opposite vectors, sum and difference vectors, position vectors and coordinates; and parametric equations for motion along a line and for motion of projectiles and objects in circular and elliptical orbits.

Unit 3 **Logarithmic Functions and Data Models** develops student understanding of logarithmic functions and their use in modeling and analyzing problem situations and data patterns.

Topics include inverses of functions; logarithmic functions and their relation to exponential functions, properties of logarithms, equation solving with logarithms; logarithmic scales and re-expression, linearizing data, and fitting models using log and log-log transformations.

Appendix continues on next page.

APPENDIX CONTINUED

Unit 4	**Counting Models** extends student ability to count systematically and solve enumeration problems, and develops understanding of, and ability to do, proof by mathematical induction. *Topics include* systematic counting, the Multiplication Principle of Counting, combinations, permutations; the Binomial Theorem, Pascal's triangle, combinatorial reasoning; the General Multiplication Rule for Probability; and the Principle of Mathematical Induction.
Unit 5	**Binomial Distributions and Statistical Inference** extends student understanding of the binomial distribution, including its exact construction and how the normal approximation to the binomial distribution is used in statistical inference to test a single proportion and to compare two treatments in an experiment. *Topics include* binomial probability formula; shape, mean, and standard deviation of a binomial distribution; normal approximation to a binomial distribution; hypothesis test for a proportion; design of an experiment; randomization test; and hypothesis test for the difference of two proportions.
Unit 6	**Polynomial and Rational Functions** extends student ability to use polynomial and rational functions to represent and solve problems from real-world situations while focusing on symbolic and graphical patterns. *Topics include* factored and expanded symbolic forms, computational complexity, connections between symbolic and graphical representations, multiplicity of zeroes, end behavior; Factor Theorem, Remainder Theorem, complex numbers and their use in the solution of polynomial equations, Fundamental Theorem of Algebra; equivalent forms of rational expressions; horizontal, vertical, and oblique asymptotes; and optimization.
Unit 7	**Functions and Symbolic Reasoning** extends student ability to manipulate symbolic representations of exponential, logarithmic, and trigonometric functions; to solve exponential and logarithmic equations; to prove or disprove that two trigonometric expressions are identical and to solve trigonometric equations; to reason with complex numbers and complex number operations using geometric representations and to find roots of complex numbers. *Topics include* equivalent forms of exponential expressions, definition of e and natural logarithms, solving equations using logarithms and solving logarithmic equations; the tangent, cotangent, secant, and cosecant functions; fundamental trigonometric identities, sum and difference identities, double-angle identities; solving trigonometric equations and expression of periodic solutions; rectangular and polar representations of complex numbers, absolute value, DeMoivre's Theorem, and the roots of a complex number.
Unit 8	**Space Geometry** extends student ability to visualize and represent three-dimensional shapes using contours, cross sections, and reliefs and to visualize and represent surfaces and conic sections defined by algebraic equations. *Topics include* using contours to represent three-dimensional surfaces and developing contour maps from data; sketching surfaces from sets of cross sections; conics as planar sections of right circular cones and as locus of points in a plane; three-dimensional rectangular coordinate system; sketching surfaces using traces, intercepts and cross sections derived from algebraically-defined surfaces; surfaces of revolution and cylindrical surfaces.

Appendix continues on next page.

Unit 9	**Informatics** develops student understanding of the mathematics of information processing, focusing on the basic issues of access, security, and accuracy. *Topics include* set theory; modular arithmetic; symmetric-key and public-key cryptosystems; error-detecting, including bar codes and check digits.
Unit 10	**Problem Solving, Algorithms, and Spreadsheets** develops student understanding and skill in use of standard spreadsheet operations for mathematical problems, while at the same time reviewing and extending many of the basic topics in Courses 1–3. *Topics include* mathematics of finance, modeling population growth, apportionment of power in representative governments, sequences and series, and numerical solution of equations.

CHAPTER 2

REVIEW OF RELATED LITERATURE

Following publication of the *Curriculum and Evaluation Standards for School Mathematics* (National Council of Teachers of Mathematics, 1989), the decade of the 1990s was characterized by efforts funded by the National Science Foundation (NSF) to develop and implement curricula that were based on interpretations of those standards. Compared to more conventional mathematics curricula, these programs not only emphasize some new mathematical and statistical topics, but they integrate topics differently, support a problem-based instructional approach, incorporate technology in new ways, and broaden conventional assessment practices (Suurtamm, Lawson, & Koch, 2008). As a result, these *Standards*-based curricula have generated a great deal of interest of researchers, not only those who study mathematics curriculum but also those who focus on mathematics teaching, learning, and teacher education (Stein, Remillard, & Smith, 2007).

The purpose of this chapter is to place the present evaluation study in the context of this body of recent research. The chapter is not intended to be an exhaustive literature review. The chapter has two main sections: a summary of the scholarly literature that provides a background for the study, and a final main section that situates the present study within that background. The first section on the background literature begins with a summary of the Stein et al. (2007) review of research on how curriculum

A Five-Year Study of the First Edition of the Core-Plus Mathematics Curriculum, pp. 23–45

influences student learning, primarily *Standards*-based curricula across all grade levels. The second section on the background literature discusses issues of content and teaching that are particularly important for development of high school mathematics curricula. The last three subsections of the background focus on studies that either involve the Core-Plus Mathematics curriculum or that are very specifically related to the present study. In particular, the first subsection describes a study that relates teacher beliefs and practices to student achievement, the second summarizes a number of comparative studies of student achievement and affective outcomes, and the final subsection describes research dealing with two important transitions—from high school mathematics to collegiate mathematics and from middle school mathematics to high school mathematics.

BACKGROUND OF THE PRESENT STUDY

Studies that compare student outcomes, especially achievement and sometimes attitudes, in different school mathematics programs have been a major part of educational research since its inception. Yet as Stein et al. (2007) noted in their review of how mathematics curriculum influences student learning in the *Second Handbook of Research on Mathematics Teaching and Learning* (Lester, 2007), there was not a similarly named chapter in the 1992 *Handbook of Research on Mathematics Teaching and Learning* (Grouws, 1992). Prior to the NSF-supported curriculum development work alluded to in the opening paragraph of this chapter, there may have been "general disillusionment among mathematics educators with the textbooks available at the time, most of which were developed by publishing companies and did not draw on research on how students learn mathematics" (Stein et al., 2007, p. 319). These reviewers go on to say that *Standards*-based materials of the 1990s "have generated particular interest of researchers because they embody an approach to mathematics teaching and learning that is qualitatively different from textbooks or instructional resources previously available" (p. 320). The findings of the Stein et al. review are briefly summarized in the next section as a context for the later discussion of research and evaluation more directly pertinent to the present study.

How Curriculum Influences Student Learning—Review in the Second Handbook of Research on Mathematics Teaching and Learning

In brief, Stein et al. (2007) found that *Standards*-based mathematics curricula differ significantly from more conventional programs that, by and large, present skill-oriented content directly and provide support for teachers who also mainly teach directly. Studies comparing student achievement in *Standards*-based versus conventional curricula, whether conducted internally or externally to a *Standards*-based development and evaluation project, consistently show that *Standards*-based curricula lead to significantly stronger results on measures of thinking, reasoning, and problem solving. On more conventional standardized tests or tests of paper-and-pencil skills, most comparisons result in no significant difference, although there are some instances of students in conventional curricula scoring higher. Since there is more emphasis on conceptual understanding, reasoning, and problem solving in *Standards*-based curricula and more time spent explicitly developing skills in conventional curricula, these findings can be partially explained by differing opportunities to learn.

However, Stein et al. (2007) present a convincing, research-based argument that there is much more to the influence of a *Standards*-based curriculum on student learning than just differences in opportunity to learn. The authors discuss differences in content presentation between conventional and *Standards*-based curricula. For example, on the same content topic, students in a *Standards*-based curriculum grapple with problem tasks designed to elucidate the more qualitative and conceptual features of the topic before being introduced to conventional procedures. Students in a conventional curriculum are generally taught the conventional procedure or concept directly. This is followed by examples of the use of the procedure or concept that students are then expected to apply to similar tasks on homework and tests. *Standards*-based curricula, unlike conventional ones, tend to integrate the mathematical topics while balancing concepts versus procedures, calculator-aided versus by-hand calculations and tabular and graphical representations.

Characteristics of the written curriculum are important, but no curriculum implements itself. How the teacher uses a *Standards*-based curriculum to plan and deliver instruction is also a crucial factor in student learning from the curriculum. (In addition to the Stein et al. review, see Superfine, 2008). Furthermore, *Standards*-based curricula are challenging for teachers to implement well, and there is a great deal of variability in how a given curriculum is implemented. Relative to the challenge of implementation, Stein et al. (2007) examine research on teachers' beliefs and knowledge and their effect on *Standards*-based curriculum implementation and on how teachers may transform the intent of the curriculum by varying content coverage or by reducing the intended richness of individual problem-based learning tasks. These reviewers also present research on how teachers themselves can and do learn mathematics and pedagogy from the use of a *Standards*-based curriculum.

This more general body of recent research on how *Standards*-based curricula influence student learning, so thoroughly reviewed by Stein et al. (2007), is consistent with many of the findings of studies in classrooms using the Core-Plus Mathematics curriculum, the focus of the present study. In fact, the Stein et al. review includes several studies that were conducted in Core-Plus Mathematics classrooms. Clearly, the distinguishing characteristics of the *Standards*-based curriculum in the present study and the teaching approach that it is designed to support, described in Chapter 1, have much in common with characteristics of *Standards*-based curricula in general, as described by Stein et al. Thus the review provides a good context for the following discussion of issues and research that are particularly relevant to the present study.

Particularly Important Issues in High School Curriculum and Evaluation

It is useful to review research on *Standards*-based curricula across all programs and all grade levels as there are many commonalties in underlying conceptions about mathematics and its teaching and learning. However, there are some issues that are especially important, or that have important nuances, for curricula at the high school level such as the following.

Issues of Mathematical Content. The mathematical content of a curriculum is the most important consideration at all school levels, but the content issues in high school differ in significant ways from those at other levels. In American comprehensive high schools there have traditionally been two kinds of mathematics curricula with distinctly different goals and content. One kind has focused on preparation of students for collegiate mathematics courses; the other has aimed at imparting a level of mathematical literacy that would serve students well in their lives outside school. Within the college preparatory mathematics programs, most high schools allow qualified students the opportunity to differentiate either by acceleration or placement into different academic tracks.

Mathematical literacy, the high school content goal that has until recently received least attention, requires more than the acquisition of an expanded list of quantitative skills. As Price (1997) argues, logical thinking, analysis of evidence, and statistical reasoning are more important for engaged citizenship in the twenty-first century than conventional mathematical skills. Perhaps this more comprehensive view of mathematical literacy is best captured in the International Life Skills Survey that defines *quantitative literacy* as reported in Steen (2001) as:

> An aggregate of skills, knowledge, beliefs, dispositions, habits of mind, communication capabilities, and problem solving skills that people need in order to engage effectively in quantitative situations arising in life and work. (p. 7)

Sometimes *mathematical literacy* and *quantitative literacy* are used interchangeably, but often they are used to denote important distinctions. For example, to distinguish between what is needed for life (quantitative) and what is needed for education (mathematical), or between what is needed for general school subjects (quantitative) and what is needed for engineering and the physical sciences (mathematical) (Steen, 2001).

A comprehensive high school mathematics curriculum for all students, as *Standards*-based curricula are designed to be, must provide a solid preparation for collegiate mathematics and, at the same time, an adequate level of mathematical or quantitative literacy. The Core-Plus Mathematics curriculum has attempted to address this dual preparation with an integrated, contextualized approach that is at once applied and theoretical, concrete and conceptual, practical and academic. Compared to more conventional college-preparatory high school curricula, most mathematics in the Core-Plus Mathematics curriculum is developed in the context of its uses, with abstraction and appreciation of mathematical structure building gradually across the four-course curriculum. Many of the topics that have received increased attention in the curriculum are often mentioned by writers as important components of mathematical literacy, including:

- Probability, which facilitates reasoning about uncertainty and assessment of risk;
- Exploratory data analysis and statistics, which facilitate reasoning about data;
- Model-building, which facilitates systematic, structured understanding of complex situations;
- Operations research, which facilitates planning of complex tasks and achieving performance objectives;
- Discrete mathematics, which facilitates understanding of most applications of computers (National Research Council, 1989; Steen, 2007).

Teacher and Teaching Issues in High School. Inadequate knowledge of mathematical content is at the root of many of the difficulties elementary school teachers experience with *Standards*-based curricula (Stein et al., 2007). However, many high school mathematics teachers were collegiate mathematics majors, so they have managed to be successful at a fairly abstract level of mathematics. Weak content knowledge is sometimes a problem, even for the mathematics majors, in areas in which teachers may have little background such as statistics and probability or discrete mathematics. The collegiate mathematics training of most high school teachers has also not prepared them well for everyday applications of mathematics or for use of contextual problem situations in teaching. Usually though, these teachers are not intimidated by the need to learn some new mathematical or statistical content, and many are stimulated by the opportunity the curriculum provides them for learning new content and gaining new perspectives on familiar mathematics.

The teacher issues that more often stand in the way of acceptance and effective implementation of high school *Standards*-based curricula are beliefs about high school mathematics, how it is learned by students, and how it needs to be organized and taught to prepare students well for college admittance and success in college mathematics courses (Arbaugh, Lannin, Jones, & Park-Rogers, 2006). Having succeeded in college mathematics themselves after a conventional curriculum in high school, some high school teachers have difficulty accepting the integration of content in a *Standards*-based curriculum. More still doubt that one curriculum can possibly serve the college preparatory and mathematical literacy needs of the full range of students.

Besides conventional beliefs about the content, organization, and target audience, research shows that teachers with advanced subject matter knowledge tend to view meaningful teaching as explaining the organizing principles and formalisms of mathematics, rather than being guided by their students' learning needs and developmental profiles (Philipp, 2007). More specifically, Nathan and Koedinger (2000a) found that secondary mathematics teachers tend to predict that students' symbolic-reasoning skills would develop first, with word-problem-solving ability developing later. According to Nathan and Koedinger, this belief is contrary to research that shows that development of students' verbal reasoning precedes the development of their symbolic reasoning, the order of development in a contextual problem-based teaching approach as used in *Standards*-based curricula. The researchers found that in two widely used conventional textbook programs, the development matched the teachers' erroneous belief, suggesting that the belief may be the result of repeated exposure to textbooks like these (Nathan & Koedinger, 2000b). Beyond the influence of conventional curricula, this erroneous belief is often deeply ingrained in the mind of a high school teacher whose career as a student and teacher has consistently reinforced the notion that symbolic procedural methods come first and word problems are only later applications of the procedural methods.

Teachers' beliefs like those described above are barriers to acceptance and high quality implementation of a *Standards*-based curriculum, but, on the positive side, the curriculum can help to change such beliefs. As a case of beliefs limiting the implementation of the Core-Plus Mathematics curriculum, Lloyd and Wilson (1998) found that a teacher's beliefs about functions limited the richness of his teaching of that topic in pertinent lessons from the curriculum. Conversely, a *Standards*-based curriculum can influence teachers' beliefs as shown by Lloyd (2002), who highlighted aspects of the curriculum that support teacher learning. Since the materials are designed to support problem-based teaching, a teacher using the curriculum will find it to be easier and more natural to use that teaching approach. To teach from the curriculum materials using direct instruction and focusing on symbol manipulation before word problems would take much more rethinking and supplementing. Thus almost in spite of their beliefs and former practices, teachers using this curriculum are likely to teach via problem solving, at least to a greater extent than they otherwise would. Seeing firsthand the positive effect the approach has on their students' learning has helped many initially somewhat reluctant teachers change their beliefs about problem-based teaching. Lloyd (1999, 2002) also found that using the curriculum over several years supported one teacher's learning or relearning of mathematical subject matter. Specifically, the teacher's understanding of graphical representations of functions became richer and more nuanced, which also improved his teaching.

Teachers' Backgrounds, Beliefs, and Practices as Predictors of Student Achievement

Evaluation work prior to the present study that was conducted by Core-Plus Mathematics evaluators was mainly intended to be formative, that is, to inform the ongoing development of the curriculum. As a curriculum development and evaluation project, not a research project, the focus of the evaluation work was necessarily on documenting the curriculum's effects mainly on student achievement, the effectiveness criterion that is demanded of innovative curricula by many stakeholder groups like parents, teachers, and mathematicians. The timely publication of the results of these studies was partially a response to pressure from various directions to provide evaluation evidence that the curriculum was at least as effective as more conventional curricula.

The first study, at least *conceptually* first, dealt with a basic question about teaching a *Standards*-based curriculum. The development of *Standards*-based curricula and the accompanying professional support for teachers proceeded under the assumption that teachers who are most faithful to the developers' intent when they implement the curriculum will be most effective, that is, their students will achieve more. If the criterion for effectiveness of a curriculum is student achievement, one would expect a positive association between the intended teaching practices and growth in student achievement. If there were no such association, the project development team would be in the awkward position of developing curriculum and teacher support materials that do not contribute to the curriculum's effectiveness. Thus a very basic question that was not answered by prior research was, "What classroom practices and teacher behaviors are associated with student achievement in *Standards*-based classrooms?"

To provide some evidence relative to this important question, project evaluators used regression techniques to identify Core-Plus Mathematics teachers' background characteristics, behaviors, and concerns that are associated with growth in student achievement. The sample consisted of 40 teachers of the field-test version of Course 1 and their 1,466 students in 26 schools. The criterion measure was the Iowa Test of Educational Development's *Ability to Do Quantitative Thinking* (*ITED-Q*). The predictor variables were teacher characteristics, beliefs, and practices from periodic classroom observations and annual surveys of teacher beliefs and classroom practices conducted during the field test of the curriculum. The teacher background variable found to be most highly correlated to achievement growth was having completed a professional development workshop focused on teaching the course effectively. Generally, teaching practices that were consistent with problem-based teaching as described in Schoen and Charles (2003) and that reflect high mathematical expectations were positively related to growth in student achievement. These practices include using more small collaborative group or pair work and less time in teacher presentations, spending minimal class time on nonacademic activities, using a variety of assessment methods including individual student interviews, having high expectations on homework and grading, giving students enough time to learn from investigations, and pressing students toward understanding the big mathematical ideas of the lesson by questioning their understanding and problem-solving strategies (Schoen, Cebulla, Finn, & Fi, 2003).

Many researchers have noted that there are clearly observable differences in teachers' implementations of a standard-based curriculum and that professional development in preparation for teaching a *Standards*-based curriculum is important (cf. Arbaugh et al., 2006; Remillard, Herbel-Eisenmann, & Lloyd, 2009; Ross, McDougall, & Hogaboam-Gray, 2002; Stein et al., 2007). The findings of Schoen et al. (2003) described above provide some assurance that implementations that are aligned with the curriculum developers' intent are, in fact, associated with higher levels of student achievement. Furthermore, strong implementations are more likely if the teacher is well prepared to teach the *Standards*-based curriculum and holds beliefs about mathematics and student learning that are aligned with beliefs implicit in the curriculum. Students in a *Standards*-based curriculum are likely to have smaller achievement gains if their teacher transforms the goals of the curriculum in ways that make its delivery much more conventional than the developers intended.

Comparing Student Achievement and Attitudes with Those in Conventional Curricula

Most of the prior studies that were overseen by the Core-Plus Mathematics internal evaluators were quasi-experimental, comparative studies of achievement and sometimes attitudes of students using a field-test version of the curriculum versus those using more conventional published curricula. These studies were either embedded in or spun off the national field test of the curriculum, which followed a year of pilot testing in 19 schools together with refinement of the curriculum materials. Each of the first three courses was field tested in 36 high schools (1994–97), and Course 4 was field tested in 28 high schools (1997–98). Eleven of the 36 field-test schools identified comparison classes that were using a conventional algebra textbook in Grade 9. Four of these 11 schools also had comparison classes that were using a conventional geometry textbook in Grade 10. The comparison classes completed the same tests and belief surveys at the same times as the Core-Plus Mathematics students, but otherwise were given no special treatment.

Field-test schools were located in 11 states—Alaska, California, Colorado, Georgia, Idaho, Iowa, Kentucky, Michigan, Ohio, South Carolina, and Texas. A broad cross-section of students from urban, suburban, and rural communities with ethnic and cultural diversity was represented. The field-test schools were encouraged to include students with a wide range of achievement and interest in mathematics and, where possible, to group students heterogeneously. Limitations at local sites did not always make this possible. Approximately one-fifth of the Course 1 teachers reported that their classes included all ninth-grade students, including honors students. The most common class (as reported by 43.0% of the teachers) was composed of students with a wide range of prior mathematics achievement and interest; however, accelerated students were generally not included because they completed a conventional ninth-grade course in Grade 8 and continued with the next course in the sequence in Grade 9.

Thus accelerated students are probably underrepresented in the field-test sample (Schoen & Hirsch, 2003a).

Quantitative results were analyzed using a standardized test, *ITED-Q*, administered at the beginning of the first course as a covariate. Students in this curriculum performed well on tasks involving statistics and probability, content that was emphasized throughout the curriculum. At the same time, there was evidence that they were at least as well prepared for the SAT and the ACT college entrance examinations as similar students in more conventional curricula. Results of the *ITED-Q* and researcher-developed posttests in Courses 1 and 2 and a test composed of released tasks from the National Assessment of Educational Progress (NAEP) in Course 3 consistently showed that students were stronger than comparison students in more conventional curricula in conceptual understanding, interpretation of algebraic representations and calculations, and problem solving in realistic contexts, but somewhat weaker in out-of-context, paper-and-pencil symbolic manipulation (Schoen & Hirsch, 2003a). This general pattern of algebraic was also confirmed by a study of matched groups of Course 3 and comparison students in conventional advanced algebra courses in six field-test schools who were tested with a researcher-developed measure of a broad range of algebraic outcomes (Huntley, Rasmussen, Villarubi, Sangtong, & Fey, 2000).

The project development team used these findings in the final revision of the first three courses prior to publication and in the development of the field-test version of Course 4. The intent was to improve the procedural algebra outcomes while maintaining the curriculum's identified strengths. For example, a section providing additional symbolic manipulation skill practice, mainly as extra preparation for college mathematics department placement tests, was included at the end of each lesson of each unit in Course 4. Partly to test whether Course 4 changes had the desired effect, a conventional college mathematics placement test was administered to students at the end of Course 4 and to several classes of conventional precalculus comparison students. There was no significant difference between group means on algebraic symbol manipulation tasks with no context. Course 4 students scored significantly better on the more conceptual and applied calculus readiness tasks (Schoen & Hirsch, 2003b). More details of this study are provided in the next section.

A later study (Nelson, 2006) examined the performance on a state mathematics assessment of students who used the published first edition of the curriculum. The pass rate on the 2004-05 Tenth-Grade Washington Assessment of Student Learning (WASL) Mathematics test for the 22 high schools in the state of Washington that were in at least their second year using the Core-Plus Mathematics curriculum was compared to that of a sample of 22 schools carefully matched on prior mathematics achievement, percent of students from low-income families, percent of underrepresented minorities, and student enrollment. The pass rate in mathematics was significantly higher in the schools using the Core-Plus Mathematics program, and the higher pass rate was evident for both students from low-income families and those from other families.

In one of the few large-scale, externally conducted comparative studies in which students were using the first edition of the curriculum, Harwell et al. (2007) compared the mathematical achievement of high school students enrolled for 3 years in one of three *Standards*-based curricula including the Core-Plus Mathematics curriculum. No significant differences on the standardized achievement subtests emerged among the *Standards*-based curricula once background variables were taken into account.

This body of evaluation studies was included in the exhaustive, "best evidence" review of hundreds of published and unpublished articles by Slavin, Lake, and Groff (2008). The review had stringent inclusion criteria for classroom studies, including only those studies that met the following criteria:

- Schools or classrooms using each program had to be compared to randomly assigned or well-matched control groups.
- Study duration had to be at least 12 weeks.
- Outcome measures had to be assessments of the mathematics being taught in all classes. Almost all are standardized tests or state assessments.
- The review placed particular emphasis on studies in which schools, teachers, or students were assigned at random to experimental or control groups.

The Core-Plus Mathematics program was one of just two *Standards*-based curricula placed in the "Limited Evidence of Effectiveness" category. All others for which evidence was reviewed were in lower categories such as "Insufficient Evidence" or "No Qualifying Studies" (Slavin et al., 2008).

In June 2009, following an extensive review of research on education-related programs by Strategic Ed Solutions for the Business-Higher Education Forum, the Core-Plus Mathematics program was recognized as one of 35 programs in the United States that increase student achievement and improve college readiness.

As for students' attitudes toward the Core-Plus Mathematics curriculum, Schoen and Pritchett (1998) compared students' attitudes in Course 2 to the attitudes of students in a conventional geometry course in the four field-test schools that had comparison geometry groups. Recognizing that there may be a novelty effect inflating attitude results, students in the

Standards-based curriculum were much more positive about Course 2 than the comparison students were about their conventional geometry course. A common perception of students was that Course 2 was challenging and made them think, but with effort it was possible for them to understand the ideas and how they apply. Students perceived that they were improving in conceptual understanding, problem solving, and reasoning. For the most part, they reported that they enjoyed and felt they learned more from working with other students in small groups. They saw the problems and investigations as more realistic than the conventional mathematics content they had experienced prior to high school. They viewed graphing calculators as a useful aid to learning and applying mathematics, and many students felt that it had a positive impact on their confidence and tenacity in doing mathematics. Attitudes were measured using The Core-Plus Mathematics Project (CPMP) Student Belief Survey, one of the student belief and attitude instruments in the present study.

Transitions Before and After a Standards-Based High School Curriculum

A major concern for *Standards*-based curriculum developers is what to assume about the focus of mathematics courses prior to and again after their target students study the curriculum under development. For high school curriculum developers, this problem has been difficult on the front-end, since there is not a well-defined middle school mathematics program. But at the back end, the problem of preparing students for college mathematics is particularly daunting.

Preparation for Collegiate Mathematics. As with middle school, part of the problem is variation in undergraduate mathematics curricula and instruction, mainly between reform programs and conventional ones. The college preparation problem is made much more challenging by the fact that so much pressure is exerted on students, teachers, school administrators, and developers of innovative high school curricula concerning preparation for and entrance into college. Understandably, many parents have strong concerns about their child's preparation for college. Entrance examinations and college mathematics department placement tests must be passed at acceptable levels. For outstanding mathematics students and their parents, passing scores on AP Calculus examinations are especially prized. Many university mathematicians who pay little attention to the school curriculum of younger children take critical notice of the college preparatory high school curriculum, since they want to be sure that their incoming clientele are well prepared mathematically.

Some findings concerning preparedness of Core-Plus Mathematics students for tests used for admission and placement in college were mentioned briefly in the previous section and are expanded upon here. In the field test, three studies investigated the college entrance examination scores of students in the *Standards*-based curriculum. Two studies, one involving SAT and the other ACT, were randomized comparisons in single schools. The other was an investigation of a 5-year trend in ACT scores of students in eight schools that began using the curriculum with all their high school students in the third year of the data collection (Schoen & Hirsch, 2003a).

In 2 of the 36 field-test schools, subsets of students were randomly placed in nearly equal numbers into Course 1 or a conventional algebra course at the beginning of ninth grade. In the first school, a suburban district in the South, as juniors, many of these students completed Course 3 ($N = 55$) or conventional advanced algebra ($N = 44$) and took the SAT college entrance examination. The Course 3 students' mean SAT Mathematics score was higher than the mean of the conventional students, but the difference was not statistically significant. In the second school, an urban school in the Midwest, many of the randomly placed students as juniors completed Course 3 ($N = 71$) or advanced algebra ($N = 42$) and took the ACT college entrance examination. The ACT means of these two groups were almost identical. Thus the mean of the *Standards*-based curriculum students did not differ from that of the conventional curricula students on either the SAT or ACT mathematics tests. The fact that the numbers of initially randomized students remaining in a college preparatory mathematics course for at least 3 years and taking a college entrance examination were considerably greater in the *Standards*-based curriculum than in the conventional ones, especially in the urban school, suggests something positive about the curriculum's effect on both college entrance examination scores and students' decisions to continue their study of mathematics (Schoen & Hirsch, 2003a).

As for the ACT trends, 5 years of ACT school data were obtained for eight schools that used the curriculum with all students beginning in the third year of data collection. Across these schools, approximately 1,000 (from 971 in 1997–98 to 1,150 in 1996–97) students per year took the ACT. As shown in Table 2.1, changes in the ACT Mathematics means were small from year to year with little change following the use of the Core-Plus Mathematics curriculum. The most consistent pattern in the data was an increase of .3 to .5 points in ACT Science Reasoning means after students began to use the curriculum (Schoen & Hirsch, 2003a). The ACT Science Reasoning test measures reasoning in contextual, quantitative, and graphical settings, also an important goal of a *Standards*-based mathematics curriculum.

Table 2.1. Five-Year Trends in ACT Means Across Eight Schools That Used Core-Plus Mathematics With All Students Beginning in 1995–96

	Conventional Curriculum		*Core-Plus Mathematics Curriculum*		
ACT Subtest	*1993–94*	*1994–95*	*1995–96*	*1996–97*	*1997–98*
Mathematics	21.3	21.8	21.9	21.5	21.6
Science Reasoning	22.2	22.4	22.7	22.6	22.8
Composite Score	21.9	22.1	22.3	22.3	22.4

In the field test, all students (N = 164) who had just finished at least six of the seven calculus preparatory units of Course 4 completed a multiple-choice placement test compiled by the mathematics department at a major Midwestern university from an item bank then available from the Mathematical Association of America. The same test was administered to students (N = 177) in field-test schools who were at the end of a conventional precalculus course and well matched with the Course 4 students on average baseline standardized achievement test scores. A graphing calculator that did not have symbol manipulation capability was allowed on all three subtests of this test. The first two subtests consisted almost entirely of algebraic manipulation tasks such as simplifying and factoring algebraic expressions, solving equations and inequalities, and finding equations for lines given sufficient conditions. The third subtest, called Calculus Readiness, measured some of the important concepts and processes that underlie calculus, such as reasoning with logarithmic and exponential equations, trigonometric functions and identities, composition of functions, rational functions and their domains, systems of nonlinear equations, and area under a curve. There was no significant difference between the means of the two groups on the algebraic subtests, but the mean of the Course 4 students was significantly higher ($p < 0.01$) on the Calculus Readiness subtest (Schoen & Hirsch, 2003b).

The study by Harwell et al. (2003) cited earlier provides some evidence relative to the performance of students in the Core-Plus Mathematics program on AP Calculus examinations. In one of the districts in that study, all high school students had experienced only *Standards*-based curricula since Grade 6 (Connected Mathematics in middle school and Core-Plus Mathematics in high school) between 1999 and 2003. This district reported that in that period the number of its high school students taking the BC level of the AP Calculus examination jumped from 50 to 67, and the passing rate with scores of 3 or better increased from 64% to 87%. For AB calculus, the number of students increased from 10 to 16 and the passing rate with a score of 3 or better increased from 30% to 81% (Harwell et al., 2003). Some of the increases in numbers of students may be part of a general national trend, but the curriculum's effect is also a likely candidate for explaining such striking increases.

With regard to variations in undergraduate curricula, the Tulane Conference on Calculus and its proceedings (Douglas, 1987) are usually considered to be a major catalyst for the calculus reform effort. The proceedings report activities of various projects to further the reform. The goals of calculus reform have much in common with school mathematics curriculum reform, including emphasis on conceptual understanding, applications, and use of computer laboratories. Pedagogical techniques most often cited as part of the calculus projects are technical writing, inquiry learning, use of multiple representations of concepts, and cooperative learning (Ganter, 2001). As in school curriculum reform, several innovative calculus curricula were developed based on interpretations of calculus reform goals. The Harvard Calculus is probably the program that has had the most use in undergraduate programs around the country, but several other reform calculus programs were developed.

Reform calculus programs have often been evaluated in terms of students' achievement test scores or performance in subsequent courses compared to more conventional calculus programs (cf. Armstrong & Hendricks, 1999; Baxter, Majumdar, & Smith, 1998; Darken, Wynegar, & Kuhn, 2000; Hurley, Koehn, & Ganter, 1999). In her review of these studies, Ganter (2001) found that most concluded that students in reform courses had better conceptual understanding, higher retention rates, higher confidence levels, and greater levels of continued involvement in mathematics than students in conventional courses. However, scores on common traditional exams yielded mixed results, making it unclear whether reform students had any significant loss of conventional skills. Even the overall reform calculus evaluation results sound similar to those of *Standards*-based school curricula.

Transition to Collegiate Mathematics—Field Test Curriculum. It would not be surprising if students who completed a *Standards*-based high school curriculum would be more comfortable, and possibly more successful, in a reform college calculus course than in a conventional one. In fact, that is exactly the conclusion that the Core-Plus Mathematics field-test teachers reached in their frequent discussions of what their students would face in their transition to college mathematics. In annual summer workshops sponsored by the project during the field test, the teachers often talked about advising their better students to attend colleges or universities that had reform mathematics programs or at least did not have a strongly traditional bias in their mathematics department placement tests and their technology policies for mathematics courses. The consensus among field-test teachers in Michigan schools was that, of the two largest state universities, the Harvard Calculus courses at the University of Michigan (U of M) were far more compatible with their high school preparation in comparison to what they perceived to be a very conventional placement test and undergraduate mathematics program at Michigan State University (MSU). There is no evidence concerning the extent to which teachers' advice of this kind affected students' decisions, but its effect, if any, would be to increase the proportion of strong Core-Plus Mathematics students attending U of M and decrease in the proportion attending MSU. This information is important for interpreting the results of some of the following studies.

Four years of mathematics course grades for entering freshman from two similar Michigan high schools in the same district were obtained from the registrar at U of M, which was using the Harvard reform calculus program. In the first 2 years of the U of M grade data, these college freshmen had used a conventional curriculum in both high schools. Beginning in the third year of the grade data, U of M freshmen from East High School had completed 4 years of the field-test version of the Core-Plus Mathematics curriculum. U of M freshmen from West High School completed a conventional mathematics curriculum in high school for all 4 years of the grade data. In the last 2 years of the available data when East High School freshmen had completed the Core-Plus Mathematics curriculum, mean grade point averages in Calculus I courses and beyond (up to and including Introduction to Differential Equations) of the freshmen from East High School graduates increased and were higher than the mean of West High School graduates each year. Over the 4 years of available grade data, the mean grade point averages for East High School graduates versus West High School graduates were 2.71 versus 2.45, 2.98 versus 3.16, 3.13 versus 2.97, and 3.08 versus 2.51 (Schoen & Hirsch, 2003a). There also was an increase in the number of U of M freshmen represented in the data from East High School but not an increase in the number of students from West High School. One partial explanation for these outcomes is a positive achievement effect of the *Standards*-based high school curriculum compared to the conventional curriculum. Another partial explanation may be that the proportion of strongly prepared East High School graduates attending U of M increased in the last 2 years of the data because of advising from teachers of the *Standards*-based curriculum. In any event, there is clearly no evidence of a negative effect of the Core-Plus Mathematics curriculum on college mathematics courses taken or grades in the courses. If anything, the effect may be positive.

In a qualitative study (external to the Core-Plus Mathematics project) of the transition from a *Standards*-based high school curriculum to a conventional undergraduate curriculum, Lewis, Lazarovici, and Smith (2001) carefully monitored the experiences of seven students who had completed

3 years and, in some cases, a fourth year of the field-test version of the Core-Plus Mathematics curriculum as they entered MSU. The students experienced varying degrees of difficulty with the transition to conventional university content expectations and teaching styles, but it is not clear how their difficulties compare with those that have always been experienced by students coming from a conventional high school curriculum. Three of these students passed conventional Calculus I with grades of B or higher, two others passed with lower grades, and a sixth student withdrew before the end of the course.

The seventh student provides evidence of both the difficult transition to conventional college mathematics courses and the relatively easy transition to reform calculus. This student encountered difficulty with conventional Calculus I, seeing the course as dramatically different from her high school classes. She transferred after two class periods to Applied Calculus, an alternative track in which a Harvard reform textbook was used. She went on to earn grades of "A" in both Applied Calculus I and II. According to the researchers,

> She quickly found that course [Applied Calculus I] and its successor ... more to her liking. The content fit perfectly with her Core experiences, the problems were the familiar situational type.... She cruised through both semesters of Applied Calculus, reporting few difficulties. (Lewis et al., 2001, p. 21)

In a qualitative study of six students who had completed 4 years of the field-test version of the Core-Plus Mathematics curriculum, Walker (2006) studied the experiences of the students as they progressed through their first semester of mathematics at two large midwestern state universities. Data for the case studies were collected from a variety of sources: two interviews and three problem-solving sessions with each student (conducted by the author), review of student work on tests and quizzes, classroom observation, and instructor interviews. The interviews occurred in August before the students entered college and in January after their first semester of college mathematics. The problem-solving sessions were evenly spaced throughout the semester and involved students in think-aloud problem-solving sessions where they solved problems similar to those they were working on in their classes. All interviews and problem-solving sessions were transcribed and coded for analysis. Classroom observations and instructor interviews were used to help determine the type of college mathematics classroom environment of each case-study student. Three of the students were enrolled in reform calculus classes, one in a traditional calculus class, and two in traditional precalculus classes.

Based upon findings of the researcher and reports of the participants, none of the students had serious problems making the transition from the *Standards*-based mathematics high school curriculum to college mathematics. All of the students found the expectations of college mathematics to be different than had been the case in high school; however, they were able to make the necessary adjustments. In interviews inquiring what the students thought would help make the transition easier for future students, four students identified the need for more algebraic skills.

The case-study analysis also identified several strengths that students brought with them to college. During high school the students developed the ability to communicate about mathematics and also understood the need to reason about mathematics and justify their thinking. They were accustomed to working through problems on their own, and so when they confronted the need to learn mathematics without the teacher first explaining it to them, they were able to do so. They also were able to explain their thinking to their peers and instructors.

Transition to Collegiate Mathematics—Published First Edition. In a follow-up to the Lewis et al. (2001) study cited in the previous subsection, Smith and Star (2007) studied the transition to MSU of students who used the first edition of the Core-Plus Mathematics curriculum in high school as compared to that of other students who had come from conventional high school programs. Compared to students entering MSU's Harvard reform courses from the *Standards*-based high school curriculum, those entering MSU's conventional courses reported struggling to be attentive in class when the dominant activity was lecture presentation. This difficulty did not, however, result in lower course grades. Smith and Star (2007)

> examined department data on the distribution of grades in [conventional] Pre-Calculus, Calculus I, and Calculus II and found no significant overall difference in the distribution of grades between [the Core-Plus Mathematics] sample and the sample of students from conventional high school programs. (p. 24)

In a recent study conducted externally to the Core-Plus Mathematics Project at the University of Minnesota, Harwell and Post (2009) used hierarchical linear modeling to compare the mathematical course-taking and grades of students at the university from different high school mathematics curricula, including 275 students who came from the first-edition Core-Plus Mathematics program. They found no overall statistically significant differences in initial college course difficulties or grades across the curriculum groups. Over time students in different high school curriculum groups did not differ in their persistence, that is, in the numbers of university mathematics courses completed and grades. Harwell and Post report the same patterns of findings within groups of students with high, medium, and low ACT Mathematics scores, contradicting the largely anecdotal criticism that *Standards*-based curricula would leave middle and high ability students unprepared for postsecondary mathematics.

Transition to Collegiate Mathematics—Discussion. The body of research described above provides solid evidence that students completing a Core-Plus Mathematics program are at least as well prepared as students from a conventional curriculum. One published study stands in sharp contrast to this body of evidence. Hill and Parker (2006) examined six consecutive years of data (1994–99) from the MSU registrar for six schools that participated in the Core-Plus Mathematics field test. In the case of four of these schools, they found a decline in the level of college mathematics courses taken and grades in those courses toward the end of the 6 years of their data. There was not a similar decline in the other two schools, but the researchers concluded that was because these schools supplemented the *Standards*-based curriculum (and presumably, but with no reported evidence, the other four schools did not). Hill and Parker concluded that "these results raise serious issues about the effectiveness of CPMP in preparing students to take college mathematics courses at MSU" (p. 920). They also note that the "difficulties might be a result of inadequate enactments of the first edition [actually field-test versions] of CPMP" (p. 920).

A strong rebuttal of this study as being misleading and conducted in an unprofessional manner appears in the August/September 2007 issue of the *American Mathematical Monthly* (Fey, Hart, Hirsch, Schoen, & Watkins, 2007, pp. 654–655). For example, many students in two of the four schools in Hill and Parker's main analysis did not use the Core-Plus Mathematics curriculum exclusively in high school (actually relatively little in one school). In spite of the authors' reference to "the first edition of CPMP" quoted above, no students in their study used the published version of the curriculum. Methodological flaws of the study are elaborated at www.wmich.edu/cpmp/LongitudinalStudy1.html

Setting aside all the serious problems of the Hill and Parker (2006) study, there is a downward trend in the data in some of their target schools. At least two of those schools actually used the prepublished version of the Core-Plus Mathematics curriculum with all students, as did the two schools that the researchers dropped from their analysis. The downward trend may be evidence of the relative difficulty that students who used a prepublished version of this *Standards*-based curriculum in high school had with the transition to a conventional college mathematics program compared to a reform mathematics program. Another partial explanation may be that more of the best graduates of these schools were heeding the advice of their high school teachers, described above, and avoiding universities like MSU that have a very conventional mathematics program.

In summary, the above studies, when taken together, suggest that across entering aptitude levels students are at least as well prepared for college entrance examinations and for success in calculus by the Core-Plus Mathematics curriculum as by more conventional high school curricula. On a mathematics department placement test, students from this curriculum did as well on average as those from conventional precalculus courses on conventional, out-of-context, algebraic symbol manipulation and did significantly better on calculus readiness concepts and applications. The data from college mathematics courses suggest that a *Standards*-based curriculum, with its emphasis on sense-making and reasoning, may prepare students especially well for reform college calculus as compared to conventional calculus courses. However, there is evidence that the distributions of conventional college mathematics course grades of students who used the first edition of the Core-Plus Mathematics curriculum and those who used conventional high school mathematics curricula did not differ significantly. It may be significant to note that all the studies described in this subsection focused on students' transition to large, midwestern state universities. More research is needed in which all students used the Core-Plus Mathematics curriculum in high school and attended a wide variety of community colleges, colleges, and universities. The present study provides evidence of this type.

Transition from Middle-School Mathematics. In 1992–93 when development of the first edition of Core-Plus Mathematics began, it seemed appropriate for the developers to assume that students would be coming into high school from a conventional middle school program or one that was somewhat more progressive like *Transition Mathematics* from the University of Chicago School Mathematics Project. In 2003, when work began on the second edition, it was decided that a more realistic starting point would be a *Standards*-based middle school program, since these programs were making strong inroads into the schools. *Connected Mathematics Project* (CMP) was assumed as the starting point, because of its similarity in philosophy and approach to the Core-Plus Mathematics program, and its particularly strong presence in the schools at that time. In the present study, students entering two of the three high schools had just completed 3 years of CMP. Students entering the third school had completed 3 years of another *Standards*-based middle school curriculum, *MATH Thematics,* developed by the Six Through Eight Mathematics (STEM) project. The content and approach of these two programs are discussed in Chapter 3. For developers' descriptions of these programs and some evaluation results of their use, see Senk and Thompson (2003). Selected evaluation studies are cited in the following paragraphs.

Students using either of these two middle school mathematics programs were found to score significantly higher in data analysis and algebra as measured by the Missouri Assessment Program than comparison students from the same three school districts who were using a conventional curriculum (Reys, Reys, Lapan, Holliday, & Wasman, 2003). In two studies, CMP students scored at the same level or higher on standardized tests than comparison students in a conventional curriculum (Cain, 2002; Riordan & Noyce, 2001). In the Riordan and Noyce study, CMP students also scored significantly better on a state mathematics test. In another study, students in the CMP curriculum were found to be particularly adept at proportional reasoning, a result that the researchers argue was attributable to the contextual problem-based teaching of the curriculum (Ben-Chaim, Fey, Fitzgerald, Benedetto, & Miller, 1998). Although this is a brief sampling of studies, this and further research evidence indicates that use of either the CMP or the STEM curricula is associated with strong student achievement.

A recent study investigated achievement of students in both CMP and STEM on the Stanford Achievement Test and the New Standards Reference Examination (Post et al., 2008). Consistent with research cited earlier in this chapter, the authors found that students in both programs learned conventional topics including computational procedures at acceptable levels, and their achievement levels were greater on open-ended and problem-solving tasks than on procedural tasks.

As *Standards*-based mathematics curricula are used to guide learning, it is important to capture not just data on achievement but also data on the way in which students respond to and interact in a *Standards*-based instructional setting. Bay, Beem, Reys, Papick, and Barnes (1999) had sixth and seventh graders write letters about their experience in CMP and one other middle school *Standards*-based curriculum. Findings suggest that across CMP classrooms students were positive toward applications, hands-on activities, and working collaboratively. Students' perceptions of their mathematics class were affected by various factors, including the teacher, the classroom norms, and the curriculum materials. In the present study, a similar data collection method was used at the end of Courses 1 and 2.

GENDER AND MATHEMATICS LEARNING

According to a recent review (Bishop & Forgasz, 2007), gender differences in mathematics achievement have narrowed recently, and the differences that remain, such as on the 2003 NAEP, are dwarfed by differences on other factors like socioeconomic status and underrepresented minority group membership. Furthermore, in recent studies, girls sometimes do significantly better than boys on mathematical achievement tests, and girls are attending college at higher rates than boys. Numbers of females in scientific, technological, medical, and legal fields that in the past were almost exclusively male domains are steadily increasing. Even single sex classes, long viewed as anachronistic, are re-appearing with a main intent of benefiting academically talented girls, although the research results are mixed.

Partly due to these recent, rather dramatic changes in the gender landscape, the *Second Handbook of Research on Mathematics Teaching and Learning* (Lester, 2007) did not have a separate chapter on gender research, instead included gender in the Bishop and Forgasz chapter reviewing research on access and equity issues. Fifteen years earlier, the gender review by Leder (1992) in the *Handbook of Research on Mathematics Teaching and Learning* (Grouws, 1992) summarized three consistent trends in the then current gender research, as follows:

- Differences in participation [by gender] continue to be observed in higher level, more intensive mathematics courses, and related applied fields.
- While there is much overlap in achievement scores by gender, when significant differences occur, they tend to favor males, particularly at higher cognitive achievement levels.
- The observed differences described in the first two bullets are often accompanied by differences in the ways males and females regard themselves, and are regarded by others, as learners of mathematics.

Among the environmental factors that have often been identified by researchers as contributing to these general findings are the more social learning styles of girls (Leder, 1992), suggesting that perhaps the problem-based, small group learning supported by *Standards*-based curricula may be especially beneficial to girls. In the present study, the gender effect in *Standards*-based classrooms is addressed by the quantitative comparison by gender of achievement and affective outcomes.

SITUATING THE PRESENT STUDY

This study adds to the growing body of evaluation studies that focus on the use of *Standards*-based mathematics curricula (cf. National Research Council, 2004; Stein et al., 2007). Most evaluations have studied the impact of field-test versions of a curriculum. Since the curriculum was so new at the time of many of these studies, students and teachers were relative novices at the use of a *Standards*-based curriculum. These earlier studies, at least those dealing with the Core-Plus Mathematics curriculum, were mainly 1 year or less in duration, although some field-test studies examined data collected over 3 years or more. Some schools in these studies used the curriculum with all students as it was intended, but students in the comparisons were typically from schools that used two mathematics curricula, including a conventional curriculum.

At the beginning of the present study (Fall 1997), the three participating schools were just completing their 4-year involvement in the Core-Plus Mathematics field test, so many of the teachers had participated in professional development programs that specifically prepared them to teach the curriculum. Many also had 1 to 3 years of experience teaching the curriculum. Virtually all high school students in each school used the curriculum, and the middle school curriculum in feeder middle schools was a *Standards*-based curriculum as well. Except for those who transferred in or out of these districts during Grades 6 through 12, students in the study's sample had completed 7 years of mathematics using *Standards*-based curricula by the end of their senior year. Thus this may be one of the first studies of the efficacy of *Standards*-based mathematics curricula with all of the following characteristics:

- The study focused on fairly stable implementations of a first-edition high school *Standards*-based curriculum that was used by all students in each school.
- It involved students who experienced up to 7 years of *Standards*-based mathematics curricula in middle school and high school.
- It monitored students' mathematical achievement, beliefs, and attitudes for 4 years of high school and 1 year after.
- Prior to the study, many of the teachers had 1 or more years of experience teaching the *Standards*-based curriculum and/or inservice education dealing with how to teach the curriculum well.
- In the study, variations in levels of implementation of the curriculum are described and related to student outcomes and teacher behavior variables.

In Chapter 3, the methods and procedures used in the study are described. This is followed by a description of the teachers and their use of the curriculum in Chapter 4.

CHAPTER 3

METHOD AND PROCEDURES

For 5 years, the Core-Plus Mathematics evaluation team monitored the mathematics course-taking patterns, grades, mathematical achievement of various types, and beliefs and attitudes of a substantial subset of the 1997 freshman class (graduating class of 2001) in three high schools. The three high schools were among the 36 schools in the field test of the curriculum conducted from 1994 through 1998, all of which were considered for possible inclusion in the present study. The three schools that were chosen met the following criteria: (a) they agreed to all conditions of participation including the testing, interviewing, and class observation schedules; (b) they used the *published* first edition of the curriculum with all students in Grades 9–12, up to AP Statistics or AP Calculus taken by some accelerated students; and (c) their feeder middle schools used a NSF-funded *Standards*-based mathematics curriculum. These settings are three instances of generally solid implementations with all students, who, with few exceptions, had completed 7 years of *Standards*-based mathematics by the end of high school.

This chapter begins with a statement of the goals of the study. The second main section describes the study's sample, including descriptions of the three communities in which the schools are located, the makeup of the student body and of the mathematics teachers in each school, each school's daily and yearly schedule and mathematics curriculum policies, the subset of students who provided the data for this study, and the *Standards*-based middle school mathematics curricula that were used in feeder

A Five-Year Study of the First Edition of the Core-Plus Mathematics Curriculum, pp. 47–59

middle schools. The third main section provides an overview of the measurement instruments, the procedures for administering them, and the methods of analyzing the resulting data.

GOALS OF THE STUDY

The main goals of this study were as follows:

- Describe the local implementations of the Core-Plus Mathematics curriculum, including the demographics of the schools and communities, the experiences and beliefs of the teachers concerning mathematics and the curriculum, and the range of teaching practices.
- Describe what students from these three high schools knew and understood mathematically at the end of each year with a focus on different types of mathematical outcomes each year.
- Describe what students believed at the end of each year about mathematics and about the curriculum and how these beliefs were related to mathematical achievement.
- Describe how mathematical achievement and beliefs differed by school, by gender, and by the level of students' mathematical aptitude and background.
- Describe the experiences and perceptions of graduates of these schools in the year after high school, especially as these relate to college mathematics.
- Describe, in detail, three student cases over the 5-year duration of the study.
- Discuss possible contributing factors and effects of a local controversy over the curriculum that occurred in one of the participating schools during the study.

SAMPLE

Communities of Participating Schools

The participating schools—Adams, Jefferson, and Washington (town and school names are pseudonyms)—were located in three small-town communities. The communities of Adams and Washington are smaller than that of Jefferson. Washington, the smallest of the three towns, has the highest median household income and the lowest percent of families

Table 3.1. Demographic Data for Target Communities from the 2000 U.S. Census

Town	*Town Population*	*Median Household Income*	*Percentage of Families Below Poverty*	*Percentage of Mgmt & Professionals*	*Percentage of Mfg & Industry*
Washington	8,835	51,901	4.2%	33.8%	4.3%
Adams	11,285	33,838	11.2%	18.6%	45.3%
Jefferson	14,532	37,330	4.8%	34.2%	9.8%

below the poverty level (see Table 3.1). However, the cost of living in Washington is higher than in either of the other two communities, so the income difference is not as pronounced as the numbers suggest. Of the three, Adams is the most "blue collar" community as indicated by the relatively high percent of employment in manufacturing and industry and the relatively low percent of people in management and professional jobs.

Participating Schools

As for the schools themselves, the largest of the three communities, Jefferson, has two high schools, each comprised of students in Grades 10–12. This study focused on just one of the high schools in Jefferson, called Jefferson High School. Ninth graders were housed in two middle schools in town that fed both of the high schools. Thus it was necessary for the purposes of this study to collect Grade 9 data in both middle schools. In later years, data were collected only at Jefferson High School, not at the other high school in town.

The communities of Washington and Adams both have just one Grades 9–12 high school. Adams High School used a semester block schedule in which students completed a course in one semester by meeting daily for extended periods (90 minutes), while the other two schools had more typical schedules with daily class meetings of 40 to 50 minutes for the entire school year. For graduation, all three schools required the successful completion of at least two mathematics courses in Grades 9 through 12.

On average, the entering mathematical achievement level of students in this study was somewhat higher than a nationally representative sample, but not outstanding. In particular, at the beginning of the study, mean scores of all Course 1 students from the three schools, Washington, Adams, and Jefferson, were at national student percentiles of 55, 65, and 65, respectively, on the Iowa Tests of Educational Development subtest, *Ability to Do Quantitative Thinking* (*ITED-Q*). Demographic data including

Table 3.2. Demographic Data for Target High Schools (1997–98)

School	*Grades in High School*	*Enrollment*	*Percentage of Free/Reduced Lunch*	*Percentage of Underrep. Minorities*	*Middle School Curriculum*
Washington	9–12	465	17.2%	27.7%	STEM
Adams	9–12	930	13.3%	4.5%	CMP
Jefferson	10–12	1,304	8.9%	3.2%	CMP

enrollment, percent of students qualified for free and reduced lunch, percent of underrepresented minorities, and middle school mathematics curriculum completed are given in Table 3.2 above.

The schools differed in their approaches to acceleration of mathematically promising students. At Washington High School, there were two opportunities for students to accelerate. First, top mathematics students at the end of Grade 8 who wanted to accelerate were given a teacher-prepared placement test. If they did well and had strong recommendations from their eighth-grade teacher, they were allowed to skip Course 1 of the high school curriculum and enroll in Course 2 in Grade 9. Approximately 20 students took advantage of this option for acceleration. Second, students in Grade 11, but not in the first accelerated group, who did well in Courses 1 and 2 could, with the teacher's approval, enroll in a block (double length) class in which Courses 3 and 4 were taught in 1 year. Students who successfully completed either of the two acceleration options were eligible to enroll in AP Calculus in Grade 12.

At Adams High School, the four Core-Plus Mathematics courses were divided into five one-semester courses. Any student could opt to complete two mathematics courses in any year, one per semester, in order to accelerate their mathematics program. Course options beyond this curriculum were AP Calculus and AP Statistics. At Jefferson High School, top mathematics students in Grade 7 who qualified could opt to complete Course 1 in Grade 8. As in the first option at Washington High School, the acceleration criteria were scores on a placement test and the recommendation of the student's seventh-grade teacher.

Jefferson High School was differentiated in another way from Washington High School and Adams High School by a situation that materialized during this study. Beginning in the first year of the study, a few dissident teachers and parents in Jefferson organized a public opposition to the *Standards*-based high school curriculum. Amid much local controversy over several years, this group succeeded in pressuring Jefferson High School administrators and faculty to provide an alternative, "conventional," mathematics track beginning in the fourth year of the study.

Some of our data from Jefferson reflect that controversy. For example, it is clear that the controversy had a major impact on some outcomes, especially on student attitudes. This controversy is referred to periodically as it is pertinent throughout this report. In Chapter 13, the local controversy at Jefferson and its impact on teachers and students is described in detail.

Participating Students and Teachers

In 1997–98, data were collected from all students who completed Course 1 in these three high schools. These students were mainly in ninth grade, and this set of students included the vast majority of the ninth-grade students in each of the schools. Data were collected from all students who completed Course 2 in 1998–99 and, in the following year, from all students who completed Course 3. These students were mainly sophomores and juniors, respectively. In 2000–01, when most students in the initial Course 1 group were seniors, data were collected from students who completed Course 4, AP Statistics, or AP Calculus. With few exceptions, AP Statistics was taken by students who had previously completed Courses 1–3, and AP Calculus was taken by students who had previously completed Courses 1–4. In the fifth year of the study (2001–02), the 2001 graduates of the three high schools were surveyed concerning their experiences in college, especially as related to mathematics courses.

As in any study conducted in public schools over a period of several years, the student populations were not identical from year to year for various reasons, although there was substantial overlap. Most of the students tested each year were in the graduating class of 2001, but some students were accelerated, some dropped out of classes or out of school, and others transferred in. For practical reasons, our paper-and-pencil instruments were administered to classes rather than to individual students. A class is typically designed for students at a target grade level, but it may include some younger, accelerated students and some older students who repeated or delayed taking the course.

In this report, results for a particular course include all students for whom course data were available. Statistical tests of changes from course to course include only those students for whom data were complete for the measures under discussion. In order to keep this report from becoming overwhelmed with detail, data tables for each analysis are included in chapter Appendices that are referenced in the body of the report. The numbers of students in each school who completed at least one cognitive or affective instrument in each of the 5 years of the study are given in Table 3.3. The numbers of students remained fairly stable in the first 2 years when a mathematics course was required. The numbers then

Table 3.3. Numbers of Students in Each School Completing at Least One Cognitive or Affective Instrument Each Year

	Year 1 1997–98	*Year 2 1998–99*	*Year 3 1999–2000*	*Year 4 2000–01*	*Year 5 2001–02*
Washington	108	88	46	38	14
Adams	223	230	143	89	25
Jefferson	374[a]	417	300	189	107

[a] Students from Jefferson middle schools who did not appear in our data set in any of Grades 10, 11, or 12 were dropped from the Year 1 sample.

Table 3.4. Teachers' Gender, Educational Preparation, and Experience by School

School	*Female (N)*	*Male (N)*	*MA (N)*	*Median Yrs. Exp.*
Washington	2	2	2	13
Adams	3	3	1	15
Jefferson (Gr. 9)	6	3	2	7
Jefferson (Gr. 10–12)	5	6	2	8
TOTAL	16	14	7	8

decreased markedly in Years 3 and 4 when mathematics was optional. The decrease in numbers in Year 5 is also understandable, since this number is the subset of graduates who went on to postsecondary education after high school and who responded to the researchers' written postsecondary survey.

A total of 30 different teachers taught the target mathematics courses at these 3 schools during the 4-year duration of the study. All of these teachers held a bachelor's degree or higher, and seven (23.3%) had a master's degree in mathematics education. On average, the teachers at Washington High School and Adams High School were more experienced than those at Jefferson High School (see Table 3.4 above). For more details about the teachers' backgrounds, beliefs, and approaches to implementing the curriculum (see Chapter 4).

Middle School Mathematics Curricula

The two middle school programs, *Connected Mathematics* from the Connected Mathematics Project (CMP) and *MATH Thematics* from the Six Through Eight Mathematics (STEM) Project, were two of the NSF-funded

Table 3.5. Units in Eighth-Grade *Connected Mathematics and MATH Thematics*

Connected Mathematics (CMP)	*MATH Thematics (STEM)*
Thinking With Mathematical Models Representing relationships: introduction to functions and modeling; slope; and finding the equation of a line	*Amazing Feats, Facts, and Fictions* Problem Solving; Data Displays; Fitted Lines; Perimeter; Circumference; Area; Volume; Equations
Looking for Pythagoras The Pythagorean theorem: investigating the Pythagorean theorem, area, irrational numbers, slope, and distance	*At the Mall* Proportions; Percents; Probability; Operations with Integers and Fractions; Inequalities; Data Displays
Growing, Growing, Growing… Exponential relationships: exponential growth and decay through data tables, graphs, and simple symbolic forms	*The Mystery of Blacktail Canyon* Measurement; Equations, Graphs, and Slope; Similar Figures; Constructions; Scientific Notation
Frogs, Fleas, and Painted Cubes Quadratic relationships: growth and quadratic functions through data tables, graphs, and simple symbolic forms	*Patterns and Discoveries* Fractals; Classifying; Quadrilaterals; Rotations; Pythagorean Theorem; Geometric Probabilities
Say It With Symbols Algebraic reasoning investigating equivalent expressions; solving linear and simple quadratic equations	*Inventions* Surface Area and Volume; Slope; Equations of Lines; Exponents; Permutations; Combinations; Probability
Hubcaps, Kaleidoscopes, and Mirrors Symmetry and transformational geometry; connecting geometry and algebra	*Architects and Engineers* Constructions; Surface Area and Volume; Parallel Lines and Transversals; Inequalities; Similarity
Samples and Populations Statistics and probability: using samples to reason about populations and make predictions; comparing samples and sample distributions	*Visualizing Change* Graphs; Functions; Linear Equations; Exponential Change; Quadratic Change; Transformations
Clever Counting Combinatorics: ways to count in application situations; using combinations, trees, and other representations	*Making an Impact* Collecting Data; Choosing and Making Data Displays; Misleading Graphs

curricula developed in response to the 1989 NCTM *Curriculum and Evaluation Standards for School Mathematics* (NCTM, 1989). Both curricula intended to change both the content and the teaching approach in middle school mathematics by emphasizing problem solving, reasoning, and mathematical connections. In eighth grade, each curriculum was organized into eight units as described in Table 3.5.

While there are many similarities between the two middle school curricula, one difference is that STEM units tend to be organized around a real-world theme with mathematics pulled in as needed, while CMP units are organized more directly around the mathematics that the students are to learn. In this regard, the Core-Plus Mathematics curriculum is more like CMP than like STEM, although either of these middle school programs should be good preparation for the Core-Plus Mathematics curriculum (see Senk & Thompson, 2003, pp. 193–224, for more details about CMP and pp. 251–296 for more details about STEM).

The present study, together with the CPMP field test, provides some evidence of the effectiveness of these middle school curricula. In the field test, the mean of all students from Washington High School and Adams High School[1] at the beginning of Grade 9 in 1994–95 was at the 51st student percentile on the ITED-Q. Those students had just completed a conventional middle school mathematics program. In this study, the mean of all Grade 9 students in 1997–98 from the same two schools increased to the 60th percentile on the same test. Socioeconomic indicators like percent of students eligible for free and reduced lunch and percent of underrepresented minorities increased in both schools over this 3-year period, so one likely explanation for this steep increase in percentile rank is a positive effect of the *Standards*-based middle school curricula that the 1996-97 students experienced.

INSTRUMENTS AND PROCEDURES

The following principles guided the choice of instruments and scheduling of their administration:

- A standardized mathematics achievement measure and an affective measure should provide a baseline prior to the study.
- At least one achievement measure and one affective measure should be administered at the end of each course and problem-based interviews of some students should be administered during each course.
- The measures taken together should assess a wide variety of cognitive and affective student outcomes.

Table 3.6. Data Sources and Their Target Samples and Administration Schedules

Data Source	*Target Sample*	*Administration Schedule*
ITED-Q	All students	Course 1, Sept. & May
Mathematics Belief Survey	All students	Course 1, Sept.; Cos. 1 & 2, May
ETS Algebra End-of Year Exam	All students	Course 2, May
TIMSS Math Literacy	All students	Course 3, May
TIMSS Advanced Math	All students	Year 4, May
CPMP Reasoning/Proof Test	All students	Year 4, May
Conceptions of Math Inventory	All students	Years 3 & 4, May
Problem-Based Interviews	30–50 students per year	Courses 1–4, periodically
Class Observations	Students and teachers	Courses 1–4, periodically
Teacher Surveys	All teachers	Courses 1-4, May
Teacher Interviews	9 selected teachers	Years 1–4, periodically
Post-High School Survey	146 respondents	Year 5, January or February

- Developers of at least some of the achievement measures should provide results from administrations of the same instruments or tasks in the instruments to groups of students comparable to those in the present study.
- Observations of classes, teacher surveys, and interviews should be conducted with some teachers each year.
- In the fifth year, graduates should be surveyed concerning their experiences in their first year of post-high school study or employment.

The instruments and schedule of data collection are summarized in Table 3.6. The measurement instruments are described in detail in the chapter in which the results for the administration of each instrument are reported. Except for published instruments, the instruments and their subtests or subscales can be accessed at http://www.wmich.edu/cpmp/evaluation.html.

At each testing time, teachers at Washington High School and Jefferson High School administered achievement assessments and affective measures on consecutive days. At Adams High School, these instruments were usually administered during the same 90-minute period. (As is usually the case with standardized tests like the *ITED-Q*, the researchers attempted to minimize teacher variation in administration contexts by providing teachers with a highly detailed written set of instructions for administration of each written assessment instrument.) For the student interviews, teachers were asked to select a group of students that represented a full range of the class's diversity. Core-Plus Mathematics evaluation staff, either professors or doctoral students, visited each school a total of at least three days per year. On these school visits, the evaluators interviewed students and teachers and observed classes. The evaluators tried to observe at least one class of each teacher each year and to conduct at least one interview with a representative subset of teachers. However, the schedules of the teachers and the evaluators and the limited time available on school visits did not always make that possible.

Data Collection and Analysis

Demographic information came from local school personnel and from data reported on NCES (National Center for Educational Statistics) and local community websites. Descriptive information concerning teachers was gathered from written surveys and one-on-one interviews of the teachers themselves. When it seemed helpful, records from the CPMP field test were used to cross check information about teachers' attendance at professional development workshops. Information about teaching practices was mainly gleaned from classroom observations.

Interviews with teachers and students were audiotaped and then transcribed for later analysis. In problem-based interviews, the paper-and-pencil work of the students was also an important data source. Interview problems were scored using a rubric that included both a score for correctness and a process category, and students' written and oral "work" was further analyzed in light of the rubric score. *NUD*IST 4* software (© 1985–1997 Qualitative Solutions & Research Pty Ltd.) was used to parse and categorize interviews, classroom observation notes, and written quotes from surveys.

Quantitative data were compiled in computer data files and analyzed using *SPSS 10* statistical software (© SPSS, Inc. 2000). The subgroups of most relevance to our goals were school, gender, and preachievement level. The last of these was defined using score intervals on the *ITED-Q* pretest (Form K, Level 15) that was administered at the beginning of Course 1 as follows:

1. *Top:* 90th percentile and above (305 up to the maximum standard score of 353)

2. *Above Average:* 67th through 89th national percentile (271 through 304 inclusive)
3. *Below Average:* 34th through 66th national percentile (236 to 270 inclusive)
4. *Bottom:* Lower third in the national norm group (154 to 235 inclusive)

These intervals were chosen partly for their logic (top 10%, remainder of top third, middle third, and bottom third) and partly because the number of students per interval was at least 100 at the beginning of the study. For the above classification of students, missing *ITED-Q* pretest scores were estimated by the least squares estimate of the pretest score as predicted by all the achievement scores that were available for the student. For convenience, these groups are referred to as PAL 1 (Preachievement Level 1), PAL 2, PAL 3, and PAL 4. By Course 3, the numbers of students in PAL 4 was too small to be reliable, so preachievement groups 3 and 4 were combined for Course 3 and all courses beyond.

Our main quantitative analyses of belief scores in a given year were conducted in the three steps described below. The quantitative analyses of end-of-year achievement results in a given year were conducted in the same three steps, with the caveat that ninth-grade *ITED-Q* pretest scores were entered into each achievement analysis as a covariate.[2]

1. The initial step was to conduct univariate or, if multiple subtests or subscales were involved, multivariate school by gender and school by PAL analyses of variance. If interactions in these analyses were significant at the 0.05 level, we described the results by gender within school and PAL group within school. If the interactions were not significant, the results of the main effect analyses are reported and interpreted. The decision was made to run two-way ANOVAs rather than a three-way, school by gender by PAL, because the latter results in some cells with very small numbers of students.
2. If interactions with school in step 1 were not significant, a gender by PAL ANOVA (or MANOVA) was conducted ignoring the school variable. If interactions were significant, the results by gender within preachievement levels were described and interpreted.
3. If gender by PAL interactions were not significant, we reported the results first by gender and then by preachievement level groups. Gender main effects are reported using the results of the school by gender analysis, and PAL main effects are reported using the results of the gender by PAL analysis.

Linear regression was the main statistical tool for analysis of the relationship between mathematical achievement and beliefs. In particular, for each gender and preachievement level group we entered the belief subscales as predictors of mathematical achievement. The large-scale quantitative statistical tests of these associations were also used to help focus our deeper, qualitative analyses. In general, if a main effect, interaction, or regression coefficient was statistically significant, we tried to describe that significant association in more detail with a deeper look at subgroup or individual performance on pertinent subtests and related interview or survey information. Conversely, if we noticed an interesting pattern in our qualitative data, we looked for quantitative evidence of the pattern in larger sets of students. Occasionally, a chi-square was used to test the significance of the distribution of frequency counts in a contingency table.

In addition to the analysis of group data, case studies of three students are reported. Data sets are essentially complete for these students, one from each school. The intent in the case studies is to provide the numerical data for each student in the context of a rich description of their experiences over the 5 years of the study.

FINAL CHAPTER NOTE

In the next chapter, the teachers' backgrounds and their practices and beliefs relative to the Core-Plus Mathematics curriculum are described. In the following four chapters (5–8), achievement patterns in each of the students' 4 years of high school are examined. Two chapters (9 and 10) that follow report affective outcomes of students during their high school years. Chapter 11 focuses on students' preparation for college as reflected in their ACT and SAT scores and their choice of mathematics courses and grades in the first year of college.

The case studies of three students are reported in Chapter 12. Chapter 13 contains a case study of one school, Jefferson High School, focusing on the local conflict about the Core-Plus Mathematics curriculum that occurred during the present study. School differences in results on students' achievement, beliefs, and attitudes are noted in previous chapters, but in Chapter 13 these differences are revisited in the context of the local controversy.

The final chapter (14) of this report is a summary and synthesis of the findings across 5 years and multiple measures in the study. Chapter 14 also includes a discussion of implications for mathematics education reform and for curriculum development and evaluation. Throughout, the authors' intent is to present the major results in a narrative style that will appeal to an audience of school personnel, mathematicians, curriculum developers, and interested parents, not just to mathematics education researchers.

Readers should be aware that this evaluation was conducted by members of the Core-Plus Mathematics Project from 1997 through 2002 under the codirection of the first and second authors with the assistance of the fourth author. The third author is the principal investigator of the Core-Plus Mathematics Project. Beginning in 2002, the second author directed the formative evaluation of the second edition of the curriculum, copyrighted 2008, 2009, and 2010, which the results of the reported study helped to inform in ways that are discussed in the last chapter of this volume.

For readers interested in more of the details about the instruments and the data analysis, the chapter appendices include the results of the main statistical tests, tasks from some assessments and how these tasks are grouped into subtests or subscales, and reliability estimates for the main assessments. Researchers who want still further details or who want to consider adapting the unpublished instruments or some of the study's procedures for use in their own research may access and download the instruments and detailed task and instrument statistics at http://www.wmich.edu/cpmp/evaluation.html.

NOTES

1. Jefferson's field test situation is not comparable to this study, since only a few of their tracked classes of better students participated in the field test.
2. Missing *ITED-Q* pretest scores were replaced with the linear regression best estimate as predicted by all posttest scores available for each student.

CHAPTER 4

TEACHERS AND THE CURRICULUM

The nature and intent of the Core-Plus Mathematics curriculum was described in introductory chapters of this volume. At the school level, the curriculum was intended for use with all students, as is the case in the present study. However, it is well known that teachers within a given school differ a great deal in how they make use of a curriculum. Thus it is important to know how individual teachers actually implemented the curriculum in their classrooms.

In this chapter, results of teacher data are reported, including results concerning teachers' backgrounds, beliefs, and knowledge and how these relate to their use of the curriculum materials. The intent is to determine how the teachers used the curriculum and its accompanying teaching and assessment resources. Beyond this, the chapter discusses how using the curriculum is related to the teachers' own learning of mathematics; their beliefs about mathematics and how it should be taught; their beliefs about their students and how they learn mathematics; and the pressures that teachers faced from students, colleagues, parents, and the community. Data sources include interviews, written surveys, and class observations. The written teacher surveys and class observation forms used in this study are available for download at http://www.wmich.edu/cpmp/evaluation.html

This chapter begins with a description of the methods used in gathering teacher data, the sample of teachers and their background, and

A Five-Year Study of the First Edition of the Core-Plus Mathematics Curriculum, pp. 61–83

similarities and differences among schools as those factors may affect teaching and the use of the curriculum. The second major section describes the results of a mainly qualitative analysis of the teacher data by noting that the teachers for whom substantial data were available fell roughly into three categories: *Experienced Supporters*, *Novices*, and *Experienced Critics*. The similarities and differences in beliefs, perceptions, and curriculum implementation practices of teachers within and across each of these categories provide the structure for the discussion.

METHOD

As a context for the following results from teachers and classrooms, recall that the curriculum in this study, *Contemporary Mathematics in Context: A Unified Approach* (Coxford et al., 1998a, 1998b, 1999, 2001), is the first published edition of a 4-year high school mathematics program developed by the Core-Plus Mathematics Project. The first three courses are designed to provide a core curriculum of broadly useful mathematics for all students. The fourth course continues the preparation of students for college mathematics. Four strands of mathematics (algebra and functions, geometry and trigonometry, statistics and probability, and discrete mathematics) are integrated throughout each course and are unified by common topics, themes, and mathematical ways of thinking. Instructional activities, homework tasks, and projects are varied in complexity so that all students can access the material at appropriate entry levels and proceed to develop mathematical understanding to their personal limits.

Designed to support teaching mathematics through problem solving (Schoen & Charles, 2003), the curriculum provides investigations based on usually realistic problem settings. The intent is for students to engage in making sense of mathematical problem situations as a vehicle for developing both an ability to reason about mathematics and a rich understanding of the mathematics embedded in the situations. Multiple representations of concepts and mathematical modeling are key features of the curriculum, and graphing calculators comparable to a TI-83 are assumed to be available at all times. Assessments are designed to engage students in problem-solving situations in both collaborative and individual settings.

Sample

A total of 30 different teachers taught mathematics to the target classes at the three schools during the 4-year duration of the study. All these teachers held a bachelor's degree or higher, and seven (23.3%) held a master's degree in mathematics education. The teachers at Washington and Adams were more experienced than those at Jefferson, with respective medians of 13, 15, and 8 years of teaching experience prior to this study. (See Table 3.4 in the previous chapter for a summary of the backgrounds of these 30 teachers.)

Since some of the 30 teachers taught just one course of the curriculum and our opportunities for gathering teacher data were limited due to considerations of time and expense, extensive data were not available for all teachers. The results that follow in this chapter are based on the 21 teachers for whom either (a) at least two data sources (surveys and interviews) from different courses were available, or (b) at least one class observation was completed. Six of these 21 teachers also taught the Core-Plus Mathematics Project (CPMP) curriculum during its national field test, and for those six teachers, data over 7 consecutive years of teaching the curriculum are available.

Teacher Backgrounds

The 21 teachers fall roughly into three categories with respect to their preparation for, experience with, and attitude about the curriculum and how to teach it. Although there is some variation within each category in the way teachers used the curriculum and in their beliefs about its use, this variation was small as compared to that across the categories. Thus in this report, we will discuss results separately within the three categories described next: *Experienced Supporters*, *Novices*, and *Experienced Critics*.

Experienced Supporters. The majority (14) of teachers were generally supportive of the use of the curriculum, had 1 to 4 years of experience teaching from a *Standards*-based mathematics curriculum at the beginning of our study, and had completed at least one summer workshop in preparation for teaching the curriculum. Three of these teachers who taught Course 1 in Grade 9 in Jefferson middle schools in this study had also taught Connected Mathematics, the reform curriculum used in the middle school. These teachers generally accepted the beliefs about mathematics and teaching that underlie the development of the curriculum. (For more details, see the Results section on Beliefs.) Finally, teachers in this first category attempted to adjust their teaching, although sometimes in different ways, to the teaching through problem-solving approach that the curriculum was intended to support. We refer to these teachers as *Experienced Supporters*, but it will be clear that the level of support varied from teacher to teacher and was not without caveats for any teacher.

Novices. Five teachers were new to the curriculum at the beginning of the study and had no professional development in preparation for teaching it.

Some of these Novices were in their early years of teaching mathematics, but others were experienced teachers of more conventional mathematics curricula.

Experienced Critics. Two experienced teachers at Jefferson High School had each completed at least one workshop to prepare to teach the curriculum, had taught the curriculum several times before the study began, but were nonetheless very critical of the curriculum and its perceived impact on students. These teachers did little to adjust their teaching to a problem-solving approach and used a great deal of skill-based material to supplement or supplant the curriculum.

The numbers of teachers by school, category, gender, and highest degree earned along with median years of experience teaching secondary school mathematics are given in Table 4.1. These data are from surveys completed by each teacher in their first year of inclusion in the study. Across all 21 teachers, 4 are from Washington High School with a median of 14 years of experience teaching secondary school mathematics, 5 are from Adams High School with a median of 23 years of experience, and 12 are from Jefferson High School (5 from middle schools and 7 from Jefferson High School) with a median of 8 years of experience. Fourteen of the teachers are classified as Experienced Supporters, 5 are Novices with respect to professional development or teaching a *Standards*-based curriculum, and 2 are Experienced Critics. Eleven of the 21 teachers are women with a median of 14 years of secondary school mathematics teaching experience, while the 10 men had a median of 11 years experience. The group of 21 teachers had a median of 12 years of secondary school mathematics teaching experience. Seven teachers had earned an MA or MS degree in mathematics education, and the 14 remaining teachers held at least a BA or BS degree.

Important School Differences

Since the three participating schools—Washington, Adams, and Jefferson—have many commonalties, results will mainly be reported across schools rather than school by school. However, school differences like those reported in the section on "Participating Schools" in the previous chapter will be noted when a school difference seems helpful for interpreting particular findings.

For example, schools differed somewhat in the curriculum units that they completed in each course, as described below, but teachers within schools were fairly consistent in this regard. The teachers at Washington High School consistently completed all seven units of each of the first three courses.[1] Unit titles and brief descriptions were given in Chapter 1

Table 4.1. Numbers of Teachers by School and Category, Gender, Highest Degree Earned, and Years of Experience Teaching Secondary School Mathematics

		Experienced Supporters			*Novices*			*Experienced Critics*		
School	*Gender*	*BA/ BS*	*MA/ MS*	*Yrs Exp*	*BA/ BS*	*MA/ MS*	*Yrs Exp*	*BA/ BS*	*MA/ MS*	*Yrs Exp*
Washington	F	–	1	15	1	–	12	–	–	–
	M	1	1	9	–	–	–	–	–	–
Adams	F	2	–	24	1	–	4	–	–	–
	M	1	1	17	–	–	–	–	–	–
Jefferson MS	F	1	1	14	–	–	–	–	–	–
	M	–	1	14	2	–	11	–	–	–
Jefferson HS	F	2	1	15	1	–	4	–	–	–
	M	1	–	8	–	–	–	2	–	17
All Schools	F	5	3	18	3	0	4	0	0	–
	M	3	3	11	2	0	11	2	0	17

(Table 1.1). The teachers at Jefferson High School completed the first six units of Course 1, with one or two starting Unit 7. The Jefferson High School teachers completed all seven units in Courses 2 and 3. At both Washington High School and Jefferson High School, Course 4 consisted of Units 1 through 7, with Jefferson High School skipping the fifth unit.

Recall from Chapter 3 that Adams High School was on a semester block schedule in which students completed a course in one semester by meeting daily for extended periods (90 minutes). Teachers at Adams High School taught the four courses of the curriculum in five semesters. Course 1 consisted of the first six units of the first course of the curriculum; Course 2 was the seventh unit of the first course plus the first five units of the second course; Course 3 was the sixth and seventh units of the second course plus Units 1–4 and sometimes Unit 6 of the third course; Course 4 included the fifth and seventh units of the third course plus the first two units of the fourth course; and Course 5 consisted of Units 3, 6, 7, and 8 of the fourth course. The content of the second, third, and fourth courses of the curriculum was clearly more "spread out" and taught over a longer period of time at Adams High School than at the other two schools.

Recall, too, that in both Washington High School and Adams High School, students in Grades 9 through 12 attended the one high school in the district, so the same teaching staff taught all four courses of the curriculum. On the other hand, in Jefferson High School, a student in Grade 9 attended one of two middle schools in the district before moving on in Grade 10 to Jefferson High School (or to a second high school in the same district). Thus the Jefferson High School teachers who taught Course 1 in this study were not in the same building as those who taught Courses 2–4. As a result, the data from the Washington and Adams high school teachers are based on a 4-year period, but the data for Jefferson teachers are either for only 1 year (Course 1) for those teaching in a middle school or for up to 3 years (Courses 2–4) for those teaching at the high school.

RESULTS

In this section, we describe the shared beliefs and implementation practices in each category of teachers, the range of beliefs and practices relative to important variables within each category, and how teachers' beliefs and implementation practices changed over time. Results are treated separately for Experienced Supporters, Novices, and Experienced Critics.

Experienced Supporters

Teachers were placed in this category because they had previous experience teaching a reform curriculum and had completed at least one professional development workshop designed to prepare them to teach the Core-Plus Mathematics curriculum. Furthermore, these teachers generally accepted the beliefs about mathematics and teaching that underlie this curriculum. These beliefs were consistent with the professional development that the teachers completed in preparation for teaching the curriculum and were reinforced by their experiences with their own students and by data collected at their schools. Since all teachers in this category shared common beliefs, we describe the beliefs in the next section with relatively few references to particular teachers' comments. Implementation practices varied much more than teachers' stated beliefs, however, so in the second section we cite many practices and quotes of teachers to illustrate ways in which these practices varied within the Experienced Supporters category.

Beliefs. These teachers all reported that they believe that understanding of mathematical concepts and methods is mainly the result of students' active attempts to make sense of mathematical problem situations in which these methods and concepts are embedded. They saw the teacher's role as providing a classroom environment that gives students the opportunity to learn mathematics in this way. They believed that some important elements of such a classroom are norms that encourage students to reason about problems, to explain their reasoning to others, to listen to the reasoning and methods used by others, and to take responsibility for their own learning. They agreed that especially important skills of teachers in such classrooms are using open-ended questions that facilitate students' efforts at sense-making and actively listening to students as they engage in mathematical activities. As one teacher (*A, ES, 2*)[2] put it, "I've learned that when students 'complain' about having to read, write, and orally communicate their understanding of mathematics, and when they 'complain' about 'having to think too much' that we and they are on the right track."

They saw this curriculum as supporting their teaching by providing a coherent collection of problem tasks that help students understand and make connections among important mathematical concepts and methods. They believed that the content and contexts that comprise this curriculum provide their students with a more useful and personally meaningful view of mathematics than is typically true of more conventional curricula. They saw the integration of the curriculum as helping to strengthen connections across mathematical content strands. They also believed that most students welcome the variety of mathematical content within a school year as it gives them breaks from content that may be especially difficult or of less interest for them.

They believed that students who complete this curriculum when it is taught well develop better habits for doing mathematics, such as reasoning through and making sense of mathematical concepts and methods; reading the textbook as an aid to understanding; asking questions of teachers and classmates; offering suggestions and answers; and, when faced with a challenging problem, working persistently on it rather than seeking help immediately or giving up easily. They believed that, as a result of these better habits, students completing the well-implemented curriculum develop a better understanding and retention of mathematical concepts, increased ability to process and solve mathematical problems, and increased inclination to enroll in future mathematics courses. They further believed that significant improvement in these outcomes can be realized with students across a wide range of entering levels of mathematical interest and background. Finally, they took satisfaction in the belief that their particular approaches to implementing the curriculum were resulting in the positive student outcomes described above.

In addition to the above pay-offs for students, teachers in the Experienced Supporters category believed that teaching through problem solving with the support of this curriculum has important pay-offs for them as teachers. The most frequently reported and, arguably, the most important of these pay-offs was their own improved understanding of high school mathematics. Teachers cited improvements in their mathematical understanding of four different types: first, deeper knowledge, and new insights into, familiar mathematical content, second, knowledge of new and unfamiliar mathematical content, third, knowledge of new and unfamiliar applications of mathematics, and fourth, deeper pedagogical content knowledge. In contrast to teachers in the first category, teachers in the second category spoke mainly of developing an understanding of topics in probability, statistics, and discrete mathematics that had previously been unfamiliar or poorly understood, although some topics in geometry (e.g., transformations and linkages) were also mentioned. One teacher (*A, ES, 1*) said, "I'm starting now to see those connections that can be made between the different areas of mathematics," and another (*A, ES, 4*) agreed by saying, "Every year in the program, I learn and think of new math concepts differently, even though I taught the material before." Some teachers found that they learned a lot from the students using this curriculum as well:

> I am absolutely amazed sometimes at the way my students will solve a problem, and I never thought about it that way. And it's like, "Group, I want you to see what this person did; I'm so excited about it." And they're thinking, "What is the big deal? We're always finding different ways to solve problems." (*J, ES, 5*)

Concerning their knowledge of new and unfamiliar applications, teachers described many of the problem contexts across content strands as new and interesting. One teacher (*A, ES, 4*) was deeply affected by the program saying, "It was the most wonderful, eye-opening experience I had had in my whole teaching career. I can't remember when I learned more about math … and figuring it out myself as a student would have is basically what I did."

Deeper pedagogical content knowledge, the fourth type of mathematical understanding listed in the previous paragraph, was seen to arise to some extent from the professional development workshops in which pedagogical content knowledge was a main focus and from the teacher support materials in which typical misconceptions and alternative ways to develop a concept or method are described. One teacher (*A, ES, 4*) explained that before the workshop training, "just to stay ahead of the kids was a real struggle." Probably the major source of the belief that their pedagogical content knowledge had deepened, however, was the realization of the teachers that teaching through problem solving gave them a better opportunity to observe and assess their students' thinking about mathematics. As one teacher (*A, ES, 3*) clarified, "If you talk to one person in the group you can find out something. You can find out what that group knows and what their weaknesses are." Understanding the strengths and gaps in their students' content knowledge provided a basis for instructional decisions. Deepening of the teachers' pedagogical content knowledge then resulted from the accumulated effect over time of repeating the process of adjustment of pedagogy informed by students' thinking. One teacher (*J, ES, 6*) reported that her entire outlook on student learning changed after using this curriculum: "When I first began [teaching this curriculum] ... I noticed what students could not do. Now I look more at what students can do."

There are areas in which some of the Experienced Supporters' beliefs differed from those that underlie problem-based or *Standards*-based teaching. While these teachers agreed that student outcomes were consistently strong in areas of understanding, application, and problem solving, there was a concern shared by some in this group about paper-and-pencil algebraic skills. To respond to these concerns, the curriculum developers provided several features including a supplementary *Reference and Practice* book for each of Courses 1 to 3 and a section called Preparing for Undergraduate Mathematics Placement (PUMP) at the end of each unit in Course 4. Many of the Experienced Supporters considered these skill practice and test preparation materials to be useful and important parts of the curriculum. Feeling pressure for their students to do well on college entrance and placement tests, some teachers believed they should, and did, provide even more supplementary materials for skill and test practice.

Finally, most of these teachers believed that teaching through problem solving is more time-consuming than teaching in a more direct way, especially with respect to the time required for assessment and grading. With experience, teachers found ways to reduce the time that they spent outside of class on grading and planning activities. Some of the ways in which teachers compensated will be described in a later section.

Implementation Practices. Of course, there was variation in how Experienced Supporters taught the curriculum, but there were many commonalities as well. These teachers all based the sequence of mathematical content they taught largely on the student textbook, with the exception of some supplementing of skill practice and testing to be described later. They also adjusted their teaching approaches in the direction of teaching through problem solving that the curriculum was designed to support, but there was considerably more variation in the specifics of their teaching approaches than in both their beliefs and their content goals. In this section, we attempt to describe what we see as salient features of that variation.

We begin with a description of the practices of a teacher (*A, ES, 1*) who seemed to do a particularly good job of teaching the curriculum through problem solving. We will call him Mr. Schulte. The following description of his implementation practices comes from six class observations (three in Course 1, two in Course 4, and one in AP Calculus), five interviews, and two written surveys collected over a 3-year period.

Mr. Schulte typically began class with a 5- to 15-minute whole-group discussion as a launch to familiarize students with the context of the investigation that they would spend most of the class time working on in groups of three or four. If his class was at the beginning of a lesson in the curriculum, he usually based his launch on the one in the student materials that was designed to provide information about and promote interest in the setting of the investigation that followed and to assess prior knowledge. He then based a discussion on the open-ended questions in the curriculum's lesson launch, called Think About This Situation. If his class started the day at a point other than the beginning of a multiday lesson, he designed his own daily mini-launch to help students recall what they did the day before and connect it with what they would be working on that day. In either scenario, his daily mini-launch often included a brief review, usually in a discussion format, of concepts and methods that would be helpful in the upcoming day's activities.

The launch involved the whole class, but students often worked together with a nearby classmate or two. Mr. Schulte sometimes asked pairs of students about hypothetical situations involving a new concept and had them reach a consensus prediction about some new properties or uses of the concepts that were to be investigated in the day's lesson. During the whole-class summary at the end of the day, students used what they learned that day to reflect on whether their prediction was accurate and how it may need to be adjusted.

When Mr. Schulte judged that students were ready, the class began to work in groups of three or four on a problem-based investigation from the student materials. Mr. Schulte circulated among the groups and spurred discussion with many open-ended questions. He asked students to compare a problem to one that they knew how to solve. He asked them how concepts and procedures were similar to or different from others. When students were using symbolic procedures as part of solving a problem, he asked them to describe what the numbers and symbols represented in the problem situation and how changes in numbers and symbols were reflected in the problem situation. He also stressed the importance of students developing multiple ways to solve a problem, and he emphasized that some questions can have more than one correct answer depending on one's assumptions.

Students in Mr. Schulte's class were, to a great extent, monitors of their own work. Students were seen coming in before class to ask questions of one another and to compare findings. Mr. Schulte also put assignments and reminders on the overhead before students came to class so they could be responsible for their own pacing. Often when students gave answers or asked questions, he asked another student if the given answer made sense, or he turned the question over to the students' small group or the whole class for discussion. Sometimes he allowed students to struggle a little by not answering their questions immediately but instead redirecting them to their groups before he intervened. This gave the students an opportunity to move toward a valid solution strategy by themselves. Mr. Schulte gave students plenty of time to complete their work and to understand the mathematical content. Often class observers stated that he seemed to be in no rush to cover material, although there was a sense that the work had to be done. Mr. Schulte devoted most of his instructional time to allowing groups to work together on in-class investigations or their assignments.

Mr. Schulte made graphing calculators available to students whenever they were needed during the class. He also used an overhead calculator when whole class discussion involved the uses of technology. In some situations, especially in later courses, he did not allow students to use calculators. He attempted to get students to make good decisions about when to use a calculator and not to be too dependent on its use. He sometimes allowed students to use a note card on in-class exams rather than insisting that they memorize all formulas. Mr. Schulte once said that he "loves the problem-based curriculum," a sentiment that is evident from the articles about the curriculum that he displayed around his classroom.

Mr. Schulte cultivated a classroom atmosphere in which students often answered questions with conceptual explanations, even when they were not specifically asked to do so. Sometimes when a student offered an incomplete definition or conjecture, Mr. Schulte asked follow-up questions and offered examples until the class was able to come to a complete and accurate formulation. Usually when students made conjectures, he asked the class for examples or counterexamples of their claims. He then used those examples as a way to direct discussion toward bigger concepts. Often Mr. Schulte used questioning and prompting to help students develop definitions of new terms on their own. When several small groups were having trouble at the same point in an investigation, Mr. Schulte reorganized the class into a whole group so that the students could discuss their issues together. He reminded the students of related problems that they knew how to solve and asked them to try to connect the problem they were working on to previously learned ideas. Even when a lesson was mostly procedurally oriented, Mr. Schulte made sure that students arrived at the procedures in a meaningful way through discussion and exploration. In other words, the emphasis of his teaching was consistently on understanding and problem solving, even when the goal was to learn procedures.

After giving students a significant portion of class time to engage in mathematical sense-making in small groups, Mr. Schulte called students back together for a whole-group discussion of what they had learned and what connections they had made among concepts and with previous content. Thus a class period always ended with a summary of the main ideas of the day's lesson. If the class period ended when students had just completed an investigation in the curriculum, this summary was usually based on a feature designed for this purpose in the student materials called a Checkpoint. If the class period ended in the midst of an investigation, Mr. Schulte designed his own "mini-checkpoint" to be sure students pulled together what they had learned before the end of the class period. If students made some predictions during the launch at the beginning of the class period, the predictions were revisited and discussed in light of the day's learning.

Mr. Schulte did not make lengthy homework assignments. He did not spend a lot of class time going over assignments or reviewing concepts and methods, because students were given enough time to learn or relearn the material. Often while students were working in groups, he checked over their homework and offered suggestions for corrections while simultaneously observing what they were presently working on.

All 13 of the other teachers in the Experienced Supporter category taught from the curriculum in ways that, at least on the surface, had many similarities with Mr. Schulte's approach, although our evidence is not as complete for all of them. Of course, each teacher brought his or her own personality to the classroom. For example, one teacher (*A, ES, 3*) made especially effective use of humor. Another (*J, ES, 6*) was very conscientious about her teaching, videotaping herself in the classroom and analyzing the tapes in an attempt to improve her questioning and monitoring techniques, which were already judged by observers to be exceptionally effective. This same teacher organized a field trip to a local manufacturing plant so the students could see a real-world use of the quality control procedures taught in one of the Course 3 units. A third teacher (*A, ES, 4*) was especially adept at using hands-on activities; for example, her students made pop-up greeting cards that operated on the flexibility property of quadrilaterals.

At a deeper level, there were also differences in how teachers handled questions and answers during student explorations, how they monitored and pressed for student understanding, and how they supplemented the curriculum. Some of the different practices appeared to encourage further sense-making by the students. For example, one teacher (*A, ES, 3*) had students write letters explaining the meaning of a mathematical concept or summarizing what was done in class that day. Another teacher (*J, ES, 5*) put a great deal of effort into developing students' independent thinking. She often allowed the class to have their own whole-group discussion, interjecting ideas and guiding them only as necessary to push the students to fully understand the mathematics under discussion. She handed back assignments that were not done satisfactorily by most in the class and had students revisit their solution methods and discuss in small groups what was wrong with them and how to correct them. Students then handed the assignment back to the teacher for further feedback. She also wrote differing student solutions on the board and had students critique the solutions together and decide which was best and why.

Some practices by other teachers provided students with more direction than Mr. Schulte often gave. For example, one teacher (*A, ES, 2*) usually started her class with a review and correction of the previous day's homework and then had a whole-class discussion, accompanied by directly teaching the important concepts and methods that were prerequisites for class that day. This took about 30 minutes, at least twice as long as a launch in Mr. Shulte's class. After the preliminary activities, students worked on an investigation in small groups, but this teacher was the obvious intellectual authority in the classroom. Much more than was true in Mr. Schulte's class, students checked regularly with this teacher to make sure they were correct, they relied on her to give them information and hints during the whole-group discussions, and they tended to ask her questions when they were working in small groups instead of asking each other. Often she gave incomplete answers such as, "You need to explain more about the math behind it," but students sometimes seemed confused when she did not follow up with any further idea of what she meant. Nevertheless, students in this teacher's class were quite open to working together and helping each other with homework problems. In several instances, a student or small group was observed explaining some mathematics to a different group.

A particularly directive teacher (*A, ES, 4*) made attempts to encourage students to monitor their own work by writing assignments and agendas on the board at the beginning of class, but some of her other practices conflicted with the self-monitoring norm she seemed to want to establish. For example, when this teacher asked a question of the class and a student answered incorrectly or gave a short or incomplete answer, she often did not follow up. When students asked her questions during small-group investigations, she often answered completely and relayed her answers to the entire class. Her "answers" were mostly direct instructions, such as "They are asking you to find an enlargement factor" or "Maybe use the distance formula?" that appeared to curtail the need for students to make sense of the problems on their own.

All of the Experienced Supporters had their students work in pairs or groups of three or four for significant portions of class time, but they varied on how, and how effectively, they did so. Much like Mr. Schulte, many of the teachers were effective with groups. For example, consider the following summary of observations of one teacher (*J, ES, 7*). Students were seated in groups of four at tables during the entire class time. The observer noted that groups worked well together during the time they were given. Occasionally students were even given partner quizzes. Students learned in a variety of settings in this teacher's classroom. She usually had a whole-group discussion along with time for individual or small-group work. Watching the class go over a test that they had taken the previous day, an observer noted, "Throughout this discussion, students are participating, answering questions, explaining their solutions." At the beginning of class, the teacher usually used the previous day's assignment as a basis for starting the current day's discussion in order to help students see the connections between topics and concepts. She used a lot of "what if" questions to help students make connections between different problems. She also made sure that students clarified their solutions by asking them questions, and she used counterexamples as a way to signal students to rework conjectures that were not quite correct.

Another example of especially effective use of small groups was by a teacher (*J, ES, 3*) who had her students seated in threes and fours at tables for whole-group and small-group discussions. In either classroom organization, she continually asked students to describe how and why they were doing things, asked them to justify their answers, and had students answer each other's questions. Students seemed eager to please her and answer her questions to the best of their ability. Sometimes students got out of their seats to ask the teacher a question instead of asking the other students at their table. When the teacher instructed the students to work together, however, they remained on task and worked well together to come to a conclusion. Every student in the class seemed comfortable with the fact that they were expected to actively participate in completing problems within their groups as well as with the fact that each group member had to present a part of their assigned problem's solution to the class.

Like Mr. Schulte and those described above, two other teachers were effective in getting students involved in their learning, but their approaches were different in potentially important ways. One of these teachers (*A, ES, 3*) always wrote an agenda on the board in advance so that students could work at their own pace and do bonus problems if they got ahead or wanted extra credit. He let students decide what they needed more work on in class. It was obvious that they felt confident enough to work through problems on their own—often questions arose that the students helped each other answer. He also let the students be responsible for checking that their solutions were correct: "My answer book is open,

I'm open, you are on your own time." This teacher often asked students to describe and explain procedures and concepts in different ways (both in groups and individually) to make sure that they had a deep understanding of the mathematics they were trying to learn.

The second teacher mentioned above (*J, ES, 2*) also was effective in facilitating student learning, but he did not insist that all students work in groups. During small-group work in his class there were always a few students who worked individually. The teacher did nothing (and felt strongly that he should not do anything) to get students to work in groups if they did not want to. Although he pressed students toward understanding big mathematical ideas, unlike Mr. Schulte his questioning was often very directed as opposed to encouraging students to struggle or discover on their own (e.g., "Do you see anything from algebra here that we can do with the formula? Starts with a D?").

By contrast, another teacher (*W, ES, 1*) often had his class form small groups, but rather than circulating among them to facilitate learning, he waited at his desk for students' questions. The students' questions were mostly to check if their answers were correct. Regarding teacher questioning and whole-class discussion, this teacher used mainly fact-based, rather than open-ended questions. In fact, some students commented on the distance and rigidity of this teacher. Both the teacher and his students seemed to view the group work as focused on working through and getting correct answers to each question in the sequence of investigation problems. They did not seem to appreciate the deeper learning that is embedded in the problem-solving activities, a disposition sometimes evident in two or three other teachers and their students. As one class observer wrote, "A difficulty with [this teacher's] approach is that he fails to get the positive student-student group effects [from the group work]." In spite of the apparent shortcomings in his work with groups, this teacher stated in a survey that he "sees the power of [group work] in action. Students learn!"

Two teachers in the Experienced Supporter category often had problems managing their students when they worked in groups, to the extent that it detracted seriously from student learning. During an observation of the first teacher's (*J, ES, 1*) class, students seemed to be working together very well, but during another observation of the same teacher, most of the students spent most of their available work time socializing. In an observation of the second teacher's (*J, ES, 4*) class, the observer wrote, "Students are busy talking—not much on task—some books open at desks—group next to me has their desks empty—socializing." The observer further noted that one group was playing cards and that the teacher spent quite a while talking to another group about topics unrelated to mathematics. This second teacher's management problems were not restricted to small-group work. Several times when this teacher was leading a whole-group discussion, the observer noted that most students were not really paying attention and that students were giving responses intended to make other students laugh.

Concerning supplementing the curriculum, most if not all of the Experienced Supporters used the *Resource and Practice* books and, in Course 4, the skill practice material in preparation for college mathematics placement examinations. They also commonly provided algebraic practice or memorization tasks for class warm-up, homework, and/or quizzes. Six teachers (*J, ES,* 4; *W, ES, 2*; *A, ES, 2*; *W, ES, 3*; *A, ES, 3*; and *A, ES, 4*) in this category mentioned supplementing as an issue in their interviews. Such supplementing seemed to be more common in Courses 1 and 2, as there was a common belief among teachers that there is not enough time given to practice in the early courses of the curriculum for students to really become proficient with some important procedures. Two of these teachers (*A, ES, 4* and *J, ES, 4*) particularly emphasized the need for supplementing basic skills review, practice, and testing. They also agreed on the importance of students memorizing rules or procedures that they would be using in later mathematics courses.

An important motivation for supplementing to strengthen skills was the issue of high stakes tests that students were required to take, including state tests, PSAT, ACT, SAT, and college mathematics placement exams. Many teachers (and parents) worried that their students would not be ready for the algebraic manipulation and factual knowledge emphasized on these tests. As one teacher (*J, ES, 4*) put it, the curriculum does not provide enough "repetition of specific math skills," and he was not sure how well it prepared students for college entrance exams. On the positive side, he believed that the more experience he had teaching the curriculum, the better he became at deciding how and when to provide supplementary material. Two teachers (*A, ES, 1* and *J, ES, 4*) also noted that, while they supplement this curriculum to some extent, they had never used a curriculum that they did not supplement in some way. They considered tailoring a curriculum to better fit their needs and the needs of their students to be an important part of good teaching.

Novices

The five teachers in this category were new to the curriculum at the beginning of this study and had no professional development in preparation for teaching it. While none of these teachers was opposed to the use of the curriculum, their understanding of its goals and their confidence in teaching it was clearly evolving as they gained experience with the curriculum materials. Both their beliefs and their implementation practices were largely idiosyncratic, so we briefly sketch each teacher's beliefs in the next section and, in the same order, each teacher's implementation practices in the section after that.

Beliefs. The evolution of the Novices' beliefs is illustrated well by a teacher (*J, N, 3*) who struggled with one of her classes that was composed of lower track students who did not attend class regularly. Many of her students had failed mathematics once or twice and had been held back. This teacher commented on her experience with the curriculum as follows:

> When I first came here I was really appalled by the idea of not having a lower-level class for these kids. And I was like, "What? You put them all in this class, and I'm supposed to teach them this stuff? You're nuts." But, you know, even my lowest kids in there, I think they have learned more this year than they would have in general math. I really do, because you stick them in those classes, and it's a storage place, and they learn absolutely no mathematics. But, you know, [in this curriculum] they have gotten something, and they have some math skills to take with them out in life. Even if it's not enough to move on [to the next course], it's definitely more than they would have gotten in those old, traditional [general math] courses.

A second teacher in the Novice group (*J, N, 1*) was a long-term substitute who replaced a regular teacher who was on leave. He was an experienced mathematics teacher (13 years), but he was new to teaching a *Standards*-based mathematics curriculum. He believed that students get more problem-solving skills using this curriculum, but he believed a combination of *Standards*-based and conventional approaches would probably be best. He thought that students seemed to feel more relaxed in *Standards*-based classrooms than in conventional ones. Some of his students indicated a preference to be in a conventional class, but he believed that their older siblings or parents influenced them negatively about the curriculum.

The third Novice teacher (*A, N, 1*) spoke favorably of the curriculum, but she believed it contained too little basic skill practice and review. She believed that students who struggled with the curriculum were often just being lazy and not doing the work as opposed to not understanding the concepts. She also believed that students who did not like the curriculum were probably influenced by negative comments from their parents. The fourth Novice (*W, N, 1*) teacher expressed much enthusiasm for the curriculum throughout this study, but her efforts to implement it were overwhelmed by classroom management problems as described in the next section.

The fifth teacher (*J, N, 2*) in the Novice category saw the curriculum as a way for students of all ability levels and learning styles to be successful.

He mentioned several times that he thought the curriculum would be a good independent study program for high ability students, but he saw group work as optional and rarely used it. In an interview, he said, "[The middle school curriculum] seems to depend more on group and class discussions than [the high school curriculum] does." This teacher complained that the curriculum did not tell teachers enough about what to do in their classrooms (i.e., when to have students work individually, what to bring up in class discussions, and so on). He reported feeling a lot of pressure from other teachers to include more drill and practice of skills so that students would be prepared for standardized tests.

Implementation Practices. Like their beliefs, the Novices' implementation practices were mixed and often evolved as the teachers gained experience with the curriculum. The first of these teachers (*J, N, 3*) was originally hired as a substitute, and although she was needed full-time, contract restrictions required that she teach only 3 days a week. The class relied on substitutes and resource teachers on the other 2 days of the week. This arrangement was sometimes problematic as on 1 day, when the observer noted that the substitute for this teacher knew "no mathematics" and so the special education resource teacher ran the class. Overall, though, this teacher facilitated understanding with open-ended questions in both whole-group discussions and small-group investigations.

Similar to Mr. Schulte, she used brief whole-group discussions at the beginning of class to review and connect back to what students had been doing and to spark interest in the day's upcoming activities. Students spent most of their class time working on investigations in small groups. Although the teacher was clearly in charge when leading large-group discussions, she let the students struggle with ideas while encouraging them as they worked together. One of her classes, mentioned in the *Beliefs* section, was composed of lower track students, many of whom didn't attend class regularly and had failed one or two previous mathematics classes. Despite the students' weak mathematics backgrounds and the regular teacher being in class only a few days per week, the students worked well together. All students worked in groups of three or four; no one worked alone. During an observation when the teacher was absent, the students got right to work, did little socializing, and were able to get through most of the investigation by collaborating.

As noted in the previous section, the second teacher (*J, N, 1*) in this group was a long-term substitute for a regular teacher who was on leave. Since he took his teaching position late in the year and was absent on the day of one scheduled observation, there was just one observation of his class. Students in his class were willing to help each other and seemed comfortable working together, although he allowed them to work on their own if they did not want to work in groups. The observer noted that students seemed to like him and to respect his authority.

The third Novice teacher (*A, N, 1*) found that she had a hard time keeping students motivated. She tried to vary activities occasionally, but she seemed to rely mostly on a brief review/presentation at the beginning of class and then putting students to work in groups on their homework. She often asked open-ended questions, such as "How do you know?" "Why did you do that?" and "What does it mean?" She admitted to having an initial difficulty with letting the students do the work themselves, but she had gotten used to it, liked the teaching approach a lot, and thought it would help the students not only learn the mathematics but also develop their social, reading, and writing skills. She held individual students accountable for their work in groups and made sure that students worked toward a group consensus before depending on her help. She expressed her own difficulty with the mathematics from time to time, and her limited understanding of some important concepts was sometimes evident. She indicated that she relied heavily on collaborating with her more experienced colleagues on both subject matter and pedagogical concerns. She considered supplementing basic skill practice and providing extra review sessions to be a necessity.

The fourth Novice teacher (*W, N, 1*) consistently expressed strong support for the curriculum. In the first two courses, she allowed time for students to struggle with the material in a manner consistent with the curriculum design. Unfortunately, she had a great deal of difficulty managing her classroom. Students were often off-task, socializing, or even listening to music on headphones. When the teacher attempted to monitor the group work, her focus was on getting through each investigation with correct answers for each question. She rarely pushed for deep understanding of the mathematical content. A student in this teacher's Course 2 class noted that he and his classmates were frustrated with the lack of class structure and of learning. Interestingly, her teaching approach changed considerably when she taught Course 4. She still had difficulty with classroom management, but she used a more direct approach to teaching. Compared to her teaching in Courses 1 and 2, she did more teacher-centered instruction at the overhead, including summaries of the mathematical content with worked out examples before students began their work on an investigation from the curriculum. These comments about Course 4, however, are based on the observation of one lesson and may have been an anomaly rather than a permanent change in teaching methodology.

The fifth teacher (*J, N, 2*) saw group work as optional. Other than occasionally having students compare answers with neighbors, he rarely used any sort of group or partner work in his classes. His teaching approach appeared to be mainly whole-group discussion. As an observer noted,

> There was little attempt made to get students to clarify answers or justify responses. Follow-up questions were asked only when a response was incorrect and sometimes it was not clear if students understood when and why they did have correct answers.

In response to perceived pressure from other teachers, he provided extra drill and practice of skills so that students would be prepared for standardized tests. For example, when his Course 1 students were working on a geometry unit, he supplemented with worksheets that had students connect dozens of geometric terms with their definitions. As a teacher in a middle school, he taught only Course 1 classes and admitted that he had never looked at the later course materials. Ironically, this teacher believed that he made effective use of the curriculum, as he complained, "We have staff members who don't deliver the curriculum the way it's meant to be delivered."

Experienced Critics

The teachers in this category were opposed to this curriculum and worked actively against its use at Jefferson High School. The teacher for whom we have the most data (*J, EC, 1*) had completed 25 years of high school mathematics teaching, and he had taught Courses 3 and 4 prior to this study. He had also participated in a 1-week workshop to prepare to teach Course 3. His class organization, assignments, and grading schemes were all very conventional. Although he called himself "a very traditionally-oriented teacher," he evidently saw several good things about the curriculum, for example, (emphases are the teacher's) "[The] curriculum does help STUDENTS to LEARN how to think. The curriculum has given me a BETTER insight on where MATH is used and how STUDENTS learn. [The curriculum] has many good points but is weak in certain areas." On the whole, he believed that the best curriculum would be a combination of *Standards*-based and conventional approaches. He regularly supplemented the curriculum with worksheets and problems that he created himself or found in conventional textbooks. He taught very conventionally as well: "I do not enjoy teaching the 'Pure Core Model Method.' It is not me."

His biggest complaint about the curriculum was that he often could not figure out what the investigation questions were asking unless he looked at the answer in the teacher's manual. He complained that students in this curriculum were not proficient enough with paper-and-pencil skills (e.g., dividing fractions or graphing a line without a calculator) and that the basic skills of his students "are terrible." In one interview he talked about how he believed it was so much easier for students to "do it with paper and pencil" (meaning in a conventional way) than it was "to set up that whole thing" (meaning work through a contextual problem). He also recalled his frustration trying to help his daughter when she was in a Course 2 class. Having never taught Course 2, he was unhappy that he had to "read all the way back to problem one to see what the heck was going on." He did admit that students in a conventional curriculum, however, just tried to fit a problem to a formula and gave up if they couldn't think of a formula. The students in the *Standards*-based curriculum, on the other hand, tried some sort of solution strategy whether they recognized the situation or not. They "will just figure out a way to make it work." Still he noted that he would prefer students who can combine these two approaches to solve problems.

This experienced critic (*J, EC, 1*) spent most of his class time in whole-group discussion. He asked the students mostly closed-ended questions, and they provided the answers. When a student's answer was incorrect or incomplete, the teacher sometimes asked another student until someone answered correctly and completely. He often assigned students part of an investigation to do at home, and the next day he led the class through the answers together. An observer noted that his class had "the feel of a really long review of homework." The only time students worked together was when they were given a few minutes to work on test corrections with a partner. When grading homework, he gave credit to students for trying all of the assigned problems. The observer noted that there were far fewer students in this teacher's class (nine) than in another section of the same course that met at the same time. Apparently at the beginning of a semester the numbers of students per section were balanced, but students were allowed to switch sections upon request during the semester.

The second experienced critic (*J, EC, 2*), a man in his 40s, had about 8 years of experience, including teaching Courses 2 and 3 prior to this study. He had also completed three 2-week workshops to prepare to teach Courses 2, 3, and 4, respectively. He seemed to deliberately avoid classroom observers, twice canceling a scheduled observation, so we have no direct evidence of what happened in his classes. However, his beliefs, along with indirect evidence from interviews with students and teacher colleagues, suggest that he taught in a conventional manner. He referred to teaching via this curriculum as "discovery learning" and he saw little value in it. On a written survey completed during Course 2, he noted [the teacher's emphases]:

> I have learned that the best balance of instruction is 20–25% discovery learning. The rest would be traditional. *Traditional learning is more efficient. Much more material can be covered using a traditional format within a year.* I've attempted (nearly 100%) the Core-Plus approach for all of CP2, CP3, and

> CP4. I've found too many students are turned off by this approach. They are less successful at mastery of material than their traditional counterparts were. *Discovery learning is not the best format for gaining knowledge of higher level math skills*.

Similar attitudes are reflected in the following quote 2 years later:

> In place of (in addition to) the MORE questions, algebraic drill is needed. They [students] not only need the drill, but need a break from the discovery learning approach.... If you develop MORE-type sections that are traditional in nature (including example problems with answer to some problems), then you will greatly improve this program.

("MORE questions" refer to the homework problems in the curriculum materials.)

CHAPTER SUMMARY AND DISCUSSION

Issues as complex as teachers' curriculum implementation practices and their beliefs about mathematics and how it should be taught are not easy to characterize. The qualitative descriptions in this chapter are intended to give an accurate general description of what teachers in this study believed about the curriculum and how they implemented it in their classrooms. Although some variation from school to school, teacher to teacher, and from course to course for a given teacher is discussed, a complete, detailed accounting of all these variations is not possible. In fact, there are other variations like those between observers and interviewers that are unavoidable limitations of our study.

Acknowledging these limitations, the picture of the beliefs and classroom practices of 21 teachers in this study suggests that all but two, the Experienced Critics, expressed generally positive beliefs about the curriculum. Many believed the curriculum had a positive impact on students' understanding and problem-solving abilities and, in some cases, on other attributes like social skills, writing and reading mathematical content, and a better understanding of more applications of mathematics. Some teachers were less sure that the curriculum provided sufficient emphasis on developing students' paper-and-pencil algebraic skills. Most of the teachers seemed to implement the curriculum in ways that would be largely acceptable to the curriculum developers, although the details of that implementation varied by teacher. The teachers consistently reported satisfaction that their teaching of the curriculum was having a positive effect on their own mathematical learning as well as on that of their students.

Several teachers emphasized and added to the developers' *Reference and Practice* books with the intent of strengthening students' algebraic skills.

Compared to the Experienced Supporters, the Novices were less sure of themselves in the classroom. This lack of confidence sometimes contributed to management problems that seriously compromised the learning environment in their classrooms. Novices were also not as sure about how well their students were learning, although they voiced generally positive initial impressions and optimism about their future use of the curriculum. By contrast, the two Experienced Critics believed that the curriculum and teaching approach were less efficient than direct teaching of a conventional curriculum. Their classrooms reflected their beliefs as they mainly used direct teaching either from a substitute conventional textbook or an answer-oriented presentation of the *Standards*-based curriculum with very little of the intended involvement of the students in making sense of the mathematical ideas.

In the following Chapters 5–8, student achievement patterns in each of the 4 years of high school are analyzed and reported.

NOTES

1. The units completed were quite consistent from teacher to teacher at Washington High School and Adams High School. The data were not as consistent for Jefferson High School since there were more teachers and less common planning and cooperation. For given teachers, there were some instances of skipping or shortening of individual lessons within units. Completion data are also missing for a few teachers.
2. Teacher ID codes have the form (*school, category, number*), where *school* is *W* = Washington High School, *A* = Adams High School, and *J* = Jefferson High School; *category* is *ES* = Experienced Supporter, *N* = Novice, and *EC* = Experienced Critic; and *number* is the individual teacher identifier 1 through 7 within the particular *school/category*.

PART II

YEARLY PATTERNS IN STUDENT ACHIEVEMENT

CHAPTER 5

ACHIEVEMENT PATTERNS IN YEAR 1

Four Content Strands

The Core-Plus Mathematics curriculum is designed so that students in Course 1 have quite different learning experiences than those in more conventional Algebra I courses. In general, Core-Plus Mathematics students are expected to spend more time making sense of problems in which mathematical ideas and methods are embedded and less time practicing individual symbol manipulation skills outside a problem context. They also are likely to spend less time on conventional algebraic topics and more time on other content (geometry, statistics and probability, and discrete mathematics) and the connections among content topics. The actual extent of differences in student experiences depends on many factors, including the level of implementation of the Core-Plus Mathematics curriculum and specific characteristics of the Algebra I curriculum and how it is taught. Nevertheless, it would not be surprising if what Core-Plus Mathematics students know and can do mathematically at particular points in time differ markedly from students in a more conventional curriculum. This chapter is intended to paint a picture of students' mathematical knowledge, understanding, and skill at the end of Course 1. How

A Five-Year Study of the First Edition of the Core-Plus Mathematics Curriculum, pp. 87–119

student results vary across teachers and their implementations is addressed further in Chapter 14.

The chapter begins with a description of the achievement assessments administered in Course 1. Results from the *ITED-Q*, a standardized test of quantitative thinking for high school students, are then reported. Next, the performance of students at the end of ninth grade on the paper-and-pencil assessment of a range of curriculum-specific objectives is described. Concepts and methods in the areas of algebra and functions, geometry, statistics and probability, and discrete mathematics are included on the assessment. The description of student performance is enriched by interview problems administered individually to a sample of students that assess a range of learning outcomes including problem-solving abilities.

ACHIEVEMENT TESTING IN COURSE 1

A standardized test (*ITED-Q*) was administered to all Course 1 students at the three schools in September 1997. During the school year, 80 students (8 at Washington, 24 at Adams, and 48 at Jefferson) were interviewed individually as they were presented with a variety of problems. Teachers were asked to select the students to be interviewed so that they represented a full range of the class's diversity. At the end of the school year in May 1998, Course 1 students were again tested using an alternate form of the *ITED-Q*. (In Adam's semester block system, Fall Course 1 students were tested in January and Spring Course 1 students were tested in May.)

Within a day of the *ITED-Q* end-of-course testing, each student completed one of three forms of a Course 1 posttest. The posttest was comprised of tasks adopted, or sometimes adapted, from tests used in the CPMP field test or from assessment tasks included in the first edition Course 1 *Assessment Resources*. The three forms together measured the main content goals of Course 1 in all four content strands: Algebra and Functions, Geometry and Trigonometry, Statistics and Probability, and Discrete Mathematics. Since only the Washington High School classes completed Unit 7 of Course 1, *Simulation Models*, content from that unit was not included on the Course 1 posttest. The three forms were distributed randomly in each classroom, so performance data on each form can be viewed as essentially equivalent to that of the entire set of students. The content breakdown in Table 5.1 was used in the construction and in the analysis of the Course 1 posttest.

In summary, the achievement measures administered in Course 1 were two paper-and-pencil tests and a set of interview problems. A nationally standardized test served as a pretest and, in alternate form, as a posttest.

Table 5.1. Content Categories and Subcategories of the Course 1 Posttest

Algebra and Functions	*Statistics and Probability*
Use of Algebraic Operations	Measures of Central Tendency
Algebraic Modeling	Box Plots and Histograms
Depicting and Understanding Graphical Representations	Scatterplots and Linear Regression
Geometry and Trigonometry	*Discrete Mathematics*
Geometric Computation	Euler Circuits and Paths
Visualization and Spatial Reasoning	Critical Paths
	Graph Coloring

A Course 1 posttest, developed by the researchers in three randomly distributed forms, tested the main goals of the course through Unit 6. The interview problems were assembled mainly from CPMP assessment material with the goal of including representative content from each strand.

Standardized Achievement Test

The standardized test was the mathematics subtest of the *Iowa Tests of Educational Development* (*ITED*), called *Ability to Do Quantitative Thinking*, or *ITED-Q* (Feldt, Forsyth, Ansley, & Alnot, 1993). Rather than testing outcomes of a particular high school curriculum, the focus of *ITED-Q* is on quantitative thinking processes that are important for anyone with at least a high school education. In particular, the *ITED-Q* assesses high school students' ability to use appropriate mathematical reasoning in situations requiring the interpretation of data, charts, or graphs that represent information related to business, social and political issues, medicine, and science. It consists of tasks that require students to select appropriate procedures, make connections among various concepts, and identify examples and counterexamples of concepts. It also includes tasks that require students to make inferences or predictions based on data or information often given in graphs or tables, as well as tasks that require students to apply quantitative procedures to relatively novel situations, reason quantitatively, and evaluate reasonableness of solutions.

The mathematical content includes whole numbers, exponents, fractions, decimals, percents, ratios, geometry, measurement, estimation, rounding, statistics, probability, tables, and graphs. Although very little symbolic algebra is required, the *ITED-Q* is quite demanding for the full range of high school students. For example, on the *ITED-Q* (Form L, Level 15) the median of the nationally representative norm group in Spring of Grade 9 is approximately 16 of 40 tasks correct, and the 99th percentile is approximately 33 of 40 tasks correct. The national norm data for this version of the *ITED-Q* was collected during the 1991–92 school year, before any of the NSF-funded reform curricula were developed. The standard score that *ITED-Q* reports is a single interval scale with approximate mean and standard deviation of 250 and 25, respectively, that allows comparisons of scores across test forms and testing times (whereas a raw score, say, 25 correct of 40 on one form and level is not necessarily comparable to 25 correct on another form or level). In this study, standard scores are used in the statistical analyses as the test authors recommend (Feldt et al., 1993).

The *ITED-Q* correlates highly with other well-known measures of mathematical achievement, such as the *Iowa Test of Basic Skills* (*ITBS*), the ACT Mathematics test, and the SAT Mathematics test. A form of the *ITED-Q* was administered as a pretest to all students at the beginning of Course 1, and alternative forms as posttests at the end of Course 1. In the present study, the alpha reliabilities of the *ITED-Q* pretest and posttest were .83 and .86, respectively.

STANDARDIZED TEST RESULTS

A school by gender ANCOVA with the *ITED-Q* pretest as covariate and the *ITED-Q* posttest as dependent variable resulted in a nonsignificant school by gender interaction. Similarly, the interactions between school and preachievement levels (PAL) and between gender and PAL were not statistically significant, so it makes sense to discuss the main effects separately. The PAL main effect was not statistically significant and is of little interest, since the posttest is an equivalent form of the pretest that was used to define the PAL groups. The school and gender main effects are discussed in the next two sections. The results of the ANCOVAs and descriptive statistics for all students who completed either the *ITED-Q* pretest or posttest by school, gender, and PAL are given in the Chapter 5 Appendix.

Results by School

Students (70 at Washington, 189 at Adams, and 353 at Jefferson) completed the *ITED-Q* (Form L, Level 15) in May. The mean scores by school were at the 52nd, 63rd, and 62nd percentile in the nationally representative norm group of students. For these same students, the school means on the *ITED-Q* (Form K, Level 15) in September were at the 55th, 65th, and 65th percentiles, respectively. In each school, standard score means increased from May to September on this test, as shown in Figure 5.1, but the growth did not differ significantly from 1 year of growth at the pretest percentile by the *ITED-Q* nationally representative norm group. The *ITED-Q* posttest means adjusted for variance in the *ITED-Q* pretest in descending order are Adams (274.2), Jefferson (273.3), and Washington (272.4). The similarity in growth across schools is evidenced statistically by a nonsignificant school effect in the ANCOVA described above with details in the Chapter 5 Appendix, Part 2.

ITED-Q was replaced by other achievement measures in subsequent years of the longitudinal study, with one exception. The *ITED-Q* (Form K, Level 16) was administered to 122 Adams students at the end of Course 2 in the fall semester. For simplicity, the main results are reported here. At the beginning of Course 1, the mean standard score of these students was 272.2, at the 66th national student percentile. At the end of Course 2, the mean standard score of the same students was 293.1, at the 73rd national student percentile. The increase in percentile rank indicates a mean growth over these 1.5 years that is significantly greater than the average of the nationally representative student norm group at this point in the distribution. In this sample of Adams students, the growth was about .23 standard deviations greater than 1.5 years growth of the norm group. Scores on the *ITED-Q* Course 2 posttest adjusted for variance in the *ITED-Q* pretest did not differ significantly by gender or by pretest achievement level. Descriptive statistics and analysis of covariance results are given in the Chapter 5 Appendix, Part 3.

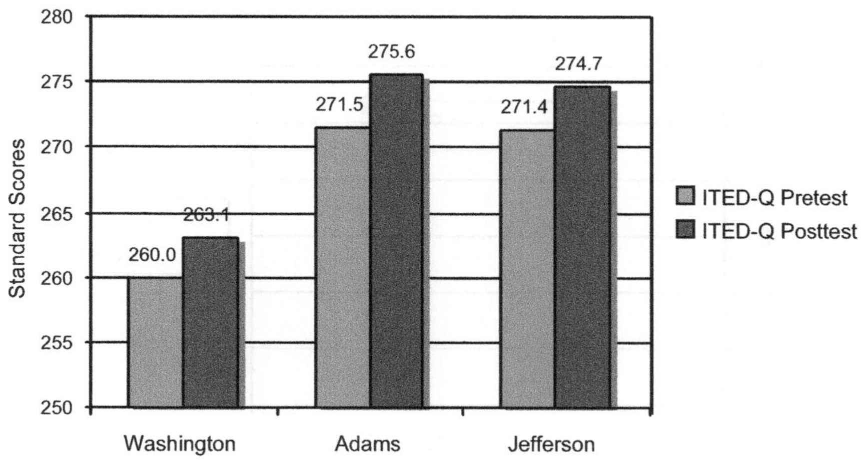

Figure 5.1. *ITED-Q* Growth in Standard Scores During Course 1 by School.

Results by Gender

As Figure 5.2 shows, for the 327 girls and 285 boys who completed the *ITED-Q* posttest, the girls' mean on the pretest was significantly lower than that of the boys, but at the end of Course 1 the means of the gender groups were almost identical. This pattern in the data is statistical significant ($p = .046$) as verified by the gender by preachievement level ANOVA. The *ITED-Q* posttest means adjusted for variance in the *ITED-Q* pretest are girls, 276.4, and boys, 271.4.

ACHIEVEMENT OF CURRICULUM-SPECIFIC OBJECTIVES

In this section, we try, within the limits of our data, to answer the question, "Mathematically, what do students know, and what are they able to do by the end of Course 1?" To address this ambitious question, we focus on the project-developed Core-Plus Mathematics posttest administered to all students at the end of the school year. Each student completed one of three forms of a Course 1 posttest. As separate tests, the 19- to 21-task forms had alpha reliability coefficients of about .84. The three forms cumulatively measured the main content goals of Course 1 in all four content strands: Algebra and Functions (25 tasks; $\alpha = .94$), Geometry and Trigonometry (13 tasks; $\alpha = .81$), Statistics and Probability (16 tasks; $\alpha = .75$), and Discrete Mathematics (7 tasks; $\alpha = .66$).[1] The three forms were distributed randomly in each classroom, so performance data on each form can be viewed as essentially equivalent to that of the entire set of students.

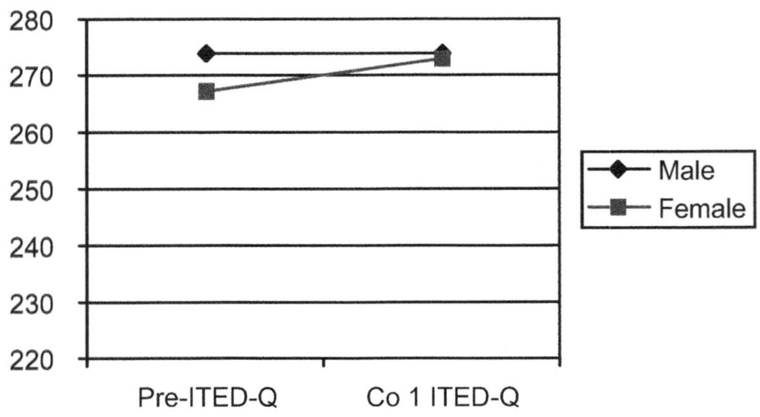

Figure 5.2. *ITED-Q* Growth in Standard Scores During Course 1 by Gender.

The subcategories within content strands were given earlier in Table 5.1. The descriptive statistics for each of these content subcategories are given in Table 5.2. Since the tasks that comprise the subtests are from different forms of the Course 1 posttest, the subtest means are computed using the mean percent correct for each item that, in turn, is based on the random set of students that completed the test form that contained the item. The subtest standard deviations are the weighted average of the standard deviations of included items from each test form. As the tabled data show, the average percent correct was highest on the Algebra and Functions subtest, especially on tasks that assess algebraic operations and algebraic modeling.

Students' performance on particular tasks forms the basis for the discussion of what they were able to do that follows. To enrich the descriptions available from students' written test responses, problem-based interviews of students in each school at various times during the school year are also analyzed and discussed. The interviews were audiotaped and transcribed, and the transcripts were analyzed along with students' written work on the interview problems. Most interview problems were identical or very similar to tasks on the written posttest. The following elaboration and discussion of the findings uses the content organization of the Course 1 posttest. The written assessment, analyses of the results by item, and the interview problems are available for examination and download at http://www.wmich.edu/cpmp/evaluation.html

Table 5.2. Numbers of Tasks, Means, and Standard Deviations by Content Category of the Course 1 Posttest

Subtest	*Tasks*	*Mean(%)*	*SD*	*Subtest*	*Tasks*	*Mean (%)*	*SD*
Algebraic Operations	11	72.4	28.9	Central Tendency	3	37.4	25.9
Algebraic Modeling	4	71.5	32.9	Box Plots, Histogr.	7	47.6	25.1
Graphical Reps.	10	56.0	29.3	Scatterplot, Lin. Reg.	6	35.5	26.3
TOTAL Alg. & Fcns.	25	66.0	25.5	TOTAL Stat. & Prob.	16	41.2	25.7
Geom. Computation	8	49.7	29.7	Euler Circuits, Paths	1	44.8	49.9
Vis. & Spatial Reas.	5	44.0	30.3	Critical Paths	3	42.2	34.2
				Graph Coloring	3	36.9	32.2
TOTAL Geom. & Trig.	13	47.5	26.3	TOTAL Disc. Math	7	40.3	35.6

Algebra and Functions

Core-Plus Mathematics Course 1 contains three units that are mainly algebraic, although connections are made to algebraic ideas to some extent in all units. Unit 2, *Patterns in Change,* builds on the data analysis ideas in the first unit to develop the idea of one variable changing as a function of another. Unit 3, *Linear Models,* uses linear functions to model and solve problems in situations that exhibit constant rate of change. Unit 6, *Exponential Models,* uses exponential functions to model and solve problems in situations that exhibit exponential growth and decay. The discussion, like the Algebra and Functions content strand, is organized as follows:

- Use of Algebraic Operations
- Algebraic Modeling
- Depicting and Understanding Graphical Representations

Use of Algebraic Operations. Algebraic symbols and operations are at the core of algebra. Computation with and manipulation of these symbols using valid operations in proficient and meaningful ways is an important part of doing and understanding algebra. Another important aspect of understanding algebraic symbols and operations is the ability to use an algebraic expression to represent a problem situation and to draw reasonable conclusions about the situation from its algebraic representation.

Students demonstrated their proficiency in algebraic computation and symbol manipulation by responding to fairly standard algebraic computation tasks such as solving an equation for a given variable and evaluating an expression given a specific value for a variable. Some of these equations arose from verbally described contexts; others were purely symbolic. About three-fourths of the students were successful on tasks of this type as illustrated in the following examples.

- Seventy-seven percent of students correctly determined the value of y associated with $x = 4$ in the equation $y = 1.5x$.
- Students were asked to use a "$y =$" (i.e., closed form) or *NOW-NEXT* (i.e., recursive) equation that they had created to model the relationship between a bouncing ball and its height if the ball returned to half its previous height on each bounce. Using either equation of their choice, 72% were able to compute the expected heights after each of the first five bounces of the ball (6.6% earned 3 of 4 possible points on this constructed-response task and 65.4% earned 4 points).

- In a series of tasks about the relationship between time and weight of pigs whose average daily weight increase was 0.76 grams per day, 77% of students were able to correctly complete a table giving an average pig's weight after 7, 14, 21, 28, and 35 days.
- In the same series of questions, 74% of students were able to compute correctly the weight of an average pig after 42 days. They were also asked to find the minimum number of days on the weight-gain program that is required before an average 25-kg pig will weigh at least 50 kg, and 71% answered correctly.

Interviews with similar tasks shed light on students' strategies and error patterns. For example, 22 of 27 interviewees (82%) were able to use algebraic operations to solve the following equation for x^2:

$$16x - 81 = 263$$

However, just 13 of 22 interviewees (59%) were able to solve the following similar equation:

$$132 = 12 - 17x$$

This difference in level of difficulty is consistent with research on learning algebra (cf. the review by Kieran, 2007). Solving a linear equation in one variable is made more difficult by the placement of a negative variable term on the right-hand side of the equation following a constant term. Of the nine students who answered incorrectly, five attempted to use a correct strategy, but misinterpreted the positive and negative terms. These five students obtained an incorrect result by adding 12 to both sides of the equation and dividing by 17.

Other tasks probed more deeply into students' understanding of algebraic representations. For example, one task that appeared on the written posttest and as an interview problem was the Motor Boat Problem[3] given in Figure 5.3.

The mean score on the first question in the Motor Boat Problem was 2.86 (71%) of 4 possible points. Some students were interviewed while completing this task, and they shared their thinking. The most successful students had a firm grasp of the meanings of 18 and –2 in this equation. One student said, "The boat has an 18 gallon tank, or has 18 gallons of gasoline, and it uses 2 gallons per mile," indicating a solid contextual understanding of this equation. However, other students who were interviewed had trouble describing the meaning of the numbers in the problem context and were particularly confused by –2. Some students said that –2 meant, "miles since filling the tank," and another commented "that maybe could be how

The number of gallons (y) of gasoline left in a large motor boat after traveling x miles since filling the tank is given by

$$y = 18 - 2x$$

1. Explain what 18 and –2 in the equation tell about the number of gallons.
2. Graph this equation. Explain the role of 18 and –2 in the graph.
3. After filling the gasoline tank, Helen drove the boat until there were 10 gallons left. How many miles had she driven? Explain how to tell from the equation and how to tell from the graph.
4. How many gallons of gasoline were left after Helen had driven the boat 8 miles? Show or explain your work.

Figure 5.3. Motor Boat Problem.

many miles he got, 2 per gallon, to his gas tank." The least successful students had trouble with both the meanings of 18 and of –2.

The second question in the Motor Boat Problem will be discussed in a later section on graphical representations. The mean score on the third question was 2.32 (58%) of 4 possible points. In interviews, some students were confident of their algebraic approach, with one saying, "I could tell that the answer to the question was 4 on the equation by making y equal 10, because y is the amount of gasoline left in the tank after driving so many miles." Another explained the problem by reasoning through the contextual information, "Well, if there is 10 gallons left, then that means 8 had to be taken away. And if you spend 2 gallons per mile, then it would be 4." Other students had trouble with this task because of their confusion between gallons and miles in the equation. One student said, "She said 18 gallons of gas ... they had 10 gallons of gas left after she drove 8 miles." Others subtracted 10 gallons from 18 gallons to get 8 miles.

On the fourth question in the Motor Boat Problem, the mean score was 2.88 (72%) of 4 possible points. Successful students recognized the similarities between this question and the previous one. A student said, "before this it gave me a number for y. And then this problem gave me a number for x. So I just put the number in, which was 8 for x. I figured it out." Others grasped the problem in terms of the context: "Well, she goes 8 miles, and it burns 2 gallons of gas every mile, so you go 8 times 2, which is 16. So if she burns 16 and the difference of 16 and 18 is 2." Again, students who had difficulties with this problem were often confusing gallons and miles. One student said,

> If there is 8 miles left there would be 10, because she had driven, Helen drove the boat until there were 10 gallons left. She hadn't driven 10 miles. There's 8 miles left. I don't know what to do with this. I don't understand.

Algebraic Modeling. Besides the ability to understand and to compute using algebraic expressions, students should be able to "use symbolic algebra to represent and explain mathematical relationships" (National Council of Teachers of Mathematics, 2000, p. 296). They should also be able to "use symbolic expressions, including iterative and recursive forms, to represent relationships arising from various contexts" (p. 296). To assess these abilities, students were asked to write or identify "y =" and "*NOW-NEXT*" equations that modeled tabled data or a given problem situation. On most tasks, 65% to 85% of students were able to do this, with a somewhat higher success rate for recursive rules than for closed form rules.

For example, a sequence of multiple-choice posttest tasks described earlier referred to a situation concerning the relationship between time and weight of pigs whose average daily weight increase was 0.76 grams per day. In response to the first task in the sequence, 75% of students chose the rule, $W = 25 + 0.76D$, for calculating weight W of an average pig as a function of the number of days D in the program.

As an example of a related assessment task, students were given the algebraic rule $y = 1.5^{X}$ for integer values of x and the table below:

x =	0	1	3	4
y =	1	1.5	1.5^2	1.5^3

In the table, it can be seen that every y value after the first is 1.5 times the previous value. Students were asked to represent this pattern using *NOW-NEXT* notation, as *NEXT* = 1.5 * *NOW* where *NEXT* is 1 when *NOW* is 0. Just 66% of students were able to do so, a success rate that is the lowest across several such posttest tasks

Both recursive and closed form rules were required in an open-ended sequence of posttest tasks that refers to a situation in which a ball dropped from a height of 10 ft onto a hard surface rebounds to half of its drop height. After finding how high the ball will bounce on the first and second bounces, 68% of students were able to write a "*NOW-NEXT*" equation that shows how to calculate the rebound height for any bounce from the height of the previous bounce. In the next task in the sequence, however, just 48% of students were able to write a correct "y =" equation that estimates the rebound height y after any number of bounces x.

In a similar problem administered in individual interviews, 13 of 14 students were able to give the correct *NOW-NEXT* rule, *NEXT* = 1.03 * *NOW*, in a population growth problem with a 3% annual growth rate, and 12 of 14 followed that with a correct "y =" rule.

Depicting and Understanding Graphical Representations. Results relating to students' ability to depict and understand graphical representations of algebraic situations were mixed. Students demonstrated understanding on some graphical problems, but on other problems their answers indicated difficulties. The reasons for the differences in success rates lie, at least in part, in characteristics of specific assessment tasks. For example, consider the two somewhat similar multiple-choice tasks shown in Figure 5.4.

Although exponential functions are usually considered to be a more advanced and difficult topic than Linear functions, 67% of students responded correctly to the Exponential task and only 34% chose the correct answer in the linear task. To explain this large difference in success rate, several of the tasks' characteristics are probably at least as important as their mathematical content. One clear difference is that the Linear task required students to choose the statement that is *not true*, which may be inherently more difficult than choosing a true statement from among five choices as in the Exponential task. Another potentially important difference is that the Exponential task is the second in a sequence of three questions. In the question immediately preceding this one, students were prompted to think of the y-values that should be entered into a table to correspond to $x = 0$ through 5 by the rule, $y = 1.5x$. So, the context of the Exponential problem led students to think of a table of whole number pairs as they considered the five given statements. The Linear task, by contrast, stood alone with no related context to influence students' thinking.

The facilitative effect for these students of a meaningful context is also evident in data from the two related tasks in Figure 5.5. Percents of students correctly answering these two questions (choices e and c, respectively) were 42% and 83%, respectively. The arbitrary constant b added a level of abstraction, making the first question more difficult, and the real-world context boosted the success rate on the second question.

How do students think about graphical representations? Recall the second question in the Motor Boat Problem given previously (Figure 5.3).

(Exponential) When the points (satisfying $y = 1.5x$) are plotted, which of the following will be true?	**(Linear)** Which of the following IS NOT TRUE of the graph of $y = 12 - 3x$?
(a) The point (0, 0) will be on the graph.	(a) The graph decreases from left to right.
(b) The points will lie on a straight line.	(b) The y-intercept is 12.
(c) The graph will be a horizontal line through the point (0, 1.5).	(c) The slope is 3.
(d) The points will increase more rapidly as you move from left to right.	(d) The graph crosses the x-axis at (4, 0).
(e) The graph will be an example of exponential decay.	(e) (6, –6) is a point on the graph.

Figure 5.4. Sample Graphical Representation Tasks.

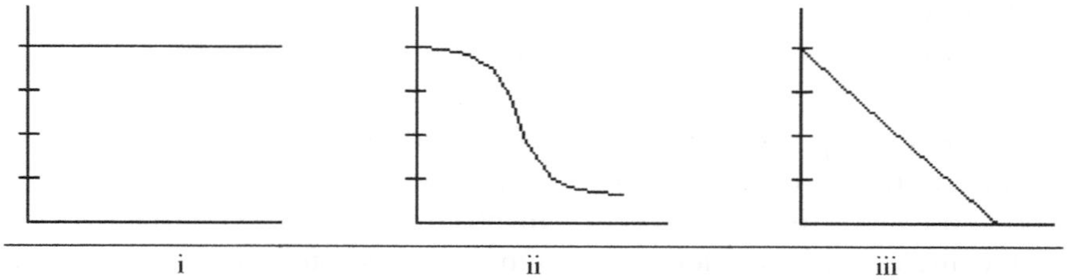

• Which of the graphs above could be part of the graph of y = 4 + bx, where b is a positive number?

(a) i only (b) ii only (c) iii only (d) both i and iii (e) none of them

• A riding lawn mower has a 4-gallon gasoline tank, and it uses gasoline at a steady rate of one gallon per hour. Which of the above graphs could represent (time, gallons of gasoline remaining) for this lawn mower?

(a) i only (b) ii only (c) iii only (d) both i and ii (e) both i and iii

Figure 5.5. Sample Tasks Illustrating the Role of Context in Graphical Representation.

On the paper-and-pencil tests, the mean on this question was 2.45 (61% of 4 possible points). In individual interviews, some of the students demonstrated an understanding of the connection between the equation and the graph, but others had difficulties involving interpreting their calculator's output. One student said,

> So I just graphed it out by looking at the table [on my calculator] and kind of using common sense. Just making sure that I was on the right track." Some students who were interviewed had trouble understanding the graph on their calculator or could not graph the equation completely. One student said he was confused by the relationship between the –2x and the graph provided by the calculator, "like in the graph it has like the positive sector, like it's positive, but I would think it would be *x* negative, positive is *y*. It's not set up like that." Still others demonstrated comfort with graphing by hand: "I went to the first point that I knew and that was the start-up point, which was 18 ... from that point on I took the –2*x* and I just went over 1 and down 2 to create the slope."

Geometry

Course 1 students completed just one unit that was primarily geometric content, Unit 5, *Patterns in Space and Visualization.* This unit examines two- and three-dimensional shapes and their properties including symmetry, area, and volume. Geometric achievement is discussed in the two main content categories of the Geometry and Trigonometry subtest as follows:

- Geometric Computation
- Visualization and Spatial Reasoning

Geometric Computation. Students were tested on their ability to compute geometric measures like perimeter and area. In this category, students were most successful with tasks that involved basic geometric shapes, such as rectangles and parallelograms. On one task, students were given a sketch of a rectangle with one diagonal drawn in. The width and length were given in inches and the diagonal was labeled as *d*. Over three-fourths of the students (76%) chose the correct area of the rectangle.

Many students (67%) were able to compute the perimeter of the parallelogram sketched in Figure 5.6, but they were less successful at computing the area of a triangle. Just 46% of students chose the correct area, 15 square inches, of a triangle with base 6 inches and altitude to that base of 5 inches. About 40% of the students selected 30 square inches, the product of the base and altitude. There was no visual cue, so a student's success depended entirely on a careful reading and verbal understanding of the task.

Students had some difficulty computing the perimeter, volume, and surface area of a nonstandard shape. Students were asked a sequence of related open-ended questions about a two-dimensional sketch that could be folded into a box in the shape of a triangular prism. (See the Box Problem in Figure 5.7.)

One question in the sequence asked:

> When determining the costs of constructing these boxes, the company is interested in how much cutting is involved to cut the shape from a large cardboard sheet. Find this length by calculating the perimeter of the flat shape as it is shown in the diagram. Show your work.

The mean on this question was 2.01 of 4 possible points (50%). Mean scores were much lower on tasks that asked students to calculate the volume (29%) and the surface area (30%) of the box. Other tasks in the Box Problem sequence will be discussed later in this chapter.

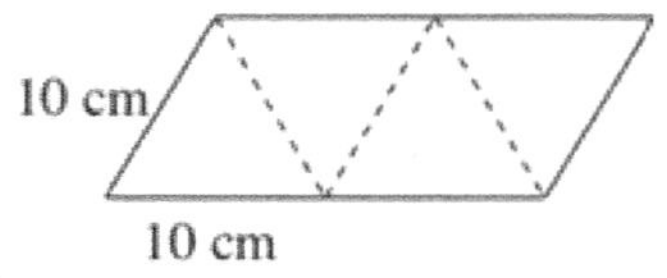

Each triangle in the figure is equilateral.

Figure 5.6. Parallelogram for a Sequence of Tasks.

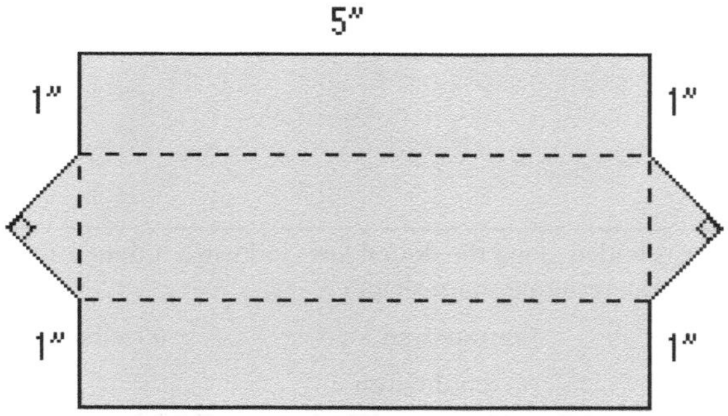

Box Problem: A manufacturing company machine constructs assorted boxes for shipping from a single sheet of cardboard by folding along dotted lines. The finished products are 3-dimensional boxes in various shapes such as the one diagrammed below.

Figure 5.7. Stem of the Box Problem.

Visualization and Spatial Reasoning. Students were asked several questions that required them to visualize two- and three-dimensional objects from different perspectives and to identify the lines of symmetry of different objects. Performance on these tasks was mixed, demonstrating that many students have difficulty with spatial visualization.

For example, most students (86%) were able to draw a correct three-dimensional representation of the folded-up box in Figure 5.7. However, students were less successful at other visualization tasks. Students scored just 46% when asked to sketch a two-dimensional diagram, or net, different from the one given in Figure 5.7, that would result in the same three-dimensional box when folded.

Fewer students still (8%) were able to name the three-dimensional figure (choice e) that results if the two-dimensional net in Figure 5.8 were folded along the dotted lines. The most common incorrect choices were (d) prism (43%) and (a) triangle (38%). It is not clear how much of the poor performance on this task was due to visualization difficulties and how much was due to unfamiliarity with the terminology. Students did very little with tetrahedra in the Course 1 curriculum.

Students were also required to identify lines and planes of symmetry of given figures. On one such problem (Figure 5.9), 38% of students chose (e), the correct answer. The most popular wrong answer was (c), chosen by 29% of the students. On an open-ended task, 24% of students were able to sketch all the planes of symmetry of the three-dimensional figure (triangular prism) that results from folding up the net given in Figure 5.7. Another 39% of students correctly sketched at least one plane of symmetry. While results on symmetry tasks like these are somewhat better than results

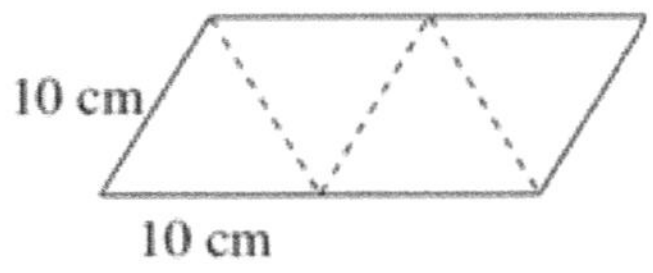

Suppose the figure is folded along the dotted lines to form a 3-dimensional space shape. What is the name of the resulting space-shape?

(a) triangle (b) trapezoid (c) cube

(d) prism (e) tetrahedron

Figure 5.8. Sample Multiple-Choice Task from Parallelogram Sequence

Which of the following is not a symmetry of rhombus ABCD?

(a) Reflection in line AC

(b) Reflection in line BD

(c) Rotation of 180° about the point of intersection of lines AC and BD

(d) Rotation of 360° about the point of intersection of lines AC and BD

(e) Reflection in the line containing the midpoints of lines AB and CD

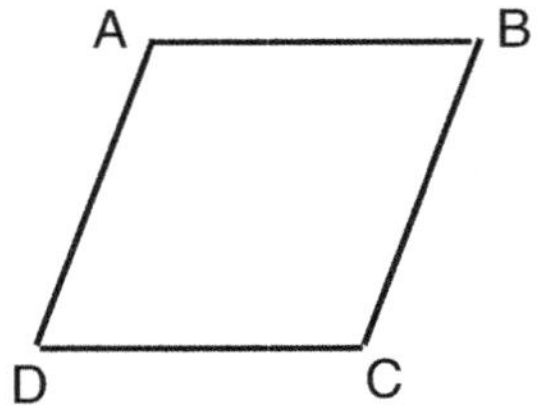

Figure 5.9. Sample Multiple-Choice Task from Parallelogram Sequence.

on some of the spatial visualization tasks reported above, success rates are still low.

To better understand how students think about symmetry, 36 students were asked in individual interviews to describe and draw all the symmetries of the sketch in Figure 5.10. Seven students (19%) correctly identified and drew all the symmetries. These students recognized that the figure had two rotational symmetries with angles of 120 and 240 degrees. They also identified the three line symmetries of the figure. One student expressed this by saying:

> There's three points of rotational symmetry and the way to find out how many degrees you have to turn to get that, you have to divide 360 by that number, so 360 divided by three points of rotation symmetry equals 120 degrees for each rotation to get the same look.

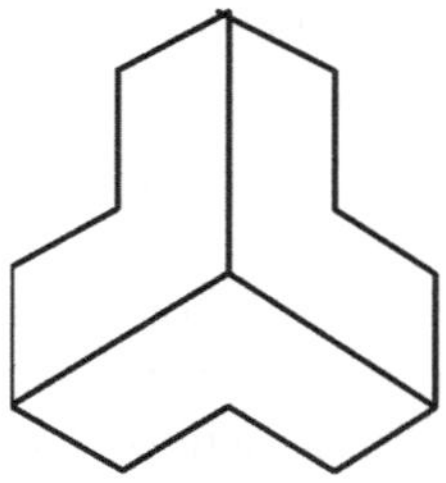

Figure 5.10. Sketch in Symmetry Interview Problem.

Sixteen students (44%) received partial credit for their work on this problem. Many students who received partial credit noted the rotational symmetry at 120 degrees but did not recognize the additional rotational symmetry at 240 degrees. One student indicated this by saying:

> It has, well, if you rotate a shape all around, that's 360, and so I divided into 3 because that's how many pieces I could divide it into to rotate and it gave me 120, so that's what I think is rotational symmetry and it didn't appear to have any other symmetries.

Students who received no credit had misconceptions, or difficulty communicating, about symmetry. One student said, "Well, I wouldn't really, if I was going to do this, I wouldn't use degrees to do it; I would just do it. I would just turn it."

Statistics and Probability

There are two units in the Statistics and Probability strand in Course 1—Unit 1, *Patterns in Data,* and Unit 7, *Simulation Models*—but few of the classes in the longitudinal study completed the latter unit. To assess their competence in statistics and probability at the end of Course 1, students were posed problems in a paper-and-pencil and an individual interview format. It should be kept in mind that the interviews were conducted at various points during the year, and the paper-and-pencil test was administered in the last few weeks of the school year. As the first unit in the course, the *Patterns in Data* content was not fresh in the minds of the students in either setting, and the unit was especially remote in time for the paper-and-pencil test. The following discussion is based on the three content categories of the Statistics and Probability subtest as follows:

- Measures of Central Tendency
- Box Plots and Histograms
- Scatterplots and Linear Regression

Measures of Central Tendency. The computation of the mean, median, and mode, the usual measures of central tendency, of a given distribution of data are standard middle school topics. The focus in Course 1 was on the interpretation and relative usefulness of these measures for describing particular data sets. One kind of interpretation is the effect of additional data on the various measures of central tendency of a given distribution as assessed by the sample task in Figure 5.11. Students were moderately successful, with 63% choosing the correct response, (a). Incorrect responses were divided fairly evenly among the other four choices, so the data are not helpful in determining what students were thinking on this problem.

Students were less successful on two other interpretive questions about the data set in Figure 5.11. The stems and choices in these questions are given in Figure 5.12. The first or left-most task is complicated by the fact that it mixes the ideas of central tendency, outliers, and dispersion (range). It also has a negatively stated question form that often makes an assessment task more difficult than it may otherwise be. On this task, 37% of students chose (b), the correct response. Although from teacher reports and homework over 90% of students have no difficulty computing the median and mean of a distribution like the given one, about one-fourth of the students chose (d).

The second question in Figure 5.12 was very difficult. The keyed correct answer, (c), was chosen by only 12% of students. The interpretation leading to choice (c) is that the median and mode are both 2, and 2 is the most typical and certainly the most frequently occurring score. However, the mean (3) is just one more than the median/mode. While there is only

Ten third-grade students competed in a contest to see who could do the most pull-ups. The number of pull-ups were as follows.

1	7	2	3	1
0	10	2	2	2

One more student enters the contest and does eight pull-ups. What effect will this new data point have on the distribution?

(a) The mean will increase. (b) The mode will increase. (c) The median will decrease.

(d) The range will increase. (e) The mean, median, and mode will not change.

Figure 5.11. Sample Central Tendency Multiple-Choice Task.

Which of the following <u>is not true</u> of the distribution of "pull-up" data?	The number of pull-ups that a typical student from this group can do is best represented by the _____.
(a) The mode is 2.	(a) mean and median
(b) 0 and 10 are outliers.	(b) mean and mode
(c) The range is 10.	(c) median and mode
(d) The median is less than the mean.	(d) mean, median, and mode
(e) Most of the data is clustered between 0 and 3.	

Figure 5.12. Two More Central Tendency Tasks.

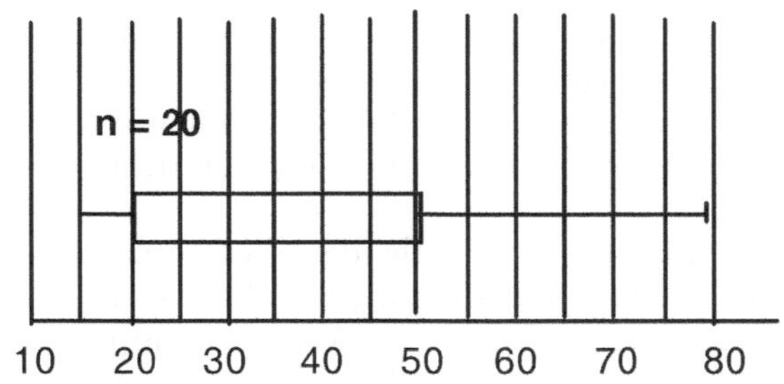

Figure 5.13. Box Plot Used in Paper-and-Pencil and Interview Formats.

one score of 3 and just two scores above 3, it could be argued that any of the three measures are acceptable as measures of central tendency. Perhaps this is what the approximately 30% of students who chose (d) were thinking. Interestingly though, even more students (about 35%) chose (a), a result that may suggest that the mean and median are more attractive to students as potential answers than the less familiar mode.

Box Plots and Histograms. Both paper-and-pencil and interview data were collected to assess students' proficiency at interpreting the meaning of a given box plot, including identifying the five statistics illustrated by the plot, namely, the minimum, first quartile, median, third quartile, and maximum. The box plot in Figure 5.13 above was presented in both a paper-and-pencil and an interview format. In the paper-and-pencil format, 88% of students chose the correct median of the plotted distribution, 60% identified the interquartile range, and 52% chose the correct range. Results of interviews reported below suggest that the lower percents in the last two cases are largely due to misunderstanding the terms *interquartile range* and *range*.

When this box plot was presented to students in a one-to-one interview, students were asked to describe as completely as they could the distribution represented by this box plot. A response was sought that included some form of the five summary statistics—minimum, first quartile, median, third quartile, and maximum. The interquartile range was accepted instead of either or both of the first and third quartiles. To earn full credit, students had to identify at least four of the five summary statistics or they had to identify three of these statistics, plus some other correct information. Most interviewed students' explanations (72%) were assigned full credit, and all earned partial credit.

Overall, the students seemed to have a fairly good understanding of the box plot representation and its associated statistical vocabulary. For example, one student summarized the box plot as follows:

> Range in the plot equals about 63 from the minimum to the maximum. The median equals 40. The lower quartile range equals 5. The interquartile range equals 30, which is 50% of the graph. Twenty-five to 75%. Upper-quartile range equals about 28 and this box plot is right [skewed].

This student's explanation correctly identified three of the summary statistics, the intequartile range, the range, and the skewness of the distribution. She even gave the ranges for the lower and upper quartiles.

Another student had many of the right ideas about the distribution represented by the box plot, but his use of statistical vocabulary was shaky.

> My description [of the distribution] is the number of people surveyed was 20, the median of this information was 40, it has an outlier from the rest of the data at 79. The quartile one is at 20, the second quartile is at 40, quartile 3 at 50 and the lower quartile is at 15 and the upper quartile, which is the outlier is 79.

This student has confused "minimum" with "lower quartile" and "maximum" with "upper quartile," and he may use "outlier" in an intuitive, rather than technically correct way. A third student showed a more serious misunderstanding of the information represented by the box plot, of the related statistical vocabulary, or both when she referred to the median as the mean and said the range was 15 to 80.

How students interpret a box plot was probed further by a question that required them to compare the box plot in Figure 5.13 to a histogram. See the task in Figure 5.14 from the paper-and-pencil assessment. Notice that the students are told that the histogram cannot describe the same distribution as the box plot, and they are required to choose the correct reason. Only 36% of students chose the keyed response (d), the only option that is a valid reason that the two plots

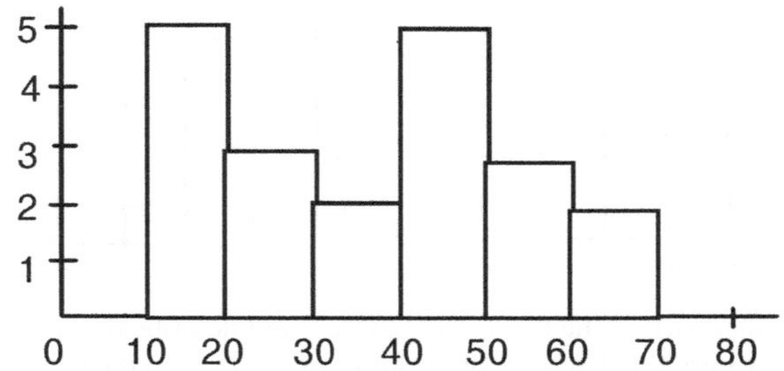

In the histogram above, a score of 30, for example, goes in the bar to the right of 30 on the number line. This histogram could not describe the same distribution as the above box plot because ______.

(a) there are too many scores between 10 and 20
(b) there are too many scores between 40 and 50
(c) there are too few scores between 60 and 70
(d) there is no score between 70 and 80
(e) there is no score between 0 and 10

Figure 5.14. Multiple-Choice Task Relating a Box Plot to a Histogram.

cannot represent the same distribution. (The box plot's maximum, 78, must be in the interval from 70 to 80.) Over 20% of students chose option (e), which is a true statement but it is also true of the box plot and so not a correct response to this task. Option (a) was also the pick of over 20% of the students, but the reason why this was an attractive option is not clear. Perhaps students were swayed by the position of the tall bar, the leftmost one in the histogram, when that interval contains only a "whisker" in the box plot. A student who made that judgment in response to the first option may have chosen (a) and, thinking it was correct, failed to give proper attention to the later options. Of course, this is speculation, as we have no direct evidence of what students were thinking as they made their choice on this task.

The 36% correct rate on the task in Figure 5.14 suggests that most students did not understand the connections between a distribution's box plot and its histogram. Before jumping to that conclusion, however, consider how students responded in interviews to the related, open-ended task in Figure 5.15. In contrast to the poor results on the multiple-choice task, 88% of the students interviewed argued correctly that the leftmost histogram could not represent the same distribution as the box plot, because the maximum on the box plot was greater than 70 and the maximum on the histogram was less than 70. The options on the multiple-choice task appear to add to its complexity and difficulty, leading students who may have a basic understanding of the connection between the two representations to become confused. The open-ended task format allows

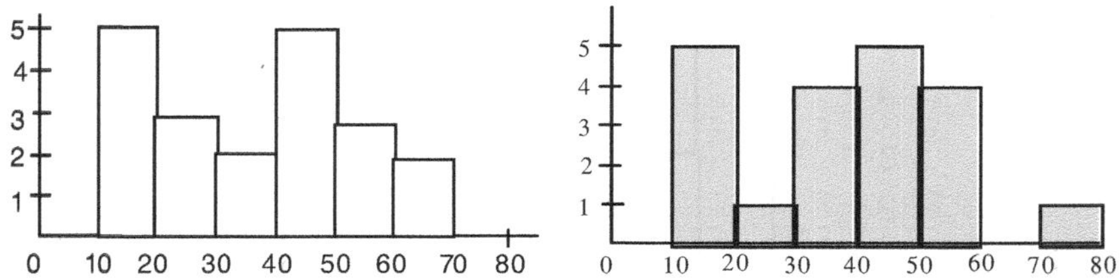

Determine whether each of the histograms above could describe the same distribution as the box plot [in Figure 5.13]. A score of 30, for example, goes in the bar to the right on the number line. Provide reasoning for your answers.

Figure 5.15. Open-Ended Task Relating a Box Plot to Histograms.

students to construct their own argument with no need to match it to one or more given arguments.

A factor that may help explain the higher success rate on the open-ended task is the tacit assumption of most students that one of the histograms could represent the same distribution as the box plot and the other could not. This is not a stated condition of the problem, but it is the case in this problem as well as in the vast majority of two-choice problems of this form that appear in school mathematics books and tests. Acting on this school-experience-based assumption, many students seemed to look for something obvious about one of the histograms that made clear that it did not match the box plot. Nearly all students noted that in the leftmost histogram there was no value in the interval that needed to contain the maximum value in the distribution represented by the box plot. Concluding that the histogram on the left could not match the box plot, they assumed that the histogram on the right could match without really analyzing in any depth why it could. Most students simply noted that there were scores in the interval from 70 to 80, so the maximum of the box plot could be there. Only a few (13%) verified that the numbers of students in the intervals of the histogram were consistent with the numbers in the quartiles of the box plot.

Scatterplots and Regression Lines. In Course 1, there is a brief introduction to scatterplots in the first unit, and an even briefer introduction to fitting lines to paired data points using linear regression. The paper-and-pencil posttest in this study included a sequence of multiple-choice tasks that assess understanding fitting lines to data especially by using linear regression. In retrospect, the questions were too detailed and complex for the treatment of the topic that the students had experienced, and as a result many students did not do well. Nevertheless, some of the patterns in the results are interesting and are presented next.

There were six questions in this sequence, all referring to the data given in Figure 5.16. The first one was stated as follows: "This data can/cannot be modeled (or fit) well by a line because _____." Students were to examine and perhaps roughly plot the data to determine whether it was approximately linear. Thirty-nine percent of students chose the keyed correct answer, "Can, because the points of the graph lie nearly in a straight line." Interestingly, nearly as many (31%) evidently read "modeled (or fit)" as meaning all points lie on a line. These students chose the option, "Cannot, because no line can go through all the points." With more experience using regression lines, this mistake would surely become less common.

Somewhat more students (45%) were able to choose a plausible regression line ($y = 2.53 + 0.20x$) for the data from among other clearly incorrect options. Presumably, most did so by estimating the slope and y-intercept using the tabled data or perhaps a rough sketch of it. Students were clearly confused about the roles of a and b in the regression line $y = b + ax$. For the role of a, about 30% of students chose the option "a is the predicted increase in average height for an increase in age of 2 years," presumably influenced by the 2, 4, 6, ... pattern of ages in the data set in Figure 5.16. Only about 16% of students chose the correct option, in which "2 years" was replaced by "1 year." As for the role of b, somewhat more students (30%) correctly chose "b is the predicted average height at birth, that is, at age = 0."

In response to "To use the linear regression equation to predict the average height of a 6-month-old boy, you would _____," about a third of students (34%) chose the correct option, "substitute 0.5 for x and solve for y, which would be the predicted height." The second most popular choice (20%) was to use the number given in the question, 6, and substitute it for x. The final question in the sequence assessed students' ability to make a real-world interpretation of the data set by asking, "The linear regression equation would/would not give an accurate prediction of the average height of 40-year-old men because ____." Nearly half (49%) correctly chose "would not, because men stop getting taller by about age 20." The second most popular choice (over 20%) was the stereotypical algebra student answer, "would, because 40 could be substituted for x, and y would be the average height."

This table gives the average height in feet of boys in the United States at the given ages (*Physician's Handbook*, 1990).

Age (years)	2	4	6	8	10	12	14
Avg. Height (feet)	2.8	3.3	3.8	4.2	4.5	4.8	5.2

Figure 5.16. (Age/Height) Data Set.

Discrete Mathematics

The curriculum also introduces students to discrete mathematics. In Course 1, topics relate to vertex-edge graphs. The content organization of the Discrete Mathematics subtest is following:

- Euler Circuits and Paths
- Critical Paths
- Graph Coloring

Students' understanding of these topics was addressed during student interviews and through the year-end Course 1 test. The interview problems were all open-ended, and the year-end test questions were in a multiple-choice format.

Euler Circuits and Paths. The only discrete mathematics assessment task that contained no context is shown in Figure 5.17. The answer options required students to determine the parity of each vertex and judge whether the graph had an Euler path or an Euler circuit. The keyed option, (e), was the choice of 45% of the students, while over 20% decided that the graph had an Euler path, but no Euler circuit (option b).

Students were given two situations including the one in Figure 5.18 in an interview setting and were asked which graph model—Euler circuits and paths, graph coloring, or critical paths—they would use to model each problem, what the vertices and edges would represent, and the reasons for their answers. All but one of the 36 students interviewed correctly selected the Euler paths and circuits to model this situation. The explanations of over 60% of the students were acceptable. For example,

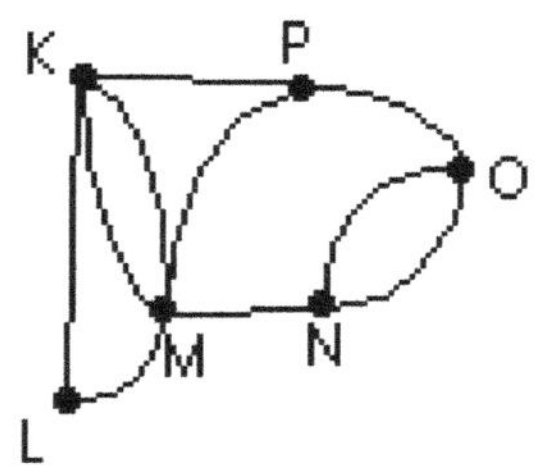

Which one of the following statements is true about the above graph?

(a) All of the vertices are even. (b) There is an Euler path, but no Euler circuit.
(c) There is an Euler circuit. (d) Exactly three of the vertices are odd.
(e) Exactly four of the vertices are odd.

Figure 5.17. Noncontextual, Multiple-Choice, Vertex-Edge Graph Problem.

Karen delivers papers to all the houses along the streets in a certain part of town. Each morning she leaves her house, which is at a street corner, delivers the papers so that she does not travel any street more than once, and ends at her friend Gina's house at another street corner. The problem is to find the corners where Karen and Gina live and a route that Karen can take.

Figure 5.18. Graph Models Interview Context I.

one student noted: "an Euler circuit is a path that hits everything and ends up at the same place. A path covers all the area, but doesn't end up in the same place." Students whose explanations were inadequate often were not clear on what the vertices and edges of their model would represent, several saying that the vertices and edges would represent houses and streets, respectively.

Critical Paths. The information given in Figure 5.19 was the basis for a sequence of questions designed to assess students' understanding of finding the shortest or critical path through a graph with weighted edges. The first question asked students to select the false statement from a list of five statements about the project. The statements discussed the timing of different stages within the project, such as how long it would take to begin a certain task in the timeline. Thirty-nine percent of students selected the keyed false statement "Candy can be sold for 5 straight days immediately after permission is granted." The second question asked students to select the earliest finish time for this project. The students had to use the information provided about task time and task order to solve this problem, but since no graphs were provided, they were able to model the situation in any manner they chose. Forty-two percent of students selected the correct finish time. The third question asked students to select the true statement from a list of five statements which dealt with critical path, slack time, and timing of the project. Forty-five percent of students selected the correct statement ("The path P-D-A-C is 13 days long"). Overall, students answered correctly 42% of the time on paper-and-pencil critical path assessment tasks.

In the interview task described in the previous section, students were given two problem situations and were asked which graph model—Euler circuits and paths, graph coloring, or critical paths—they would use to model each problem, what the vertices and edges would represent, and the reasons for their answers. The first of the problem situations was given in Figure 5.18, and it required an Euler paths and circuits model. The second problem situation is given in Figure 5.20 above.

As in the first situation, 35 of 36 interviewed students recognized the model that would most useful in this situation, in this case, a critical path. In addition, 60% of the students were able to adequately explain

Task	*Task Time (Days)*	*Immediate Prerequisite*
Permission (P)	2	None
Decide Type and Amount (D)	3	P
Ordering and Receiving Candy (O)	4	D
Put up Ads (A)	3	D
Set up Booth (B)	1	D
Selling Candy (C)	5	O, A, B

Suppose that your club is selling candy for a fund-raising project and the tasks listed above must be completed.

Figure 5.19. Complex Task Information for Critical Path Assessment.

A building contractor is planning to restore a historic mansion. She has a list of 15 tasks that need to be completed, the length of time each task takes, and the prerequisites for each task (that is, which need to be completed before others can be started). The problem is to plan the entire job in order to minimize the length of time it will take.

Figure 5.20. Graph Models Interview Context II.

their rationale for selecting a critical path model. Students recognized that the "critical path shows how long each task takes, its prerequisite tasks, and how long it will take to do all the tasks," as in the given situation. These students also correctly identified the vertices in the graph with the tasks and the edges as connections between tasks and their prerequisites. The minority of students who gave inadequate explanations had difficulty describing the meaning of the vertices or the edges in their model.

Graph Coloring. Students were given the information in Figure 5.21 and asked questions about using graph coloring to find the least number of meeting times. Asked what the vertices in a graph model of this situation would represent, 52% chose the keyed response, Committees. About 29% chose acceptable responses to the question of what the edges would represent and 30% indicated correctly that the least number of meeting times was 2. More (40%) thought that 3 meeting times would be needed.

The last part of the interview problem described in the two previous sections (see Figures 5.18 and 5.20) asked students to provide their own example of a real-life situation that would use the third graph model, which turned out to be graph coloring. Students were also expected to explain how their situation was modeled correctly by graph coloring, including the meaning of the vertices and edges in the graphs. Twenty-seven students attempted this problem. Students provided a variety of sit-

Suppose the Olympic skating club has the following membership on committees:	
Finance—Kerrigan, Hamilton, Lupinski, Stoyko	Publicity—Hamilton, Lupinski, Chu
Social—Fleming, Kerrigan, Boitano	Membership—Fleming, Button
Standards—Button, Yamaguchi, Blair	

Figure 5.21. Conflicting Committees Information for Graph Coloring Assessment.

uations; the most common responses involved radio frequencies based on distance between radio stations, or zoo animals that could safely be put into the same cages. Fifty-nine percent of students provided an acceptable situation, justification, and choice for the vertices and edges of their model. Students who received full credit recognized that an edge represented some sort of conflict between two vertices in their respective models. One student who provided the radio station example clarified this by saying, "the ones that don't touch can have the same channel because they don't interfere with each other."

Seventy percent of interviewed students received at least half credit for their example and justification on this problem. A common difficulty for students not receiving full credit was their belief that an edge represented a lack of conflict between two vertices. One student who received partial credit indicated that the edges in his example represented "what radio stations could be on the same frequency." Students who received little or no credit had difficulty describing a correct graph-coloring situation. One student demonstrated this difficulty when she attempted to model a scheduling problem: "Sara is in basketball and soccer. Sometimes she has a meeting for both clubs the same day and can't go to both of them. Find the days she can go to soccer and the days she can go to basketball."

Overall, students were very successful in selecting one of the three graph models that is appropriate for a given situation and moderately successful at constructing their own situation to fit a graph-coloring model. They were also somewhat successful in explaining and justifying their choice and the components of the model relative to the real-life situation.

CHAPTER SUMMARY

This chapter presents the results for Course 1 students on a standardized test, *ITED-Q*, and on tests of curriculum-specific objectives, supplemented by problems in individual interviews. A summary of the main findings in this chapter follows.

- In September, before they had experienced the Core-Plus Mathematics curriculum, students at Washington, Adams, and Jefferson were above the national average in mathematical achievement (55th to 65th national student percentiles, on average).
- Average growth in standardized test achievement in each school from September to May did not differ significantly from 1 year's growth of the nationally representative norm sample. Average growth of the Fall Course 2 students at Adams High School was substantially (nearly a quarter of a standard deviation) greater than the average growth of the norm group over the same 1.5-year period.
- Using the pretest score as covariate, posttest *ITED-Q* means did not differ significantly by school or by prior mathematical achievement level. The school by gender, school by prior mathematical achievement level, and gender by prior mathematical achievement level interactions were also not statistically significant.
- Boys scored significantly higher on the pretest than girls, but the posttest means of the gender groups were nearly identical, suggesting a more positive effect of Course 1 on the achievement of girls than of boys.

The remainder of the chapter provides a sketch of students' mathematical knowledge, skill, and understanding at the end of Course 1. Students generally scored better on algebra tasks (especially on algebraic operations and algebraic modeling) than on tasks that assessed the other three content strands, a finding that also reflects the relative levels of emphasis of the content of the course.

The fact that students averaged over 40% on tasks in each of Geometry, Statistics, and Discrete Mathematics indicates that their learning in these strands was certainly greater than zero, though far from mastery level. It is important to note that students in conventional first-year algebra classes could not be expected to learn any of the content of these three strands as it would not be included in their syllabus. It is likely, however, that students would have the opportunity in many first-year algebra courses to learn algebra topics like factoring trinomials and the quadratic formula that are in the second course of the first edition of the Core-Plus Mathematics curriculum.

In the next chapter, students' achievement patterns in Course 2 are described with the main focus on algebraic skill and understanding.

NOTES

1. The alpha reliability coefficients of the four content subtests are estimates computed by applying the Spearman-Brown formula to the reliability of the most reliable portion of each subtest that is contained in a single form of the Course 1 posttest.
2. As an informal comparison, CPMP field-test students in 1994-95 scored 62% on an item that had them solve a similar equation, $5x + 20 = 36$, at the end of Course 1, and conventional first-year algebra comparison students in the field test scored 75%. Scores for the same two groups when asked to solve $126 = 84 - 14x$ were 54% and 69%, respectively.
3. The Motor Boat Problem had also been administered in the CPMP field test at the end of Course 1. Field test students, who were using a prepublication version of the curriculum, did not score as well as the students in the present study. CPMP field-test students scored 65%, 61%, 59%, and 67% on the respective parts of the problem. Averaging across the four parts, the students in this study scored 66%, Core-Plus Mathematics students in the field test scored 63%, and conventional first-year algebra comparison students in the field test scored 40%.

APPENDIX

1. *ITED-Q* Pretest and Posttest Descriptive Statistics for Standard Scores of all Students Who Completed the Course 1 *ITED-Q* Posttest

		ITED-Q Pretest		*ITED-Q Course 1 Posttest*	
Group	*N*	*Mean (%-Tile)*	*SD*	*Mean (%-Tile)*	*SD*
Washington	70	260.0 (55)	35.8	263.1 (52)	44.8
Adams	189	271.5 (65)	34.2	275.6 (63)	40.2
Jefferson	353	271.4 (65)	33.1	274.7 (62)	39.9
Females	327	267.0 (61)	33.8	273.2 (61)	39.2
Males	285	273.7 (67)	33.8	274.1 (61)	42.5
PAL 1	95	315.4 (95)	7.8	316.5 (93)	16.5
PAL 2	219	289.5 (80)	8.2	289.2 (75)	27.7
PAL 3	196	255.8 (51)	11.7	259.6 (50)	33.5
PAL 4	102	213.9 (16)	12.6	227.3 (23)	33.9
TOTAL	612	270.1 (64)	33.9	273.6 (61)	40.7

Appendix continues on next page.

2. ANCOVAs With *ITED-Q* Pretest as Covariate and *ITED-Q* Course 1 Posttest as Dependent Variable

School by Gender ANCOVA

Source	Type III Sum of Squares	df	Mean Square	F	Sig.
Corrected Model[a]	424379.257	6	70729.876	84.861	.000
Intercept	25072.868	1	25072.868	30.082	.000
Pre-*ITED-Q*	418660.920	1	418660.920	502.308	.000
SCHOOL	294.629	2	147.314	.177	.838
GENDER	2342.966	1	2342.966	2.811	.094
SCHOOL*GENDER	247.767	2	123.884	.149	.862
Error	446742.481	536	833.475		
Total	41685628.000	543			
Corrected Total	871121.738	542			

[a] $R^2 = .487$ (Adjusted $R^2 = .481$)

School by Gender Adjusted Posttest Means

	Females			Males			TOTAL	
School	N	Adj. Mean	SE	N	Adj. Mean	SE	Adj. Mean	SE
Washington	30	276.6	5.21	40	268.2	4.50	272.4	3.45
Adams	101	276.5	2.83	88	272.0	3.03	274.2	2.07
Jefferson	196	275.5	2.03	157	271.1	2.28	273.3	1.52
TOTAL	327	276.2	2.09	286	270.4	1.96		

School by Preachievement Level ANCOVA

Source	Type III Sum of Squares	df	Mean Square	F	Sig.
Corrected Model[a]	424914.923	12	35409.577	42.059	.000
Intercept	2219.730	1	2219.730	2.637	.105
Pre-*ITED-Q*	36307.816	1	36307.816	43.126	.000
SCHOOL	4.096	2	2.048	.002	.998
PAL	1343.563	3	447.854	.532	.661
SCHOOL * PAL	1297.744	6	216.291	.257	.956
Error	446206.815	530	841.900		
Total	41685628.000	543			
Corrected Total	871121.738	542			

[a] $R^2 = .488$ (Adjusted $R^2 = .476$)

Appendix continues on next page.

School by Preachievement Level Adjusted Posttest Means

	Washington			Adams			Jefferson			TOTAL		
PAL	*N*	*Adj. Mn.*	*SE*	*N*	*Adj. Mn.*	*SE*	*N*	*Adj. Mn.*	*SE*	*N*	*Adj. Mn.*	*SE*
1	6	278.6	12.64	29	287.0	7.54	60	278.3	6.29	95	281.3	6.80
2	23	274.3	6.42	74	271.8	3.91	122	274.9	3.42	219	274.1	3.32
3	20	275.0	6.61	60	271.6	4.04	116	270.3	3.08	196	271.2	3.11
4	21	273.6	8.79	26	274.9	8.91	55	272.9	7.35	102	270.4	7.17
TOTAL	70	272.3	3.95	189	276.3	1.62	253	274.1	1.62			

Gender by Preachievement Level ANCOVA

Source	*Type III Sum of Squares*	*df*	*Mean Square*	*F*	*Sig.*
Corrected Model[a]	429500.152	8	53687.519	64.918	.000
Intercept	1952.602	1	1952.602	2.361	.125
Pre-*ITED-Q*	38310.470	1	38310.470	46.324	.000
GENDER	2647.667	1	2647.667	3.202	.074
PAL	2614.391	3	871.464	1.054	.368
GENDER*PAL	2657.710	3	885.903	1.071	.361
Error	441621.587	534	827.007		
Total	41685628.000	543			
Corrected Total	871121.738	542			

[a] $R^2 = .493$ (Adjusted $R^2 = .485$)

Appendix continues on next page.

Gender by Preachievement Level Adjusted Posttest Means

	Females			Males			TOTAL		
PAL	N	Adj. Mean	SE	N	Adj. Mean	SE	N	Adj. Mean	SE
1	38	280.4	6.79	57	280.8	6.40	95	280.6	5.90
2	120	277.6	3.38	99	269.2	3.60	219	273.4	2.91
3	107	271.9	3.15	89	269.9	3.44	196	270.9	2.60
4	162	275.7	7.36	40	265.8	7.67	102	270.8	6.95
TOTAL	327	276.4	1.75	285	271.4	1.79			

3. *ITED-Q* Pretest and Course 2 Posttest Descriptive Statistics for Standard Scores of Adams High School Fall Semester Course 2 Students

		ITED-Q Pretest		ITED-Q Course 2 Posttest	
Group	N	Mean (%-tile)	SD	Mean (%-tile)	SD
Females	68	269.1 (63)	29.8	288.6 (69)	32.3
Males	54	276.1 (69)	34.2	298.8 (78)	37.5
PAL 1	16	319.7 (97)	10.7	336.1 (98)	16.5
PAL 2	50	287.4 (78)	8.4	306.1 (83)	22.3
PAL 3	40	257.2 (52)	11.5	279.3 (61)	24.2
PAL 4	16	214.9 (17)	15.6	244.1 (32)	29.3
TOTAL	122	272.2 (66)	31.9	293.1 (73)	34.9

Gender by Preachievement Level ANCOVA

Source	Type III Sum of Squares	df	Mean Square	F	Sig.
Corrected Model[a]	93,873.597	8	11,734.200	24.735	.000
Intercept	4,007.055	1	4,007.055	8.447	.004
Pre-*ITED-Q*	3,822.015	1	3,822.015	8.057	.005
GENDER	295.917	1	295.917	.624	.431
PAL	1,476.532	3	492.177	1.037	.379
GENDER*PAL	4,523.949	3	1,507.983	3.179	.027
Error	53,606.017	113	474.390		
Total	10,628,677.000	122			
Corrected Total	147,479.615	121			

[a] $R^2 = .637$ (Adjusted $R^2 = .611$)

Appendix continues on next page.

Gender by Preachievement Level Adjusted Posttest Means

	Females			Males			TOTAL		
PAL	*N*	*Adj. Mean*	*SE*	*N*	*Adj. Mean*	*SE*	*N*	*Adj. Mean*	*SE*
1	5	294.6	13.05	11	318.2	11.12	16	306.4	10.61
2	32	295.3	4.71	18	303.0	5.99	50	299.1	4.32
3	22	284.2	5.68	18	291.1	5.61	40	287.6	4.43
4	9	284.8	13.03	7	261.3	13.44	16	273.0	12.04
TOTAL	69	289.7	3.46	54	293.4	3.20			

4. Core-Plus Mathematics Course 1 Posttest Results by Test Form (1 Maximum Point for Each Item)

Form	*No. Items*	*N*	*Mean (%)*	*SD*	*Reliability* (α)
C	19	163	55.3	22.8	.85
D	21	181	48.7	21.6	.85
E	21	170	53.8	20.3	.83

CHAPTER 6

ACHIEVEMENT PATTERNS IN YEAR 2

Algebra and Functions

In Course 1, the achievement focus was on measuring what students knew and were able to do mathematically across all four content strands using written and oral assessments developed by the researchers. Arguably, the most important achievement outcomes in high school mathematics are in the area of algebra. By the end of Course 2, students should have completed many of the algebraic topics that are typically covered in the first 2 years of a conventional mathematics curriculum. Thus the main Course 2 achievement assessment focuses on describing students' algebraic knowledge, understanding, and skill.

This chapter begins with an analysis of scores on the Educational Testing Service's (ETS) *Algebra End-of-Course Examination* (EoC). The EoC assesses the algebraic understanding and performance of students at the end of a year of elementary algebra. Results are reported in terms of ETS's subtest categories, by comparison to first-year algebra students, and by school and gender. At the time of this testing, May 1999, the EoC was under development, so the most current (1999) version of the test was administered. Since then, ETS has published the EoC.

A Five-Year Study of the First Edition of the Core-Plus Mathematics Curriculum, pp. 121–147

Going beyond algebra, the performance of selected students is also described on paper-and-pencil interview problems that measure curriculum specific objectives in three of the four content strands: Algebra and Functions, Geometry and Trigonometry, and Discrete Mathematics. Especially in Course 2, these strands are tightly integrated, so the interview problems were deliberately written to assess the integration of the strands. Because probability, an important part of the fourth content strand, is not so closely integrated with the other strands in this course and because some classes did not complete the probability unit (Unit 7, *Patterns in Chance*), no statistics and probability problems were used in the Course 2 interviews.

ALGEBRA END-OF-COURSE EXAMINATION DESCRIPTION AND RESULTS

According to ETS, "the *Algebra End-of-Course Examination* (EoC) is designed to reflect the way first-year algebra is taught in today's mathematics classrooms—emphasizing not only mastery of important skills, but also understanding of fundamental concepts." The EoC is kept secure, so the actual test items were not available for analysis. However, ETS provided brief verbal descriptions of the content assessed by each item, and they categorized the EoC items into three subtests: Concepts, Processes, and Skills. According to ETS's descriptions, the Concepts subtest included problems measuring students' understanding of functions, data analysis, linearity, variables, and equality. The Processes subtest included problems involving multiple representations, deductive reasoning, analogical reasoning, quantitative reasoning, and inductive reasoning. Problems on the Skills subtest required students to solve, construct, evaluate, and simplify algebraic equations or expressions. The individual item specifications provided by ETS are in Part 5 of the Chapter 6 Appendix. In this study, alpha reliability coefficients for the three subtests were .74, .75, and .41, respectively. Table 6.1 describes the content and the percentage and number of items for each subtest.

The 1999 developmental version of EoC was administered to 585 students in May 1999 at the end of Course 2. The exam was in two parts that could be completed in two 45-minute class periods or one 90-minute block period. The first part consisted of 25 multiple-choice questions, and students were not allowed to use calculators. Students were allowed to use scientific or graphing calculators on the second part consisting of 6 constructed-response items. Calculators that included Computer Algebra Systems (CAS) were not allowed on any part of the test.

Table 6.1. Content and Percent of Items on Each EoC Subtest[a]

Subtest	*Content*	*No. (%) of Items*
Concepts	Functions, data analysis, linearity, variables, equality	14 (45%)
Processes	Multiple representations, deductive reasoning, analogical reasoning, quantitative reasoning inductive reasoning	13 (42%)
Skills	Solve, construct, evaluate, simplify algebraic equations or expressions	8 (26%)

[a]Total percentage is greater than 100 because some questions have multiple parts and therefore were given multiple classifications.

Table 6.2. Mean Percent Correct[a] (*SD*) of Course 2 Students and First-Time First-Year Algebra Students With Effect Sizes

Subtest	*Course 2 Students (N = 585)*	*Algebra Students (N = 8,874)*	*Effect Size[b]*
Concepts	50% (20.1)	39%	.55
Processes	39% (22.1)	31%	.36
Skills	43% (20.6)	41%	.10
Total	45% (18.8)	39%	.32

[a] Performance is expressed as a percentage of questions answered correctly on the EoC.
[b] Effect size is computed by dividing the difference between group means by the standard deviation of the Course 2 group, the only standard deviation available.

Comparison With Baseline Algebra Students

As a baseline for comparison, ETS provided the percent correct on each subtest for all 8,874 first-year algebra students in the country who completed this exam. ETS makes no claims that these algebra students are a representative national sample, but the differing subtest score patterns for the students in this study compared to the first-year algebra students shown in Table 6.2 above is interesting. The Skills mean scores of the two groups differ by just a little, but the Concepts and Processes means of the Course 2 students are much higher than those of the first-year algebra students.

Differences between the Course 2 and first-year algebra groups' means may not be attributable to a curriculum effect, since, for example, one group may have been mathematically stronger than the other prior to experiencing any algebra curriculum. However, the achievement profiles of the two student groups across the three subtests do seem to differ markedly. If the differences were due to an initial gap in mathematical aptitudes of the two groups of students, one would hypothesize that the 3 Course 2 subtest means would increase at about the same rates. In other words, the effect sizes for each of the 3 subtests would be equal to the Total EoC effect size (.32). If this hypothesis is true, each Course 2 subtest expected mean would be greater than the Algebra students means by an amount equal to .32 times the standard deviation of that subtest. The hypothesized subtest means would be about 45% for Concepts, 38% for Processes, and 48% for Skills (see Figure 6.1).

To test the hypothesis that the three subtest effect sizes are equal (resulting in the hypothesized means for Course 2 students), a three-way, repeated measures ANOVA was run using students' subtest effect sizes as the 3 dependent variables. The subtest repeated measure effect was significant beyond the .0005 probability level. Pairs of scores also differed significantly ($p < .0005$ for each pair), so the hypothesis that the three subtest effect sizes are equal is clearly rejected. Such large differences in effect sizes would not occur by random chance. Compared to the subtest means of the first-year algebra sample, all 3 Course 2 subtest means are higher, but the relative differences are greatest for the Concepts means, followed by the Processes mean, and then the Skills mean.

The Course 2 group is not just a uniformly more mathematically adept group than the first-year algebra group. Rather they are relatively strongest on conceptual understanding, followed by algebraic processes, and slightly better than the first-year algebra group on algebraic skills. These results seem to increase the likelihood that a curriculum effect is at least a partial explanation, since this sort of pattern—similar on algebraic skills but much stronger on conceptual understanding and problem solving—is

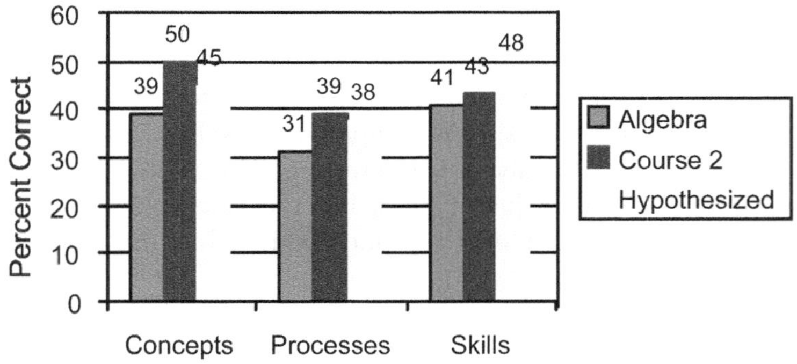

Figure 6.1. Means for First-Year Algebra and Course 2 Actual and Hypothesized on Each EoC Subtest.

consistent with findings in many studies of the impact of *Standards*-based mathematics curricula (cf. review by Stein, Remillard, & Smith, 2007) including the curriculum in the present study (Schoen & Hirsch, 2003a).

School, Gender, and PAL Effects With *ITED-Q* Pretest Scores as Covariate

To analyze the school, gender, and PAL effects on the EoC subtests in a way that takes into account variance in entering mathematics achievement level, the *ITED-Q* pretest administered at the beginning of Grade 9 was used as a covariate. The analysis of covariance is a statistical test of the differences in means on each EoC subtest after adjustment for variance in the *ITED-Q* pretest scores. Three school-by-gender analyses of covariance were run with each subtest as dependent variable. No school-by-gender interactions were statistically significant. Similarly, in three school-by-PAL and three gender-by-PAL ANCOVAs, the interactions between school and PAL and between gender and PAL are not statistically significant. Thus the school, gender, and PAL main effects are discussed separately. Complete descriptive statistics and ANCOVA tables are provided in the Chapter 6 Appendix, Parts 2–4.

School Effects. The percents correct in each school on each EoC subtest adjusted for variance in the *ITED-Q* pretest are plotted in Figure 6.2. The descending order by school of the adjusted means—Washington, Adams, and Jefferson—is consistent across subtests. However, not all mean differences are statistically significant beyond the .05 probability level. The statistical analyses of mean differences based on the school-by-gender ANCOVA are as follows:

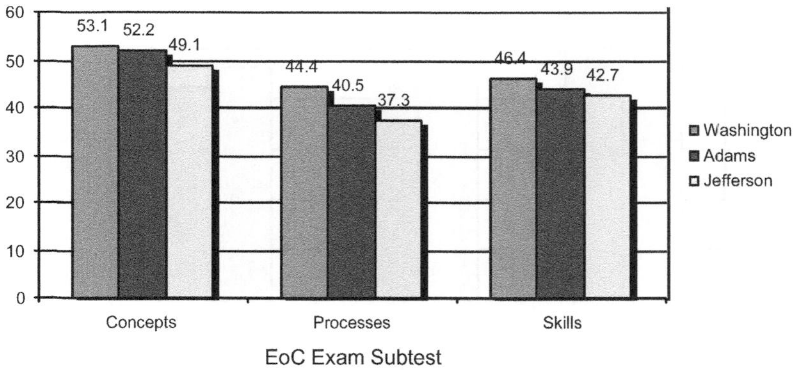

Figure 6.2. Percents Correct in Each School on Each EoC Subtest Adjusted for Variance in the *ITED-Q* Pretest.

- On the Concepts subtest, the overall school effect is significant (p = .021), but the only significant pairwise difference is Washington greater than Jefferson (p = .020).
- On the Processes subtest, the overall school effect is significant (p < .001), but again, the only significant pairwise difference is Washington greater than Jefferson (p < .001).
- On the Skills subtest, the overall school effect is not statistically significant (p = .137).

In summary, the school main effect was significant on the Concepts and Processes subtests, but not on the Skills subtest. Adjusted mean percents correct of Washington and Adams did not differ significantly on any subtest, while those of Washington were significantly greater than Jefferson's on Concepts and Processes subtests. On both these subtests, Adams' mean was greater than Jefferson's at a level approaching significance (p = .054 and p = .067, respectively).

Gender Effects. The percents correct for boys and girls on each EoC subtest adjusted for variance in the *ITED-Q* pretest are plotted in Figure 6.3. On each subtest, the adjusted mean of the girls is greater than that of the boys. Based on the school-by-gender ANCOVA, the difference in adjusted means is statistically significant on the Processes (p = .006) and Skills (p = .010) subtests, but not on the Concepts subtest (p = .162).

PAL Effects

For a variable like PAL that is defined by intervals of a baseline measure, it is important to be aware of the "regression to the mean" effect.

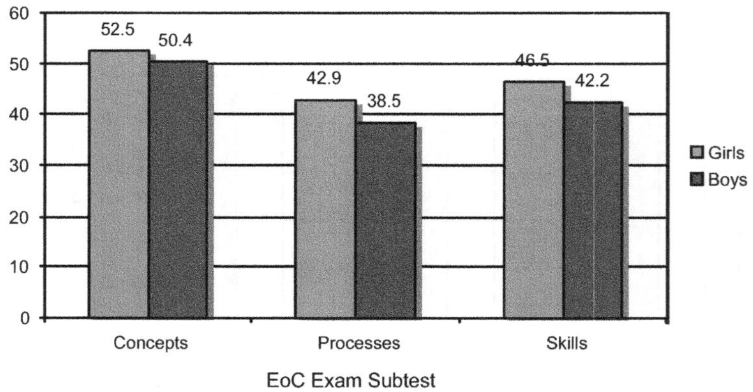

Figure 6.3. Percents Correct for Girls and Boys on Each EoC Subtest Adjusted for Variance in the *ITED-Q* Pretest.

Because of random error that is part of any test score, the "true scores" of students who are placed in either extreme group on a variable like PAL are more likely to be closer to the mean than further away. Hence, on a second test that is positively correlated with PAL's basis measure (*ITED-Q* pretest), it should be kept in mind that students in PAL 1 may be expected to have somewhat lower means, and students in PAL 4 may be expected to have somewhat higher means just because of regression to the mean.

The percents correct in each PAL group on each EoC subtest adjusted for variance in the *ITED-Q* pretest are plotted in Figure 6.4. Results are from the gender-by-PAL ANCOVA. The descending order by PAL group of the adjusted means on both the Concepts and Processes subtests is 1, 4, 2, and 3, but this switched to 4, 1, 3, and 2 on the Skills subtest. The overall PAL effect was statistically significant ($p < .001$) on each of the three subtests, but only the pairwise mean differences listed below are statistically significant beyond the .05 probability level.

- On the Concepts subtest, PAL 1 > PAL 3 ($p = .026$).
- On the Processes subtest, PAL 1 > PAL 2 ($p = .002$), PAL 1 > PAL 3 ($p = .005$), and PAL 4 > PAL 3 ($p = .015$).
- On the Skills subtest, PAL 1 > PAL 2 ($p = .016$), PAL 4 > PAL 2 ($p = .012$), and PAL 4 > PAL 3 ($p < .001$).

In summary, the PAL main effect was highly significant on each of the three subtests. The lowest preachieving group, PAL 4, did well compared to the two middle PAL groups, especially on the Processes and Skills test. However, this finding should be interpreted with care since

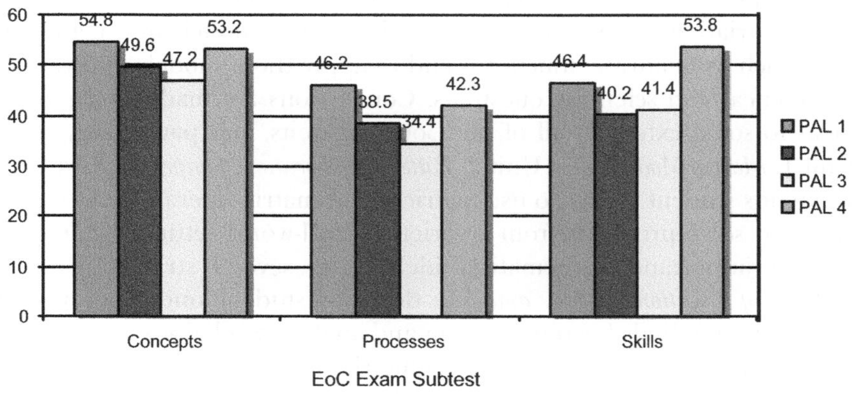

Figure 6.4. Percents Correct for PAL Groups on Each EoC Subtest Adjusted for Variance in the *ITED-Q* Pretest.

the PAL 4 scores may be inflated due to regression to the mean. On the other hand, the highest preachieving group, PAL 1, did well relative to the two middle groups on all three subtests. In the case of PAL 1, the finding is less tenuous since a regression to the mean effect would suggest that "true" adjusted means may be even higher than those PAL 1 students obtained.

ACHIEVEMENT OF CURRICULUM-SPECIFIC OBJECTIVES

As in Course 1, selected students were administered problem-based interviews at various times during Course 2. The interviewer was typically either a research assistant or a professor working on the research project.[1] Sixty-five different students worked on one or more of the seven problems chosen by the interviewers. With 20–30-minute time constraints on each interview, a given student rarely worked on all seven of the problems and sometimes did not complete all parts of attempted problems. Interview problems were analyzed based on the students' written work and the transcripts of the taped interviews. Students' quotations that appear in the following discussion were obtained from the transcripts of the interview sessions. The interview problems fall into three categories that generally align with three of the four content strands of the curriculum: Algebra and Functions, Geometry and Trigonometry, and Discrete Mathematics.

Course 2 contains one unit that is almost entirely algebraic, Unit 4, *Power Models.* According to Coxford et al. (1997), this unit develops student ability to recognize data patterns that involve both direct and inverse power variations, to construct and analyze those models and combinations such as quadratic functions, and to apply those models to a variety of practical and scientific questions. Connections are made to algebraic ideas to some extent in all of the Course 2 units, and particularly so in Unit 1, *Matrix Models,* and Unit 2, *Patterns of Location, Shape and Size*. Unit 1 extends student ability to use matrices and matrix operations to represent and solve problems from a variety of real-world settings while connecting important mathematical ideas from several strands. Unit 2, *Patterns of Location, Shape, and Size* develops student understanding of coordinate methods for representing and analyzing relations among geometric shapes, and for describing geometric change. Coordinate methods are perhaps the most important and basic connection between algebra and geometry in that they provide a way to represent both geometric ideas algebraically and algebraic ideas geometrically.

Problem-by-Problem Performance

Interview problems measured outcomes from the above units in an integrated manner. Thus the results are discussed problem by problem rather than by content strand as in the Course 1 chapter. Algebraic topics (e.g., modeling and symbol manipulation), geometric topics (e.g., two-dimensional shapes and spatial relationships), and discrete mathematics topics (e.g., matrix operations and vertex-edge graphs) are discussed as they arise in each problem.

Shortest Distance Problem. The first interview problem, given in Figure 6.5, required students to construct a geometric model, sum straight-line distances, and then apply the Pythagorean Theorem to determine a shortest distance. Twenty-one of the 29 students interviewed were assigned either partial or full credit. Those receiving full credit recognized that the two points could be plotted on a coordinate plane to represent Emmet's location and the neighbor's ranch and that a right triangle could be used with vertices that connected the two points. While using the Pythagorean Theorem, one student stated the underlying fact that "the shortest distance between two points is always a straight line."

Although most students recognized that the shortest distance between the two points was the line segment connecting them, those who had difficulty with this problem did not recognize that the Pythagorean Theorem could be used to compute the distance between these two points. These students used a vaguely defined estimation to determine the distance, such as one student who said, "I just figured that out by just drawing a diagram and estimating the length."

Triangle in a Coordinate Plane Problem. Students were given the vertex matrix and sketch of a triangle, as shown in Figure 6.6, and then asked a sequence of questions about the setting. Fourteen of the 32 students interviewed with this problem received full credit for Part a, and an additional 14 students received partial credit. The most successful students understood that since the slopes of the sides are negative reciprocals, the sides were perpendicular; thus the triangle is a right triangle. Nearly all students

---

To drive a car to his neighbor's ranch, Emmet travels 2 miles south, 3 miles east, and then 4 miles south.

(a) Draw a diagram showing the route Emmet takes to his neighbor's ranch. Mark the given distances on your diagram. Using this route, how far is it to the neighbor's ranch?

(b) If Emmet released a homing pigeon at his neighbor's ranch, what is the shortest distance it could fly to return to Emmet's house? Explain your answer.

Figure 6.5. Shortest Distance Problem.

Triangle $ABC = \begin{bmatrix} 0 & 3 & 2 \\ 0 & 3 & 4 \end{bmatrix}$ is sketched below.

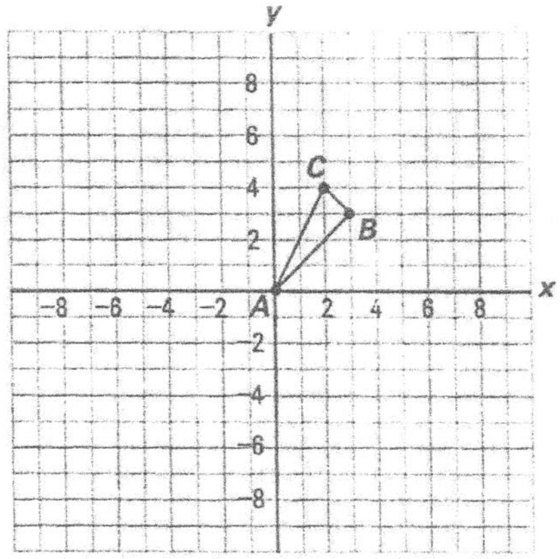

(a) ΔABC appears to be a right triangle. Check by finding the slopes of lines AB and BC. Is ΔABC a right triangle? Explain your reasoning.

(b) Find the lengths of sides AB, AC, and BC. Explain how to use these lengths to determine whether ΔABC is a right triangle.

(c) Write an equation for line AC. Show your work.

(d) Draw the image of ΔABC under each given transformation. Label it $A'B'C'$.

i. Reflection across y-axis

ii. Reflection across x-axis

iii. Clockwise rotation of 90° centered at the origin

iv. Size transformation of magnitude 2

(e) Describe the effect on $\Delta ABC$of the transformation represented by $\begin{bmatrix} 0.5 & 0 \\ 0 & 0.5 \end{bmatrix}$.

(f) Find the area of ?ABC. Show or explain your work.

(g) Consider $\Delta A'B'C'$, the size transformation of magnitude 2 of ΔABC that you sketched in Part d. Explain how to find the area of $\Delta A'B'C'$ from the area of ΔABC without computing the lengths of any sides of $\Delta A'B'C'$.

Figure 6.6. Triangle in a Coordinate Plane Problem.

were able to calculate the slopes correctly, but some had difficulty using the slopes to determine if the sides were perpendicular.

Seven of the 32 students interviewed with this problem earned full credit on Part b, and an additional 8 students received partial credit. Students who were unsuccessful with this problem had a variety of misconceptions. Many who received partial credit could find the lengths of the legs of the triangle, but they could not or did not use this information to determine whether it was a right triangle. One student who received no credit overemphasized the importance of the longest side in a triangle, seeming to think that the angle opposite the longest side is always a right angle. In his words, "You could use the lengths to prove that it's a right triangle because the longest side, which is the hypotenuse, is always across from the right angle." Another student confused isosceles and right triangles, incorrectly concluding that the triangle was not a right triangle because its two shorter sides were not the same length.

Seven of the 32 students interviewed with this problem found the correct equation for the line AC in Part c. The successful students demonstrated their ability to use the slope-intercept formula to solve this problem by using the graph to find the y-intercept and the two points from the given matrix to find the slope. Students who were not successful with this part often did not know how to incorporate the slope, which they had found earlier, into an equation.

In Part d of the Triangle in a Coordinate Plane Problem, 14 of the 32 students interviewed could draw the reflection of the given triangle across the y-axis, and 13 of the 32 could draw a second reflection across the x-axis as well. Students were more successful with size transformations. Sixteen of the 32 students could correctly draw the image of a triangle under a size transformation of magnitude 2. With one of the vertices at the origin, many of the students correctly recognized that they could multiply each vertex by two in order to get the correct size transformation. One student demonstrated her understanding that any size transformation preserves angles and, therefore, similar shape by saying, "No matter how big you get it, the angles would still be the same." Rotations, however, proved to be more difficult for students. In the most difficult part of this problem, only 2 of the 32 students could correctly draw the image of a triangle under a clockwise 90-degree rotation centered at the origin. The majority of students who had difficulty drew a reflection over the x-axis rather than a rotation of 90 degrees. Some who drew a reflection over the x-axis knew that their answer was incorrect, but they were unsure of how to correct it.

In Part e of the Triangle in a Coordinate Plane Problem, students were asked to describe the effect of a size transformation on the triangle, represented by the given 2 x 2 matrix (see Figure 6.6). Eight of the 32 students who worked on this problem provided correct solutions. Those who had difficulty with Part e were mostly confused by the matrix representation of the transformation and were unsure of how to apply this to the original triangle.

Students were asked to find the area of the triangle in Part f of the Triangle in a Coordinate Plane Problem. This part of the problem was complicated by the fact that the triangle's base and height were not given. The students were required to use their side-length calculations from a previous part of the problem and recognize that these calculations represented the base and height of the triangle. Seven of the 32 students interviewed received full credit. A few students creatively used the property that two right triangles make a rectangle, found the area of the rectangle, and divided their rectangle area in half to find the area of the triangle. Some students misused this connection and incorrectly thought that the area of the triangle would be the length of the base multiplied by the height.

In the last part, Part g, students needed to show their understanding of the effect of a size transformation of magnitude 2 on the are of a triangle. Four of the 32 students interviewed were able to determine the larger triangle's area in terms of the smaller triangle's area (4 to 1) using symbolic algebra to represent and transform the side lengths of the smaller triangle and then compute and compare areas. Students who had difficulty with this part recognized that the side lengths of the image triangle would be twice those of the original, but they concluded incorrectly that the area would increase by a factor of 2 as well.

Parallelogram Problem. Another task that required students to write equations given coordinate information is the Parallelogram Problem in Figure 6.7. In Part a of this problem, 13 of 30 students interviewed wrote a correct equation for the line containing the two coordinate points (4, 0) and (6, 3). The most successful students were able to compute the slope using these two points and then determine the y-intercept. Others were able to correctly determine the equation using their graphing calculator and estimation skills. Students who were unable to determine a correct equation typically had difficulty finding the proper y-intercept or relied solely on their calculators for an equation.

In Part b of the Parallelogram Problem, students had difficulty identifying whether the given parallelogram was a rhombus due to their uncertainty about the definition of a rhombus. Nine of the 30 students who worked on this problem were able to correctly answer the question. Students displayed a variety of beliefs about the definition of a rhombus ranging from "all equal sides" to "like a square but tilted." Few students completely understood the properties of this shape.

In Part c of the Parallelogram Problem, students were asked to find the equations of the lines containing the diagonals of the given parallelogram. Although the algebraic process was the same as that used in Part a, students were additionally required to understand the meaning of a diagonal. Twelve of 30 students correctly determined the two equations that represented the parallelogram's diagonals. The majority of those who were unable to find correct equations mistakenly identified a pair of parallel sides of the parallelogram as the diagonals of the shape.

It is important to note that Part d of this problem relied heavily on the slopes that students computed in Pard a. As a result, only 5 of the 30 students who worked on the problem received full credit for their answers.

A parallelogram $ABCD$ has vertex matrix $ABCD = \begin{bmatrix} 0 & 2 & 6 & 4 \\ 0 & 3 & 3 & 0 \end{bmatrix}$,

(a) Write an equation for the line containing the side of the parallelogram determined by (4, 0) and (6, 3). Show your work.

(b) Is the parallelogram a rhombus? Justify your response.

(c) Find equations of the lines containing the diagonals of the parallelogram. Show your work.

(d) Are the diagonals of the parallelogram perpendicular? Explain your reasoning.

(e) Find the midpoint of each diagonal. What do these results tell you about the diagonals?

Figure 6..7. Parallelogram Problem

Nine others received partial credit, typically for recognizing that slopes of two perpendicular lines are negative reciprocals, even though their slopes in Part a were not correct. Those who did not receive any credit for this problem had a variety of misconceptions about perpendicular lines, with some indication that their slopes should be the same.

In Part e of the Parallelogram Problem, only 2 of the 30 students received full credit with an additional 7 students receiving partial credit. Again, this problem was dependent on correct answers in previous steps, but partial credit was given if students understood that the diagonals of the parallelogram would meet at their common midpoint. Some students who were unable to calculate the correct midpoints had some understanding of the general concept, with one student explaining, "I knew that it was halfway between the x and halfway between the y, and I know there's an equation for how to do it, I just can't remember the equation." Students who were successful on the problem understood that the coordinates of the midpoint would be the average values of the x-coordinates and y-coordinates of the endpoints, respectively. Many of these students performed this calculation mentally.

Solving Two Linear Equations in Two Variables. In the third interview problem, students were asked to solve the following system of two equations algebraically, using matrices and any other method they chose:

$$3x + 2y = 15$$

$$x - y = 2$$

Fourteen of 35 students received partial credit, and another 5 students received full credit. Many students used some form of linear combination to isolate one of the variables, but other students were unsure of how to approach the problem. One student who tried to use linear operations said, "I think that there's just a lot of steps. That's what gets me confused is all the steps you have to do to get the answer." Although over half of the students interviewed received at least partial credit on this problem, many struggled. Some were able to get started by representing the system of equations as a matrix, but they were unable to solve for the final answer. Other students tried but were unable to represent the system as a matrix, and a few indicated a preference for using other methods for solving systems of equations.

Equipment Request Problem. Students were very successful in their efforts to explain the meaning of matrices in contextual problems such as the Equipment Request Problem, given in Figure 6.8. In Part a, 28 of the 29 students interviewed for this problem were able to find the total equipment cost matrix. Their success on this problem is evidence of their ability not only to identify matrix multiplication as the correct operation to use but also to correctly perform the multiplication.

In Part b of this problem, 25 of the 29 students received full credit for their responses indicating their ability to interpret the meaning of matrices and find the relevant entries in this contextual situation. Twenty-four of the 29 students were also able to use their total cost matrix to find the savings for all five schools in Part c. The mean score on this part was .83 (83%) out of 1 possible point. Many of the students expressed their comfort with the tasks in this problem; however, that comfort was less evident in the last part, Part d.

In Part d, students were asked to construct and properly label a cost matrix with high quality football helmet prices and average quality prices for the other equipment, then find a matrix for the total cost per school. Seventeen of the 29 students received full credit for their cost matrix on this part of the task. Sixteen of 29 students were additionally able to find a matrix for the total cost per school. Students who had difficulty with this task did not relate the correct order of prices in their matrix to the previous matrices in the problem. Some of the students were able to correct their own mistakes when they compared their matrices to other matrices in the problem. However, many of the students did not recognize the meaning of the order of the entries in the matrices and so were unable to correct their error.

Matrix Operations. According to the National Council of Teachers of Mathematics *Standards* (NCTM, 2000), students should be able to compute with matrices both on paper and with their calculator. To assess this ability, students were given some matrix operations to perform with no context. The students interviewed were successful with various matrix operations, particularly with the multiplication of matrices. Often the matrices in the given problems were large, so most students completed the matrix multiplication on their calculators, but many of these students

The North Lamar School District Athletic director is writing a funding proposal to the school board for new athletic equipment for the five middle schools (I-V) in the district. She decides that the schools need a variety of equipment including baseball bats (BB), volleyballs (VB), and football helmets (FH). The matrix Equipment Request below summarizes her request.

Equipment Request by School

$$\begin{array}{c} \\ BB \\ VB \\ FH \end{array}\begin{array}{c} \begin{array}{ccccc} I & II & III & IV & V \end{array} \\ \begin{bmatrix} 2 & 3 & 1 & 0 & 4 \\ 5 & 3 & 0 & 2 & 2 \\ 12 & 7 & 5 & 4 & 10 \end{bmatrix} \end{array}$$

(a) The equipment can be ordered at different levels of quality and cost. The matrix below gives the cost in dollars.

Cost of Equipment (in dollars)

$$\begin{array}{r} \\ \text{High Quality} \\ \text{Average Quality} \end{array}\begin{array}{c} \begin{array}{ccc} BB & VB & FH \end{array} \\ \begin{bmatrix} 25 & 14 & 55 \\ 17 & 10 & 42 \end{bmatrix} \end{array}$$

Use a matrix operation to complete the total equipment cost matrix below. Show how you obtained this answer.

Total Equipment Cost (in dollars by school)

$$\begin{array}{r} \\ \text{High Quality} \\ \text{Average Quality} \end{array}\begin{array}{c} \begin{array}{ccccc} I & II & III & IV & V \end{array} \\ \begin{bmatrix} \_\_ & \_\_ & \_\_ & \_\_ & \_\_ \\ \_\_ & \_\_ & \_\_ & \_\_ & \_\_ \end{bmatrix} \end{array}$$

(b) If school V orders average quality equipment, instead of high quality equipment, how much will they save? Show your work.

(c) Find the total savings if the athletic director orders average quality equipment for all schools.

(d) The athletic director decides to order high quality football helmets for safety reasons, but only average quality baseball bats and volleyballs.

- Construct a 1 by 3 cost matrix that gives the cost of each piece of equipment that is requested. Be sure to properly label your matrix.
- Then find a matrix for total cost per school. Indicate the matrices to be multiplied and explain why you chose the ones you did. Be sure to properly label your total cost per school matrix.

Figure 6.8. Equipment Request Problem.

were able to explain how to perform matrix multiplication by hand were able to do so. One student explained how critical it is to recognize the order of matrices when multiplying: "There's a property where the communicative [sic] property of multiplication doesn't apply."

Twenty-three of 26 students were able to correctly complete the following matrix multiplication task:

$$\begin{bmatrix} 2 & 4 & -1 \end{bmatrix} \begin{bmatrix} 2 & 6 & -2 \\ 0 & 2 & 1 \\ 1 & -3 & 0 \end{bmatrix}$$

Twenty-one of the 26 students were able to correctly square the following matrix:

$$\begin{bmatrix} -3 & 0 \\ 4 & 1 \end{bmatrix}$$

A common mistake made by those students who could not square the given matrix was to square each entry in the matrix. Once prompted, most students were able to correct their error.

However, many students had difficulty finding the matrix B given the following:

$$A = \begin{bmatrix} 5 & 7 \\ 2 & 3 \end{bmatrix} \text{ and } A \times B = \begin{bmatrix} 1 & 0 \\ 0 & 1 \end{bmatrix}$$

Only a few students recognized that A × B was the identity matrix and, consequently, that B is the inverse of the matrix A. Only six of 26 students were able to correctly determine the matrix B. Some students tried to divide A × B by A on their calculator, and others communicated similar thoughts about how to algebraically solve for B. Other students recognized that A × B was the identity matrix, but they were unsure about its properties. One student, in particular, knew that there was a function that could be used on the calculator, but she did not remember which function would work.

Tennis Tournament Problem. The NCTM (2000) *Standards* recommend that students be able to use vertex-edge graphs to model and solve problems as well as use matrices to represent and analyze vertex-edge graphs. Students had the opportunity to demonstrate their understanding of vertex-edge graphs with a sequence of questions in the Tennis Tournament Problem given in Figure 6.9. Seventeen of the 34 students who worked on this problem received full credit and an additional 10 students received partial credit. Successful students understood how a vertex-edge graph could model this tournament and conveyed their understanding through their drawings and descriptions. Most students were able to use a vertex-edge graph representation in some manner, although describing the graph verbally was difficult for some. Consequently, some students produced a correct vertex-edge graph but were unable to explain the representation correctly. Others had a clearer explanation but had an incomplete vertex-edge graph.

Part b of the Tennis Tournament Problem tested students' ability to use a matrix to represent the vertex-edge graph they had already prepared and also required them to demonstrate multiple representations of the same event. Twenty-one of the 34 students interviewed with this problem received full credit and an additional 6 students received partial credit. Successful students demonstrated a good understanding of the meaning of both of these representations. One student even created the vertex-edge graph and the matrix together in the first part of the problem without being explicitly asked for both.

A tennis tournament involved four girls, each of whom was to play every other girl. However, the tournament was rained out after 6 matches. The results so far are given below.

Aretha beat Stacey and Lindsay

Stacey beat Lindsay and Juanita

Lindsay beat Juanita

Juanita beat Aretha

(a) Draw a vertex-edge graph that represents this situation. Describe what the vertices and edges represent.

(b) Construct a matrix that represents this situation. Explain the entries in your matrix.

(c) After these 6 matches, how would you rank these 4 tennis players, with no ties? Explain how to use the matrix in part (b) to help justify your ranking.

Figure 6.9. Tennis Tournament Problem.

In Part c of the Tennis Tournament Problem, students were asked to use their matrix to rank the four tennis players after the six matches were completed. Many of the students knew to consider the row sums and the square of the matrix, but they often failed to break ties by referring to individual matches between the players. Students who received partial credit usually did not determine the correct ranking of the tennis players, but their explanations and work showed some conceptual understanding of the meaning of the entries in the matrix.

CHAPTER SUMMARY

A summary of this chapter's main findings on the ETS *End-of-Course Algebra Examination* follows. "Adjusted means" refers to means adjusted for variance on the *ITED-Q* pretest at the beginning of Grade 9.

- Compared to the first-year algebra sample, the Course 2 students were much stronger on conceptual understanding, stronger on algebraic processes, and slightly stronger on algebraic skills.
- Washington's adjusted mean percents correct were significantly greater than Jefferson's on the Concepts and Processes subtests, but not on Skills. Other pairwise school differences were not significant.
- The adjusted mean of girls was significantly higher than that of boys on the Processes and Skills subtests, but not on Concepts.
- In spite of adjustment for their high pretest scores and a possible negative regression to the mean effect, students in the top 10% of pretest scores did significantly better than the average and below average student groups.

The first-year algebra comparison group was not necessarily nationally representative and there is no way to know how their entering mathematical aptitude compared to the Course 2 students. However, this sort of pattern of results—similar on algebraic skills but much stronger on conceptual understanding and problem solving—is consistent with findings in many studies of the impact of *Standards*-based mathematics curricula including the curriculum in the present study. It seems likely that curriculum effect is at least a partial explanation for the highly statistically significant differences in subtest results.

The finding that students with higher entering mathematical achievement learned more than other students may be partially due to the fact that a high proportion of these students were in accelerated classes. In Course 2, 34% of PAL 1 students were in accelerated classes compared to 11% of students in lower preachievement groups. Research on tracking has consistently shown that, compared to regular college preparatory classes, classes considered by teachers and students to be in the higher academic track have higher expectations and content coverage, richer student-student and teacher-student interactions, and higher mathematical achievement (cf. reviews by Kulik & Kulik, 1982; Slavin, 1990). Whether class interactions were enriched in the accelerated classes in this study is not clear from the data, but these classes typically covered at least one unit more of content and adjusted achievement scores were significantly better than in regular classes. The tracking variable is a very important issue for quasi-experimental curriculum comparison studies, and one that is often overlooked. (See the further discussion in Chapter 14.)

Following the reporting of the quantitative EoC examination results, the remainder of the chapter describes the performance of selected students who were interviewed as they attempted to solve a variety of mathematical problems like those in the curriculum. The results are not easily summarized, but some of the main results are the following. In the Algebra and Functions strand, students showed a variety of strengths and weaknesses in their understanding and application of algebraic concepts. Many students were able to successfully represent situations that could be modeled using the Pythagorean Theorem, but problems that required them to represent and analyze mathematical structure using algebraic symbols were difficult for many students. Students demonstrated much success when asked to provide an equation for a given line, but they struggled when asked to solve a system of equations algebraically.

In the Geometry strand, many of the interview problems required students to use the coordinate plane to analyze geometric situations, particularly to understand and represent geometric transformations. Students demonstrated a solid understanding of the coordinate plane and were able to represent reflections and size transformations, but some had difficulty drawing the image of a triangle under a rotation. Many students had difficulty with a problem that required them to recognize the characteristics of a rhombus, but they had a variety of valid methods for successfully calculating the area of a triangle.

Overall, in the Discrete Mathematics strand, students were consistently able to perform matrix operations, particularly matrix multiplication. They demonstrated a good understanding of the meaning and properties of matrices as representations of contextual, verbally stated problems. Students also showed a good understanding of how to apply and interpret vertex-edge graphs in a contextual situation. However, some students had difficulty with the identity matrix and the inverse of a matrix, and few were able to solve a noncontextual system of two linear equations in two variables using matrices.

In the next chapter, students' achievement in Course 3 is summarized with a main focus on mathematical literacy as measured by released items from the Third International Mathematics and Science Study (TIMSS, 1997) and interview problems from the Balanced Assessment project (Balanced Assessment, 2007).

NOTES

1. Time and travel restrictions required a few interviews to be conducted by a classroom teacher, who was a former graduate student of one of the researchers and a former codirector of Core-Plus Mathematics inservice workshops for other teachers. Before conducting her own interviews, she observed a researcher-conducted interview and was observed and critiqued by the researcher as she conducted her first interview.

APPENDIX

1. *ITED-Q* Pretest and EoC Subtest Descriptive Statistics for all Students Completing the EoC

	ITED-Q Pretest			*Concepts* ($\alpha = .74$)		*Processes* ($\alpha = .75$)		*Skills* ($\alpha = .41$)	
Group	*N*	*Mean (%-Tile)*	*SD*	*Mean*	*SD*	*Mean*	*SD*	*Mean*	*SD*
Washington	87	270.5 (65)	33.4	51.3	19.8	42.2	21.1	44.6	19.7
Adams	1,051	282.9 (75)	27.7	56.3	20.1	45.5	23.5	48.3	20.7
Jefferson	393	271.1 (65)	32.0	48.3	19.9	36.5	21.6	41.9	20.6
Females	314	272.0 (66)	32.4	50.5	20.6	39.8	22.8	44.1	20.5
Males	271	274.4 (67)	31.0	49.8	19.6	37.9	21.3	42.7	20.6
PAL 1	97	315.4 (95)	7.3	72.5	14.4	65.2	17.8	66.1	17.8
PAL 2	212	289.9 (80)	8.5	56.8	15.8	46.2	16.5	48.2	16.6
PAL 3	200	256.5(52)	11.1	40.2	14.5	26.9	15.3	33.6	15.6
PAL 4	76	216.3 (18)	11.7	29.4	12.4	16.9	9.8	27.1	14.5
TOTAL	585	273.1 (65)	31.8	50.2	20.1	38.9	22.1	43.4	20.6

[a] Recall from Chapter 5 that the Fall semester students at Adams completed an alternate form of the *ITED Q*, not the EoC. These 105 Adams students are those who completed Course 2 in the Spring.

Appendix continues on next page.

2. ANCOVAS With *ITED-Q* Pretest as Covariate and EoC Concepts Subtest as Dependent Variable

School by Gender ANCOVA; Dependent Variable EoC Concepts Scores

Source	Type III Sum of Squares	df	Mean Square	F	Sig.
Corrected Model[a]	118,203.182	6	19,700.530	96.556	.000
Intercept	35,774.837	1	35,774.837	175.340	.000
Pre-*ITED-Q*	112,043.946	1	112,043.946	549.151	.000
SCHOOL	1,578.476	2	789.238	3.868	.021
GENDER	399.128	1	399.128	1.956	.162
SCHOOL * GENDER	631.963	2	315.982	1.549	.213
Error	117,929.989	578	204.031		
Total	1,707,991.263	585			
Corrected Total	236,133.170	584			

[a] R^2 = .501 (Adjusted R^2 = .495)

School by Gender Adjusted Concepts Means

	Females			Males			TOTAL		
School	N	Adj. Mean	SE	N	Adj. Mean	SE	N	Adj. Mean	SE
Washington	35	56.0	2.42	52	50.1	1.98	87	53.1	1.56
Adams	63	51.4	1.81	42	52.9	2.21	105	52.2	1.43
Jefferson	216	50.0	0.98	177	48.1	1.07	393	49.1	0.73
TOTAL	314	52.5	1.06	314	50.4	1.05			

School by Preachievement Level ANCOVA; Dependent Variable EoC Concepts Scores

Source	Type III Sum of Squares	df	Mean Square	F	Sig.
Corrected Model[a]	122,026.982	12	10,168.915	50.975	.000
Intercept	2,893.601	1	2,893.601	14.505	.000
Pre-*ITED-Q*	9,568.135	1	9,568.135	47.964	.000
SCHOOL	1,188.895	2	594.448	2.980	.052
PAL	2,566.514	3	855.505	4.289	.005
SCHOOL * PAL	649.954	6	108.326	.543	.776
Error	114,106.189	572	199.486		
Total	1,707,991.263	585			
Corrected Total	236,133.170	584			

[a] R^2 = .517 (Adjusted R^2 = .507)

Appendix continues on next page.

School by Preachievement Level Adjusted Concepts Means

	Washington			Adams			Jefferson			TOTAL		
PAL	*N*	*Adj. Mn.*	*SE*	*N*	*Adj. Mn.*	*SE*	*N*	*Adj. Mn.*	*SE*	*N*	*Adj. Mn.*	*SE*
1	11	60.9	4.96	25	57.9	3.82	61	53.4	3.12	97	56.8	3.14
2	33	49.4	2.68	43	53.3	2.37	136	49.2	1.54	212	50.2	1.58
3	27	50.0	2.96	34	46.9	2.71	139	46.2	1.56	200	48.2	1.65
4	16	56.7	4.89	3	52.2	8.86	57	51.3	3.93	76	54.3	4.59
TOTAL	87	54.3	1.67	105	52.7	2.32	393	50.1	0.81			

Gender by Preachievement Level ANCOVA; Dependent Variable EoC Concepts Scores

Source	*Type III Sum of Squares*	*df*	*Mean Square*	*F*	*Sig.*
Corrected Model[a]	120,718.992	8	15,089.874	75.309	.000
Intercept	2,980.674	1	2,980.674	14.876	.000
Pre-*ITED-Q*	9,515.887	1	9,515.887	47.491	.000
GENDER	196.760	1	196.760	.982	.322
PAL	4,254.102	3	1,418.034	7.077	.000
GENDER * PAL	211.716	3	70.572	.352	.788
Error	115,414.179	576	200.372		
Total	1,707,991.263	585			
Corrected Total	236,133.170	584			

[a] $R^2 = .511$ ($R^2 = .504$)

Gender by Preachievement Level Adjusted Concepts Means

	Females			Males			TOTAL		
PAL	*N*	*Adj. Mean*	*SE*	*N*	*Adj. Mean*	*SE*	*N*	*Adj. Mean*	*SE*
1	48	55.2	3.29	49	54.4	3.26	97	54.8	2.94
2	112	51.2	1.70	100	48.0	1.73	212	49.6	1.41
3	108	47.7	1.65	92	46.7	1.85	200	47.2	1.43
4	46	53.3	4.08	30	53.2	4.26	76	53.2	3.83
TOTAL	314	51.9	0.90	271	50.6	1.00			

Appendix continues on next page.

3. ANCOVAs With *ITED-Q* Pretest as Covariate and EoC Processes Subtest as Dependent Variable

School by Gender ANCOVA; Dependent Variable EoC Processes Scores

Source	*Type III Sum of Squares*	*df*	*Mean Square*	*F*	*Sig.*
Corrected Model [a]	151,990.786	6	25,331.798	109.685	.000
Intercept	67,727.871	1	67,727.871	293.256	.000
Pre-*ITED-Q*	142,349.594	1	142,349.594	616.362	.000
SCHOOL	3,700.591	2	1,850.296	8.012	.000
GENDER	1,777.473	1	1,777.473	7.696	.006
SCHOOL * GENDER	792.704	2	396.352	1.716	.181
Error	133,489.902	578	230.951		
Total	1,171,947.103	585			
Corrected Total	285,480.688	584			

[a] R^2 = .532 (R^2 = .528)

School by Gender Adjusted Processes Means

	Females			*Males*			*TOTAL*		
School	*N*	*Adj. Mean*	*SE*	*N*	*Adj. Mean*	*SE*	*N*	*Adj. Mean*	*SE*
Washington	35	48.9	2.57	52	39.9	2.11	87	44.4	1.66
Adams	63	41.2	1.93	42	39.8	2.35	105	40.5	1.53
Jefferson	216	38.7	1.04	177	36.0	1.14	393	37.3	0.77
TOTAL	314	42.9	1.12	314	38.5	1.12			

School by Preachievement Level ANCOVA; Dependent Variable EoC Processes Scores

Source	*Type III Sum of Squares*	*df*	*Mean Square*	*F*	*Sig.*
Corrected Model[a]	159,673.632	12	13,306.136	60.498	.000
Intercept	4,513.134	1	4,513.134	20.520	.000
Pre-*ITED-Q*	10,447.496	1	10,447.496	47.501	.000
SCHOOL	2,336.248	2	1,168.124	5.311	.005
PAL	5,018.312	3	1,672.771	7.605	.000
SCHOOL * PAL	1,380.778	6	230.130	1.046	.394
Error	125,807.056	572	219.942		
Total	1,171,947.103	585			
Corrected Total	285,480.688	584			

[a] R^2 = .559 (Adjusted R^2 = .550)

Appendix continues on next page.

School by Preachievement Level Adjusted Processes Means

	Washington			Adams			Jefferson			TOTAL		
PAL	N	Adj. Mn.	SE	N	Adj. Mn.	SE	N	Adj Mn.	SE	N	Adj. Mn.	SE
1	11	49.1	5.22	25	53.7	4.02	61	43.3	3.29	97	48.7	3.30
2	33	43.2	2.87	43	40.2	2.53	136	37.3	1.62	212	40.3	1.66
3	27	39.6	3.05	34	32.9	2.80	139	33.5	1.63	200	35.3	1.73
4	16	46.0	5.14	3	44.5	9.31	57	40.6	4.14	76	43.7	4.82
TOTAL	87	44.5	1.75	105	42.8	2.43	393	38.7	0.85			

Gender by Preachievement Level ANCOVA; Dependent Variable EoC Processes Scores

Source	Type III Sum of Squares	df	Mean Square	F	Sig.
Corrected Model[a]	157,361.933	8	19,670.242	88.434	.000
Intercept	5,078.955	1	5,078.955	22.834	.000
Pre-*ITED-Q*	10,973.961	1	10,973.961	49.337	.000
GENDER	1,176.936	1	1,176.936	5.291	.022
PAL	8,611.185	3	2,870.395	12.905	.000
GENDER * PAL	679.406	3	226.469	1.018	.384
Error	128,118.754	576	222.428		
Total	1,171,947.103	585			
Corrected Total	285,480.688	584			

[a] $R^2 = .551$ (Adjusted $R^2 = .545$)

Gender by Preachievement Level Adjusted Processes Means

	Females			Males			TOTAL		
PAL	N	Adj. Mean	SE	N	Adj. Mean	SE	N	Adj. Mean	SE
1	48	49.2	3.47	49	43.1	3.43	97	46.2	3.10
2	114	40.7	1.79	101	36.3	1.83	215	38.5	1.49
3	106	34.6	1.74	91	34.1	1.95	197	34.4	1.51
4	46	43.1	4.30	30	41.6	4.49	76	42.3	4.03
TOTAL	314	41.9	0.94	271	38.8	1.05			

Appendix continues on next page.

4. ANCOVAs With ITED-Q Pretest as Covariate and EoC Skills Subtest as Dependent Variable

Source	Type III Sum of Squares	df	Mean Square	F	Sig.
Corrected Model[a]	99,587.060	6	16,597.843	65.022	.000
Intercept	32,640.556	1	32,640.556	127.869	.000
Pre-*ITED-Q*	93,897.185	1	93,897.185	367.842	.000
SCHOOL	1,020.188	2	510.094	1.998	.137
GENDER	1,707.374	1	1,707.374	6.689	.010
SCHOOL * GENDER	795.470	2	397.735	1.558	.211
Error	147,543.116	578	255.265		
Total	1,350,932.977	585			
Corrected Total	247,130.176	584			

[a] $R^2 = .403$ (Adjusted $R^2 = .397$)

School by Gender Adjusted Skills Means

	Females			Males			TOTAL		
School	N	Adj. Mean	SE	N	Adj. Mean	SE	N	Adj. Mean	SE
Washington	35	50.2	2.70	52	42.7	2.22	87	46.4	1.75
Adams	63	46.1	2.03	42	41.7	2.47	105	43.9	1.60
Jefferson	216	43.2	1.09	177	42.1	1.20	393	42.7	0.81
TOTAL	314	46.5	1.18	314	42.2	1.18			

School by Preachievement Level ANCOVA; Dependent Variable EoC Skills Scores

Source	Type III Sum of Squares	df	Mean Square	F	Sig.
Corrected Model[a]	108,125.217	12	9,010.435	37.078	.000
Intercept	4,779.808	1	4,779.808	19.669	.000
Pre-*ITED-Q*	11,689.798	1	11,689.798	48.103	.000
SCHOOL	983.141	2	491.571	2.023	.133
PAL	6,099.772	3	2,033.257	8.367	.000
SCHOOL * PAL	923.547	6	153.925	.633	.704
Error	139,004.959	572	243.016		
Total	1,350,932.977	585			
Corrected Total	247,130.176	584			

[a] $R^2 = .438$ (Adjusted $R^2 = .426$)

Appendix continues on next page.

School by Preachievement Level Adjusted Skills Means

	Washington			Adams			Jefferson			TOTAL		
PAL	*N*	*Adj. Mn.*	*SE*	*N*	*Adj. Mn.*	*SE*	*N*	*Adj. Mn.*	*SE*	*N*	*Adj. Mn.*	*SE*
1	11	47.9	5.49	25	50.2	4.22	61	44.7	3.46	97	47.6	3.47
2	33	41.2	3.02	43	41.4	2.66	136	39.9	1.71	212	40.8	1.75
3	27	42.7	3.20	34	40.5	2.94	139	41.3	1.71	200	41.5	1.82
4	16	59.6	5.40	3	58.8	9.79	57	51.5	4.35	76	56.6	5.07
TOTAL	87	47.8	1.84	105	47.8	2.56	393	44.3	0.90			

Gender by Preachievement Level ANCOVA; Dependent Variable EoC Skills Scores

Source	*Type III Sum of Squares*	*df*	*Mean Square*	*F*	*Sig.*
Corrected Model[a]	108,095.714	8	13,511.964	55.978	.000
Intercept	5,016.904	1	5,016.904	20.784	.000
Pre-*ITED-Q*	11,811.721	1	11,811.721	48.934	.000
GENDER	516.692	1	516.692	2.141	.144
PAL	9,478.537	3	3,159.512	13.089	.000
GENDER * PAL	894.745	3	298.248	1.236	.296
Error	139,034.463	576	241.379		
Total	1,350,932.977	585			
Corrected Total	247,130.176	584			

[a] $R^2 = .437$ (Adjusted $R^2 = .430$)

Gender by Preachievement Level Adjusted Skills Means

	Females			Males			TOTAL		
PAL	*N*	*Adj. Mean*	*SE*	*N*	*Adj. Mean*	*SE*	*N*	*Adj. Mean*	*SE*
1	48	49.2	3.62	49	43.6	3.58	97	46.4	3.23
2	112	42.2	1.86	100	38.2	1.90	212	40.2	1.55
3	108	41.4	1.81	92	41.4	2.03	200	41.4	1.57
4	46	53.1	4.48	30	54.4	4.67	76	53.8	4.20
TOTAL	314	46.5	0.98	271	44.4	1.09			

Appendix continues on next page.

5. EoC Subtest Item Specifications

Concepts Subtest

- Interpret the point of intersection of the graphs of two lines.
- Compute an expected value, in context.
- Given the graph of an absolute value function, find the value of the function for a specific value in the domain.
- Given two relationships involving ratio, determine a third ratio from this information.
- Interpret the meaning of the slope of a line graph, in context.
- Identify a solution of a quadratic equation in factored form.
- Interpret a distance/time graph.
- Identify the equation of a line that is parallel to a given line.
- Given the graph of a line, identify its equation.
- Identify the graph of an inequality.
- Find the x-intercepts of a parabola, given its equation.
- Extend a geometric pattern and represent the pattern algebraically.

Processes Subtest

- Identify the equation that represents data given in a table.
- Find the maximum value of the equation of a parabola, given the equation.
- Identify a domain value for which the values of two different functions will be equal.
- Simplify an algebraic expression by combining like terms.
- Identify an equivalent form of a quadratic equation.
- Solve a linear inequality.
- Find a term of an arithmetic sequence, given two other terms in that sequence.
- Generate a table of data that satisfy given conditions and write an equation that describes the data.
- Apply the Pythagorean Theorem in context.
- Extend a geometric pattern and represent the pattern algebraically.
- Represent relationships involving dimensions and volumes of rectangular prisms algebraically.
- Represent a recursive relationship algebraically.

Skills Subtest

- Identify the graph of a function.
- Evaluate an algebraic expression.
- Identify an equation that expresses the relationship between earned income and tax paid.
- Solve a system of linear equations.
- Simplify an algebraic expression using rules of exponents.
- Generate a table of data that satisfy given conditions and write an equation that describes the data.
- Represent a recursive relationship algebraically.

CHAPTER 7

ACHIEVEMENT PATTERNS IN YEAR 3

Mathematical Literacy

The achievement goals, especially those in algebra and geometry, measured in Courses 1 and 2 are typically classified as college preparatory mathematics. A comprehensive high school mathematics curriculum for all students must provide a solid preparation for collegiate mathematics, even though not all students study more mathematics after high school. However, all students will need to make use of basic mathematics in their daily lives, and so they should all possess an adequate level of *mathematical literacy*. Mathematical literacy requires more than the acquisition of an expanded list of quantitative skills. As Price (1997) argues, logical thinking, analysis of evidence, and statistical reasoning are more important for engaged citizenship in the twenty-first century than conventional mathematical skills. Steen (2001) further cautions that mathematical literacy is not necessarily a by-product of conventional college preparatory high school mathematics programs.

This chapter begins with an analysis of a mathematical literacy test that was compiled from released TIMSS (Third International Mathematics and Science Study) mathematical literacy tasks (TIMSS, 1997) and administered to all students at the end of Course 3. Results are reported in

A Five-Year Study of the First Edition of the Core-Plus Mathematics Curriculum, pp. 149–170

comparison to TIMSS' nationally and internationally representative samples of students in the last year of secondary school and also by school, gender, and preachievement levels within the present study's sample. To provide further insight into students' levels of mathematical literacy, the performance of selected students is described on six paper-and-pencil interview problems that are drawn from the Balanced Assessment Project's collection of non-routine problems for high school students (Balanced Assessment, 2007).

THE CURRICULUM'S APPROACH TO MATHEMATICAL LITERACY

The Core-Plus Mathematics curriculum has attempted to address preparation for both college mathematics and mathematical literacy in an integrated, contextualized approach that is at once applied and theoretical, concrete and conceptual, practical and academic. Compared to more conventional college preparatory high school curricula, most mathematics is developed in the context of its uses, with the abstraction and appreciation of mathematics as a deductive logical system building slowly across the four-course curriculum. Many of the topics that have received increased attention in the curriculum are often mentioned by writers as important components of mathematical literacy, including:

- Probability, which facilitates reasoning about uncertainty and assessment of risk;
- Exploratory data analysis and statistics, which facilitate reasoning about data;
- Model-building, which facilitates systematic, structured understanding of complex situations;
- Operations research, which facilitates planning of complex tasks and achieving performance objectives;
- Discrete mathematics, which facilitates understanding of most applications of computers.

MATHEMATICAL LITERACY TEST

During 1995, TIMSS assessed the mathematics and science knowledge of a half-million students from 41 nations at three levels of schooling. In the present report, the focus is on the TIMSS assessment of mathematics general knowledge. Students who completed this test during TIMSS were in the last year of secondary school, including in representative numbers those who had taken advanced courses as well as those who had not. Mathematics general knowledge items were chosen by TIMSS

> based on their likelihood of arising in real-life situations and not on their connection to a particular curriculum. However, they can be described in terms of common mathematics curriculum topics, such as number sense, including fractions, percentages, and proportionality; algebraic sense; measurement and estimation; and data representation. (U.S. Department of Education, 1998, p. 30)

Clearly, mathematical literacy as discussed earlier has much in common with the TIMSS mathematics general knowledge framework, and TIMSS documents seem to use the terms interchangeably as well (IEA TIMSS, 1998).

The complete TIMSS mathematics general knowledge or mathematical literacy assessment consisted of test booklets that each contained 34 multiple-choice items and 10 free-response items. The assessment was administered to a representative sample of all students at the end of secondary school (12th grade in the United States) in 21 participating countries. U.S. 12th graders performed below the international average, significantly below 14 countries, and significantly above just 2 countries. The mean performance of students in the Netherlands was the highest among the 21 countries. (See Chapter 7 Appendix, Part 2.)

Following the administration of the TIMSS assessments, many test items were released for use by researchers or school personnel. Scoring rubrics, answer keys, and detailed performance data by country were also made available for all released items (IEA TIMSS, 1998).

Procedures

In the present study, 12 released TIMSS mathematics general knowledge items were chosen that provided representation across TIMSS's content categories and performance expectation categories. (See Table 7.1 for the matrix of items selected for this study.) To maintain a split between multiple-choice and free-response items proportional to that used by TIMSS, 10 of the items chosen were multiple-choice and 2 were free-response. For purposes of the following analysis of the scores, the items were separated into two 6-item subtests, Number (percent, ratio and proportion, and numbers and operations) and Geometry (geometric measurement and graphical interpretation).

As during the actual administration of TIMSS, students had access to a calculator and were given a time limit that allowed an average of about 2 minutes per item. This test was administered to 371 students at the end of

Table 7.1. Numbers of Selected Items in Each Content Category by Performance Expectation

	Content Category					
Performance Expectation	*Percent*	*Rat. & Prop.*	*Nos. & Ops.*	*Geom. Meas.*	*Graph Interp.*	*Total*
Knowing		1		1	1[a]	3
Rout. Proc.	1					1
Compl. Proc.	1		1	1	1	4
Solving Probs.		1	1	1		3
Justifying					1[a]	1
Total	2	2	2	3	3	12

[a] This is a constructed-response item.

Course 3. The scoring rubrics and answer key provided by TIMSS were used to score the students' completed tests. Multiple-choice items were scored as correct (1 point) or incorrect and the two open-ended items were scored using 2-point rubrics provided by TIMSS.

The 12 mathematical literacy items were administered as a part of a 20-item posttest. The other 8 items were selected from TIMSS' set of released advanced mathematics items. These were administered at the end of Year 3 and again at the end of Year 4 to measure students' growth during Year 4. The analysis of growth on the advanced mathematics items is reported in Chapter 8.

Comparisons with Representative TIMSS Groups

TIMSS provides data on each released item for their nationally and internationally representative groups of students. By averaging the percent correct across the 12 items, it is possible to compute a good estimate of how these groups would perform on the mathematical literacy test from this study. Clearly, the comparison of these results to those in the present study is limited in its interpretation because of likely noncomparability of the groups of students and differences in testing conditions. The sample in the present study was mainly juniors, not seniors as in the TIMSS sample, and this study's sample included only students who were at the end of Course 3. Furthermore, this study's sample was not representative of all students at this point in school, even in the three schools in the study, as it excluded students who were not enrolled in a third year of mathematics. The sample may also underrepresent accelerated juniors, some of whom were in

Course 4 or even an AP Calculus or AP Statistics course. While group differences should not necessarily be attributed to the curriculum, they may be of interest in the present climate of international competition.

Means by content subtest of the 371 Course 3 students and the TIMSS samples from the United States, the Netherlands, and the 21-country compilation are presented in Figure 7.1. The subtest means of the Course 3 students were consistently higher than the United States and international samples and were similar to the Netherlands, the highest performing country. Individual items together with performance statistics can be found in the Chapter 7 Appendix, Parts 5 and 6

To further examine the group differences by subtest, the effect size for each subtest and for each of the three comparison groups were computed. (see Table 7.2). The effect size is the number of standard deviations by which the present study's sample subtest mean differed from each of the TIMSS comparison groups. Here the standard deviation is that of the Course 3 group.

Effect size (ES) = (Course 3 mean – TIMSS group mean) / (Course 3 standard deviation)

As Table 7.2 shows, this study's sample means were similar to those of the Netherlands overall—slightly higher on the Number subtest and lower on the Geometry subtest. The means of this study's sample were much higher than those of the representative U.S. 12th-grade sample with effect sizes of .74 and .99. Students in this study also scored considerably better than the international average on all subtests, with effect sizes of .43 and .80. Compared to the subtest means of the U.S. TIMSS sample, both Course 3 subtest means are much higher, but the difference in Number means is relatively greater than the difference in Geometry means.

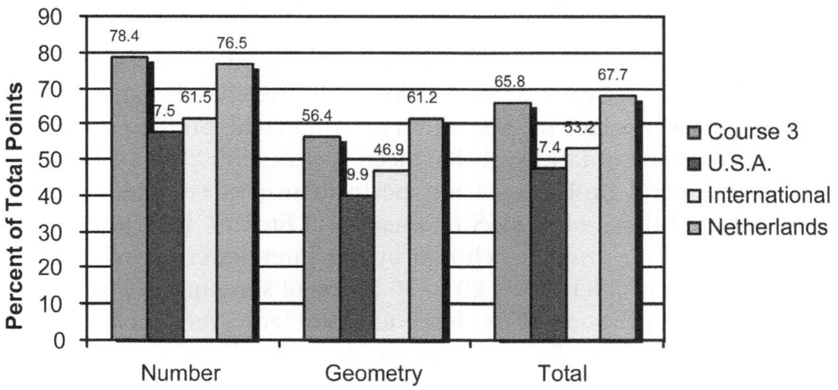

Figure 7.1. Mathematical Literacy Subtest Means.

Table 7.2. Subtest Means and Effect Sizes for Course 3 (*N* = 371) and TIMSS Groups

	Course 3		*United States*		*International*		*Netherlands*	
Subtest	*Mean*	*SD*	*Mean*	*ES*	*Mean*	*ES*	*Mean*	*ES*
Number	78.4	21.1	57.5	.99	61.5	.80	76.5	.09
Geometry	56.4	22.3	39.9	.74	46.9	.43	61.2	–.22
Total	65.8	18.7	47.4	.98	53.2	.67	67.7	–.10

This pattern may be at least partially the result of relatively more emphasis on algebraic and numerical content as compared to geometric content in the curriculum.

School, Gender, and PAL Effects With *ITED-Q* Pretest Scores as Covariate

As in previous courses, to analyze the school, gender, and preachievement level effects on the dependent variables, the *ITED-Q* pretest administered at the beginning of Grade 9 was used as a covariate. Three multivariate analyses of covariance—school-by-gender, school-by-PAL, and gender-by-PAL—were run with the Number and Geometry subtests as dependent variables. No multivariate interactions or main effects were statistically significant at the .05 level indicating that the adjusted mathematical literacy means did not differ significantly with respect to school, gender, or PAL.

PERFORMANCE ON SPECIFIC MATHEMATICAL LITERACY TASKS

In addition to the TIMSS-based test completed by all spring Course 3 students, 63 students at various times throughout the school year were interviewed as they worked on six different contextual problems from the Balanced Assessment task pool (Balanced Assessment, 2007). These tasks measured general problem-solving performance in content areas that complemented those of TIMSS mathematical literacy. Individually, each student worked on problems chosen by the interviewers, rarely working on all six of the problems, but 20 to 30 different students attempted each problem. As in previous years, interview problems were scored using a rubric that focused on the strategies employed by the students. Students were awarded partial credit on tasks and subtasks that were worth more than 1 possible point. The interview problems were scored using students' written work and transcripts of their audio-recorded verbal conversation. Student quotations that appear in the following discussion were obtained from transcripts of the interview sessions. Two of the interview problems fit generally with the Number subtest of the mathematical literacy test, and four of them fit with the Geometry subtest (although numerical or algebraic methods may be useful, too). The following discussion is based on this classification.

Number Problems

The Father-Son Race interview problem involved ratio and proportion as well as rates (see Figure 7.2). On the paper-and-pencil test, ratio and proportion was an area of strong performance by the students in the present study. On two written tasks, they scored an average of 88.5% compared to 85% by Netherlands' students. Students who were interviewed were also very successful on the first task of the Father-Son Race problem.

Although students' strategies for solving Part a of this problem varied, many chose to use 40-meter intervals, either by breaking the 100-meter race down into 40-meter intervals or by adding up the necessary 40-meter intervals to determine the speed of the 100-meter race. One student clarified:

> Since the father started at 20 meters, he would only be running 80 meters, and he ran 40 meters in 9 seconds. So I just doubled that to get 18 seconds for his total run. The son ran the 40 meters in 6 seconds, so I doubled that to get 12 seconds. And then you have 20 meters still to go, and half of 40 meters is 20 meters so I cut his time in half as well, and I got 3 seconds. So I had the son finishing in 15 seconds, which is 3 seconds ahead of his father.

A father and his son want to have a 100 meter foot race. In practice runs it is found that

- The father runs 40 meters in about 9 seconds.
- The son runs 40 meters in about 6 seconds.

Because they want to cross the finish line at about the same time, they decide that the father should run a shorter distance than the son. In answering the following questions, assume that in the race each runner will run at a constant rate close to his rate in the practice runs.

(a) The son proposes that his father start 20 meters in front of him in the 100 meter race. Show that this will not result in a close race.

(b) Suppose they want to make the race as close as possible. How far in front should the father start?

Figure 7.2. Father-Son Race Problem.

This type of reasoning was a very common and successful approach for students. Interviewed students were also consistently able to demonstrate understanding of the meanings of their calculations by relating mathematical results to the contextual situation.

Other students had less success with Part a, finding the meters-per-second rates for the father and son and then multiplying these by the distance of the race. Some students were able to correct themselves after realizing that a seconds-per-meter rate would be needed. One student elaborated:

> I was trying to find the meters that they would each run per second, and instead I inverted it and did things wrong. But after I did it right, I found the seconds-per-meter and then multiplied that by the distances they were running.

Overall, 89% of students interviewed with Part a of this problem were successful at reasoning through this task.

The second task in the Father-Son Race problem presented a bigger challenge to most students. Since the majority of students used 40-meter intervals to solve Part a, many students used this 40-meter-interval rate and a guess-and-check strategy working backwards. Although these students demonstrated their understanding of the problem's meaning, this method did not result in a precise answer. Part b was more accessible to students who were able to compute and use a unit rate, rather than the rate per 40 meters that was provided in the problem. Most students, however, did not seem to recognize the usefulness of a unit rate. The students interviewed with Part b of this problem achieved a mean rubric score of 1.07 (54%) of 2 possible points.

The Handedness interview problem also fits into the Number problem category requiring numerical tables, percent, and logical reasoning about the intersection of two sets (see Figure 7.3). On four TIMSS tasks that required percent and/or other numerical reasoning on the mathematical literacy test, students in Course 3 like those from the Netherlands scored about 73%.

In Part 1 of the problem, every student interviewed was able to accurately read and interpret the information in the table and determine how many people in the study were right-handed. In Part 2, about 71% of interviewees successfully used a combination of division and multiplication to determine the correct percentage. As one student explained, "There's a total of 2,237 people total, and 28 of them are ambidextrous, so I took 28 divided by 2,237, and then I multiplied by 100 to get a percent." Students who had difficulty with Part 2 had a weak understanding

The table below comes from a study on handedness in the United States. It shows the number of men and women in the study who are right-handed or left-handed. For example, the table shows that there were 92 left-handed women in the study. The table also shows the number of men and women in the study who are ambidextrous. (Ambidextrous people use either their right hand or left hand with equal ease.)

	Men	*Women*	*Total*
Right-handed	934	1,070	2,004
Left-handed	113	92	205
Ambidextrous	20	8	28
Total	1,067	1,170	2,237

1. How many people in the study are right-handed?
2. What percentage of people in the study is ambidextrous?
3. Using this table, estimate the number of ambidextrous people in a population of 1,000,000.

Figure 7.3. Handedness Problem.

of place value and percentages. One student said, "I took 28 divided by 2,237 and got .012 percent."

In Part 3 of this problem, nearly all students were able to use the correct procedure for computing a percent of a number. The most common error was rounding 1.25%, the percentage of ambidextrous people in Part 2, to 1%. This resulted in an underestimate of 2,000 ambidextrous people and was scored as incorrect.

Geometry Problems

Students in Course 3 did not score as well on Geometry problems as they did on Number problems, either in absolute terms or in comparison to the U.S. TIMSS sample. On the six TIMSS geometry problems, students in Course 3 earned 56.4% of possible points, compared to 39.9% for the TIMSS U. S. students and 61.2% for the Netherlands students (see Table 7.2 for details). Interviewed students' performance on the four Geometry interview problems may help to explain their geometric thinking.

The Window Design Problem in Figure 7.4 asked students to find (a) the perimeter, and (b) the area of a window that incorporated rectangular and circular shapes in terms of the width *W* of one of the window's panels. Although this problem's main focus was on geometric concepts, symbolic reasoning was needed as well. Nearly all students correctly represented the

The diagram shows a design for a window. The top is a semicircle. The bottom is made up of six squares. These windows come in different sizes. The size is specified by giving the length W of the side of one of the squares.

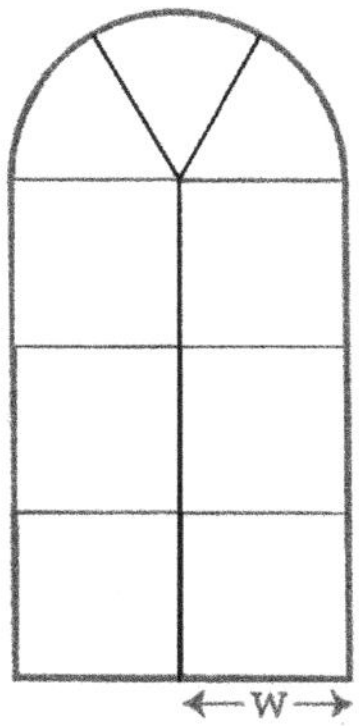

(a) A special lighting strip goes around the perimeter of the window. In terms of W, how long is this strip?

(b) To figure the amount of light let in by the window, the total window area needs to be known. In terms of W, what is this total area?

Figure 7.4. Window Design Problem

perimeter. Students' primary strategy was to calculate the perimeter of the window by separately considering the semicircle and the rectangle. One student described such a strategy for finding the window's perimeter:

> Well, the perimeter is how far around it is all the way, and so it's all addition. So you would add W plus W plus W, and all the squares added equals eight W ... and then you have this half-circle, or semicircle, up here. And you need the circumference, which is the outside of the circle, and that equals 2 times π times r for a full circle. Seeing as how it's only a half circle, I need to divide it by 2.

In Part b of this problem, students used strategies similar to those used to find the perimeter in Part a, that is, breaking the window into smaller, familiar geometric shapes. One student explained:

> I figured that the area was the number of windows that are squares. There's 6 of those, so I said $6W$ squared. And the formula for the area of a circle is π times r squared, r meaning W. So I divided that by two to find the area.

Overall, students were very successful in representing the area of the window; the mean rubric score was 1.86 (93%) of 2 possible points.

Students were also very successful solving the Bandana problem given in Figure 7.5. In order to solve this problem, students needed to recognize that each fold of the cloth did not change its horizontal length. Ultimately, the length of the bandana was the length of the diagonal of the original square of cloth.

Most students recognized that these folding steps did not change the length of the bandana. One such student commented, "I looked at the square of cloth, the original one, and I looked at the steps. And the length of the bandana isn't folded, it remains the same." Students approached this problem in several different ways, but all students used properties of right triangles to find a solution. Some students used trigonometric ratios and one even used the Law of Sines. The most common approach, however, was to use the Pythagorean Theorem. For the few students who failed to solve this problem, the most common error was to assume that every measurement in the square bandana was the same, including the diagonal.

The four diagrams on the right show the way a bandana is folded from a square of cloth.
In steps 2, 3, and 4, the bottom of the cloth is folded up to meet the top edge.
The original square is 40 inches by 40 inches.
Calculate the length of the bandana.

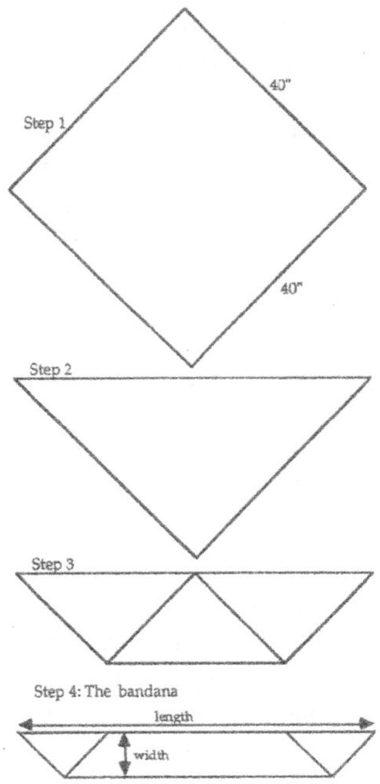

Figure 7.5. Bandana Problem.

The Folded Paper interview problem given in Figure 7.6 required both a geometric and, in Part c, an algebraic or symbolic perspective. In Part a, students were asked to find the area of the original piece of paper. Most students assumed that the paper was folded once in each direction. After considering the dimensions of the unfolded paper, students were successfully able to double the 5 cm by 6 cm dimensions of the folded rectangle and find the area of the original paper. A few students realized that the area of the unfolded paper would be four times the area of the folded paper, and simply multiplied the area of the folded rectangle by 4.

Students who were most successful on the second task of the Folded Paper problem understood that each fold affected only one dimension of the paper. Many students were able to find the dimensions of the paper after unfolding the paper once in each direction, but the most successful students also considered folding twice in the same direction, "It asks for two possibilities, so I said my first one, and also that if you folded your paper the skinnier way and then folded it the skinnier way again." Other students, however, focused only on the case of one fold in each direction. One such student said, "I am going to say not applicable because if you end up with five centimeters by six centimeters working backwards, there is only one original shape of paper." The mean rubric score on both Parts a and b was 1.48 (74%) of 2 possible points.

In Part c, students were mixed in their ability to generalize their results in terms of L and W. Some students had no difficulty with this task and were comfortable using symbolic expressions to generalize their results. One such student demonstrated her understanding of the generalized notation after working through an example with a five-by-six piece of paper:

Ken took a piece of paper. He folded it in half, and then folded it in half again. The result was a 5 cm by 6 cm rectangle.

(a) What is the area of the original piece of paper?

(b) There are several possibilities for the shape of the original piece of paper. Write down two possibilities. Illustrate each with a sketch that shows the length and width of the original piece of paper.

Consider a piece of paper. Imagine that it is folded in half, and then folded in half again. Suppose the result is an L cm by W cm rectangle.

(c) In terms of L and W, list all possible pairs of dimensions of the piece of paper before folding.

Figure 7.6. Folded Paper Problem.

> I'm going to go ahead and go with my three ways. So I'm going to replace 5 and 6 with L and W. And the end result for one of the ways would be $4L$ and that would be multiplied by W. And then in my second case I ended up with $2L$ and $2W$. And in my third case I ended up with $1L$ and $4W$.

Most students were able to make the algebraic generalizations if they first worked with an example piece of paper. Other students who were partially successful with this task gave only one algebraic generalization, typically $2L \times 2W$. Students who were unable to finish with the other dimensions were not having algebraic difficulties; rather they failed to consider other possible sets of dimensions. The mean rubric score on Part c was 1.30 (65%) of 2 possible points.

In the Tri-Tex Logo interview problem given in Figure 7.7, students were again asked to complete a combination of geometric and algebraic tasks. In Part a, the most successful students recognized that doubling the dimensions of the square logo resulted in four times as many tiles. They are asked to find the number of each color of tile needed for the larger logo and are told that doubling the number of tiles of the smaller logo is not sufficient. The most successful students recognized that doubling the dimensions of the square logo resulted in four times as many tiles. One student explained, "When I realized for the red, I multiplied both sides by two. So in all actuality, I was multiplying the area before times four." Many students were able to make this generalization, but some did not correctly calculate the number of each color of tiles needed. The mean rubric score on this part of the problem was 1.59 (53%) of 3 possible points.

In Part b of this problem, a few students were able to determine the correct size of the larger sign using proportional reasoning. One such successful student explained:

> If before, 1152 was my area after my size transformation, I divided that by my original and got 4 because I had a size transformation of 2 on both sides. So I took 7200 divided by 288 which gave me 25. I then knew that I had done a size transformation of 5 on each dimension.

Other students used educated guesses or a guess-and-check method. One student assumed that all 7,200 red tiles would be used and knew that each square foot contained 144 tiles: "So I basically, at first tried multiples of twenty-four. So I figured I'd just go up by twelve's and then for some reason I guessed 120 by sixty and it gave me 7200." Several students calculated the increase in area of red tiles but were unable to finish the problem. One student demonstrated her knowledge of proportions but had difficulty translating the red tiles to the entire logo:

Anita has designed a company logo for the Tri-Tex corporation. Here is her proposal:

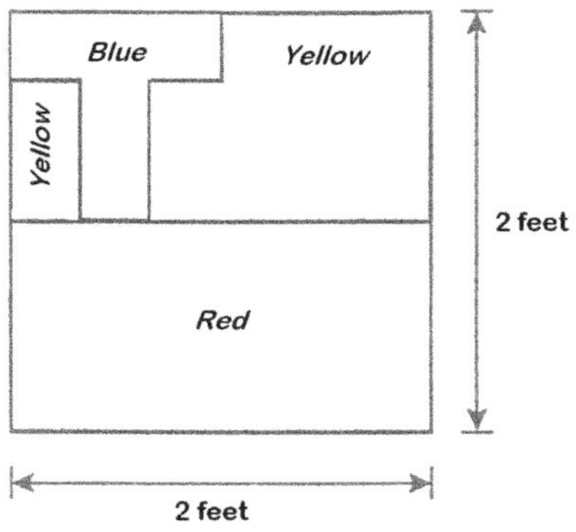

- The logo is 2 feet long and 2 feet wide.
- It is made from tiny tiles of colored glass.

  The red section uses 288 red tiles.

  The blue section uses 96 blue tiles.

  The yellow section uses 192 yellow tiles.
- When the logo is mounted on the building, it will be framed by a black border. This border will consist of a single band of 40 long black tiles.

Anita's boss likes the logo, and wants one that is 4 feet long and 4 feet wide. He tells Anita to order twice as many of each color of tile. Anita does NOT think that will be enough tiles. Anita is correct. Twice as many will NOT be enough tiles.

(a) Find out how many of **each color** will be needed to make a logo that is 4 feet long and 4 feet wide. For full credit show how you arrived at your answer.

(b) Suppose Anita has plenty of blue and yellow tiles, but only 7,200 red tiles. What are the dimensions of the largest logo that she can make? For full credit show how you arrived at your answer.

Figure 7.7. Tri-Tex Logo Problem.

> It said that she had 7200 red tiles, and with just the regular 2-foot by 2-foot logo, she had 288 red tiles. So I divided that by 288, and I got 25 and took the square root of that number, and I got that she could make 5 logos.

Very few students chose to represent the situation algebraically. Students found the Tri-Tex Logo Problem, especially Part b, to be the most difficult of the interview problems.

CHAPTER SUMMARY

A summary of this chapter's main findings on the mathematical literacy test follows. "Adjusted means" refers to means adjusted for variance on the *ITED-Q* pretest at the beginning of Grade 9.

- The mean of students at the end of Course 3 was nearly a full standard deviation above that of the U.S. TIMSS sample and about three-fourths of a standard deviation higher than the international mean.
- On the Number subtest, the mean of Course 3 students was slightly higher than that of the Netherlands, the highest scoring country, and on the Geometry subtest, their mean was about one-fifth of a standard deviation lower than that of the Netherlands.
- Adjusted means of schools did not differ significantly by school, gender, or PAL group on the two subtests combined.

Following the reporting of the quantitative mathematical literacy test results, the remainder of the chapter is a discussion of the performance of selected students who were interviewed as they worked on six different contextual problems from the Balanced Assessment task pool. These tasks measured general problem-solving performance in content areas that complemented those of the written mathematical literacy test. Two of the tasks fit into the Number category and four were mainly Geometry tasks, although several of the tasks drew on more than one mathematical content area. A brief summary of some of the main results follows.

On the Number problems, students showed a great deal of facility with proportional thinking, although one problem involving computing and applying a unit rate was challenging. Students were able to read information from a table, compute percents, and find percentages of numbers. Students also were comfortable with a wide range of problem-solving strategies, including guess-and-check, checking the reasonableness of an intermediate answer and adjusting if needed, working backwards, and computation. Many students demonstrated a clear understanding of the connection between the problem context and the mathematical strategies that they were using.

On the Geometry problems, nearly all students were able to find a correct symbolic expression for the perimeter and area of a figure that involved a partly linear and partly circular boundary. Students were also able to explain their thinking about decomposing the figure into smaller areas and computing perimeters and areas of the parts, then combining the areas. Nearly 90% of students correctly interpreted a sequence of figures illustrating the folding of a square handkerchief along its diagonal and then computed the length of the diagonal mainly, but not exclusively, using the Pythagorean Theorem.

In another Geometry problem, a piece of paper is folded in half and then folded in half again resulting in a rectangle of given numerical dimensions. About three-fourths of the interviewed students were able to reason to a correct area and more than one possible shape of the original paper, and about 65% were able to list the pairs of dimensions of the original paper when the folded rectangle's dimensions were given as *L* and *W*. The most complex and difficult problem involved a logo covered by different-colored square tiles with a great deal of information giving all the problem's parameters. Interviewed students worked hard on the problem, and over half of them solved one or both of the parts correctly. Students who had difficulty had a basic understanding of the problem but often got bogged down with the amount and complexity of information they needed to process. Persistence was clearly evident.

In the next chapter, students' achievement in Course 4 is summarized with a main focus on advanced mathematics as measured by released items from TIMSS. A second focus in Course 4 was reasoning and proof as measured by a paper-and-pencil test and interview problems that require reasoning and proof.

APPENDIX

1. *ITED-Q Pretest* and TIMSS Mathematical Literacy Descriptive Statistics for all Students Completing the TIMSS-Based Posttest

	ITED-Q Pretest				*Number Subtest* ($\alpha = .49$)		*Geometry Subtest* ($\alpha = .51$)	
Group	*N*	*Mean*	*SD*	*%-Tile*	*Mean*	*SD*	*Mean*	*SD*
Washington	46	281.8	32.0	74	80.8	23.3	58.4	20.3
Adams	56[a]	283.2	27.5	75	81.0	17.5	58.3	20.0
Jefferson	269	279.8	29.3	72	77.4	21.4	55.7	23.2
Females	204	278.1	30.2	71	76.0	22.1	54.0	21.8
Males	167	283.5	28.0	75	81.3	19.4	59.3	22.7
PAL 1	82	315.6	7.6	95	91.7	12.4	73.3	20.8
PAL 2	150	290.0	8.1	80	82.4	18.4	60.3	18.3
PAL 3[b]	139	249.7	20.4	46	65.2	21.6	42.2	18.3
TOTAL	371	280.5	29.3	72	78.4	21.1	56.4	22.3

[a] These 56 Adams students are those who completed Course 3 in the Spring semester.
[b] Beginning in Course 3, PAL 3 includes all students with *ITED-Q* pretest scores below the 67th percentile.

Appendix continues on next page.

2. TIMSS Mathematics General Knowledge Achievement by Country

Nations With Average Scores Significantly Higher Than the United States		*Nations With Average Scores Not Significantly Different From the United States*	
Nation	*Average*	*Nation*	*Average*
Netherlands	560	Italy	476
Sweden	552	Russia Federation	471
Denmark	547	Lithuania	469
Switzerland	540	Czech Republic	466
Iceland	534	United States	461
Norway	528		
France	523		
New Zealand	522		
Australia	522	*Nation with Average Scores Significantly Lower Than the United States*	
Canada	519	*Nation*	*Average*
Austria	518	Cyprus	446
Slovenia	512	South Africa	356
Germany	495		
Hungary	483	International Average = 500	

Appendix continues on next page.

3. MANCOVAs (Pillai's Trace) With *ITED-Q* Pretest as Covariate and Mathematical Literacy Number and Geometry Subtest Scores as Dependent Variables

School by Gender Multivariate Tests; Dependent Variables Mathematical Literacy Number and Geometry

Source	*Value*	*F*	*Hypotheses df*	*Error df*	*Sig.*
SCHOOL	.002	.222	4	728	.926
GENDER	.012	2.175	2	363	.115
SCHOOL * GENDER	.021	1.931	4	728	.103

School by Gender Tests of Between-Subjects Effects; Dependent Variables Mathematical Literacy Number and Geometry

Source	*Dependent Variable*	*Type III S.S.*	*df*	*Mean Square*	*F*	*Sig.*
SCHOOL	Number	209.291	2	104.645	.330	.719
	Geometry	76.149	2	38.074	.110	.896
GENDER	Number	1,308.593	1	1,308.593	4.126	.043
	Geometry	.505	1	.505	.001	.970
SCHOOL * GENDER	Number	989.697	2	494.849	1.560	.211
	Geometry	1,415.021	2	707.510	2.046	.131

Gender by PAL Multivariate Tests; Dependent Variables Mathematical Literacy Number and Geometry

Source	*Value*	*F*	*Hypotheses df*	*Error df*	*Sig*
GENDER	.011	2.099	2	363	.124
PAL	.019	1.741	4	728	.139
GENDER * PAL	.005	.488	4	728	.744

Gender by PAL Tests of Between-Subjects Effects; Dependent VariableS Mathematical Literacy Number and Geometry

Source	*Dependent Variable*	*Type III S.S.*	*df*	*Mean Square*	*F*	*Sig.*
GENDER	Number	832.047	1	832.047	2.599	.108
	Geometry	861.795	1	861.795	2.515	.114
PAL	Number	47.768	2	23.884	.075	.928
	Geometry	2,338.951	2	1,169.475	3.413	.034
GENDER * PAL	Number	161.333	2	80.666	.252	.777
	Geometry	362.338	2	181.169	.529	.590

Appendix continues on next page.

4. Mathematical Literacy Number Subtest Tasks With Performance Data

1. Experts say that 25% of all serious bicycle accidents involve head injuries and that, of all head injuries, 80% are fatal. What percentage of all serious bicycle accidents involve fatal head injuries?

A. 16%	**CPMP**	**77%**
B. 20%	**U.S.**	**57%**
C. 55%	**International**	**65%**
D. 105%	**Netherlands**	**83%**

2. In a school election with three candidates, Joe received 120 votes, Mary received 50 votes, and George received 30 votes. What percentage of the total number of votes did Joe receive?

A. 60%	**CPMP**	**86%**
B. 66%	**U.S.**	**62%**
C. 80%	**International**	**63%**
D. 120%	**Netherlands**	**80%**

3. If there are 300 calories in 100 grams of a certain food, how many calories are there in a 30-gram portion of that food?

A. 90	**CPMP**	**88%**
B. 100	**U.S.**	**68%**
C. 900	**International**	**71%**
D. 1,000	**Netherlands**	**84%**
E. 9,000		

4. From a batch of 3,000 light bulbs, 100 were selected at random and tested. If 5 of the light bulbs in the sample were found to be defective, how many defective light bulbs would be expected in the entire batch?

A. 15	**CPMP**	**89%**
B. 60	**U.S.**	**62%**
C. 150	**International**	**66%**
D. 300	**Netherlands**	**85%**
E. 600		

5. In a vineyard there are 210 rows of vines. Each row is 192 m long and plants are planted 4 m apart. On average, each plant produces 9 kg of grapes each season. The total amount of grapes produced by the vineyard each season is closest to

A. 10,000 kg	**CPMP**	**71%**
B. 100,000 kg	**U.S.**	**50%**
C. 400,000 kg	**International**	**55%**
D. 1,600.000 kg	**Netherlands**	**67%**

Appendix continues on next page.

6. A school club is planning a bus trip to the wildlife park. A bus which will hold up to 45 people will cost $600 and admission tickets cost $30 each. If the cost of the trip, including bus and admission ticket, is set at $50 per person, what is the minimum number of people who must participate to ensure that these costs are covered?

A. 12	**CPMP**	60%
B. 20	**U.S.**	45%
C. 30	**International**	50%
D. 45	**Netherlands**	61%

5. Mathematical Literacy Geometry Subtest Tasks With Performance Data

1

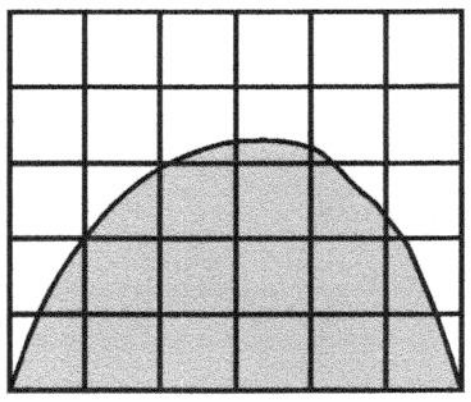

Each of the small squares in the figure is 1 square unit. Which is the best estimate of the area of the shaded region?

A. 10 square units	**CPMP**	81%
B. 12 square units	**U.S.**	54%
C. 14 square units	**International**	60%
D. 16 square units	**Netherlands**	75%
E. 18 square units		

2. Stu wants to wrap some ribbon around a box as shown and have 25 cm left to tie a bow. How long a piece of ribbon does he need?

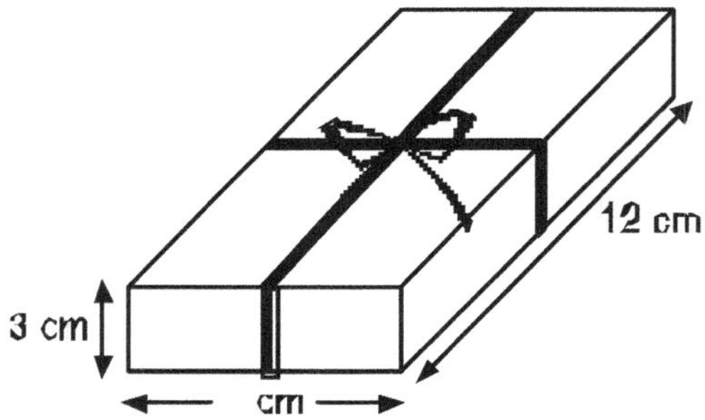

Appendix continues on next page.

A. 46 cm	**CPMP**	**66%**
B. 52 cm	**U.S.**	**32%**
C. 65 cm	**International**	**45%**
D. 71 cm	**Netherlands**	**62%**
E. 77 cm		

3. Brighto soap powder is packed in cube-shaped cartons. A carton measures 10 cm on each side. The company decides to increase the length of each edge of the carton by 10%. How much does the volume increase?

A. 10 cm^3	**CPMP 3**	**40%**
B. 21 cm^3	**U.S.**	**17%**
C. 100 cm^3	**International**	**31%**
D. 331 cm^3	**Netherlands**	**50%**

4. If the population increases by the same rate from the year 1990 to the year 2000 as in the years from 1980 to 1990, approximately what is the expected population by the year 2000?

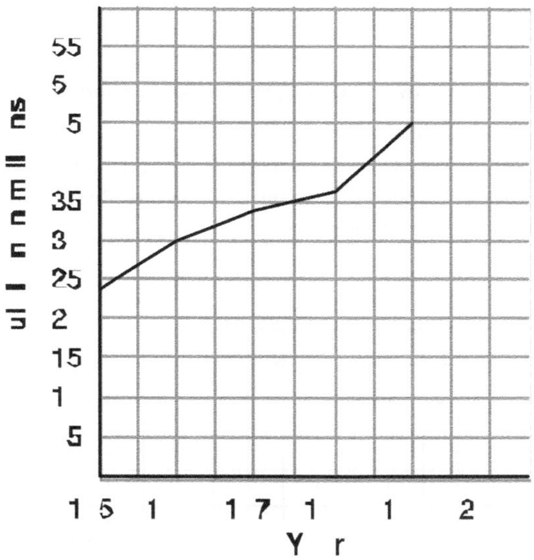

A. 47 million	**CPMP**	**73%**
B. 50 million	**U.S.**	**69%**
C. 53 million	**International**	**71%**
D. 58 million	**Netherlands**	**85%**

Appendix continues on next page.

5. A TV reporter showed this graph and said: "There's been a huge increase in the number of robberies this year."

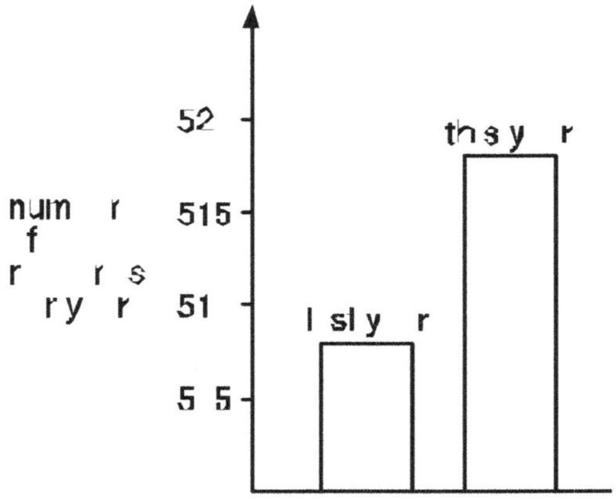

Do you consider the reporter's statement to be a reasonable interpretation of the graph

Yes ___ No ___

Briefly explain.

CPMP (51%) U.S. (42%) International (41%) Netherlands (58%)

Percents are of 2 possible points.

6. Using the set of axes below, sketch a graph which shows the relationship between the height of a person and his/her age from birth to 30 years. Be sure to label your graph, and include a realistic scale on each axis.

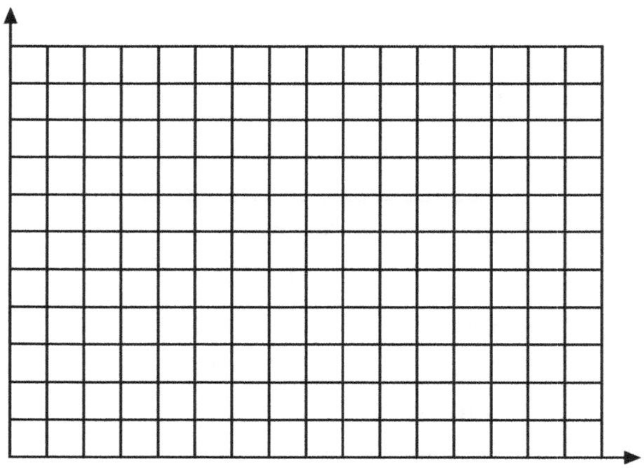

CPMP (45%) U.S. (32%) International (44%) Netherlands (51%)

Percents are of 2 possible points.

CHAPTER 8

ACHIEVEMENT PATTERNS IN YEAR 4

Advanced Mathematics, Reasoning, and Proof

In their fourth or fifth year of high school mathematics, many students are concerned about their level of preparation for college and, in particular, for collegiate mathematics courses. In the United States, these students are usually enrolled in a course that is designed to prepare them for calculus, and others are in an advanced placement course in either calculus or statistics. The advanced mathematics test administered in 1994-95 by TIMSS (Third International Mathematics and Science Study) was designed to test the content of these courses and more broadly of the mathematics courses that students typically encountered in the countries in the TIMSS advanced mathematics sample. Reasoning and proof, a cornerstone area of mathematical thinking measured by some TIMSS advanced mathematics tasks, is worthy of special attention in the evaluation of a high school mathematics curriculum.

This chapter begins with an analysis of the results of a mathematics test that was compiled from released TIMSS advanced mathematics tasks and administered to all students in college preparatory mathematics courses at the end of the fourth year of the present study. Results are reported in

A Five-Year Study of the First Edition of the Core-Plus Mathematics Curriculum, pp. 171–199

comparison to TIMSS' U.S. and international means on the same tasks. A separate reasoning test was administered to approximately the same sample of students. Both of these tests were also administered to students in a more conventional precalculus course in two comparison schools whose demographic data were similar to the three schools in this study. Results of a comparative analysis of Core-Plus Mathematics Course 4 students versus more conventional precalculus students are presented for each test. In addition to the usual school, gender, and preachievement level analysis for each test, the results of an analysis of the third-year to fourth-year growth are presented on nine TIMSS advanced mathematics tasks administered at the end of both years. Finally, to provide further insights into students' reasoning and proof abilities, the performance of selected students is described on five paper-and-pencil interview problems involving proof and/or complex reasoning.

ADVANCED MATHEMATICS AND REASONING TESTS

At the end of Year 4 of the present study, two achievement tests were administered. One consisted of released advanced mathematics tasks from TIMSS. The second was a test of reasoning and proof. Each test was administered in a 45-minute class period.

Advanced Mathematics Test

During the 1994–95 school year, the Third International Mathematics and Science Study (TIMSS) assessed the mathematics and science knowledge of a half-million students from 41 nations at three levels of schooling. In this chapter, the focus is on the TIMSS assessment of advanced mathematics. Students who completed this test during TIMSS were in advanced mathematics courses in the last year of secondary school. In the United States, the sample included students in representative numbers in precalculus, calculus (AP or not), and a few other fourth-year courses such as AP Statistics.

Advanced mathematics items measure outcomes that would be typical of objectives in fourth-year mathematics courses in the participating countries. The mathematical content of each task was in one of the following areas: Numbers, Equations and Functions; Geometry, Probability and Statistics; and Calculus. TIMSS developers also classified advanced mathematics tasks by performance expectations as follows: Knowing, Routine Procedure, Complex Procedure, Solving Problems, and Justifying. U.S. twelfth graders in the TIMSS study scored below 15 of the 16 participating countries and significantly below 11 countries. The mean performance of students in France was the highest among the 16 countries (see Chapter 8 Appendix, Part 3).

Following the administration of the TIMSS advanced mathematics assessment, many test items were released for use by researchers or school personnel. Scoring rubrics, answer keys, and detailed performance data by country were also made available for all released items (IEA TIMSS, 1998). Twenty released TIMSS advanced mathematics items were chosen for the Course 4 TIMSS-based test that provided representation across TIMSS' content categories and performance expectation categories (with the exception of Justifying, which was measured in the reasoning test). In general, the chosen items were also judged by the evaluators to measure content that students in Year 4 courses would have had the opportunity to experience at least at an introductory level (see Table 8.1 for the matrix of items selected for this test). To maintain a split between multiple-choice and free-response items roughly proportional to that used by TIMSS, 15 of the items chosen were multiple-choice and 5 were free-response. Seven of the 20 items on the test were also included on the Year 3 mathematical literacy test and are, along with an eighth item on the reasoning test, the basis for the analysis of growth reported later in this chapter.

Reasoning Test

This test was developed as the main instrument for measuring an important focus in Year 4, reasoning and proof. Items were drawn from three sources, released items from the TIMSS advanced mathematics pool, released items from the SAT Mathematics test, and two doctoral

Table 8.1. Numbers of Selected Items on the Advanced Mathematics Test in Each Content by Performance Expectation Category

Performance Expectation	*Content Category*				
	No, Eq & Fcn	*Geometry*	*Prob & Stat*	*Calculus*	*Total*
Knowing		2		1	3
Rout. Proc.	2	3[a]	1	1	7
Compl. Proc.	1	1[a]	2[a]		4
Solving Probs.	5[a]	1	1	1	8
Total	8	7	4	3	22

[a] At least one open-ended task in each of these categories.

dissertations on proof and reasoning in high school mathematics (Kahan, 1999; Senk, 1983). The reasoning test consists of 18 multiple-choice and 6 free-response items. The test has two main content subtests, with items distributed as shown in Table 8.2. The first is Geometry, which includes reasoning steps and some complete proofs like those in conventional high school Euclidean geometry proofs. The second subtest, called Number and Algebra in this chapter, is made up of all other reasoning items on the test. These items mainly have to do with number or with symbols representing numbers, and one item involves a purely verbal logic pattern.

Procedures

Teachers administered each test during a class period in the last week of the fourth year of the present study. Students had access to their graphing calculators and were given a 45-minute time limit for each test that allowed an average of about 2 minutes per item. The numbers of students completing each test by course and school are given in Table 8.3. Scoring rubrics and answer keys provided by the source of each task were used to score the tests. Multiple-choice test items were scored as correct (1 point) or incorrect. Some free-response items were scored using rubrics that awarded 2 or more points for complete answers and fewer points for partially correct answers. Descriptive statistics for each subtest and total scores on both tests by school, gender, preachievement level, and mathematics course completed can be found in the Chapter 8 Appendix, Parts 1 and 2.

Table 8.2. Numbers of Items on the Reasoning Test in Each Content by Item Source Category

	Content Category		
Source of Item	*Geometry*	*Number and Algebra*	*Total*
TIMSS	2[a]	2[a]	4
SAT	1	10	11
Senk Dissertation	7[a]	0	7
Kahan Dissertation	0	2[a]	2
Total	10	14	24

[a] At least one open-ended task in each of these categories.

Table 8.3. Numbers of Students Completing Each Year 4 Test by School and Course[a]

	Advanced Mathematics Test				Reasoning Test		
School	*Course 4*	*AP Calculus*	*AP Statistics*	*Total*	*Course 4*	*AP Calculus*	*Total*
Washington	23	11	0	34	23	14	37
Adams	88	0	0	88	88	0	88
Jefferson	79	23	65	167	82	32	114
Total	190	34	65	289	193	46	239

[a] Washington and Adams had no AP Statistics classes. The AP Statistics students at Jefferson failed to complete the reasoning test and the AP Calculus students at Adams failed to complete either test because of misunderstandings by the teachers.

Comparison of Advanced Mathematics Test Results With Representative TIMSS Groups

TIMSS provides data on each released item for their nationally and internationally representative groups of students. By averaging the percent correct across the 20 items, it is possible to compute a good estimate of how these groups would perform on the TIMSS-based advanced mathematics test used in this study. Clearly, as with the TIMSS mathematical literacy test used in Course 3, the comparison of these results to those in the present study is limited in its interpretation because of likely noncomparability of the groups of students and variations in testing conditions. While group differences should not necessarily be attributed to the curriculum, they may be of interest in the present climate of international competition.

Means by content subtest of the 289 Year 4 students and the TIMSS samples from the United States and the 16-country international compilation are presented in Figure 8.1. Three of the four subtest means of the Year 4 students in this study were higher than the U.S. sample and lower than the international group mean. Interestingly, the Probability and Statistics subtest mean for the Year 4 students was higher than the international mean. Some individual items together with performance statistics can be found in the Chapter 8 Appendix, Part 7.

To further examine the group differences by subtest, the effect size was computed for each subtest and for each of the three comparison groups relative to the U.S. and international TIMSS advanced mathematics samples (see Table 8.4). The effect size is the number of standard deviations by which the present study's sample subtest mean differed from each of

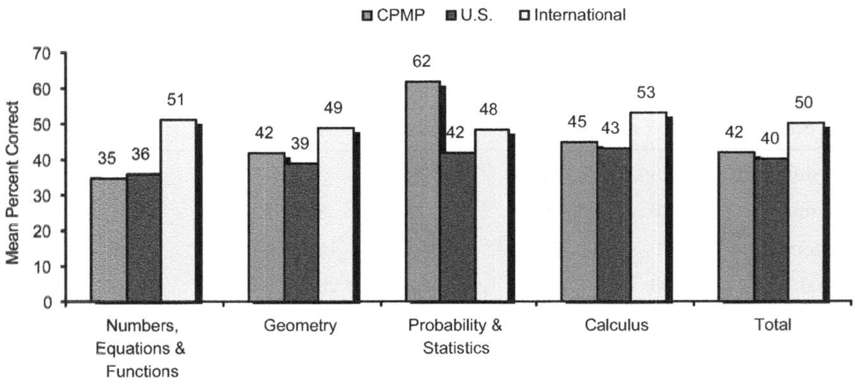

Figure 8.1. Advanced Mathematics Subtest Means.

Table 8.4. Subtest Means and Effect Sizes for Year 4 (N = 289) of This Study and TIMSS Groups

	Year 4		*U.S.*		*International*	
Subtest	*Mean*	*SD*	*Mean*	*ES*	*Mean*	*ES*
Nos., Eqs.,Fcns	34.7	18.4	36.2	–.08	50.8	–.88
Geometry	42.3	19.8	39.1	.16	48.6	–.32
Prob. & Stat.	62.1	23.1	41.8	.88	48.3	.60
Calculus	44.8	32.2	43.0	.06	53.0	–.25
Total	42.1	15.2	40.3	.12	50.0	–.52

the TIMSS comparison groups. Here the standard deviation is that of the Year 4 group.

Effect size (ES) = (Year 4 mean – TIMSS group mean) / (Year 4 standard deviation)

As Table 8.4. shows, this study's Year 4 sample total mean was .12 standard deviations higher than the U.S. sample and about one-half of a standard deviation lower than the international sample. An exception to the pattern is that this study's sample mean on the Probability and Statistics subtest was much higher (.88 and .60 standard deviations, respectively) than those of either of the two TIMSS groups. The relatively strong performance of this study's students in Probability and Statistics is consistent with findings in other studies (Schoen & Hirsch, 2003a). Although the design of this study does not allow for causal inference, this result seems likely to be at least partially a consequence of the stronger emphasis on this content area throughout the 4 years of the Core-Plus

Mathematics curriculum as compared to more conventional mathematics curricula in this country and in many other countries.

Comparison of Course 4 Students With More Conventional Precalculus Students

A precalculus comparison group was recruited from two Iowa schools to provide another comparison of scores on the two Course 4 tests. One comparison school was located in a rural setting near a small city, and the other was located in a midsize city of about 100,000 people. The first of these schools had 1,038 students in Grades 9–12 in 2000–01, 14.4% of the students were eligible for free or reduced lunch, and 4.3% were members of underrepresented minority groups. The second comparison school had 2,344 students in Grades 9–12, 30.7% of the students were eligible for free or reduced lunch, and 13.9% were members of underrepresented minority groups. The comparison schools do not differ greatly from the three schools in this study, although the second comparison school was somewhat more rural and larger than any of the three in this study. For reference, the demographics of Washington, Adams, and Jefferson schools are given in Table 3.2.

The comparison classes at both schools used the North Carolina precalculus, so the curriculum and instruction were not completely traditional but were more conventional than the Core-Plus Mathematics curriculum. As is true in nearly all Iowa high schools, students in these two schools complete the *ITED-Q* each year, and school personnel agreed to release the fall ninth-grade scores of the comparison group students for use in this study. The comparison class teachers administered both the advanced mathematics test and the reasoning test using the same guidelines as teachers in the three longitudinal study schools.

The total scores on each test of students in the comparison precalculus classes and those in the Course 4 classes were compared statistically using a one-way analysis of covariance with fall ninth-grade *ITED-Q* scores as covariates. The ANCOVA tables can be found in Part 4 of the Chapter 8 Appendix. Descriptive data and adjusted means are provided in Table 8.5. On both tests, the Course 4 adjusted mean was significantly higher than that of the comparison group, in each case at the .003 probability level.

An examination of Table 8.5 shows that the *ITED-Q* pretest means of the precalculus students were one-third to one-half of a standard deviation higher than those of the Course 4 students, and the means of the two groups on both posttests differed by only a percentage point or two. Thus the significant differences on the ANCOVAs are due mainly to variance in the covariate, that is, the pretest. The precalculus group was more

Table 8.5. Descriptive Statistics and Adjusted Data for Course 4 and Precalculus Groups on the Advanced Mathematics Test and the Reasoning Test

	ITED-Q Pretest				*Advanced Mathematics Total*		*Adjusted Data*	
Group	*N*	*Mean*	*SD*	*%-tile*	*Mean*	*SD*	*Mean*	*SE*
Course 4	190	289.7	24.3	80	40.0	18.8	41.5	0.90
Precalculus	118	301.7	15.9	88	39.3	12.5	37.0	1.15
TOTAL	308	294.3	22.2	83	39.7	14.0		
	ITED-Q Pretest				*Reasoning Total*		*Adjusted Data*	
Group	*N*	*Mean*	*SD*	*%-tile*	*Mean*	*SD*	*Mean*	*SE*
Course 4	193	293.7	21.3	83	42.3	15.4	43.5	0.81
Precalculus	117	301.4	15.9	88	41.6	11.5	39.6	1.05
TOTAL	310	296.6	19.8	85	42.0	14.0		

mathematically able at the beginning of Grade 9 than the Course 4 group, yet the latter group's means were slightly higher on both the advanced mathematics test and the reasoning test at the end of Course 4.

School, Gender, and PAL Effects With *ITED-Q* Pretest Scores as Covariate

As in previous courses, to analyze the school, gender, and PAL effects on the dependent variables in a way that takes into account variance in entering mathematics achievement level, the *ITED-Q* pretest administered at the beginning of Grade 9 was used as a covariate. School-by-gender, school-by-PAL, and gender-by-PAL analyses of covariance were run on the Course 4 student scores with each of the advanced mathematics test and the reasoning test for Course 4 as dependent variable. AP Calculus and AP Statistics students were excluded from this analysis since they were not distributed evenly across school, gender, and preachievement levels. Thus their inclusion would introduce a confounding variable, mathematics course completed.

No school-by-gender, school-by-PAL, or gender-by-PAL interactions were statistically significant for either the advanced mathematics test or the reasoning test on any of the ANCOVAs. Thus the school, gender, and PAL main effects are discussed separately.

School Effects. The percents correct in each school on each Course 4 test adjusted for variance in the *ITED-Q* pretest are presented in Figure 8.2. The descending order by school of the adjusted means—Adams,

Washington, and Jefferson—is the same on both tests and all pairwise mean differences are statistically significant beyond the .05 probability level. The statistical analysis of mean differences based on the school-by-gender ANCOVA is as follows:

- On the advanced mathematics test, the overall school effect is significant ($p < .001$), Adams is greater than Washington ($p = .011$), Adams is greater than Jefferson ($p < .001$), and Washington is greater than Jefferson ($p = .049$).
- On the reasoning test, the overall school effect is significant ($p < .001$), Adams is greater than Washington ($p = .010$), Adams is greater than Jefferson ($p < .001$), and Washington is greater than Jefferson ($p = .007$).

Gender Effects. The means for boys and girls on each Course 4 test adjusted for variance in the *ITED-Q* pretest are plotted in Figure 8.3. The adjusted mean of the boys is greater than that of the girls on the advanced mathematics test ($p = .015$), but means on the reasoning test do not differ significantly ($p = .889$). Results are based on the school-by-gender analyses of covariance; see details in the Chapter 8 Appendix, Parts 5 and 6.

PAL Effects. The means for preachievement level groups on each Year 4 test adjusted for variance in the *ITED-Q* pretest are plotted in Figure 8.4. The adjusted mean of the PAL groups do not differ significantly on the advanced mathematics test. On the reasoning test, the PAL main effect is statistically significant ($p < .001$). The adjusted mean of the top 10% of students (PAL 1) is significantly greater than that of PAL 2 ($p < .001$), but

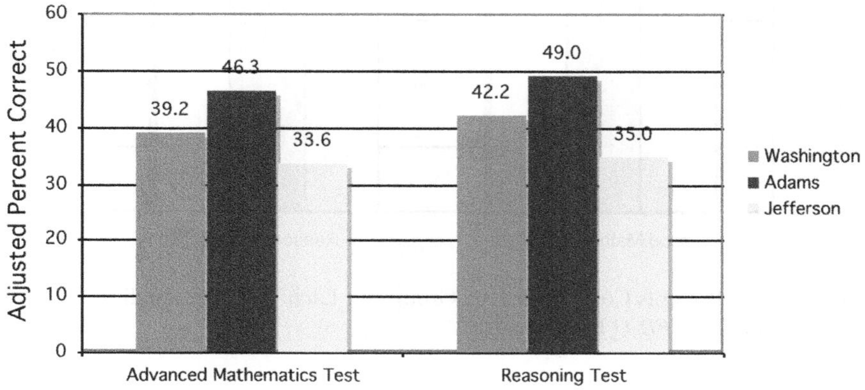

Figure 8.2. Percents Correct in Each School on Each Year 4 Test Adjusted for Variance in the *ITED-Q* Pretest.

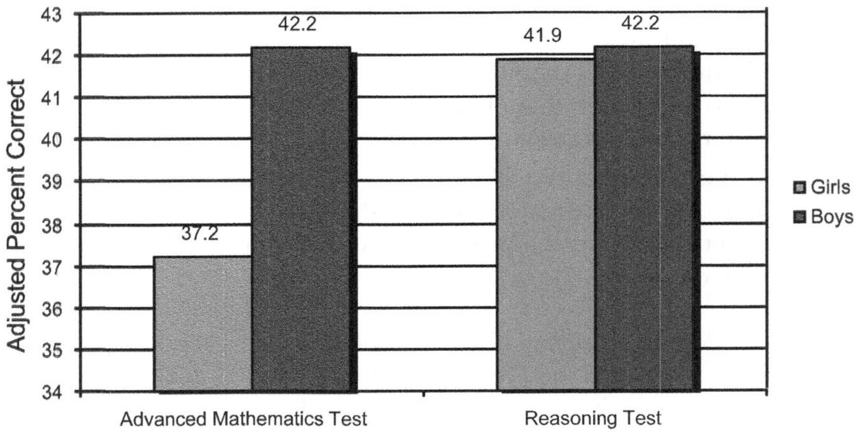

Figure 8.3. Percents Correct for Girls and Boys on Each Year 4 Test Adjusted for Variance in the *ITED-Q* Pretest.

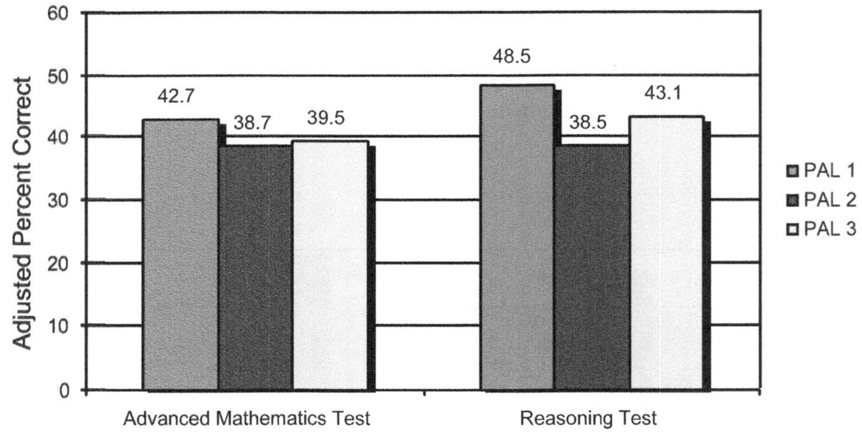

Figure 8.4. Percents Correct for PAL Groups on Each Year 4 Test Adjusted for Variance in the *ITED-Q* Pretest.

no other pairwise differences are significant. Results are based on the gender-by-PAL analyses of covariance (see details in the Chapter 8 Appendix, Parts 5 and 6).

Growth on TIMSS Advanced Mathematics Tasks From Third to Fourth Year

Nine TIMSS advanced mathematics tasks, including each part of a two-part task, were on both the Course 3 TIMSS-based test and one of the Year 4 tests. A total of 187 students completed 8 of the common tasks at the end of both years, and 134 of these students completed the ninth task (item 2 in Table 8.6) at the end of both years. This section compares the performance of these students from year to year with U.S. and international item data from the TIMSS advanced mathematics samples as baselines. On these 9 tasks, the students grew an average of 4 percentage points from Year 3 to Year 4, less than a 10th of the average standard deviation per task. The Year 4 mean on the nine tasks was .21 standard deviations higher than the U.S. nine-task mean. Interestingly, there was a decline from Year 3 to Year 4 on three tasks, and the U.S. TIMSS sample scored higher than the Year 4 students on four tasks.

The individual items and item data are provided in the Chapter 8 Appendix, Part 7, and reference to them will be helpful when reading the

Table 8.6. Descriptive Statistics of Common Items From Year 3, Year 4, the U.S. TIMSS, and the International TIMSS Advanced Mathematics Samples

Item[a]	*Year 3*	*Year 4*	*SD (4)*	*Growth*	*U.S.%*	*Internat. %*	*ES (U.S.)*
1[a]	68	74	44	6	36	51	.86
1[b]	84	88	32	4	48	63	1.25
2	77	86	34	9	70	76	.47
3	69	59	49	–10	42	52	.35
4	50	57	50	7	47	56	.20
5	51	66	48	15	67	85	–.07
6	20	16	36	–4	21	28	–.14
7	28	35	48	7	47	56	–.25
8	51	50	50	–1	68	74	–.36
Mean	55	59	43	4	50	60	.21

[a] For item 2, N = 134 in Years 3 and 4. For all other items, N = 187.

following discussion. Students in this study had both good growth and high percents correct relative to the U.S. and international samples on items 1a, 1b, 2, and 4. The two-part item 1 is a statistics problem involving finding a best fit line from data points in a scatterplot and using it to make a prediction. Item 2 is a deductive logic problem, and item 4 involves geometric transformations. This study's students also did well compared to the U.S. and international samples on a second geometric transformation problem, item 3, but the percent correct declined by 10% from Year 3 to Year 4. A likely explanation for the decline is that none of the courses in the fourth year include any new transformation geometry content.

This study's students grew well in year 4 on items 5 and 7, but their percents correct were lower than those of the U.S. sample. Item 5 is a symbolic algebra item, and item 7 requires coordinate geometry to determine if an angle is a right angle. On items 6 and 8, this study's students declined in year 4, and their percents correct were lower than those of the U.S. sample.

Item 8 is a noncontextual, algebraic symbol manipulation task, and item 6 requires students to compute the probability of the union of two events. In light of the overall outstanding performance of this study's students on probability and statistics tasks, the item 6 data may seem surprising at first. However, it should be noted that only about one-fifth of students in the U.S. sample and one-fourth in the international sample chose the correct answer to this item. By far the most frequent choice by all student groups was the product of the two given probabilities.

PERFORMANCE ON SPECIFIC MATHEMATICAL REASONING TASKS

In addition to the advanced mathematics test and the reasoning test, 42 Course 4 students were interviewed at various times during the year as they worked on 5 reasoning problems. Very few students worked on all 5 of the problems. Interviewers chose the problems each student worked on, and 12 to 20 different students worked on each interview problem. As with the previous years' interviews, problems were scored using a rubric that focused on the strategies the students chose to use. Students received some credit for partially correct work on tasks that were worth more than 1 possible point. The scoring of the interview problems was based on both the students' written work as well as transcripts of their verbal conversation with the person interviewing them. These conversations were audio-recorded and later transcribed. The student quotations in the following discussion were obtained from the transcripts of the interview sessions. The interview problems are discussed next, organized in sections depending on whether the problem involved mainly algebraic reasoning, geometric reasoning, or statistical reasoning.

Algebraic Reasoning. According to the National Council of Teachers of Mathematics (NCTM) *Standards* (2000), students should be able to generalize patterns using explicitly defined functions and to represent and analyze mathematical situations using algebraic symbols. Students showed a variety of strengths and some weaknesses when interviewed with problems that required the use of algebraic reasoning. When interviewed with the Calendar Problem in Figure 8.5, for example, students were very successful. The overall mean score for the entire Calendar Problem was 3.47 (86.8%) of 4 possible points, the highest mean score of the Course 4 interview problems.

All of the students who worked on this problem were able to correctly answer the first two parts. Most students were also successful formalizing their pattern in the third part of the problem. Students who received full credit on this part used mainly generalized algebraic equations to determine that the pattern will always be true. It was particularly important that students express this equation using the least amount of variables possible, as when one student explained:

> I am thinking it should hold because if you've got Wednesday and that was your first number that would be n. Thursday would be $n + 1$ and then when you get below that you have $n + 7$ and $n + 8$. When you do the diagonals you end up with the same amount.

Sunday	*Monday*	*Tuesday*	*Wednesday*	*Thursday*	*Friday*	*Saturday*
			1	2	3	4
5	6	7	8	9	10	11
12	13	14	15	16	17	18
19	20	21	22	23	24	25
26	27	28	29	30		

The above table is a calendar for November 2000. Several 2 by 2 blocks of four numbers have been emphasized.

- In each emphasized block, calculate the sum of the entries that are diagonally opposite. (For example, in the upper right block, $3 + 11 = 14$ and $10 + 4 = 14$.
- What pattern(s) do you notice in the results?
- Will these patterns hold true in any 2 by 2 block of numbers for any calendar square for any month of any year? If so, how would you convince a doubter? If not, why are you not convinced?

Figure 8.5. Calendar Problem.

Students who were less successful on the third part of the Calendar Problem focused on specific numbers or tried to test every group of numbers, rather than trying to generalize algebraically. One such student said, "I'm not quite sure about all calendars because it would take like really long to actually verify all those." Overall, most students were successful in finding the pattern and used algebra to generalize this pattern.

When interviewed with the Sevens Problem in Figure 8.6, students were also required to examine a number pattern. The overall mean score for this problem was 6.37 (63.7%) of 10 possible points. All students who worked on this problem were able to correctly answer the first part. Students also did well on the second part of the problem. Most students who were successful on the second part of the problem tested many or all of the numbers generated with Gary's method. Students who had difficulty with this part of the problem believed that Gary's method worked, but they had trouble justifying their answer.

On the third part of the problem, many students discovered that the number 59 was in the list **L** but was not provided by the given method. They then concluded that not *every* number could be found with this method. Many students who were less successful with this problem, however, initially believed that Brenda's method was correct until interviewer prompting led them to find a counterexample.

On the fourth part of the problem, successful students were able to clearly articulate the difference between "always" and "every." As one student explained, "There may be digits in between the ones given by a

---

This question is about positive integers for which the sum of the digits can be divided evenly by 7.

34 is such a number because 3 + 4 = 7.

185 is such a number because 1 + 8 + 5 = 14, and 14 can be divided by 7.

If we make a list **L** of all such numbers that are less than or equal to 70, the start of it looks like this: 7, 16, 25, 34.

- Write down the next larger number in the list **L**.
- Gary says, "If you start with 7 and keep adding nines until the sum is 70 you always get a number in the list **L**."

  Is Gary right? Justify your answer.
- Brenda says, "If you start with 7 and keep adding nines until the sum is 70 you get every number in list **L**."

  Is Brenda right? Justify your answer.
- Julie says, "What Brenda said means the same thing as what Gary said."

  Is Julie right? Justify your answer.

Figure 8.6. Sevens Problem.

method, so 'always' and 'every' give different results." The less successful students either had difficulty finding a counterexample, or they just assumed that there was no difference between "always" and "every." A few students had trouble working within the constraints of the problem and found counterexamples that did not meet the requirements of the original problem, such as one student who tried working with decimals.

Interviewed students had more difficulty working with a pattern in the Slope Problem given in Figure 8.7. Overall, this was the most difficult Course 4 interview problem with a mean score of 1.39 (46.3%) of 3 possible points. Students who were successful with this problem were able to use the standard definition of slope in a flexible manner. One student explained:

> I said the pattern will always work in the case of linear equations because the coefficient of x is always either added or subtracted, depending on the original sign. To get y by itself, the new coefficient of x is divided by the coefficient of y.

Students who were awarded partial credit for their work focused on specific examples rather than generalized algebraic justifications. Students who struggled with the Slope Problem either disagreed with the method but gave no justification, or they did not have a strong understanding of slope in its algebraic form. An example of the latter is a student who remarked, "I don't know where he is coming from thinking that he can get the slope out of the two numbers given, because I don't think they have anything to do with slope."

Chris is an algebra student. His teacher gives a quiz in which students are to find the slope of the line that is the graph of four given equations.

The first equation is $3x + 5y = 15$, and Chris correctly finds that the slope is –3/5. The second equation is $2x - 7y = 20$, and again Chris finds the correct slope, 2/7.

He then sees a pattern that if he divides the coefficient of x by the coefficient of y and reverses the sign, he gets the slope. Showing no work for equations 3 and 4, Chris writes

3. slope of $4x + 15y = 28$ is –4/15

4. slope of $15x - 12y = 20$ is 5/4

When the quizzes are returned, Chris receives no credit for questions 3 and 4. When Chris says he used a pattern, the teacher dismisses it as lucky but not mathematically convincing.

Write an argument that Chris could use to convince his teacher that the pattern will always work or describe how the teacher could convince Chris that it will not.

Figure 8.7. Slope Problem.

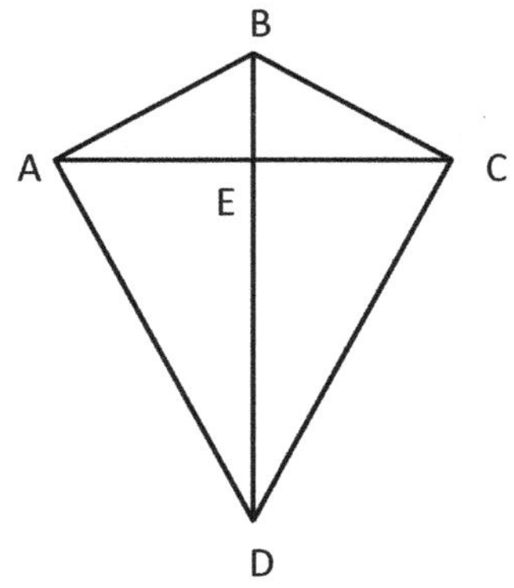

Mary Ann has a kite store. She shapes her kites by taking 2 sticks (represented by segments AC and BD in the above diagram) of equal length, aligning them so they are perpendicular, and stretching material around them (as represented by quadrilateral ABCD). She says this way she always makes a kite shape, and that, in particular she is guaranteed that segments AB and BC will have the same length.

Gunnar says Mary Ann's method is not a foolproof way to make a kite, and in particular that it does not guarantee that AB and BC will have the same length. Gunnar and Mary Ann call on you, the town mathematician, to resolve their debate.

- Is Mary Ann correct or is Gunnar?
- If you said Mary Ann was correct, give an argument that would convince Gunnar. If you said

Figure 8.8. Kite Problem.

Geometric Reasoning

Students were generally successful providing a convincing geometric argument when interviewed with the Kite Problem in Figure 8.8. Overall, the mean score on this Kite Problem was 1.38 (69.2%) of 2 possible points.

Seven students (53.8%) received full credit for their work on this problem. Successful students understood that one counterexample was sufficient to disprove a given statement. Many of these students also provided the necessary conditions for the statement to be true. For example, one student explained, "I am thinking that if she was to say that, she would have to say that the length of has to equal the length $\overline{AE}$ of $\overline{EC}$."

Four students (30.8%) who received partial credit were able to justify their answer, but their answer was based on assumptions that were not given in the original problem. Often these assumptions came from an overgeneralization of the given diagram. One student explained, "Therefore, Gunnar would be right, because it doesn't mention that it has to be the same length. I just automatically thought that, because the picture showed it." Eventually, all students who received partial credit realized that their assumptions were not supported by the problem statement and adjusted their answers accordingly. Only two students (15.4%) received no credit because of their inability to fully understand the constraints of the problem. For example, one of these students needed significant prompting before she realized she could re-position the kite sticks.

Statistical Thinking

The NCTM *Standards* (2000) recommend that students should be able to recognize how transformations of data affect the shape, center, and spread of the data. Students had some difficulty with these ideas when they were interviewed with the Mean Transformation Problem, given in Figure 8.9. The mean score on this problem was 1.0 (50%) of 2 possible points.

Two students (16.7%) received full credit for their work on this problem. These students used algebraic reasoning and had a strong understanding of the mean of a distribution. As one student explained, "If you multiply the mean by a number, it is the same as multiplying each individual number by the multiple and then taking the mean. The same is true with addition."

The average (mean) income before taxes of 100 employees at a CD company in the year 1998 was *m* dollars. In 1999, the company had a CD that was a major hit and that gave a big boost to profits. Company management decided to share some of the extra profits with these 100 employees by giving each a 10% raise in 1999 and a bonus of $2,500.

For example, an employee who made $30,000 in 1998 would make 30,000 + (10% of $30,000) + $2,500 or $35,500 in 1999. A clerk used similar operations on the 1998 mean income *m* of these 100 employees to compute their mean 1999 income, getting $1.1m$ + 2,500.

Is the clerk right? Or does he need to compute all 100 salaries for 1999 and then find the mean of these new salaries? Explain your reasoning.

Figure 8.9. Mean Transformation Problem.

Eight students (66.7%) received partial credit for their work on this problem. These students either used specific examples to justify their reasoning or gave a vague verbal explanation, such as the student who explained, "I was thinking about using variables or something because that would, you know, prove it for everything, but that is kind of complicated." The two students (16.7%) who received no credit for this problem had difficulty understanding the context of the problem, such as one student who thought that the problem could not be solved without access to the employees' individual salaries.

CHAPTER SUMMARY

Two paper-and-pencil achievement tests were administered at the end of the fourth year of this study, a test composed of released TIMSS advanced mathematics tasks and a reasoning test composed of tasks from three sources. A summary of the main findings from the results of these two tests follows. As in previous chapters, "adjusted means" refers to means adjusted for variance on the *ITED-Q* pretest at the beginning of Grade 9.

- The advanced mathematics test mean of students in this study was greater than that of the U.S. TIMSS advanced mathematics sample on three of the four content subtests and 1.5 percentage point less on the fourth subtest.
- On the Probability and Statistics subtest of the advanced mathematics test, students in this study scored much higher than either the U.S. or the international TIMSS advanced mathematics sample.
- On both tests, the adjusted mean of Course 4 students was significantly higher than that of students from more conventional precalculus classes in comparison schools.
- On both tests, the adjusted means of Course 4 students in the three schools were in the following order: Adams, Washington, and Jefferson. All pairwise differences in school means were also significant on both tests.
- On the advanced mathematics test, the adjusted mean of Course 4 boys was significantly higher than that of Course 4 girls, but there was not a significant gender effect on the reasoning test.
- There was not a significant preachievement level effect on the advanced mathematics test. On the reasoning test, the adjusted mean of students in the top 10% of pretest scores was significantly higher than that of the average student group.
- Nine TIMSS advanced mathematics tasks were administered at the end of both Year 3 and Year 4. Students who completed the items

both years grew an average of 4% per item from Year 3 to Year 4 and scored about one-fifth of a standard deviation higher on these tasks than the U.S. advanced mathematics sample.

Results of the school comparison of Course 4 students should be interpreted with care, since about 30% of the Adams students were in accelerated Course 4 classes. In the other two schools, there were no accelerated Course 4 classes. When compared directly, adjusted means of the accelerated Adams students were higher than those of the regular Course 4 students (p = .058) on the advanced mathematics test, but the mean difference between accelerated and regular Adams students did not approach significance on the reasoning test. Thus the tracking effect discussed at the end of Chapter 6 may have contributed to higher scores at Adams, especially on the advanced mathematics test. As in other years, the tracking effect may also be a contributing factor in higher adjusted achievement scores of PAL 1 students.

The item-by-item analysis of the nine common TIMSS advanced mathematics tasks provided some interesting insights into the strengths and weaknesses of the students in Year 4. Students in this study had both good growth and high percents correct relative to the U.S. and international samples on a statistics problem involving a best-fit line for data in a given scatterplot, a deductive logic problem, and a problem involving geometric transformations. On another geometric transformation problem, students did very well compared to the U.S. and international samples, but the percent correct actually declined from Year 3 to Year 4. A likely explanation for the decline is that none of the courses in the fourth year include any new transformation geometry content. Students in this study tended to exhibit growth on tasks involving symbolic algebra, and their fourth-year item means were mainly similar to or higher than those of the U.S. TIMSS sample.

Following the reporting of the quantitative test results, the remainder of the chapter describes the performance of selected students who were interviewed as they worked on five different reasoning problems. These tasks measured reasoning ability and complemented the written test of reasoning. Three of the tasks involved algebraic reasoning, and one each involved geometric and statistical reasoning. A brief summary of the main results follows.

On the algebraic reasoning interview problems, about three-fourths of students were able to recognize and generalize patterns and represent the patterns using algebraic symbols. Most students were able to reason correctly about a fairly complex method for generating a number pattern, but some were confused about the difference between "always" and "every" in two similar sounding formulations of the method. In another problem, some students showed confusion about the connection of the slope of a line to the implicit symbolic form of a linear function, that is, $ax + by = c$.

The geometric reasoning problem involved the checking of a proposed method for making a kite that would guarantee pairs of equal sides. About 70% of students understood the method and most of them produced a counterexample to disprove it. The students who had difficulty made the mistake of assuming the equality of some segment lengths based on their appearance in the given figure. Finally, the statistical reasoning problem involved transforming the mean of a distribution by multiplying all values by the same number. Some students had difficulty with this computational idea. Even though they knew how to compute a mean, many students did not have a flexible enough understanding to see how the distributive property could be used in conjunction with the computational procedure for computing the mean of the transformed data set. Interviewed students scored around 50% on this problem.

This chapter completes Section III, *Longitudinal Patterns in Student Achievement*. The next section reports on the attitudes, perceptions, and beliefs of students during high school. In the next chapter, Chapter 9, results concerning the attitudes of students about their experiences in Courses 1 and 2 are reported.

APPENDIX

1. *ITED-Q* Pretest and TIMSS Advanced Math Subtest Descriptive Statistics for all Students Completing TIMSS 4

	ITED-Q Pretest				*No., Eq. Subtest ($\alpha = .49$)*		*Geometry Subtest ($\alpha = .24$)*	
Group	*N*	*Mean*	*SD*	*%-Tile*	*Mean*	*SD*	*Mean*	*SD*
Washington	34	299.6	24.2	87	38.2	18.6	45.8	20.1
Adams	88	296.8	19.3	85	41.6	18.6	46.8	19.2
Jefferson	167	289.2	24.8	80	30.3	17.0	39.3	19.6
Females	157	289.5	24.9	80	32.5	17.0	40.0	18.8
Males	132	296.7	21.1	87	37.2	19.7	45.0	20.8
PAL 1	96	316.1	8.7	95	45.1	19.3	50.9	20.3
PAL 2	142	290.5	7.9	81	31.5	16.0	39.9	18.4
PAL 3[a]	51	255.1	18.6	50	23.9	13.1	32.8	16.7
Course 4	190	289.7	24.3	80	32.5	18.4	40.5	19.7
AP Calc	34	301.6	17.2	88	42.9	17.5	50.4	19.3
AP Stat	65	297.0	22.3	85	36.7	17.8	43.3	19.7
TOTAL	289	292.7	23.5	82	34.7	18.4	42.3	19.8

[a] Beginning in Course 3, PAL 3 includes all students with *ITED-Q* pretest scores below the 67th percentile.

Appendix continues on next page.

Group	P & S Subtest (α = .24)			Calculus Subtest (α = .33)		Adv. Math Total (α = .68)	
	N	*Mean*	*SD*	*Mean*	*SD*	*Mean*	*SD*
Washington	34	66.9	24.4	52.9	28.6	46.4	15.4
Adams	88	66.8	21.0	47.3	31.4	47.6	13.7
Jefferson	167	58.7	23.4	41.7	33.1	38.4	14.9
Females	157	58.3	23.6	38.6	31.7	39.2	14.1
Males	132	66.7	21.8	52.0	31.4	45.6	15.8
PAL 1	96	72.9	20.4	53.5	33.7	51.9	14.9
PAL 2	142	58.3	22.8	43.4	29.4	39.3	12.5
PAL 3[a]	51	52.5	21.4	32.0	32.6	31.6	12.3
Course 4	190	59.3	23.3	42.8	31.9	40.0	14.8
AP Calc	34	66.9	24.4	65.7	29.0	51.2	14.2
AP Stat	65	67.7	20.6	39.5	31.1	43.6	15.1
TOTAL	289	62.1	23.1	44.8	32.2	42.1	15.2

[a] Beginning in Course 3, PAL 3 includes all students with *ITED-Q* pretest scores below the 67th percentile.

2. *ITED-Q* Pretest and Math Reasoning Subtest Descriptive Statistics for all Students Completing Math Reasoning

Group	ITED-Q Pretest			Geom. (α = .53)		No. & Al. (α = .59)		Total (α = .69)	
	N	*Mean (%-tile)*	*SD*	*Mean*	*SD*	*Mean*	*SD*	*Mean*	*SD*
Washington	37	302.5 (89)	15.5	40.7	11.8	53.9	17.2	47.1	11.6
Adams	88	301.5 (88)	17.6	50.6	18.2	52.4	14.9	51.5	13.9
Jefferson	114	288.6 (80)	22.1	29.4	13.0	42.8	16.1	35.9	12.5
Females	123	291.9 (82)	22.5	37.9	18.4	48.0	17.1	42.8	15.5
Males	116	299.3 (86)	17.8	40.1	17.1	48.1	16.0	43.9	14.0
PAL 1	77	315.5 (95)	8.8	51.9	19.5	60.5	14.2	56.1	13.5
PAL 2	134	292.5 (82)	8.1	34.4	12.7	43.3	13.7	38.7	10.6
PAL 3	28	254.6 (50)	17.3	25.4	12.4	36.2	15.2	30.7	11.3
Course 4	193	293.7 (83)	21.3	38.3	18.6	45.9	16.6	42.3	15.4
AP Calculus	46	303.0 (89)	15.5	39.5	14.1	57.0	12.9	48.0	11.1
TOTAL	239	295.5 (84)	20.7	39.0	17.8	48.0	16.6	48.4	14.8

Appendix continues on next page.

3. TIMSS Advanced Mathematics Achievement by Country

Nations With Average Scores Significantly Higher Than the United States		*Nations With Average Scores Not Significantly Different From the United States.*	
Nation	*Average*	*Nation*	*Average*
France	557	Italy	474
Russian Federation	542	Czech Republic	469
Switzerland	533	Germany	465
Australia	525	United States	442
Denmark	522	Austria	436
Cyprus	518	*Nation With Average Scores Significantly Lower than the United States*	
Lithuania	516		
Greece	513	*Nation*	*Average*
Greece	513	NONE	
Sweden	512		
Canada	509	International Average = 501	
Slovenia	475		

4. ANCOVA for Course 4 versus Conventional Precalculus With *ITED-Q* Pretest as Covariate and Course 4 TIMSS-Based Test and Course 4 Reasoning Test as Dependent Variables

Group (Course 4 Versus Precalculus) ANCOVA; Dependent Variable TIMSS-Based Test Total Scores

Source	*Type III Sum of Squares*	*df*	*Mean Square*	*F*	*Sig.*
Corrected Model[a]	14,380.327	2	7,190.163	48.000	.000
Intercept	4,785.826	1	4,785.826	31.949	.000
Pre-*ITED-Q*	14,348.771	1	14,348.771	95.790	.000
GROUP	1,357.330	1	1,357.330	9.061	.003
Error	45,687.058	305	149.794		
Total	54,6671.598	308			
Corrected Total	60,067.385	307			

[a] $R^2 = .239$ (Adjusted $R^2 = .234$)

Appendix continues on next page.

Group (Course 4 versus Precalculus) ANCOVA; Dependent Variable Reasoning Test Total Scores

Source	Type III Sum of Squares	df	Mean Square	F	Sig.
Corrected Model[a]	21,918.561	2	10,959.281	86.977	.000
Intercept	9,908.245	1	9,908.245	78.635	.000
Pre-*ITED-Q*	21,890.484	1	21,890.484	173.730	.000
GROUP	1,103.153	1	1,103.153	8.755	.003
Error	38,682.828	307	126.003		
Total	607,929.240	310			
Corrected Total	60,601.390	309			

[a] $R^2 = .362$ (Adjusted $R^2 = .358$)

5. ANCOVAs With *ITED-Q* Pretest as Covariate and TIMSS-Based Test Total as Dependent Variable

School by Gender ANCOVA; Dependent Variable Course 4 TIMSS-Based Total Scores

Source	Type III Sum of Squares	df	Mean Square	F	Sig.
Corrected Model[a]	16,787.272	6	2,797.879	20.593	.000
Intercept	660.261	1	660.261	4.860	.029
Pre-*ITED-Q*	4,636.154	1	4,636.154	34.123	.000
SCHOOL	5,948.373	2	2,974.186	21.890	.000
GENDER	811.215	1	811.215	5.971	.015
SCHOOL * GENDER	259.652	2	129.826	.956	.387
Error	24,863.615	183	135.867		
Total	34,5650.888	190			
Corrected Total	41,650.888	189			

[a] $R^2 = .403$ (Adjusted $R^2 = .383$)

School by Gender Adjusted Course 4 TIMSS-Based Total Means

	Females			Males			TOTAL		
School	N	Adj. Mean	SE	N	Adj. Mean	SE	N	Adj. Mean	SE
Washington	12	34.8	3.37	11	43.6	3.52	23	39.2	2.44
Adams	49	43.9	1.68	39	48.6	1.89	88	46.3	1.28
Jefferson	40	32.9	1.95	39	34.4	1.87	79	33.6	1.36
TOTAL	101	37.2	1.40	89	42.2	1.47			

Appendix continues on next page.

School by Preachievement Level ANCOVA; Dependent Variable Course 4 TIMSS-Based Total Scores

Source	*Type III Sum of Squares*	*df*	*Mean Square*	*F*	*Sig.*
Corrected Model[a]	16,817.492	9	1,868.610	13.544	.000
Intercept	177.660	1	177.660	1.288	.258
Pre-*ITED-Q*	1,178.173	1	1,178.173	8.540	.004
SCHOOL	4,036.078	2	2,018.039	14.627	.000
PAL	561.876	2	280.938	2.036	.134
SCHOOL * PAL	418.759	4	104.690	.759	.553
Error	24,833.395	180	137.963		
Total	345,650.888	190			
Corrected Total	41,650.888	189			

[a] $R^2 = .404$ (Adjusted $R^2 = .374$)

School by Preachievement Level Adjusted Course 4 TIMSS-Based Total Means

	Washington			*Adams*			*Jefferson*			*TOTAL*		
PAL	*N*	*Adj. Mn.*	*SE*	*N*	*Adj. Mn.*	*SE*	*N*	*Adj. Mn.*	*SE*	*N*	*Adj. Mn.*	*SE*
1	11	41.1	3.94	31	48.6	2.91	13	33.8	3.82	55	41.2	2.59
2	10	34.8	3.72	48	44.8	1.70	38	32.0	1.91	96	37.2	1.50
3	2	48.3	9.23	9	43.2	4.56	28	35.8	3.63	39	42.4	4.40
TOTAL	23	41.4	3.36	88	45.5	1.59	79	33.9	1.49			

Gender by Preachievement Level Adjusted Course 4 TIMSS-Based Total Means

Source	*Type III Sum of Squares*	*df*	*Mean Square*	*F*	*Sig.*
Corrected Model[a]	11,085.159	6	1,847.527	11.061	.000
Intercept	361.279	1	361.279	2.163	.143
Pre-*ITED-Q*	1,602.188	1	1,602.188	9.592	.002
GENDER	230.255	1	230.255	1.379	.242
PAL	394.521	2	197.261	1.181	.309
GENDER * PAL	107.190	2	53.595	.321	.726
Error	30,565.729	183	167.026		
Total	345,650.888	190			
Corrected Total	41,650.888	189			

[a] $R^2 = .266$ (Adjusted $R^2 = .242$)

Appendix continues on next page.

Gender by Preachievement Level Adjusted Course 4 TIMSS-Based Total Means

	Females			Males			TOTAL		
PAL	*N*	*Adj. Mean*	*SE*	*N*	*Adj. Mean*	*SE*	*N*	*Adj. Mean*	*SE*
1	28	40.9	3.25	27	44.5	3.29	55	42.7	2.77
2	48	36.7	1.87	48	40.6	1.87	96	38.7	1.32
3	25	39.6	4.31	14	39.5	4.24	39	39.5	3.65
TOTAL	101	39.1	1.41	89	41.5	1.55			

6. ANCOVAs With *ITED-Q* Pretest as Covariate and Reasoning Test Total as Dependent Variable

School by Gender ANCOVA; Dependent Variable Course 4 Reasoning Total Scores

Source	*Type III Sum of Squares*	*df*	*Mean Square*	*F*	*Sig.*
Corrected Model[a]	23,136.640	6	3,856.107	32.486	.000
Intercept	1,856.015	1	1,856.015	15.636	.000
Pre-*ITED-Q*	6,553.190	1	6,553.190	55.208	.000
SCHOOL	6,836.668	2	3,418.334	28.798	.000
GENDER	2,300	1	2.300	.019	.889
SCHOOL * GENDER	111.995	2	55.997	.472	.625
Error	22,078.028	186	118.699		
Total	38,9781.478	193			
Corrected Total	45,214.667	192			

[a] $R^2 = .512$ (Adjusted $R^2 = .496$)

School by Gender Adjusted Course 4 Reasoning Total Means

	Females			Males			TOTAL		
School	*N*	*Adj. Mean*	*SE*	*N*	*Adj. Mean*	*SE*	*N*	*Adj. Mean*	*SE*
Washington	12	40.5	3.15	11	43.9	3.30	23	42.2	2.28
Adams	50	49.6	1.56	38	48.3	1.82	88	49.0	1.22
Jefferson	40	35.6	1.87	42	34.4	1.69	82	35.0	1.27
TOTAL	102	41.9	1.31	91	42.2	1.38			

Appendix continues on next page.

Gender by Preachievement Level ANCOVA; Dependent Variable Course 4 Reasoning Total Scores

Source	*Type III Sum of Squares*	*df*	*Mean Square*	*F*	*Sig.*
Corrected Model[a]	19,476.487	6	3,246.081	23,458	.000
Intercept	773.817	1	773.817	5,592	.019
Pre-*ITED-Q*	2,225.817	1	2,225.817	16,085	.000
GENDER	339.254	1	339.254	2,452	.119
PAL	3,082.757	2	1,541.378	11,139	.000
GENDER * PAL	118.452	2	59,226	.428	.652
Error	25,738.181	186	138.377		
Total	389,781.478	193			
Corrected Total	45,214.667	192			

[a] The School by PAL ANCOVA is omitted because one of the cells contained just one student.
[b] $R^2 = .431$ (Adjusted $R^2 = .412$)

Gender by Preachievement Level Adjusted Course 4 Reasoning Total Means

	Females			*Males*			*TOTAL*		
PAL	*N*	*Adj. Mean*	*SE*	*N*	*Adj. Mean*	*SE*	*N*	*Adj. Mean*	*SE*
1	27	50.8	2.90	33	46.3	2.76	60	48.5	2.38
2	58	39.1	1.57	50	37.9	1.67	108	38.5	1.15
3	17	45.2	4.68	8	41.0	5.24	25	43.1	4.27
TOTAL	102	45.0	1.50	91	41.7	1.71			

Appendix continues on next page.

7. Growth on Common Tasks of Matched Set of 184 Students From End of Course 3 to End of Senior Mathematics Course

1. Scientists have observed that crickets move their wings faster in warm temperatures than in cold temperatures. By noting the pitch of cricket chirps, it is possible to estimate the air temperature. Below is a graph showing 13 observations of cricket chirps per second and the associated air temperature.

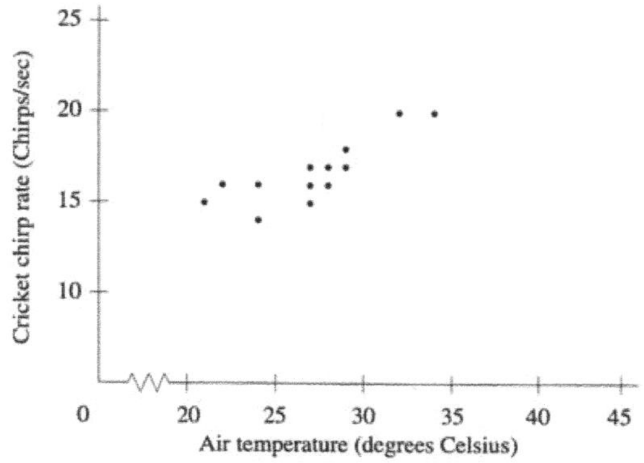

(a) On the graph, draw in an estimated line of best fit for these data.

CPMP Yr. 3 – 68% **Yr. 4 – 74%** **U.S. – 36%** **International – 51%**

(b) Using your line, estimate the air temperature when cricket chirps of 22 per second are heard.

CPMP Yr. 3 – 84% **Yr. 4 – 88%** **U.S. – 48%** **International – 63%**

2. The Smith sisters made these statements. If Vera told the truth, who else must have told the truth?

Lucy: "If the rug is in the car, then it is not in the garage."
Sally: "If the rug is not in the car, then it is in the garage."
Vera: "If the rug is in the garage, then it is in the car."
Cherry: "If the rug is not in the car, then it is not in the garage."

A. Lucy
B. Sally
C. Cherry
D. none need have told the truth.

	Yr. 3	Yr. 4
CPMP	77%	**86%**
U.S.		**70%**
International		**76%**

3. A translation maps $A(2, -3)$ onto A' (-3, -5). Under the same translation, find the coordinates of B?, the image of B(1, 4).

CPMP Yr. 3 – 69% **Yr. 4 – 59%** **U.S. – 42%** **International – 52%**

Appendix continues on next page.

4.

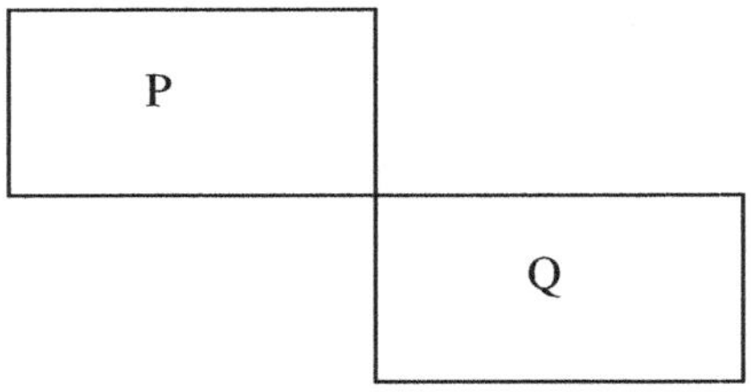

The rectangle labeled Q CANNOT be obtained from the rectangle labeled by means of a

A. reflection (about an axis in the plane of the page)

B. rotation (in the plane of the page)

C. translation.

D. translation followed by a reflection

	Yr. 3	Yr. 4
CPMP	50%	57%
U. S.		47%
International		56%

5. If $xy = 1$ and x is greater than 0, which of the following statements is true?

A. When x is greater than 1, y is negative.

B. When x is greater than 1, y is greater than 1.

C. When x is less than 1, y is less than 1.

D. As x increases, y increases.

E. As x increases, y decreases.

	Yr. 3	Yr. 4
CPMP	51%	66%
U.S.		67%
International		85%

6. A warning system installation consists of two independent alarms having probabilities of operating in an emergency of 0.95 and 0.90 respectively. Find the probability that at least one alarm operates in an emergency.

A. 0.995

B. 0.975

C. 0.95

D. 0.90

	Yr. 3	Yr. 4
CPMP	20%	16%
U.S.		21%
International		28%

Appendix continues on next page.

7. The vertices of the triangle PQR are the points $P(1, 2)$, $Q(4, 6)$ and $R(-4, 12)$. Which of the following statements about triangle PQR is true?

   A. PQR is a right triangle with the right angle $\angle P$.

   B. PQR is a right triangle with the right angle $\angle Q$.

   C. PQR is a right triangle with the right angle $\angle R$.

   D. PQR is not a right triangle.

	Yr. 3	Yr. 4
CPMP	28%	35%
U.S.		47%
International		56%

8. What are all values of x for which the inequality $5x + \frac{5}{3} \leq -2x - \frac{2}{3}$ is true?

   A. $x \leq -\frac{7}{9}$

   B. $x \leq -\frac{1}{3}$

   C. $x \geq 0$

   E. $x \geq \frac{9}{3}$

	Yr. 3	Yr. 4
CPMP	51%	50%
U.S.		68%
International		74%

PART III

ATTITUDES, BELIEFS, AND CONCEPTIONS OF STUDENTS

CHAPTER 9

ATTITUDES ABOUT THE CURRICULUM AND PEDAGOGY

Years 1 and 2

A mathematics curriculum's effect can be measured not only by students' achievement, but also by their attitudes about the curriculum and instruction that they experience and by their more general beliefs about mathematics. Such variables are of interest in their own right, and also with regard to the nature of their association with achievement. In this study, the researcher-developed *Student Belief Survey* (SBS), consisting of six scales measuring different aspects of beliefs about mathematics, was administered at the beginning and end of Course 1 and at the end of Course 2. A seventh scale focusing on students' specific attitudes about their experience in the mathematics course they just completed was included in the SBS survey at the end of each of these courses.

Results on the general belief scales are reported in Chapter 10. In this chapter, the focus is on the specific attitudes of students about their experience in their Course 1 and Course 2 mathematics classes. The chapter begins with a description of the portion of the written instrument that measures specific attitudes. Quantitative results on the Attitude scale are

A Five-Year Study of the First Edition of the Core-Plus Mathematics Curriculum, pp. 203–226

then reported over time, school, gender, and preachievement level. The quantitative scale results are enriched by responses to individual scale items and to an open-ended question asking students to describe their experiences in their mathematics class.

ATTITUDES ABOUT COURSES

The SBS at the end of both Courses 1 and 2 included 11 items that measured students' attitudes about the mathematics course they just completed. These items solicited the following student attitudes:

- Whether students believed that their mathematics course helped them to understand mathematical ideas and make better sense of mathematics
- Whether students were confident in their problem-solving abilities and mathematical reasoning skills
- Whether students believed that their mathematics course helped them to better talk about and write about mathematics
- Whether students found working cooperatively in groups to be helpful and enjoyable
- Whether students found the problems to be representative of realistic situations
- Whether students believed the textbook was easy to read
- Whether students believed that using calculators was enjoyable

In this section, the quantitative results of the Attitude scale by course, school, gender, and preachievement level are reported.

For a positively stated item on the course Attitude scale, 1 corresponds to "strongly disagree," 2 to "disagree," 3 to "not sure," 4 to "agree," and 5 to "strongly agree." Therefore, in the following analysis, a score of 3 can be thought of as a neutral attitude, 5 as very strongly positive, and 1 as a very strongly negative attitude. In the statistical analyses, scores were treated as real number data, rather than categorical data. This data treatment may increase the power of the statistical tests. In the following, most probability levels are reported, and the reader may decide to view mean differences with probability levels greater than 0.01 with caution. Descriptive statistics for all students who completed the Attitude scale each year are given in the Chapter 9 Appendix, Part 1.

School, Gender, and PAL Effects Across Courses

To analyze the school and gender effects, two school-by-gender analyses of variance were run with each course Attitude scale score as dependent variable. As in previous chapters, school-by-PAL and gender-by-PAL analyses of variance were also run with each course Attitude scale as dependent variable. Unlike with achievement dependent variables described in earlier chapters, no covariate was entered into the analyses. The ANOVA tables are provided in the Chapter 9 Appendix, Part 2. The statistically significant effects are discussed next.

School Effects. No interactions involving the school variable were statistically significant, but the school main effects were highly significant ($p < .001$) for each course Attitude scale. The scale means for each school in each course are plotted in Figure 9.1. After each course, Adams students had the most positive mean attitude ($p < .001$) compared to each of the other two schools. In addition, Jefferson's Course 2 mean was significantly greater than that of Washington ($p = .027$).

Gender-by-PAL Interaction. The gender main effect was not significant in either course, but the interaction between gender and preachievement level on the Course 1 Attitude scale was statistically significant ($p = .019$). In the PAL 1 and PAL 3 groups, boys had more positive attitudes than girls, but in the PAL 2 group girls were more positive about Course 1 than boys (see Figure 9.2). One might conjecture that, consistent with many gender studies, brighter boys are more positive about mathematics than brighter girls, but there does not seem to be a ready explanation for the gender interaction in the two middle PAL groups.

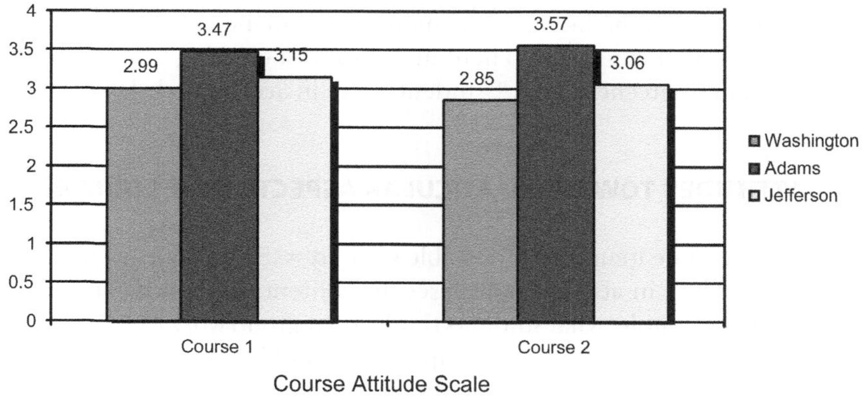

Figure 9.1. Course 1 and Course 2 Attitude Scale Means for Students in Each School.

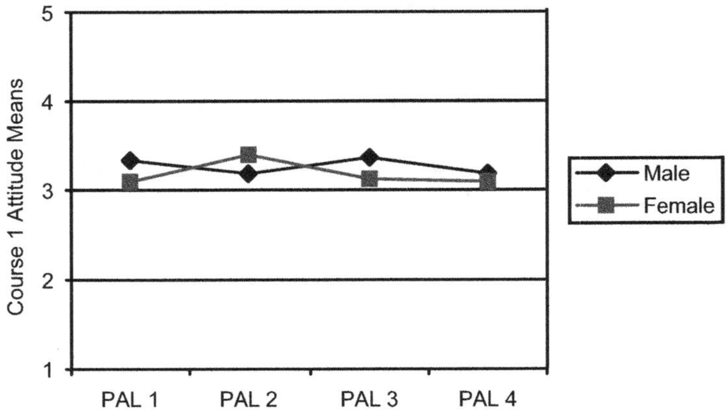

Figure 9.2. Course 1 Attitude Scale Means by Gender and PAL.

PAL Main Effects. The Attitude scale means for each course by PAL group are displayed in Figure 9.3. The PAL main effect for Course 1 was not statistically significant. In Course 2, the PAL main effect was highly significant ($p < .001$), reflecting a positive correlation between attitudes about Course 2 and the *ITED-Q* pretest scores. The following pairwise PAL group mean attitude differences in Course 2 are all statistically significant: PAL 1 > PAL 3 ($p = .006$), PAL 1 > PAL 4 ($p < .001$), PAL 2 > PAL 4 ($p = .001$), and PAL 3 > PAL 4 ($p = .021$). It is also clear in Figure 9.3 that the top preachievement students were more positive about Course 2 than they had been about Course 1, and the reverse trend was true for low preachievement students.[1] A plausible explanation for this course-to-course pattern is that the increasing mathematical sophistication of the content is more to the liking of the more able students than to those who are less able mathematically. There may also be a tracking effect at work, since a higher percent of PAL 1 students were in accelerated classes.

ATTITUDES TOWARD PARTICULAR ASPECTS OF A COURSE

While the attitude items form a reliable scale ($\alpha = .82$ in Course 1 and $\alpha = .84$ in Course 2), in at least some cases the content of a specific item is of interest. For example, what students think about group work or calculators, or whether they believe they have improved in problem solving, reasoning, and reading and writing mathematics is of individual interest. To help describe responses to individual items by gender and preachievement level, a gender-by-PAL level multiple analysis of variance with the 11

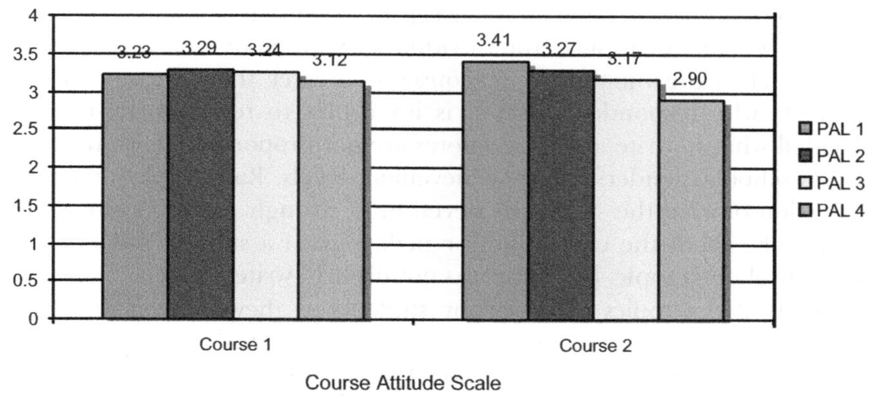

Figure 9.3. Course 1 and Course 2 Attitude Scale Means for Students in Each PAL Group.

Course 1 attitude items as dependent variables was run, followed by the same statistical test with the 11 Course 2 attitude items as dependent variables. The statistically significant results of these analyses form the basis for the discussion of quantitative item results, but to keep within space limitations and to make the reading more interesting, the data from the tests are not reported in this book. The interested reader can find the data from these statistical tests posted at http://www.wmich.edu/cpmp/evaluation.html

In this section, individual item responses at the end of each course are analyzed by percents of students choosing each response. These quantitative item data are enriched by students' responses to the open-ended statement concerning their experiences in mathematics class during the year. Since the general pattern of higher attitudes for students in higher preachievement levels applies to nearly all scale items, when students are quoted concerning a topic, their preachievement level will be identified. For the few items that are exceptions to this positive association, the students' preachievement level remains of interest to the discussion because these items are exceptions.

After Course 1, 477 of 604 students wrote about their course experience, and 624 of 692 did so after Course 2. Student written comments were coded by topic and tone. The quantitative results of the coding are given in the Chapter 9 Appendix, Part 3. As a gross descriptor of the set of quotes in Course 1, the percents of quotes that were favorable, neutral, and unfavorable were 45.6%, 21.4%, and 33.0%, respectively. In Course 2, the respective percents were 49.2%, 13.4%, and 37.4%. In the Appendix and in the following discussion, a *response* refers to a student's written quote coded under a single topic. Keep in mind that students may mention more than one topic in their written description of their course experience. Thus the number of responses is greater than the number of students who responded. Also, it is important to realize that students decided what to write about, so quotes are not proportionally distributed across schools, genders, or preachievement levels. Rather they may be a reflection of what the student believed most strongly, either positively or negatively, about the curriculum or pedagogy. If a student did not feel strongly about a topic, he or she was not likely to write about it.

Many of the topics discussed by students as they wrote about their experience in a course overlapped with the SBS attitude items. Students, however, brought up several additional topics such as their teacher, their effort in the class, and their homework. The next section is a presentation of the quantitative Attitude scale item results and a discussion of these results enriched by related comments. The other topics that students wrote about are discussed in a later section.

Results and Discussion of Attitude Scale Items

There were 11 items on the Attitude scale each year, and students wrote about many of the topics in those items when they described their experiences in the course. Results of these items and a discussion of the related comments are described in this section.

Understanding and Making Sense of Mathematics. An important pair of related attitude items are, "I understood the mathematical ideas in this course" and "This course helped me see that mathematical ideas make sense." Means and percents of students choosing each response on each item for each course are displayed in Figure 9.4. Students were above the

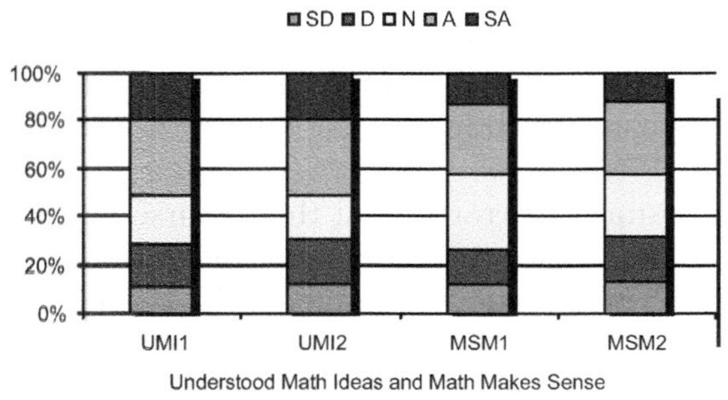

	%A/SA	%D/SD	Mn
UMI1	50.8	28.5	3.31
UMI2	51.5	30.2	3.29
MSM1	42.8	26.6	3.18
MSM2	42.9	31.2	3.10

Figure 9.4. Percent of Each Response and Mean of *Understanding Mathematics* (UMI1 and UMI2) and *Making Sense of Mathematics* (MSM1 and MSM2) Items at the End of Course 1 and Course 2.

neutral level on both items with a somewhat more positive response to the first item. Evidently some students who agreed that they understood the mathematical ideas in this course did not agree that the course helped them see that mathematical ideas, in general, make sense. There was little change on either item from Course 1 to Course 2. As demonstrated in the previous section, students' preachievement level was positively correlated with their attitudes about the courses, and this correlation is also evident as they wrote about their experiences.

Following Course 1, a PAL 1 student indicated that he learned to view mathematics as a coherent body of knowledge. "This year I learned a lot. It seemed like all the big math ideas came together." Two PAL 2 students found enjoyment in their understanding, writing, "This year I understood math better than last year and I think this kind of math was easy, interesting, and it wasn't hard to understand if you pay attention and get the hang of it" and "I now enjoy math because I understand it better. Math can be fun." Students from lower PAL groups, however, did not find as much enjoyment, writing such things as "I really had a hard time in math. I understood very little." A PAL 4 student prepared to avoid mathematics as soon as possible, writing, "I don't like or understand Core Plus Math, and I plan to get my two credits and not take any more."

There was a similar mix of students' written responses at the end of Course 2. A PAL 1 student wrote, "My experience in math class this year brought me to better understand and know how to figure out different mathematical ideas." A PAL 2 student agreed, writing, "Math this year actually helped me understand the logics or theories of mathematics." Another PAL 2 student emphasized that Course 2 helped her make more sense of mathematics:

> I think that my experience this year in math was good. In the beginning it seemed really hard, but I kept with it and it makes a lot more sense now. I usually am pretty good in math and don't have to try really hard, but this course made me think more. I learned a lot of new helpful things.

Other Course 2 students, especially those at lower levels of preachievement, were not so positive about their experiences. A PAL 3 student thought that Course 2 took away from her understanding of mathematics. "Math is not my best subject. I'm really good in some areas of math. But then other areas I just won't understand at all. I always did really well in math until they started using the Core program. I don't really like the Core program." Another PAL 3 student described a very negative mathematical experience: "I have always struggled in math. It is hard for me to comprehend mathematical situations and equations. I dread going to my math class and it makes me feel stupid. Math scares me." A PAL 4 student agreed by writing, "I struggle everyday to comprehend even the basic situations. I wish I never had to take math class my whole life."

Problem Solving and Mathematical Reasoning. Problem solving and reasoning are two of the key processes involved in doing mathematics. The following two survey items measured students' attitude and confidence in these areas: "This course helped me feel confident that I can solve math problems" and "I learned to reason mathematically." Means and percents of students choosing each response on each item for each course are displayed in Figure 9.5. Students were above the neutral level on both items with a somewhat more positive response to the reasoning item. There was a decline in the mean response to the problem-solving item in Course 2.

Again students' written comments were similar by course, but varied by the students' preachievement level. Concerning problem solving, a PAL 1 student wrote at the end of Course 2, "My experience in mathematics class this year has proven to me that I can solve mathematical equations and problems." A PAL 2 student recognized an improvement in problem-solving ability, writing, "Core 2 has taught me how to solve mathematical problems, and now I find it easier to do many other things that involve math."

With regard to mathematical reasoning, a PAL 1 student remarked:

> I have learned how to reason with other's ideas and how to put our ideas and answers together to form one sensible answer. I enjoyed being with friends and also communicating with other people. I made great accomplishments and learned new things and how to solve advanced mathematical problems.

A PAL 3 student, however, disagreed concerning the enjoyment of reasoning through a problem. "I like math better the old way it was taught where

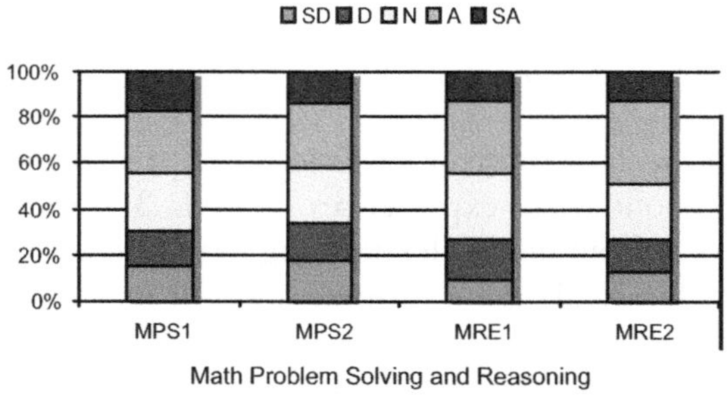

	%A/SA	%D/SD	Mn
MPS1	44.7	30.2	3.17
MPS2	42.3	33.2	3.05
MRE1	44.2	26.5	3.21
MRE2	48.6	27.0	3.22

Figure 9.5. Percent of Each Response and Mean of *Mathematical Problem Solving* (MPS1 and MPS2) and *Mathematical Reasoning* (MRE1 and MRE2) Items at the End of Course 1 and Course 2.

you would learn a formula and how to use it, and how it worked instead of trying to figure it out for yourself."

Talking and Writing About Mathematics. Two attitude survey items measured students' attitudes about how the courses affected their ability to communicate about mathematics: "This course made me better at talking about mathematical ideas" and "This course made me better at writing about mathematical ideas." Means and percents of students choosing each response on each item for each course are displayed in Figure 9-6. On both items, mean responses were slightly above the neutral level, and there was a modest decline in Course 2.

A PAL 2 student wrote that talking to others was helpful for learning mathematics. "I like to work in groups, it made me feel like I could answer a question and talk about it more." A PAL 1 student agreed that communicating with others brought enjoyment. "This year in math, the questions and ideas are a little tougher than last year, but I like that because it gives me a chance to think for myself and to express my own ideas and opinions." A PAL 3 student explained how not talking can have a limiting effect on understanding. "In mathematics this year, I did not do too well mainly because I'm so quiet and don't ask a lot of questions when I don't understand something, if I would ask more questions I would probably be doing a lot better in class." Another PAL 2 student was not happy with all of the required writing. "This year I have found that this mathematics class has been sometimes good and a lot of times bad. All the writing problems that we had to do were pointless. What is this a language class?"

More on the Gender-by-PAL Interaction in Course 1. The significant gender-by-preachievement level interaction on the Course 1 Attitude scale was discussed earlier in this chapter. Just four individual items contributed to that interaction: confidence in problem solving, understanding the mathematical ideas in the course, writing about mathematics, and

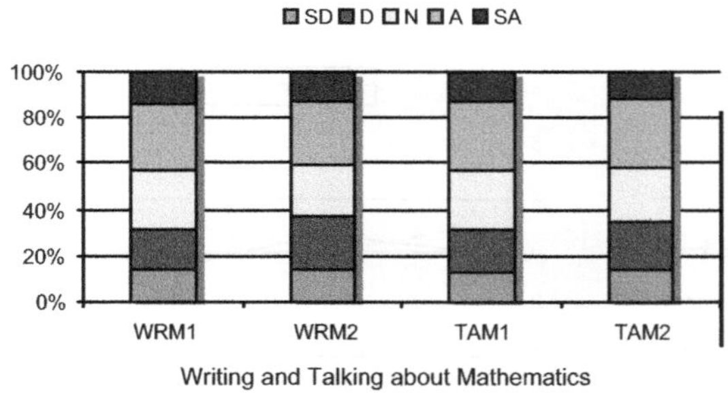

	%A/SA	%D/SD	Mn
WRM1	43.5	31.4	3.12
WRM2	40.6	37.2	3.01
TAM1	43.0	31.0	3.13
TAM2	41.5	35.2	3.05

Figure 9.6. Percent of Each Response and Mean of *Writing About Mathematics* (WRM1 and WRM2) and *Talking About Mathematics* (TAM1 and TAM2) Items at the End of Course 1 and Course 2.

reading about mathematics. The gender-by-PAL means for those four items are plotted in Figure 9.7.

As the plots show, among students in the top 10% of preachievement, boys were somewhat more positive than girls with regard to all four items. That was not the case in the above average group (67th to 89th percentile); in fact, at this level, the girls tended to be more positive than the boys. Interestingly, in the lower preachievement groups, especially the 33rd to 66th percentile group, boys were more positive than girls.

It seems unlikely that the curriculum caused such interactions. A more plausible explanation lies in the beliefs about themselves and mathematics of teenage boys compared to teenage girls. Boys tend to think of mathematical ability as a male domain that is, to a large extent, genetically determined, and, partly for this reason, they have a tendency to express an inflated view of their own abilities. Boys in the above average preachievement group (PAL 2) may see themselves as being in competition with the top students, but falling short for genetic reasons (not having enough of the math gene). Thus their view of themselves in mathematics may be overly.

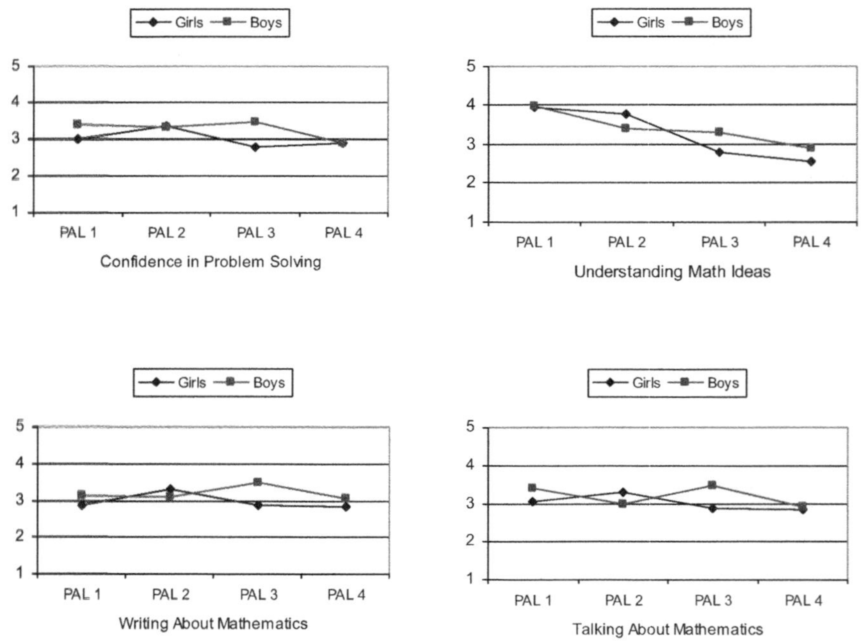

Figure 9.7. Significant Gender by PAL Interactions on Course 1 Attitude Scale Items.

Another notable aspect of the plots is that there was a general decline across PAL groups on the understanding mathematical ideas item, but not on the other three items. This result is likely to be due to an important difference in the item statements. "I understood the mathematical ideas in this course" refers to the level of understanding actually achieved by the student. The other three items all refer to whether the course led to an improvement in the focus area, that is, problem solving, talking about mathematics, and reading about mathematics. The results on these items suggest that the more mathematically able students correctly viewed themselves as achieving more in a course than those who are less mathematically inclined. However, students at all preachievement levels recognized that the course helped them to improve on their own prior understanding and skill.

Cooperative Group Work. Two of the SBS attitude items addressed different aspects of working in cooperative groups: "Group work helped me learn mathematics" and "The group work was enjoyable." Means and percents of students choosing each response on each item for each course are displayed in Figure 9.8. On both items, mean responses were well above the neutral level with somewhat more students agreeing that group work was enjoyable than that it was helpful for learning mathematics. On both items, Course 1 and Course 2 means were nearly equal.

These two items are exceptions to the positive association between attitude item means and preachievement level. At the end of Course 1, three of the four PAL groups had positive mean responses to the helpfulness of the cooperative group work. Only the PAL 1 mean response was slightly below neutral. With the exception of PAL 3 compared to PAL 4, students in lower preachievement groups consistently found cooperative group work to be significantly more helpful than students in higher PAL groups. A similar trend, though less pronounced, was evident in the responses to

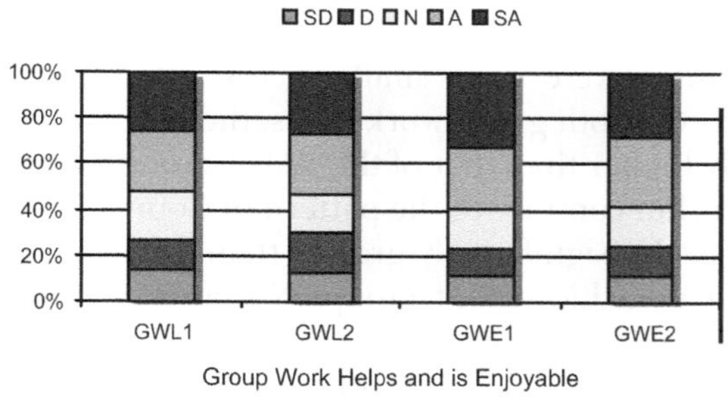

	%A/SA	%D/SD	Mn
GWL1	52.6	27.3	3.36
GWL2	53.9	29.7	3.39
GWE1	59.4	23.4	3.57
GWE2	58.7	25.0	3.50

Figure 9.8. Percent of Each Response and Mean of *Group Work Helps Learn* (GWL1 and GWL2) and *Group Work Is Enjoyable* (GWE1 and GWE2) Items at the End of Course 1 and Course 2.

"The group work was enjoyable." The only pairwise statistically significant differences were that both PAL 3 and PAL 4 means were greater than the mean of PAL 1.

The pattern of responses in Course 1, it seems, strongly suggests that less mathematically able students see themselves as both profiting from and enjoying the experience of group work more than those who are more able. Commenting on the helpfulness of group work in Course 1, a PAL 4 student remarked, "I really enjoyed math class this year, I really learned a lot that I did not know. Even though some of the work and problems we did were hard but I still got through math. I loved working in our groups because it helped me to understand things better." Two PAL 1 students disagreed. One of these students wrote, "I think that group work needs to be fixed. I am an A/B student and the others in my group just try to copy off of my work or have me do all of the figuring out." The other wrote,

> Group work does not help! If people won't learn then it's slowing down everyone. The ones that understand get frustrated and sometimes give up because of the "slackers" in the group. If people aren't going to work, groups won't help.

Comments about group work being fun in Course 1 were similar. One PAL 3 student wrote, "This year I am doing good and feel I have learned quite a bit. It helps to enjoy and discuss math problems when sitting with my friends." A PAL 2 group student agreed that working in groups was enjoyable but emphasized troubles with productivity: "It was fun to work in groups but we never got work done. All around me people were messing around and cheating and not getting their work done. I learned a little but not very much."

Interestingly, the responses by PAL group to the same items in Course 2 are less easily explained. Generally, all students felt more positively than neutral that group work helped them learn and that group work was enjoyable, but students' attitudes were more similar across PAL groups than was the case in Course 1. On both group work items, the mean of the PAL 3 group was significantly higher than that of the PAL 1 group as predicted by the Course 1 results, but contrary to the pattern in Course 1, the mean of the PAL 3 group was also significantly greater than the mean of the PAL 4 group, the lowest preachievement group. No other pairwise mean differences were statistically significant.

As for some representative comments from Course 2, one PAL 3 student found the security of groups to be enjoyable: "I learned a lot [more] this year than in previous years. I think by working in groups you learn more from your friends that know how to explain things just for you. Also some kids don't enjoy asking questions in front of a class and this way they can ask a group member." A PAL 1 student, however, found little enjoyment in small group work, writing, "My experiences in math class were mainly good. I do not enjoy working in groups, because I feel it makes people want to copy more than do work. I like working with the whole class rather than little groups."

Textbook Problems and Reading Level. Two of the SBS attitude items addressed characteristics of the textbook: "Most of the problems in the course are realistic" and "The textbook materials in this course were easy for me to read."[2] Means and percents of students choosing each response on each item for each course are displayed in Figure 9.9. On average, students were approximately neutral about the realism of the problems, slightly above neutral in Course 1 and slightly below in Course 2. Course 1 students, on average, tended to slightly disagree that the textbook was easy to read, although in Course 2 the level of agreement increased to nearly neutral.

On the attitude item concerning the realism of the problems, no significant mean differences were found by PAL group at the end of Course 1, but there were significant differences at the end of Course 2. Overall in Course 2, students from higher PAL groups had more favorable responses than students in lower PAL groups with regard to the realism of problem situations. A PAL 1 student found future benefits in the realism of the problems:

> I have taken math and advanced math for my entire life and this was just difficult to adjust to. I was taught the standard $y = ax + b$ type equation and I liked those better, but I fail to see how that would affect my adult life. Core has helped me to do that.

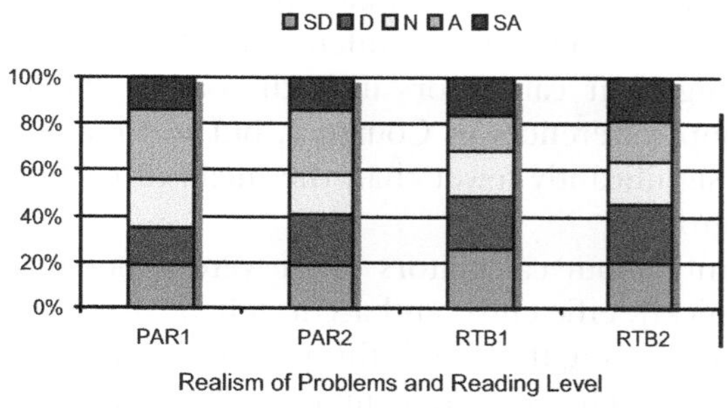

	%A/SA	%D/SD	Mn
PAR1	44.4	35.2	3.05
PAR2	41.8	40.7	2.96
RTB1	31.6	47.6	2.74
RTB2	37.0	45.4	2.92

Figure 9.9. Percent of Each Response and Mean of *Problems Are Realistic* (PAR1 and PAR2) and *Reading Textbook* (RTB1 and RTB2) Items at the End of Course 1 and Course 2.

Two PAL 3 students, however, disagreed with the future usefulness of most of the problems, writing "I learned nothing I'm going to use when I grow up or to make money" and "Well, many of the ideas in Core Plus math seem to be unrealistic and that we won't use them, even though math is used in most every career."

In both courses, students in higher preachievement level groups considered the textbook to be significantly easier to read. At the end of Course 1, one PAL 4 student indicated that one of the most difficult parts about mathematics class was deciphering the textbooks: " the problems in the books were quite hard to understand and sometimes didn't make sense." Two PAL 2 students agreed, writing, "I feel that the books we use are useless. They do not explain anything and they seem to go on and on forever" and "For the past year I have always had trouble with the text." Even PAL 1 students, who had the least difficulty reading the books, had trouble making sense of some of the content. As one such student remarked, "I think the wording in the books is too confusing and that the books don't teach, they just ask you to figure it out." At the end of Course 2, a PAL 3 student commented, "If the questions were written better, then I'm sure I would do better in math. After all, if you don't understand the question how can you answer it?"

At the end of both courses, very few comments made about the textbooks were positive. Evidently the readability of the textbook was not a topic that students chose to write about unless their attitude was strongly negative. Many of the negative comments suggest that the students who wrote about the book would have preferred more of a conventional reference-type textbook, so they could locate information and full explanations more easily.

Calculators. An SBS attitude item asked students about the use of calculators, namely, "I enjoyed using the calculator in this course." Means and percents of students choosing each response for each course are displayed in Figure 9-10. Of the 11 items on the Attitude scale, the mean response each year was most positive on this item. Students at all levels of preachievement enjoyed using their calculators in both courses. There were no significant PAL group differences in Course 1, but in Course 2 the PAL 4 group mean was significantly lower than the mean of each of the other three higher PAL groups.

Favorable written comments about calculators often were about how students could work more quickly, efficiently, and accurately by using the calculators, such as "I've enjoyed using the TI82's this year. It's helped me figure out equations much easier." One student commented on becoming more confident with a calculator: "I feel more confident while using my calculator. I was afraid of it, but I can see how to make it work for me." Many of the students pointed out specific uses for a calculator: "I was able

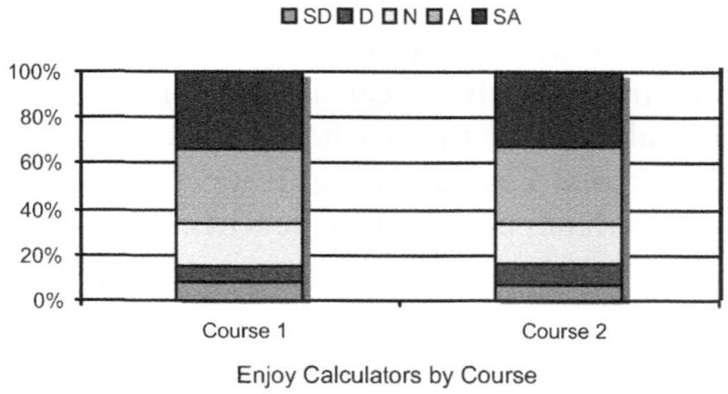

	%A/SA	%D/SD	Mn
Co. 1	65.7	15.3	3.75
Co. 2	66.3	16.0	3.75

Figure 9.10. Percent of Each Response and Mean of the Calculator Item at the End of Course 1 and Course 2.

to learn new ideas using graphs, tables, and equations ... the calculators were helpful because they allowed me to learn faster and quicker." Some students made remarks about how the calculator makes class more fun: "I think that math was fun because we did some pretty cool things on the calculators" and "My experience in mathematics class this year is enjoyable ... the best part is that we do fun things with the calculator."

The few negative responses about calculators usually had to do with students feeling too dependent on the calculators. One student remarked, "We should also do more things not using a calculator because I don't even remember how to do long division," and another student agreed, writing, "Yes, I believe math is important but I think we need to learn mental math, not just how to do the problems on the calculator." Some students feared the consequences of using the calculator so much, as one student said, "[the class] uses the calculator too much because if we use the calculator how will we be able to do this stuff on our own."

Other Open-Ended Responses About the Courses

The written descriptions of students' experiences in their courses were not restricted to the topics in the Attitude scale. Many students wrote about their teacher, their own effort or lack of it, and a number of other, usually more general, observations were made about the course and its effectiveness. What the students had to say about these topics is described in this section.

The Role of the Teacher. Although there was no SBS attitude item that asked the students specifically about their teacher, many students made comments about her or him or about how the class was taught. Many students praised their teachers with responses indicating how helpful their teacher was. For example, one student wrote, "I think I did better in math this year because of the teachers mostly. The teachers get involved and help out and answer questions in a way that I can understand." Other responses praised the teaching abilities of the teacher, such as, "This is the first year in which I really felt that I was learning. It was the teacher that really taught me." Another student compared the teacher to teachers in previous classes:

> I enjoyed math this year much more than I have in years past. This is because teaching techniques used by our teacher were extremely effective. I have learned much more about various concepts through her one year of teaching than I could have through many years of my former instructors teaching.

All of the comments in the previous paragraph indicate that students enjoyed the class more when they understood the material. The converse of this statement is also true. When students did not understand the material, they often viewed the class as a waste of time and many indicated that their teacher was the cause of their angst. One student wrote:

> I felt that the curriculum was well planned out, but I felt we could have been taught better and more efficiently. I felt that this year has cheated me from the mathematical knowledge I should have absorbed, a waste of my time. If taught better it would have been useful.

Some comments indicated that students wanted the teacher to explain more clearly or spend more time "teaching." Examples of such comments are "I think I would understand more if it was explained better ... I might have enjoyed math class a little more" and "I hope in years to come I will have better class experience—I have in past years, I just need a teacher to teach."

Students' Effort

None of the Attitude scale items asked students about their effort in their mathematics class, but many students made one of three types of comments about effort. Students commented that (1) the courses were easy in the beginning but became progressively more difficult, (2) they should have worked harder in order to do better in the class, and (3) content was more accessible when they worked harder or paid more attention in class.

Although a few students commented that the course was too easy or too difficult, many students commented on the courses' progressive difficulty.

One student wrote, "Math class this year was easy in the beginning and then gradually got harder!" Another student agreed, writing, "This class is somewhat easy (very), but the newest stuff is getting harder." After Course 1, one student specifically stated that "At first it was easy ... chapters 5 & 6 were more difficult and I didn't do so well."

Other students commented that they could have done better if they had tried harder. Many students who did poorly in class felt that they had only themselves to blame. One student wrote, "My experience was difficult and confusing because I was lazy and stupid, because I didn't study, and I didn't do a lot of my homework." Another student was also honest about his or her class performance:

> I am a student with bad habits. I turned in no work or late work. Most of the time I understand all the material but I don't do the [homework]. I do okay, I think, on normal tests, but notebook quizzes aren't what they could be. It's not a hard course, I made it out to be.

Similar to working harder on homework, other comments focused on the students' lack of paying attention. One student wrote, "Mathematics was a little hard for me this year because of my not paying attention and not understanding." Another student was more specific about the negative repercussions for not paying attention in class: "I found once I thought I knew what we were doing I shouldn't have stopped paying attention, because I got way behind."

Many students felt that more work on their part would have led to better understanding of the material. One student commented that class was difficult, but hard work led to success: "My experience in math this year was good, I really did better than I thought I would, because I worked hard." Another student wrote, "Math was challenging for me this year but with extra work and trying hard to understand I was able to get through it just fine." In a similar vein, some students attributed their success to paying attention in class. One such student wrote, "This year math has managed to teach me many new things. One of the most important things that I learned was that paying attention in class will help you more than anything else."

Other Student Comments. Several students commented on other topics, such as homework, but the number of responses in each topic category was low. Since these infrequently occurring responses were often vague and not easily categorized, they were put into an *Other* category.

Interestingly, many students who praised the program found it challenging, such as one student who wrote, "My overall experience has been interesting, yet challenging." Other students criticized the curriculum for being too easy, as one student said, "At first the math was so easy, and I didn't mind doing it. Then as the year dragged on I got very bored and stopped doing a lot of work."

Some favorable responses were very general, such as "Math can be fun." Other responses described the generally helpful aspects of the curriculum, such as "Well, it was a class that helped one to learn about more mathematics and helped me to get along well with others. In the long run it helped me in every way." The unfavorable responses were sometimes more specific. One complaint from several students was that the curriculum was repetitive. Other students simply said they did not like or did not do well in their mathematics courses. Some sample negative comments are: "I am not good at math. I don't enjoy it," "I did not enjoy doing any work, thank god it's over," and "I got much better grades but don't like math!"

Some students also commented negatively about their homework, indicating that there was too much homework or that the homework they did was not substantial. One student commented, "What I did not care for was the amount of homework we were given, it was an awful lot." Another student observed, "If I don't get my school work [done] and I have to take it home it is understandable, but just assigning a couple of pages to keep me busy at night was absurd."

CHAPTER SUMMARY

The 11-item Attitude survey reported on in this chapter refers specifically to aspects of the mathematics course that students just completed. A summary of the chapter's main findings follows.

- Of the three schools, Adams students had the most positive mean attitude scores about both Course 1 and Course 2. In Course 2 only, Jefferson students had more positive attitudes than Washington students.
- Girls and boys did not differ significantly with respect to their overall attitudes toward either Course 1 or Course 2.
- There was a significant gender-by-preachievement level interaction in attitudes toward Course 1, but not toward Course 2. In PAL 1 and PAL 3, boys were more positive about Course 1 than girls, but in PAL 2 girls were more positive than boys.
- The preachievement level effect was not significant in Course 1. In Course 2, the PAL effect was highly significant with higher PAL groups consistently having more positive attitudes than lower PAL groups.

Following the reporting of the quantitative Attitude scale results, the remainder of the chapter is a discussion of responses to the individual scale items enriched by related student comments from their written descriptions of their experiences in the mathematics course they just completed. Students tended to be somewhat positive about understanding of mathematics in the course, problem-solving and reasoning skills, skills at reading and talking about mathematics, and their level of agreement that the problems in the curriculum were realistic. Students were particularly positive about the helpfulness and enjoyment of group work and of the use of calculators. The one item with overall negative means had to do with the readability of the textbook. More students found the textbook difficult, rather than easy, to read.

There were significant preachievement level differences on many individual items. In general, students with higher preachievement levels were more positive about the content of the item. The notable exceptions to this pattern were in attitudes toward helpfulness and enjoyment of cooperative group work, especially in Course 1. Higher PAL students were less positive than lower PAL students about working in small groups. The significant gender-by-PAL interaction on the Course 1 Attitude scale was due mainly to four items: understanding the mathematics in the course, confidence in problem solving, reading mathematics, and writing mathematics.

In addition to writing about the topics in the Attitude scale items, students expressed a variety of attitudes about their teachers, more positive than negative. They also discussed their own level of effort in the course and how it related to their success or lack of success in the course. Finally, a few students mentioned other aspects of the curriculum like homework and level of challenge.

It is interesting to note that specific attitudes toward Courses 1 and 2 were positive in this study, but not as positive as they had been in the field test of this curriculum (Schoen & Pritchett, 1998). In the field test, it was not uncommon for students to make strongly positive comments about their experience in the brand new *Standards*-based curriculum as compared to their negative experiences in a conventional curriculum just a year or two before. These comments most often were about how much better the student understood mathematical ideas and their usefulness than they ever had before. In the present study, the newness of the curriculum was no longer a factor. Most of these students had experienced a *Standards*-based curriculum since sixth grade. A *Standards*-based curriculum was all that they had experienced in mathematics in their recent memory. They had generally positive attitudes about this curriculum and teaching approach, but there was no longer a novelty effect as there had been during the field test.

In the next chapter, the general Beliefs About Mathematics scales administered as part of the SBS at the end of Course 1 and Course 2 will be analyzed and discussed. The results of the Conceptions of Mathematics inventory administered at the end of Course 3 and Course 4 will also be reported. Of interest, too, is the relationship of these scales to each other and to yearly achievement measures.

NOTES

1. A caveat to this course-to-course comparison, the samples for Course 1 and Course 2 are not identical, but there is a great deal of overlap.
2. The actual item was negatively stated, "The textbook materials in this course were difficult for me to read." In order to be consistent with the other items in which "good" responses correspond to the high categories, A = 4 and SA = 5, students responses on this item were reversed. For discussion of the item responses, it is easiest to think of the item stated positively. The higher a student's score on the item, the more strongly he or she believed that the book was easy to read.

APPENDIX

1. Attitude Scale Descriptive Statistics for all Students Completing the Scale at the End of Course 1 and Course 2

	Attitude Toward Course 1 ($\alpha = .82$)			*Attitude Toward Course 2 ($\alpha = .84$)*		
Group	*N*	*Mean*	*SD*	*N*	*Mean*	*SD*
Washington	64	2.99	.827	85	2.85	.771
Adams	187	3.47	.618	225	3.57	.708
Jefferson	340	3.15	.798	374	3.06	.794
Females	322	3.21	.753	373	3.20	.783
Males	269	3.27	.784	311	3.21	.837
PAL 1	91[a]	3.23	.830	109[a]	3.42	.703
PAL 2	218	3.29	.773	254	3.27	.747
PAL 3	191	3.24	.763	221	3.17	.853
PAL 4	90	3.12	.693	85	2.90	.850
TOTAL	591	3.24	.767	684	3.20	.808

[a] A few students completed the attitude scale but no achievement scale so, there is no basis to classify them in PAL groups. Thus the PAL N-counts total 590 for Course 1 and 669 for Course 2.

Appendix continues on next page.

2. ANOVAs With *ITED-Q* With Course 1 and Course 2 Attitude Scale as Dependent Variable

School by Gender ANCOVA; Dependent Variable Course 1 Attitude Total Scores

Source	*Type III Sum of Squares*	*df*	*Mean Square*	*F*	*Sig.*
Corrected Model[a]	17.958	5	3.592	6.389	.000
Intercept	3,832.019	1	3,832.019	6,817.086	.000
SCHOOL	16.420	2	8.210	14.606	.000
GENDER	7.183E-02	1	7.183E-02	.128	.721
SCHOOL * GENDER	.440	2	.220	.392	.676
Error	328.840	585	.562		
Total	6,534.843	591			
Corrected Total	346.798	590			

[a] $R^2 = .052$ (Adjusted $R^2 = .044$)

School by Preachievement Level ANCOVA; Dependent Variable Course 1 Attitude Total Scores

Source	*Type III Sum of Squares*	*df*	*Mean Square*	*F*	*Sig.*
Corrected Model[a]	23.969	11	2.179	3.901	.000
Intercept	2,758.076	1	2,758.076	4,938.136	.000
SCHOOL	20.654	2	10.327	18.489	.000
PAL	1.743	3	.581	1.040	.374
SCHOOL * PAL	5.835	6	.972	1.741	.109
Error	322.828	578	.559		
Total	6,524.132	590			
Corrected Total	346.796	589			

[a] $R^2 = .069$ (Adjusted $R^2 = .051$)

Appendix continues on next page.

Gender by Preachievement Level ANCOVA; Dependent Variable Course 1 Attitude Total Scores

Source	*Type III Sum of Squares*	*df*	*Mean Square*	*F*	*Sig.*
Corrected Model[a]	8.004	7	1.143	1.964	.058
Intercept	5,026.816	1	5,026.816	8,635.396	.000
GENDER	1.001	1	1.001	1.720	.190
PAL	1.373	3	.458	.786	.502
GENDER * PAL	5.829	3	1.943	3.338	.019
Error	338.792	582	.582		
Total	6,524.132	590			
Corrected Total	346.796	589			

[a] R^2 = .023 (Adjusted R^2 = .011)

School by Gender ANCOVA; Dependent Variable Course 2 Attitude Total Scores

Source	*Type III Sum of Squares*	*df*	*Mean Square*	*F*	*Sig.*
Corrected Model[a]	49.618	5	9.924	17.003	.000
Intercept	4,651.074	1	4,651.074	7,969.031	.000
SCHOOL	45.516	2	22.758	38.993	.000
GENDER	5.361E-03	1	5.361E-03	.009	.924
SCHOOL * GENDER	1.411	2	.706	1.209	.299
Error	395.710	678	.584		
Total	7,458.917	684			
Corrected Total	445.329	683			

[a] R^2 = .111 (Adjusted R^2 = .105)

Appendix continues on next page.

School by Preachievement Level ANCOVA; Dependent Variable Course 2 Attitude Total Scores

Source	*Type III Sum of Squares*	*df*	*Mean Square*	*F*	*Sig.*
Corrected Model[a]	58.112	11	5.283	9.352	.000
Intercept	3,777.069	1	3,777.069	6,686.372	.000
SCHOOL	31.533	2	15.766	27.910	.000
PAL	7.067	3	2.356	4.170	.006
SCHOOL * PAL	2.815	6	.469	.830	.546
Error	371.133	657	.565		
Total	7,328.298	669			
Corrected Total	429.245	668			

[a] $R^2 = .135$ (Adjusted $R^2 = .121$)

Gender by Preachievement Level ANCOVA; Dependent Variable Course 2 Attitude Total Scores

Source	*Type III Sum of Squares*	*df*	*Mean Square*	*F*	*Sig.*
Corrected Model[a]	15.073	7	2.153	3.437	.001
Intercept	5,360.492	1	5,360.492	8,555.112	.000
GENDER	5.011E-02	1	5.011E-02	.080	.777
PAL	12.381	3	4.127	6.587	.000
GENDER * PAL	.976	3	.325	.519	.669
Error	414.172	661	.627		
Total	7,328.298	669			
Corrected Total	429.245	668			

[a] $R^2 = .035$ (Adjusted $R^2 = .025$)

Appendix continues on next page.

3. Summary of Number of Quotes by Course, Topic, and Tone

	Course 1			*Course 2*		
Topic	*Favorable*	*Neutral*	*Unfavorable*	*Favorable*	*Neutral*	*Unfavorable*
Group Work	58	15	13	72	1	14
Teacher	37	10	19	55	0	25
Realism	12	6	27	18	1	36
Prob. Solve	22	8	12	23	0	8
Calculators	11	2	9	19	2	8
Textbooks	3	7	16	2	0	27
Effort	23	18	24	14	1	10
Other	90	54	65	152	92	131
Total	256	120	185	355	97	270

CHAPTER 10

BELIEFS AND CONCEPTIONS ABOUT MATHEMATICS

Years 1–4

In addition to the Attitude scale reported in the previous chapter, the researcher-developed *Student Belief Survey* (SBS) included six scales that measured generalized beliefs about mathematics or about self in relation to mathematics. These generalized scales were administered three times: at the beginning of Year 1, at the end of Year 1, and at the end of Year 2. In order to get a somewhat different affective perspective, a second survey called *Conceptions of Mathematics Inventory* (CMI) was administered to mathematics students at the end of each of the last 2 years of high school. The CMI consists of seven scales that collectively measure the level to which a student's conceptions of mathematics and how it is learned agrees with the conceptions implicit in a *Standards*-based curriculum (Grouws, Howald, & Colangelo, 1996).

In this chapter, the results of the administrations of the SBS and CMI will be reported. The chapter begins with a description of the SBS mathematics beliefs scales and the quantitative results by school, gender, and preachievement level at each administration time. This is followed by a similar treatment of the CMI for Year 3 and Year 4. Finally, the associations

A Five-Year Study of the First Edition of the Core-Plus Mathematics Curriculum, pp. 227–265

among the scales of the two instruments and the yearly achievement measures are examined using regression analysis.

STUDENT BELIEFS ABOUT MATHEMATICS IN COURSES 1 AND 2

The six SBS scales, a total of 35 items, were administered at the beginning of Course 1, at the end of Course 1, and at the end of Course 2. The scales are named and described briefly below in descending order of the average scale score in Course 2.

- *Self-Assessment*—measures students' confidence in their mathematical ability and their intentions to complete more mathematics in high school and college. A higher score on this scale indicates greater confidence in one's mathematical ability and intentions to complete more mathematics. Example items are "I feel confident about my mathematical ability" and "I expect to take some math courses in college."
- *Creativity*—measures the extent to which students see and enjoy the creative and original side of mathematics. A higher score on this scale indicates a greater enjoyment of the creative aspects of mathematics. An example item is "Doing math allows room for original thinking and creativity."
- *Cooperation*—measures the extent to which students value cooperating with others in learning and doing mathematics. A higher score on this scale indicates a greater valuing of cooperating with others. An example item is "I feel really pleased doing math at school when we help each other solve problems."
- *Genetic*—measures the extent to which students believe that natural or genetic and gender-linked ability is the main determiner of success in mathematics. In this report, a higher score on this scale indicates stronger disagreement with a genetic view of success in mathematics. Example items are "In general, boys tend to be naturally better at math than girls" and "Math is a subject in which natural ability matters more than effort."
- *Challenge*—measures the extent to which students enjoy the challenge of mathematics as opposed to preferring that it be easy. A higher score on this scale indicates a greater enjoyment of the challenging aspects of mathematics. An example item is "I feel really pleased doing math at school when the teacher challenges me to think."

- *Competition*—measures the extent to which students enjoy the competitive aspect of mathematics, that is, they are pleased when they know more than others, finish before others, have more correct answers, and so forth. Since the curriculum under study values cooperative forms of learning over competitive ones, a higher score on this scale is defined to indicate lesser pleasure in these competition-based outcomes. An example item is "I feel really pleased doing math at school when I get more right answers than my friends." High agreement with this example item would correspond to a low score.

The scales were scored like the Attitude scale, described in Chapter 9. For a positively stated item on the SBS, 1 corresponds to "strongly disagree," 2 to "disagree," 3 to "not sure," 4 to "agree," and 5 to "strongly agree." Therefore, in the following analysis, a score of 3 can be thought of as a neutral belief, 5 as very strongly positive, and 1 as a very strongly negative belief. In the statistical analyses, scores were treated as real number data, rather than categorical data. This data treatment may increase the power of the statistical tests. In addition, many tests were run, again increasing the probability that some statistically significant results are due to chance. Most probability levels are reported in the chapter, and the reader may decide to view mean differences with probability levels greater than 0.01 with caution. In the section that follows, the results are summarized descriptively across scales and administration times. The results are then summarized for each generalized belief scale by school, gender and preachievement level (PAL) group.

Descriptive Results Across Belief Scales

Comparisons of means across scales should be considered with caution, since the scales are measuring different affective constructs. Similarly, comparisons of overall means across administration times should also be interpreted with care, as the samples are not identical. In addition, when considering either comparison—by scale or over time—keep in mind that there are many significant school, gender, and preachievement level main effects and interactions that will be presented in the next section and will add to the power to explain the findings. However, a broad descriptive look at the overall scale means will help to provide a context for the more detailed analyses of each scale by school, gender, and preachievement level to follow later. In Figure 10.1, the overall scale means are plotted for each scale at each administration time.

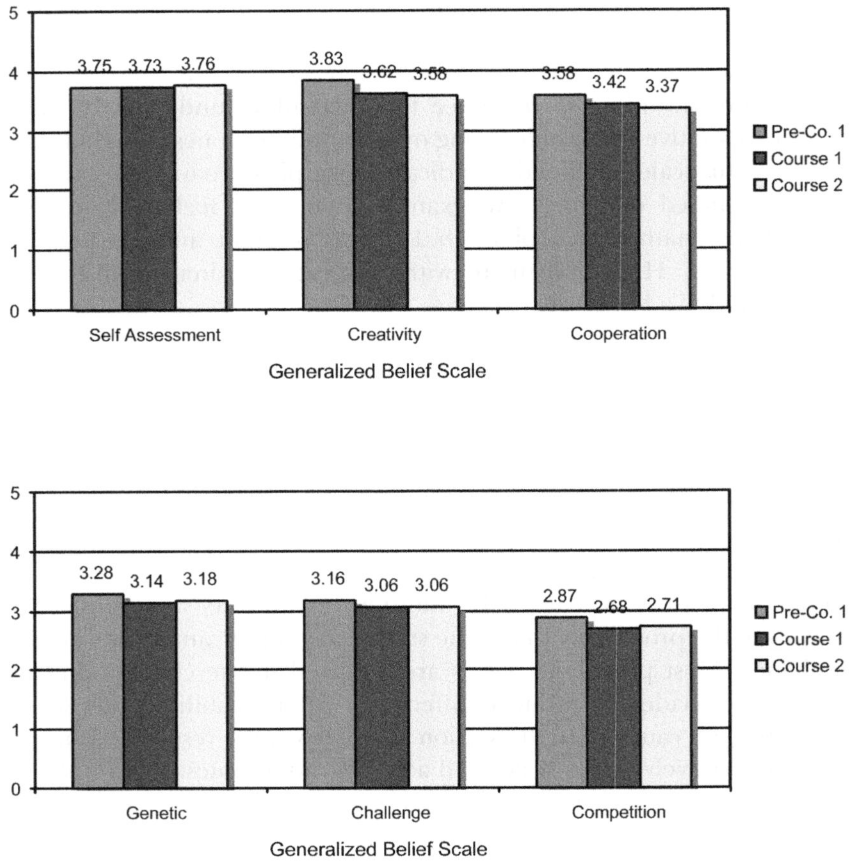

Figure 10.1. Overall Means on Each Belief Scale at Each Administration Time in Descending Order of the Course 2 Mean.

Overall, students were most positive about their assessment of their own mathematical abilities, and this assessment was stable across administration times. On the other five scales, means were higher on the Pre-Course 1 administration than at the end of either course. This result is expected as research on affect in mathematics education shows that students tend to score lower on affective measures at the end of a school year than at the beginning, and they also tend to score lower as they advance through their mathematics courses (cf. the review by McLeod, 1992).

Students were considerably more positive than the neutral response (3.0) in their view of mathematics learning as both a creative and a cooperative activity. They also tended to see mathematics learning as not strongly linked to genes or gender, although their responses were not as strongly positive as on the first two scales. Overall, students were slightly more positive than the neutral response concerning valuing the challenge of mathematics learning. The only scale for which the overall means were below the neutral score was Competition. Recall that a positive response was defined as disagreeing that competition with classmates was enjoyable or helpful. Thus the results on the Competition scale mean that students tended to consider competition in mathematics to be a good thing, and they were stronger in that opinion after each course than they had been prior to Course 1.

Another way to describe the SBS scales is to measure the strength of their associations with one another. The Pearson product-moment correlations between each pair of the six belief scales and the course Attitude scale for Course 1 and Course 2 are given in Table 10.1. The strongest association is between Cooperation and Creativity, suggesting that students who value the cooperative approach to learning and doing mathematics also appreciate the creativity involved in mathematics. The Competition scale has perhaps the most unusual pattern of association with the other scales. It is negatively associated with Self-Assessment, Creativity, and Cooperation and positively associated with the Genetic and Challenge scales. These correlations suggest that students who value the competition involved in mathematics tend to have a higher self-assessment of their mathematical ability, to value the creative aspects of mathematics, and to value cooperation in doing and learning mathematics. However, students who value the competition involved in mathematics tend not to value the challenge of

Table 10.1. Pearson Product-Moment Correlations for the Belief Scales and the Course Attitude Scale for Course 1 (N = 585) and Course 2 (N = 677)

	Self-Assess	*Creativity*	*Cooperation*	*Genetic*	*Challenge*	*Competition*
Self-Assess	–	.661[b]	.366	.146	.339	–.225
Creativity	.629[a]	–	.695	.151	.392	–.174
Cooperation	.400	.706	–	.047	.311	–.094
Genetic	.107	.057	–.096	–	.100	.148
Challenge	.278	.342	.254	.084	–	.225
Competition	–.266	–.244	–.211	.233	.246	–
Co. Attitude	.431	.622	.557	–.016	.259	–.111

[a] If $|r| > .106$ for $N = 585$, r is significant at the .01 level. If $|r| > .081$, r is significant at the .05 level. Course 1 correlations are below the diagonal.

[b] If $|r| > .099$ for $N = 677$, r is significant at the .01 level. If $|r| > .075$, r is significant at the .05 level.

mathematics (preferring for it to be easy), and they tend, relative to other students, to see mathematical ability as at least partially determined genetically and by gender.

Related to the pairwise associations of the belief scales is the question, "What do students who are positive about their experiences in Course 1 and Course 2 tend to believe about mathematics?" To answer this question, a stepwise linear regression was run for both Course 1 and Course 2 data with Course Attitude as the independent variable and the six belief scales as dependent variables entered in descending order of their pairwise correlation with Course Attitude. At each step, a dependent variable was included if $p < .05$ and excluded if $p > .10$.

In Course 1, the following regression equation predicted Course 1 Attitude with adjusted $R2 = .410$:

$$\textit{Co 1 Attitude} = .461(\textit{Creativity}) + .246(\textit{Cooperation}) + .726$$

In short, the most strongly held belief of students who liked Course 1 was that doing and learning mathematics are creative processes. Second, students who liked Course 1 valued learning mathematics cooperatively with others.

In Course 2, the prediction equation involved the same variables at the first two steps, but two other belief scales added significantly to the predictive power of the equation in steps 3 and 4 of the regression process. The following regression equation predicted Course 2 Attitude with adjusted $R^2 = .507$:

$$\textit{Co 2 Attitude} = .294(\textit{Creativity}) + .370(\textit{Cooperation}) + .245(\textit{Self-Assessment}) + .059(\textit{Competition}) - .177$$

As in Course 1, the two primary predictors of attitude toward Course 2 were Creativity and Cooperation. In addition, students who like Course 2 tended to have a relatively high assessment of their own mathematical ability, and, to a lesser extent, they did not like the competitive aspects of doing and learning mathematics.

Results by School, Gender, and PAL for Each Scale

To analyze school, gender, and PAL main effects and interactions, school-by-gender, school-by-PAL, and gender-by-PAL multiple analyses of variance were initially run with the six scales at each of the three testing times as dependent variables. If the multivariate F was significant at the .01 level, univariate ANOVAs were run with each individual scale as dependent variable. Since there are so many statistical tests, space limitations prohibit including them in this book. The statistical tables can be found at http://www.wmich.edu/cpmp/evaluation.html. In this section, the results are presented by belief scale.

Assessing One's Own Mathematical Ability. A higher score on the Self-Assessment scale indicates greater confidence in one's mathematical ability and intentions to complete more mathematics in high school and college. The Self-Assessment means did not differ significantly by gender at any of the survey administration times. The school effect was significant at the end of both Course 1 (p = .019) and Course 2 (p < .001). Means by school on Self-Assessment are displayed in Figure 10.2. At the end of both courses, Adams's mean was significantly greater than either mean of the other two schools with p < .001.

The PAL means over administration time are shown in Figure 10.3. At each administration time, students of higher preachievement levels had higher means on the Self-Assessment scale, a result that is expected. Nearly all main effect and pairwise probabilities were significant beyond the .001 level. Furthermore, mean differences by PAL increased over time, resulting in a significant time-by-PAL interaction. There were large declines over time in the mean of the PAL 4 group, coupled with increases in the means of students in the PAL 1 and PAL 2 groups.

The above results for PAL groups should be interpreted in light of a significant gender-by-PAL interaction after Course 1 (p = 0.011). As Figure 10.4 shows, in the PAL 1 group, boys had higher Self-Assessment means than girls, but the reverse was true for students who were in the PAL 2 group. This interaction was not significant at either of the other two administration times.

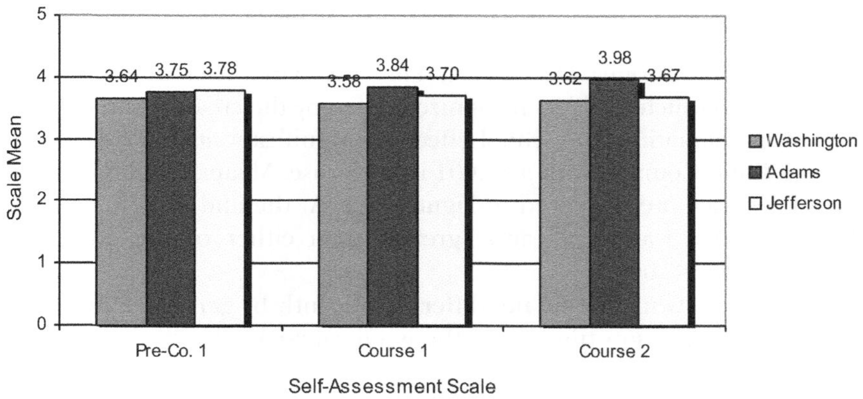

Figure 10.2. Self-Assessment Scale Means by School and Administration Time.

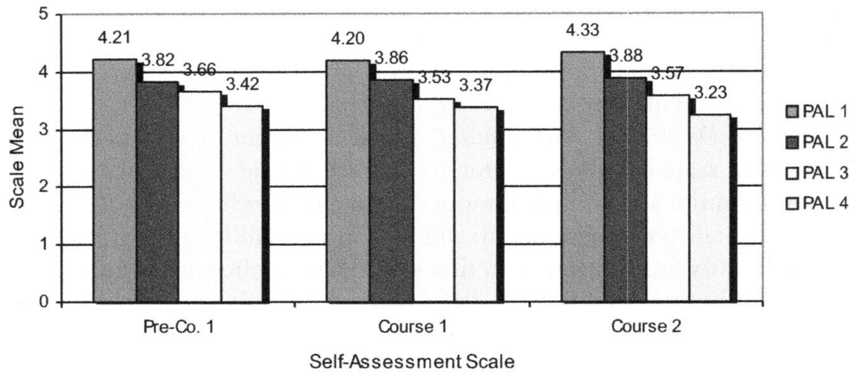

Figure 10.3. Self Assessment Scale Means by Preachievement Level and Administration Time.

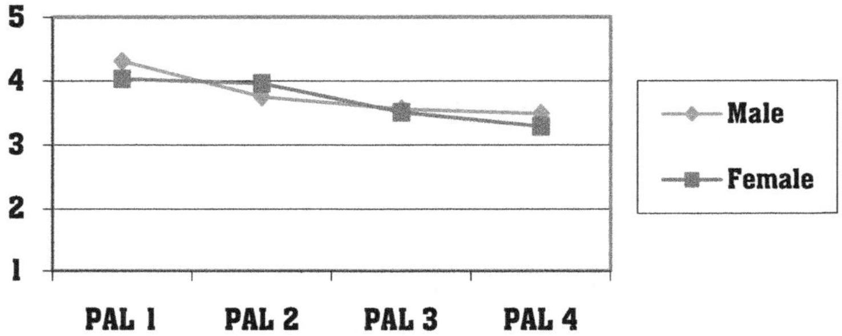

Figure 10.4. Self-Assessment Scale Means at the End of Course 1 by Gender and Pre Achievement Level.

Creativity in Learning Mathematics. The Creativity belief scale measures the extent to which students recognize and enjoy the creative and original side of mathematics. The school effect was significant at the end of both Course 1 and Course 2 with $p < .001$ in each case. Means by school on the Creativity scale are displayed in Figure 10.5. At the end of both courses, Adams's mean was significantly greater than either of the other two schools with $p < .001$.

The Creativity means did not differ significantly by gender at any of the survey administration times, and the gender-by-PAL interaction was not significant. Means by PAL and time are shown in Figure 10.6. Means on the Creativity scale aligned with students' PAL levels at each administration time, but the differences between means of adjacent PAL groups on Pre-

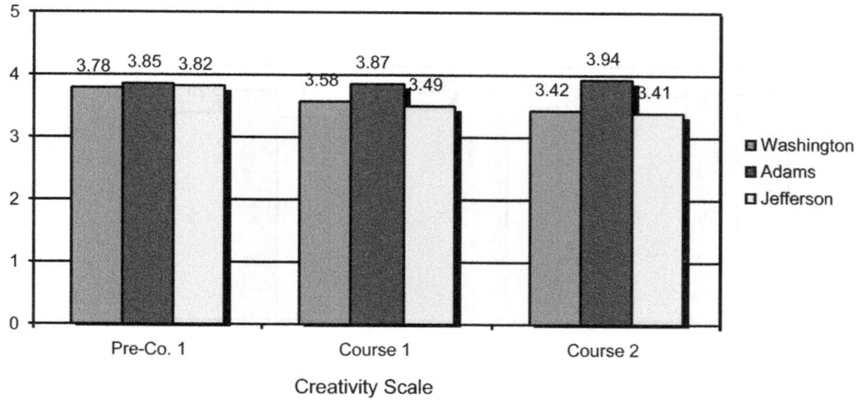

Figure 10.5. Creativity Scale Means by School and Administration Time.

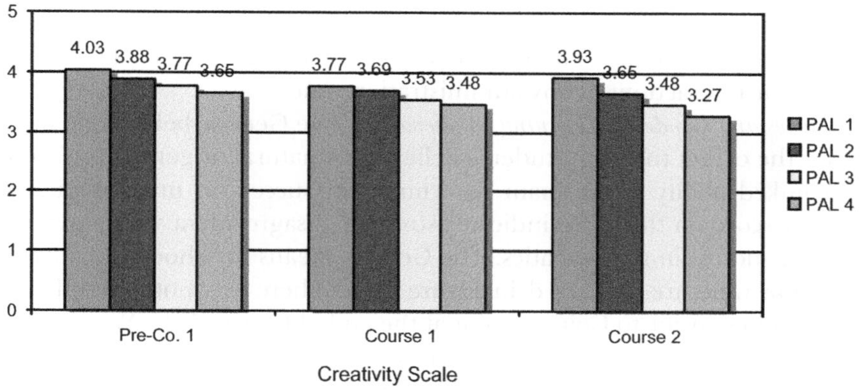

Figure 10.6. Creativity Scale Means by Preachievement Level and Administration Time

Course 1 SBS and Course 1 SBS were not large. Specifically, on both Pre-Course 1 SBS and Course 1 SBS, the PAL 1 mean was significantly greater than those of both PAL 3 and PAL 4. Following Course 2, differences in adjacent PAL group means were highly significant, with the exception of the two middle groups whose means differed at the 0.058 level.

Cooperation in Mathematics Learning. The Cooperation scale measures the extent to which students value cooperating with others in learning and doing mathematics. Higher scores on this scale indicate a greater valuing of cooperation with others. The school effect was significant at the end of both Course 1 and Course 2 ($p < .001$ at both times). Means by school on the Cooperation scale are displayed in Figure 10.7. At the end

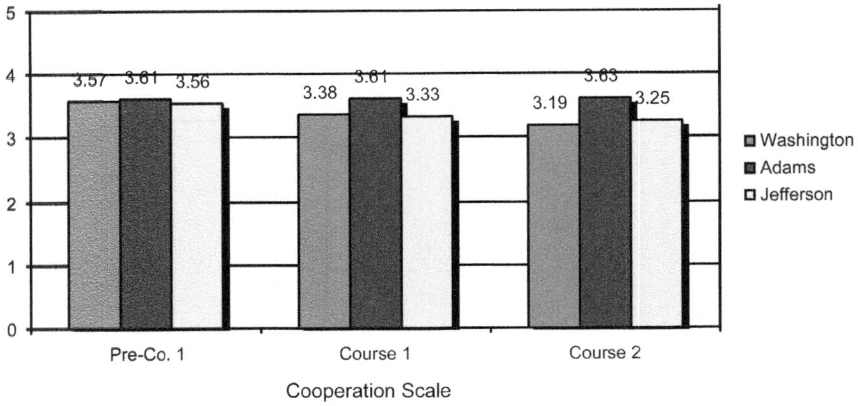

Figure 10.7. Cooperation Scale Means by School and Administration Time.

of both courses, Adams's mean was significantly greater than that of both of the other schools. There were no significant gender or PAL main effects or interactions at any administration time.

Genes and Gender in Learning Mathematics. The Genetic belief scale measures the extent to which students believe that natural or genetic and gender-linked ability is the main determiner of success in mathematics. A higher score on this scale indicates stronger disagreement with a genetic view of success in mathematics. The Genetic means by school and administration time are displayed in Figure 10.8. There was not a significant school effect prior to Course 1, but at the end of Course 1 the Washington mean was greater than that of either of the other two schools ($p < .001$). At the end of Course 2, both Washington's mean ($p < .001$) and Adams's mean ($p = .001$) were significantly greater than Jefferson's mean.

Although the multivariate gender effect on all scales was not statistically significant, the gender effect was especially strong on this scale. Male students were essentially neutral, while girls were more likely to discount the role of genetics and gender in learning mathematics. See Figure 10.9. The probability level of the difference between boys and girls at each administration of the survey is less than 0.001. The mean difference following Course 1 is particularly large, accounting for significant ordinal gender-by-time interaction ($p = 0.013$). Across all students, the mean on the Pre-Course 1 SBS was greater than that of both Course 1 and Course 2 ($p = 0.002$), but there was no significant difference between means for the latter two administrations of the Genetic scale. This change over time is much more evident for boys; girls' means decreased only slightly from one survey administration to the next.

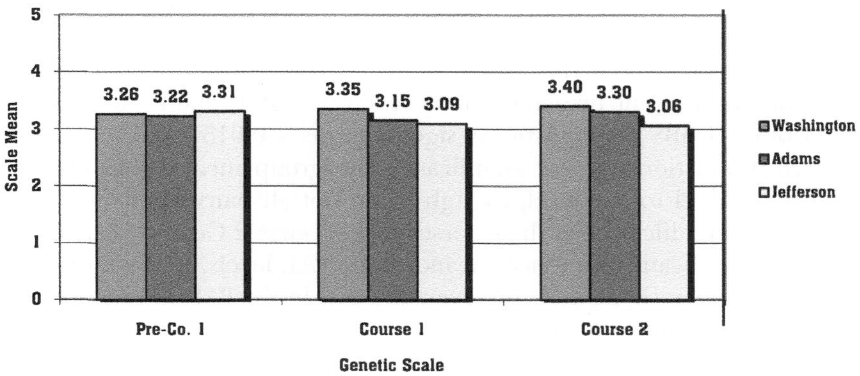

Figure 10.8. Genetic Scale Means by School and Administration Time.

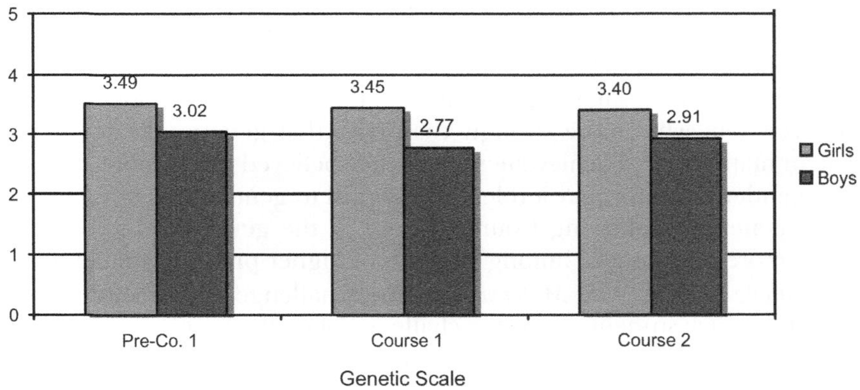

Figure 10.9. Genetic Scale Means by Gender and Administration Time.

It is also important to point out, and perhaps not surprising, that gender differences were especially evident in students' responses to the statement, "In general, boys tend to be naturally better at math than girls." Responses to this statement differed by gender beyond the .001 probability level at each administration time. Gender differences in responses to the statement, "Math is a subject in which natural ability matters more than effort," also favored girls, but at the .425, .002, and .022 probability levels before Course 1, after Course 1, and after Course 2, respectively. Girls also disagreed to a greater extent than boys to the statement, "To be good at math, you need to have a kind of mathematical mind," before Course 1 (p = 0.001) and after Course 1 (p = 0.031). At the end of Course

2, however, mean responses to this last statement were essentially identical by gender ($p = 0.947$).

As for beliefs about the role of genetics in learning mathematics for students of different preachievement levels, the PAL main effect on the Pre-Course 1 SBS was statistically significant ($p = 0.015$), and the *gender-by-PAL* interaction was not significant. The group means were ordered from high level to low level, though again not all pairwise mean differences were significant. On the Course 1 and Course 2 Genetic scale, there were no significant differences in means by PAL levels. At each of these latter administration times, however, the gender-by-PAL interaction was statistically significant (Course 1: $p = 0.018$; Course 2: $p = 0.007$).

Interestingly, though, these interactions are significant only because of responses to the first of the above statements concerning mathematics as a male domain. When responses to that item alone are analyzed, the interactions are highly significant ($p = 0.001$ after Course 1 and $p = 0.008$ after Course 2). When responses to the other two statements were analyzed separately, no gender-by-PAL interactions were statistically significant. The two interactions involving mathematics as a male domain are shown in Figure 10.10.

In short, the results suggest that at the end of both courses girls believed somewhat more strongly than boys that genetics do not play a role in mathematical achievement, and they believed much more strongly that gender does not play a role. With regard to gender (but not genetics more generally) following Courses 1 and 2, the gender differences are much more pronounced among students of higher preachievement level.

Challenge in Learning Mathematics. The Challenge scale measures the extent to which students enjoy the challenge of mathematics as opposed to preferring that it be easy. The higher the score on this scale, the more the student enjoys challenge in learning mathematics. The school effect was significant at the end of both Course 1 ($p = .018$) and Course 2 ($p = .002$). Means by school on the Challenge scale are displayed in Figure 10.11. At

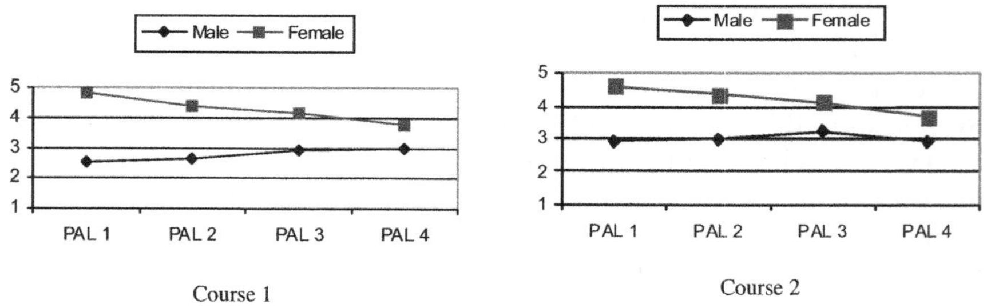

Figure 10.10. Mean Responses to the Math as a Male Domain Statement at the End of Course 1 and Course 2 by Gender and Preachievement Level.

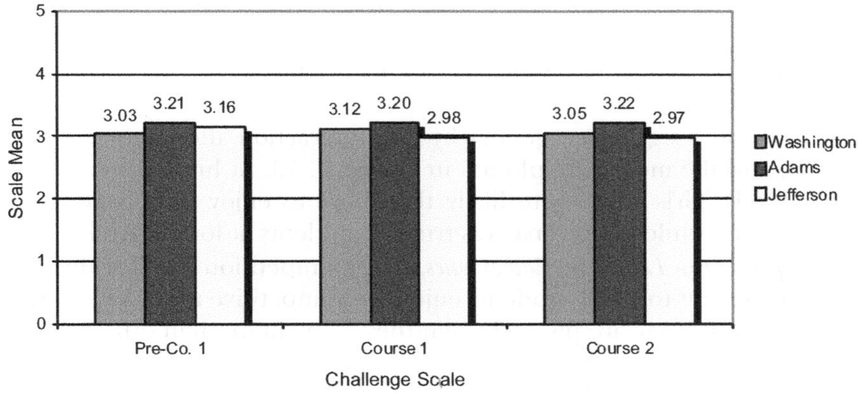

Figure 10.11. Challenge Scale Means by School and Administration Time.

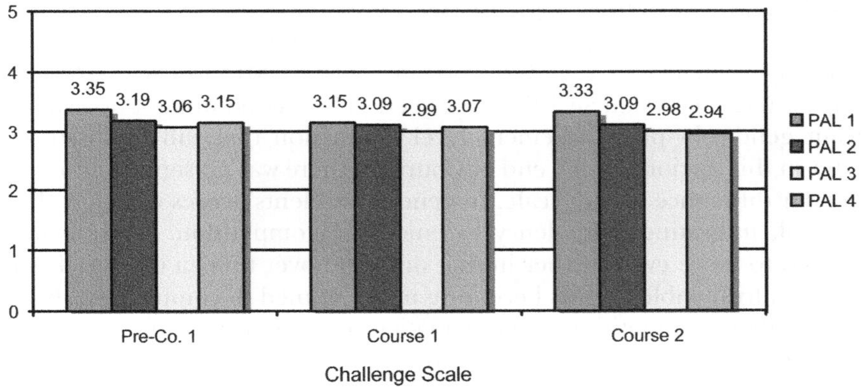

Figure 10.12. Challenge Scale Means by Preachievement Level and Administration Time.

the end of both courses, Adams's mean was significantly greater than Jefferson's, but none of the other pairs of school means differed significantly.

The Challenge means did not differ significantly by *gender* at any of the survey administration times. Means on this scale for preachievement level groups over time are shown in Figure 10.12 above. The PAL main effect is significant at Pre-Course 1 SBS ($p = 0.045$) and at the end of Course 2 ($p = 0.002$), but not at the end of Course 1. The *gender*-by-*PAL* interaction is not significant at Pre-Course 1 SBS or after Course 2, so the PAL mean differences can be interpreted directly. At Pre-Course 1 SBS, the PAL 1 mean is significantly greater than that of PAL 3 ($p = 0.005$), and other pairwise mean differences are not significant. After Course 2, the PAL 1 mean is significantly greater than PAL 2 ($p = 0.005$), PAL 3 ($p = 0.001$), and PAL 4 ($p = 0.003$). Other pairwise mean differences are not statistically significant.

There was a significant gender-by-PAL interaction after Course 1 ($p = 0.001$), and the means are plotted in Figure 10.13. At higher preachievement levels, girls were more likely than boys to enjoy the challenge of mathematics while the reverse was true for students at lower PAL levels.

Competition in Learning Mathematics. The Competition belief scale measures the extent to which students enjoy the competitive aspects of mathematics, that is, they are pleased when they know more than others, finish before others, have more right answers, and so on. A higher score on this scale is defined to indicate lesser pleasure in these competition-based outcomes. On the Competition scale, there were no significant interactions involving school and no significant differences by school at any of the administration times. Concerning the gender variable, gender means are displayed in Figure 10.14.

Male students indicated more enjoyment of the competitive aspects of learning mathematics at both the beginning ($p < .001$) and end of Course 1 ($p = .042$). The Course 1 findings need to be viewed in light of a significant gender-by-preachievement level interaction that will be discussed later in this section. By the end of Course 2, there was no significant mean gender difference on this scale. In general, students' scores were less than neutral, indicating a tendency to enjoy the competition. Their beliefs tended to move even further in that direction over time, a change that is mainly attributable to girls becoming more attuned to competition. Boys' beliefs about competition in mathematics were about the same at the end of Course 2 as they had been prior to Course 1.

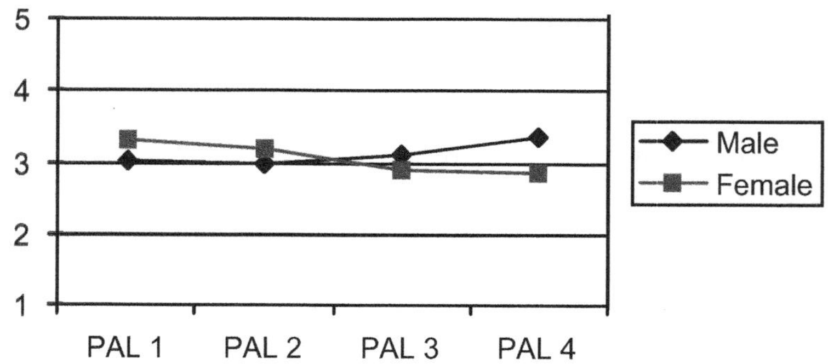

Figure 10.13. Challenge Scale Means at the End of Course 1 by Gender and Preachievement Level.

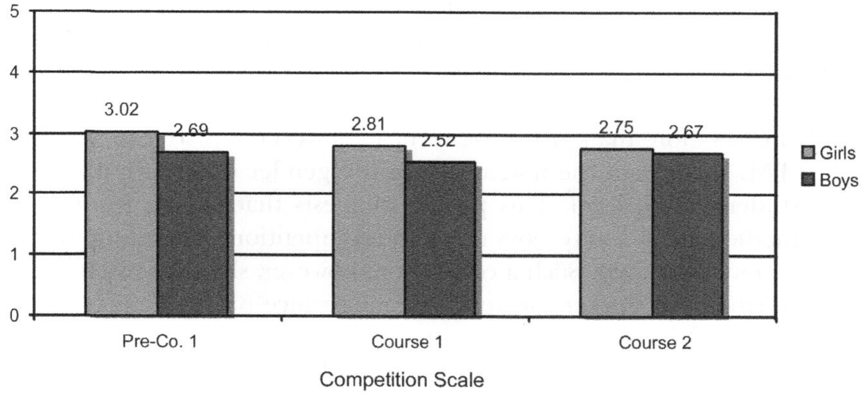

Figure 10.14. Competition Scale Means by Gender and Administration Time.

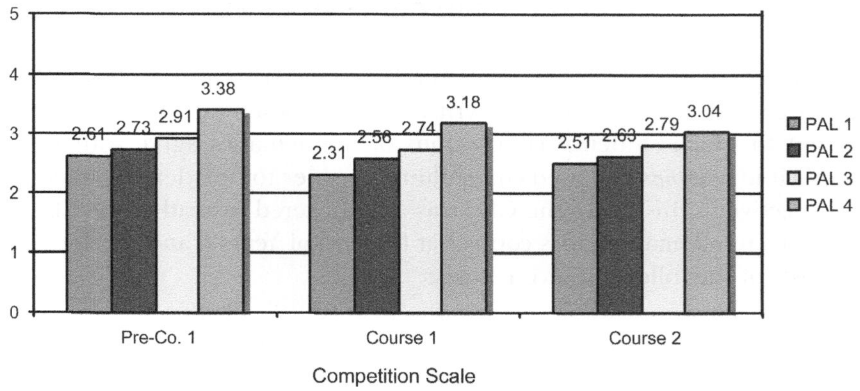

Figure 10.15. Competition Scale Means by Preachievement Level and Administration Time.

As for beliefs about competition in learning mathematics for students of different preachievement levels, the time-by-PAL interaction was not statistically significant, so means over time are directly interpretable. As Figure 10.15 above shows, means on the Competition scale tended to align in reverse order with the PAL groups, that is, students in higher preachievement levels tended to see competition in learning mathematics in a more positive light. The probability levels of the pairwise differences in PAL group means are omitted here, but the trend is clear from the plot.

The above results for gender and PAL levels should be interpreted in light of the fact that the gender-by-PAL interaction was statistically significant after Course 1 ($p = 0.011$). As Figure 10.16 shows, on average, at the low preachievement level (PAL 4), boys disliked competition in learning mathematics more than girls. The reverse, however, was true at the other three PAL levels, and the magnitude of the gender difference increased with students' PAL level. This pattern suggests that among students of high mathematical ability, boys enjoy the competition of learning mathematics more than girls. Such a conclusion, however, should be stated with caution since this interaction reached significance on the Course 1 SBS survey only. The same trend, but not approaching statistical significance, appeared on the Pre-Course 1 ($p = 0.201$) and the Course 2 survey data ($p = 0.218$).

STUDENTS' CONCEPTIONS OF MATHEMATICS IN COURSES 3 AND 4

The Conceptions of Mathematics Inventory (CMI) (Grouws, Howald, & Colangelo, 1996) is a 56-item written survey designed to measure the extent to which students' conceptions of mathematics agree with those implicit in a *Standards*-based curriculum. In order to broaden the affective perspective in this study, the CMI was administered instead of the SBS to students in all mathematics courses at the end of Years 3 and 4. The CMI consists of the following seven scales:

- *Usefulness of Mathematics*—measures the extent to which students find mathematics to be a worthwhile tool for use in their future

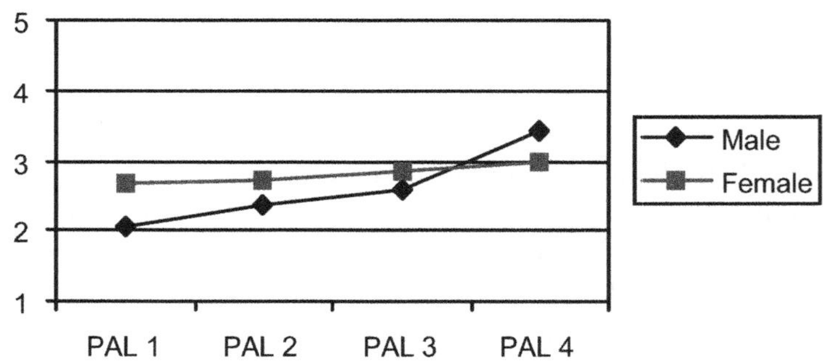

Figure 10.16. Competition Scale Means at the End of Course 1 by Gender and Preachievement Level.

lives. Students with a lower score on this scale believe that mathematics will not be pertinent to their lives outside of school. The following is an example item indicating such a belief: "Taking mathematics is a waste of time." Students with a higher score on this scale believe that mathematics will be useful in their future careers and activities outside of school. The following is an example item indicating such a belief: "I will use mathematics in many ways as an adult."

- *Structure of Mathematical Knowledge*—measures the extent to which students believe that mathematics consists of connected topics and relationships between ideas. Students with a lower score on this scale have a stronger belief that diagrams and graphs do not relate to operations or equations, problems are not usually related to one another, and different mathematical topics have little in common. The following is an example item indicating such a belief: "Finding solutions to one type of mathematics problem cannot help you solve other types of problems." Students with a higher score on this scale have a stronger belief that one concept can explain a variety of formulas, that ideas in one mathematics class can be used in other mathematics classes, and that most mathematical ideas are related. The following is an example item indicating such a belief: "Mathematics is mostly thinking about relationships among things such as numbers, points, and lines."
- *Doing Mathematics*—measures the extent to which students believe that solving mathematics problems is a process that could be reasoned through or made sense of through problem solving. Students with a lower score on this scale believed that knowing formulas is the key to solving mathematics problems. The following is an example item indicating such a belief: "If you knew every possible formula, then you could easily solve any mathematical problem." Students with a higher score on this scale believe that understanding concepts and ideas and relating different parts of mathematics is the key to solving mathematics problems. The following is an example item indicating such a belief: "When working mathematics problems, it is important that what you are doing makes sense to you."
- *Validating Ideas in Mathematics*—measures the extent to which students believe that they themselves can be an intellectual authority in the classroom. Students with a lower score believe that teachers or textbooks are the only way to know if a solution is correct or flawed. The following is an example item indicating such a belief: "In mathematics, the teacher has the answer and it is the student's job to

figure it out." Students with a higher score believe that students can work individually or work collaboratively with other students to confirm the strength of a solution and that multiple solution methods are possible. The following is an example item indicating such a belief: "When your method of solving a problem is different from your teacher's method, your method can be as correct as your teacher's."

- *Status of Mathematical Knowledge*—measures the extent to which students believe mathematics is still an evolving and growing field of study. Students with a lower score on this scale believe that mathematics is a fixed and unchanging subject. The following is an example item indicating such a belief: "When you do an exploration in mathematics, you can discover something already known." Students with a higher score on this scale believe that mathematics is an area where people are still making new discoveries and that learning new mathematics can change the way people think about old mathematics. The following is an example item indicating such a belief: "Students can make new mathematical discoveries, as well as study mathematicians' discoveries."
- *Learning Mathematics*—measures the extent to which students believe that learning mathematics is about memorizing formulas and emulating similar example problems. Students with a lower score on this scale believe that students learn mathematics by being shown how to do individual problems and by memorizing steps in a process. The following is an example item indicating such a belief: "Learning mathematics involves memorizing information presented to you." Students with a higher score on this scale believe that students learn mathematics by asking questions, analyzing mistakes, and thinking carefully about mathematical relationships. The following is an example item indicating such a belief: "Memorizing formulas and steps is not that helpful for learning how to solve mathematical problems."
- *Composition of Mathematical Knowledge*—measures the extent to which students believe that mathematical knowledge is about the connections between ideas and concepts as opposed to knowing procedures and facts. Students with a lower score on this scale believe that mathematics is more about knowing what rules to follow and the manipulation of symbols instead of working with ideas. The following is an example item indicating such a belief: "There is always a rule to follow when solving a mathematical problem." Students with a higher score on this scale believe that mathematics is more about problem solving than computation and that although

formulas are important, the ideas behind the formula are more important. The following is an example item indicating such a belief: "Mathematical knowledge consists mainly of ideas and concepts and the connections among them."

The scoring of the CMI is slightly different from the SBS. For an item on the CMI, a response of 1 corresponds to a "strongly disagree," 2 to "disagree," 3 to "slightly disagree," 4 to "slightly agree," 5 to "agree," and 6 to "strongly agree." Unlike SBS items, students do not have the option of a "neutral" choice. On average, though, a neutral score would correspond to a mean across scale items of 3.5. In the section that follows, the data are treated like the data from the SBS scales. The results are summarized descriptively across scales and administration time, the descriptive statistics and associations by CMI scale are presented, and the results by school, gender, and PAL group are summarized. In addition, Course 3 CMI scale results are correlated with the Course 2 SBS scales over the intersecting sample of students in order to provide a descriptive link between the SBS and the CMI.

Descriptive Results Across CMI Scales

As was true of the SBS belief scales, comparisons of means across scales should be considered with caution, since the scales are measuring somewhat different affective constructs. Similarly, overall means across administration times should also be compared with care, as the samples are not identical. In Year 4 especially, it is important to differentiate between students in Course 4 and those in AP Calculus or AP Statistics courses. In addition, when considering either comparison—by scale or over time—keep in mind that there are many significant school, gender, and preachievement level main effects and interactions that will be presented in the next section and will add to the power to explain the findings. However, a broad descriptive look at the overall scale means will help to provide a context for the more detailed analyses of each scale by school, gender, and preachievement level to follow later. In Figure 10.17, the overall scale means are plotted for each scale at the end of each course.

Overall, students were most positive about the usefulness of mathematics, the structure of mathematical knowledge, and doing mathematics. Students tended to believe that mathematics will be useful in their future careers and activities outside of school. They tended to have a strong belief that one concept can explain a variety of formulas, that ideas in one mathematics class can be used in other mathematics classes, and that most mathematical ideas are related. Students also tended to

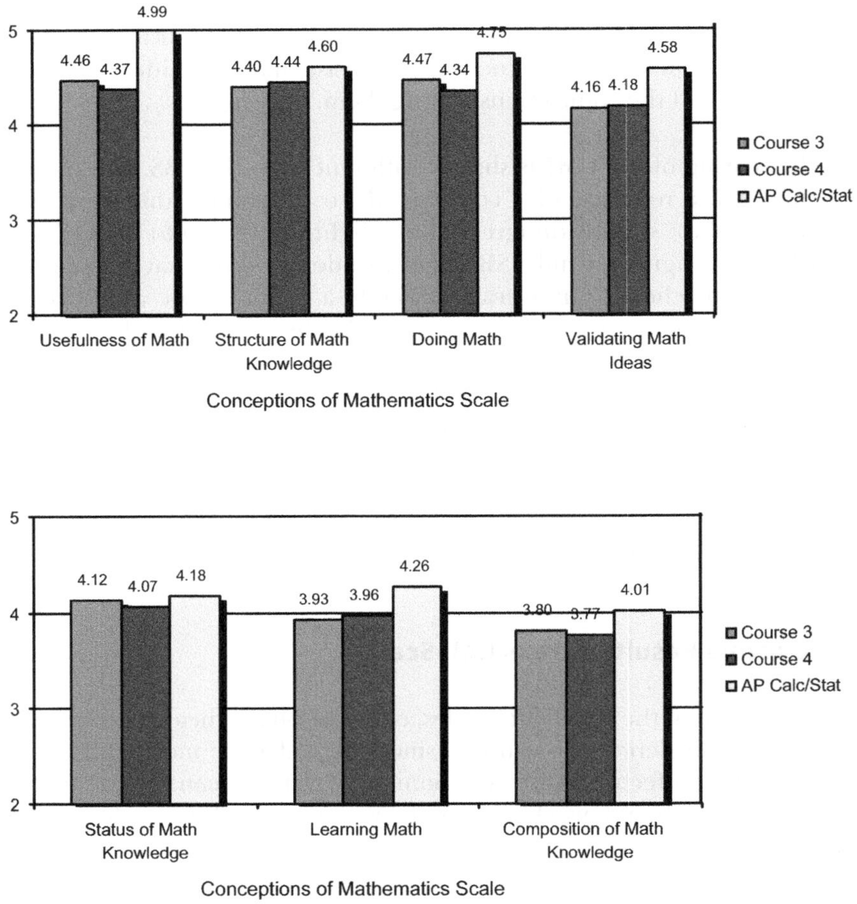

Figure 10.17. Overall Means on Each CMI Scale at the End of Each Course in Descending Order of the Course 4 Mean.

believe that understanding concepts and ideas and relating different parts of mathematics is the key to solving mathematics problems. Means on all scales were essentially the same for Course 3 students as compared to Course 4 students, but means for students in AP Calculus or AP Statistics were considerably higher than the other two course groups on all scales. This result is expected and is largely due to the fact that AP students, on average, have a higher mathematical aptitude and achievement level than students in either Course 3 or Course 4.

Students were considerably more positive than the neutral response (3.5) on all CMI scales. The lowest mean score of 3.80 was on the

Composition of Mathematical Knowledge. Students tended to believe that mathematics is more about problem solving than computation and that although formulas are important, the ideas behind the formula are more important. However, this conception was not as strongly agreed upon as the constructs measured by the other CMI scales.

Another way to describe the CMI scales is to measure the strength of their associations with one another. The Pearson product-moment correlations between each pair of the seven CMI scales for Course 3 and Course 4 (including AP Calculus and AP Statistics students) are given in Table 10.2. All correlations are positive and highly significant. Correlations greater than .500 are generally found among the following scales: Usefulness of Mathematics, Structure of Mathematics, Validating Mathematical Ideas, Doing Mathematics, and Learning Mathematics. Doing Mathematics and Validating Mathematical Ideas were also very highly correlated with Composition of Mathematical Knowledge. These high correlations indicate that the scales are measuring similar constructs.

The next analysis will help to explain the nature of what is measured, as will the later analysis that relates CMI scales to yearly achievement outcomes. A sample of 383 students completed both the SBS at the end of Course 2 and the CMI at the end of Course 3. Correlations within this sample of the Course 2 belief scales and the Course 3 Conception scales are presented in Table 10.3. Using $r = .300$ as a somewhat arbitrary criterion, it is clear from the table that the Cooperation, Competition, and Genetic scales in Course 2 were not highly correlated to any of the Course 3 Conceptions scales. Evidently, the affective construct measured by each of these scales is substantially different from that measured by any of the

Table 10.2. Pearson Product-Moment Correlations for the CMI Scales for Course 3 (N = 450) and Course 4 (N = 192)

	Use of Math	*Structure Math Knowledge*	*Doing Math*	*Validating Math Ideas*	*Status of Math*	*Learning Math*	*Composition of Math Knowledge*
Use of Math[a]	–	.499	.442	.382	.374	.314	.307
Struct Math Kn	.502	–	.661	.575	.421	.504	.455
Doing Math	.463	.543	–	.631	.458	.540	.496
Val Math Ideas	.488	.594	.605	–	.489	.556	.422
Status of Math	.208	.231	.288	.295	–	.390	.331
Learning Math	.385	.475	.507	.566	.302	–	.528
Comp Math Kn	.339	.318	.439	.410	.245	.493	–

[a] All correlations in the table are statically significant beyond the .01 level. Course 1 correlations are below the diagonal.

Table 10.3. Pearson Product-Moment Correlations for the CMI Scales for Course 3 and the SBS Scales for Course 2 (N =383)

	Use of Math	*Structure Math Knowledge*	*Doing Math*	*Validating Math Ideas*	*Status of Math*	*Learning Math*	*Composition of Math Knowledge*
Self Assess[a]	.390	.365	.211	.392	.025	.267	.179
Creativity	.393	.415	.281	.381	.106	.293	.146
Cooperation	.230	.230	.183	.180	.138	.153	.029
Genetic	.132	.240	.235	.173	.142	.238	.209
Challenge	.317	.313	.275	.253	.169	.329	.191
Competition	.015	.048	.114	−.030	.145	.113	.072
Co. Attitude	.278	.338	.141	.222	.062	.186	.110

[a] If $|r| > .131$, r is significant at the .01 level. If $.130 > |r| > .099$, r is significant at the .05 level, but not at .01.

Course 3 CMI scales. Similarly, the following Course 3 Conceptions of Mathematics scales appear to be measuring substantially different constructs than any of the Course 2 belief scales: Doing Mathematics, Status of Mathematical Knowledge, and Composition of Mathematical Knowledge.

Again using $r = .300$ as criterion, the following relatively strong associations can be seen in the table:

- Students with high assessments of their own mathematical ability in Course 2 tended, in Course 3, to believe that mathematics will be useful in their future careers and activities outside of school, that one concept can explain a variety of formulas, that ideas in one mathematics class can be used in other mathematics classes, that most mathematical ideas are related, and that students can work individually or work collaboratively with other students to confirm the strength of a solution and that multiple solution methods are possible.
- Students who valued the creative aspects of mathematics in Course 2 can be described in the same terms relative to the Course 3 Conceptions scales as those who were high on the Self-Assessment scale.
- Students who valued the challenging aspects of mathematics in Course 2 tended, in Course 3, to believe that mathematics will be useful in their future careers and activities outside of school; that one concept can explain a variety of formulas; that ideas in one mathematics class can be used in other mathematics classes; that most mathematical ideas are related; and that students learn math-

ematics by asking questions, analyzing mistakes, and thinking carefully about mathematical relationships.

- Students who had a positive attitude about Course 2 tended, in Course 3, to believe that one concept can explain a variety of formulas, that ideas in one mathematics class can be used in other mathematics classes, and that most mathematical ideas are related.

Results by School, Gender, and Preachievement Level

To analyze school, gender, and PAL main effects and interactions, school-by-gender, school-by-PAL, and gender-by-PAL multiple analyses of variances were initially run with the seven CMI scales at each survey administration time as dependent variables. Recall that there are just three levels of PAL in Courses 3 and 4: PAL 1—students who scored at or above the 90th percentile on the *ITED-Q* pretest; PAL 2—students who scored from the 67th to the 90th percentile; and PAL 3—students who scored at or below the 66th percentile. To avoid the confounding variable of course taken, the sample in Year 4 was restricted to students enrolled in Course 4.

If the multivariate F was significant at the .01 level, univariate ANOVAs were run with each individual scale as dependent variable. Since there are so many statistical tests, space limitations prohibit including them in this book. The statistical tables can be found at http://www.wmich.edu/cpmp/evaluation.html. No two-way multivariate interactions were statistically significant, so all statistically significant main effects are discussed separately. Since the Conceptions scales are so highly correlated, the results are presented on all scales first by school, then by gender, and finally by PAL.

Results by School. The multivariate school main effect was significant with $p < .007$ at the end of each course. Furthermore, the univariate F was statistically significant for each scale at each testing time with probability level ranging from $p < .001$ to $p = .008$. In general, scale means of Washington and Adams were higher than those of Jefferson, and on some scales Adams's mean was also higher than Washington's. Pairwise school mean comparisons and their probability levels are summarized in Table 10.4. Students from Adams scored highest on nearly every scale at the end of both Courses 3 and 4. However, the difference between Adams and Washington reached significance on only 3 of the 14 scale mean comparisons with probability levels between .03 and .05, and in each case the significant difference on a scale in 1 year was matched by no significant difference on the same scale in the other year. Thus there are no

Table 10.4. Directions and Probability Levels of Pairwise Comparisons of Washington (W), Adams (A), and Jefferson (J) Means by Conceptions Scale and Time of Administration

Scale	*Course*	*W vs A (p-level)*	*W vs J (p-level)*	*A vs J (p-level)*
Usefulness of Mathematics	3	NSD	W > J (.006)	A > J (.033)
	4	NSD	W > J (.003)	A > J (.009)
Structure of Math Knowledge	3	A > W (.034)	NSD	A > J (< .001)
	4	NSD	W > J (.001)	A > J (< .001)
Doing Mathematics	3	NSD	W > J (< .001)	A > J (< .001)
	4	NSD	W > J (.003)	A > J (< .001)
Validity of Mathematical Ideas	3	NSD	NSD	A > J (< .001)
	4	A > W (.030)	W > J (.023)	A > J (< .001)
Status of Math Knowledge	3	NSD	NSD	A > J (.003)
	4	NSD	W > J (.049)	A > J (< .001)
Learning Mathematics	3	NSD	W > J (.025)	A > J (< .001)
	4	A > W (.049)	NSD	A > J (< .001)
Composition of Math Knowledge	3	NSD	W > J (.001)	A > J (.005)
	4	NSD	W > J (< .001)	A > J (< .001)

consistently significant differences between the means of Washington and Adams on any of the CMI scales.

On three of the scales (Usefulness of Mathematics, Doing Mathematics, and Composition of Mathematical Knowledge), Washington's students were significantly more positive than those from Jefferson in both years. On the other four scales, Washington's mean was significantly greater than Jefferson's at one administration of the scale, and there was no significant difference in means at the other administration. Washington's superiority was more consistent in Course 4 than in Course 3, as evidenced by the fact that just one (Learning Mathematics) of the four nonsignificant mean differences was in Course 4. All four nonsignificant differences also favored Washington.

The comparisons of the scale means of Adams and Jefferson were very strongly and consistently in favor of Adams. Students from Adams were significantly more positive than those from Jefferson on both administrations of all seven scales. In 10 of the 14 comparisons, the difference was beyond the .001 probability level. In all but one comparison, the difference in means was beyond the .01 level.

Results by Gender. The multivariate gender main effect was statistically significant ($p > .001$) in Course 3 but not in Course 4, so the analysis here is restricted to Course 3 data. On the univariate tests of individual Course 3 scales, the gender effect was significant at the .05 level on four of the seven scales: Structure of Mathematical Knowledge ($p = .001$), Doing Mathematics ($p = .011$), Learning Mathematics ($p = .002$), and Composition of Mathematical Knowledge ($p = .042$). The means by gender on these scales are presented in Figure 10.18. As the figure shows, differences favored boys on the Structure of Mathematical Knowledge scale, and girls had higher means on the other three scales.

To interpret these results, at the end of Course 3 boys had a stronger belief than girls that one concept can explain a variety of formulas, that ideas in one mathematics class can be used in other mathematics classes, and that most mathematical ideas are related. Girls had a stronger belief than boys that understanding concepts and ideas and relating different parts of mathematics is the key to solving mathematics problems. Girls also had a stronger belief than boys that students learn mathematics by asking questions, analyzing mistakes, and thinking carefully about mathematical relationships. Finally, girls believed more strongly than boys that mathematics is more about problem solving than computation and that although formulas are important, the ideas behind the formula are more important. By the end of Course 4, the conceptions of mathematics of girls and boys did not differ significantly.

Results by Preachievement Levels. Like the gender effect, the multivariate PAL main effect was statistically significant ($p > .001$) in Course 3 but not in Course 4, so the analysis here is restricted to Course 3 data. On the

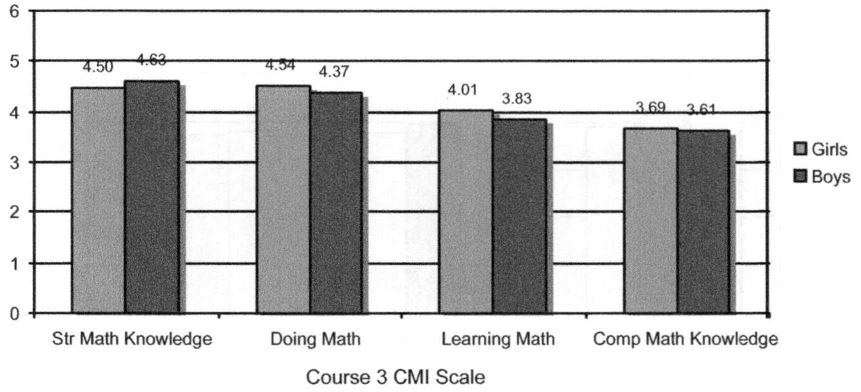

Figure 10.18. Means by Gender on the Course 3 Scales With Statistically Significant Mean Differences.

univariate tests of individual Course 3 scales, the PAL effect was significant at the .05 level on six of the seven scales, the only exception being the Status of Mathematical Knowledge scale. Of the six other scales, the PAL effect was significant at the .006 level on Doing Mathematics and beyond the .001 level on the remaining five scales. The means by PAL group on the six scales with significant differences are presented in Figure 10.19.

Pairwise PAL group mean comparisons and their probability levels are summarized in Table 10.5. Students in the PAL 1 group, that is, the high preachievement level, scored highest on each of these six scales at the end of Course 3. However, the difference between PAL 1 and PAL 2 reached significance on just two of the six scale mean comparisons. Keeping in mind that the PAL effect was not significant in Course 4, it seems reasonable to conclude there are no consistently significant differences between the means of the PAL 1 and PAL 2 groups on any of the CMI scales.

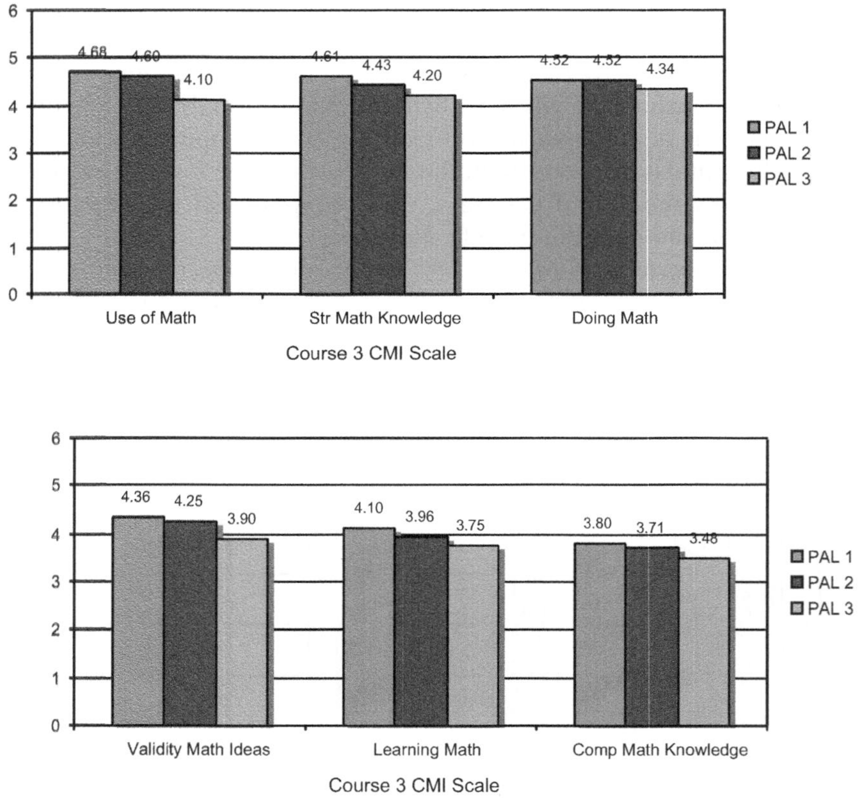

Figure 10.19. Means by Preachievement Level on the Course 3 Scales With Statistically Significant Mean Differences.

Table 10.5. Directions and Probability Levels of Pairwise Comparisons of PAL 1, PAL 2, and Pal 3 Means by Course 3 Conceptions Scale

Scale	*P1 vs P2 (p-level)*	*P1 vs P3 (p-level)*	*P2 vs P3 (p-level)*
Usefulness of Mathematics	NSD	P1 > P3 (< .001)	P2 > P3 (< .001)
Structure of Mathematical Knowledge	P1 > P2 (.006)	P1 > P3 (< .001)	P2 > P3 (.001)
Doing Mathematics	NSD	P1 > P3 (.006)	P2 > P3 (.004)
Validity of Mathematical Ideas	NSD	P1 > P3 (< .001)	P2 > P3 (< .001)
Learning Mathematics	P1 > P2 (.023)	P1 > P3 (< .001)	P2 > P3 (.001)
Composition of Mathematical Knowledge	NSD	P1 > P3 (< .001)	P2 > P3 (< .001)

Clearly, in Course 3 students in the lowest preachievement level were much less positive than those in the two higher groups on all six scales. The differences are so large that it may at first seem difficult to explain why they disappeared in Course 4. The most likely explanation is that the number and percent of students in the PAL 3 group decreased dramatically from Course 3 to Course 4. In Course 3, 134 of 436 students (30.7%) in the gender–by-PAL analysis were in PAL 3. By the end of Course 4, this number had gone down to 27 of 145 PAL 3 students (18.6%). Considering that the PAL 1 and PAL 2 students did not differ much on the CMI scales in Course 3, and the PAL 3 group size was greatly reduced in Course 4, the nonsignificant PAL effect in Course 4 is perhaps less surprising than it may seem at first.

RELATING MATHEMATICAL BELIEFS AND CONCEPTIONS TO ACHIEVEMENT

Having analyzed mathematical affective and achievement outcomes at the end of each year of high school, a natural and interesting question arises. "What do students who achieve better than expected in Courses 1, 2, 3, and 4 tend to believe about mathematics?" To answer this question, linear regression equations were constructed with *ITED-Q* pretest scores as independent variable and each of the five main achievement measures as dependent variables. Using these prediction equations, a residual score (actual score minus predicted score) was computed for each student on each achievement measure. The residual score is a measure of a student's actual achievement score as compared to the achievement score predicted by his or her ITED-Q pretest score. Finally, a stepwise linear regression was run with the residual scores for each of the achievement total scores as the independent variable. The dependent variables in Years 1 and 2 are the seven SBS scales for Courses 1 and 2, and the dependent variables in Years 3 and 4 are the seven CMI scales in Courses 3 and 4. In each regression analysis, the dependent variables were entered in descending order of their pairwise correlation with the independent variable. At each step, a dependent variable was included if $p < .05$ and excluded if $p > .10$. Regression tables can be found in the Chapter 10 Appendix, Parts 2 and 4. The resulting equations are presented below.

In Course 1, the independent variable is the *ITED-Q* posttest residual score. The following regression equation predicted the Course 1 *ITED-Q* posttest standard score with adjusted $R^2 = .053$:

$$\textit{Co 1 ITED-Q Residual} = 8.9(\textit{Self-Assessment}) - 32.7$$

Students who did better than expected on the *ITED-Q* posttest saw themselves as good mathematics students. No other belief scale contributed significantly to this prediction, and the above equation explains only about 5% of the variance in the residual score.

In Course 2, the independent variable is the residual total score on the End of Year Algebra Examination (EoC). The following regression equation predicted the EoC residual with adjusted $R^2 = .089$:

$$\textit{Co 2 EoC Residual} = 4.4(\textit{Self-Assessment}) + 1.8(\textit{Challenge}) - 1.9(\textit{Cooperation}) - 15.1$$

As in Course 1, the primary predictor of the residual score is Self-Assessment. In addition, students who did well on the EoC tended to value the challenge of mathematics and to dislike learning mathematics cooperatively. However, this equation is a weak predictor explaining about 9% of the variance in the EoC residual scores.

In Course 3, the independent variable is the residual of the total score on the TIMSS-based mathematical literacy test (Math Lit) and the predictors are the seven CMI scales. The following regression equation predicted the mathematical literacy residual score with adjusted $R^2 = .033$:

$$\textit{Co 3 Math Lit Residual} = 4.5(\textit{Doing Math}) - 19.8$$

In general, the CMI scales were not strong predictors of the mathematical literacy residual score explaining a little more than 3% of the variance. To interpret the equation, students who did better than expected on the mathematical literacy test tended to have stronger beliefs that understanding concepts and ideas and relating different parts of mathematics is the key to solving mathematics problems. No other CMI scale contributed significantly to the prediction of the mathematical literacy residual score.

In Course 4, two regression analyses were run, with residual score for the TIMSS-based advanced mathematics test (Co 4 Adv Math) and the Course 4 reasoning test (Co 4 Reas) as respective independent variables. In each analysis, the predictors are the seven CMI scales. Student data were restricted to students in Course 4 only, excluding students in AP Calculus or AP Statistics. The following regression equation predicted the advanced mathematics residual score with adjusted $R^2 = .036$:

$$\textit{Co 4 Adv Math Residual} = 4.2(\textit{Learning Math}) - 15.9$$

Students who did better than expected on the TIMSS advanced mathematics test tended to have stronger beliefs about Learning Mathematics (thinking carefully, asking questions, and so on). No other scale was a significant predictor of scores on this test.

The following regression equation predicted the Course 4 reasoning residual score with adjusted $R^2 = .160$:

$$\textit{Co 4 Reas Residual} = 1.4(\textit{Str Math Kn}) + 1.2(\textit{Val Math Ideas}) - 11.4$$

Interestingly, the CMI scales are considerably better predictors of the reasoning test residual score than of either of the two TIMSS-based tests as measured by R^2. Students who did better than expected on the Course 4 reasoning test tended to have stronger beliefs about the Structure of Mathematical Knowledge (interrelatedness of mathematical ideas) and Validating Mathematical Ideas (students can work to validate ideas in math). It seems reasonable that both of these variables would be good predictors of success on a test of mathematical reasoning.

CHAPTER SUMMARY

This chapter consists of three main sections. The first section reports the results of administrations of the general belief scales of the Student Belief Survey at the end of Courses 1 and 2. The second section reports the results of the administrations of the Conceptions of Mathematics Inventory at the end of Courses 3 and 4. The third section relates these affective scales to the main written measures of mathematical achievement in each course. A summary of this chapter's main findings on the SBS in Courses 1 and 2 follows.

- Students were considerably more positive than the neutral response of 3 on all scales, except Competition (as they tended to value competition in learning mathematics).
- With the exception of the Self-Assessment scales, responses at the end of Courses 1 and 2 were somewhat less positive than at the beginning of Course 1. Self-Assessment scale responses were stable across the three administrations.
- Creativity and Cooperation were the two belief scales that were the best predictors of students' attitudes about their experience in the course.
- Although schools did not differ significantly on the belief scales at the beginning of Course 1, at the end of each course Adams students were significantly more positive than students from the other two schools on Self-Assessment, Creativity, and Cooperation. On the Challenge scale, Adams students were significantly more positive than Jefferson students. On the Genetic scale, Washington students were significantly more positive than students from the other two schools. On the Competition scale, school means did not differ significantly.
- At the end of both courses, girls believed somewhat more strongly than boys that genetics does not play a role in mathematical achievement, and they believed much more strongly that gender does not play a role. This latter belief was particularly strong among girls at the highest preachievement level.
- Boys enjoyed the competitive aspects of mathematics more than girls at the beginning of and at the end of Course 1, but by the end of Course 2 there was no significant gender difference.
- Students in higher preachievement levels had higher assessments of their own mathematical ability. This same general trend was true of the extent to which they valued each of creativity, competition, and challenge of mathematics, but means on the Cooperation and Genetic scales did not differ significantly by preachievement level.

Next, the main findings on the Conceptions of Mathematics Inventory administered at the end of Course 3 and Course 4 are summarized.

- Students were considerably more positive than the neutral response of 3.5 on all scales, and the scales were highly correlated with one another. Students in AP Calculus and AP Statistics classes were more positive on all the scales than students in either Course 3 or Course 4.

- In general, CMI scale means of Washington and Adams were higher than those of Jefferson at each administration and on nearly all scales.
- At the end of Course 3, the mean of boys was significantly higher on the Structure of Mathematical Knowledge, but the means of girls was significantly higher on Doing Mathematics, Learning Mathematics, and Composition of Mathematical Knowledge. The gender effect was not significant at the end of Course 4.
- At the end of Course 3, there was a significant preachievement level effect on six of the seven CMI scales, excluding Status of Mathematical Knowledge. In general, the order of means from highest to lowest was PAL 1, PAL 2, and PAL 3, although the differences between the means of PAL 1 and PAL 2 were not consistently significant. The PAL effect was not significant at the end of Course 4.

The belief scales and conceptions scales that were significant predictors of stronger than expected scores on each of the main achievement measures are given next in the order of the strength of their prediction. In general, the belief scales and conceptions scales were not strong predictors of achievement residuals predicting from 3.3 to 16.0% of the variance.

- Predictor(s) of the Course 1 *ITED-Q* posttest: Self-Assessment
- Predictor(s) of the Course 2 End of Year Algebra Examination: Self-Assessment, Challenge, and Cooperation (negatively)
- Predictor(s) of the Course 3 TIMSS-based mathematical literacy test: Doing Mathematics
- Predictor(s) of the Course 4 TIMSS-based advanced mathematics test: Learning Mathematics
- Predictor(s) of the Course 4 reasoning test: Structure of Mathematical Knowledge and Validating Mathematical Ideas.

This chapter completes Part III, "Attitudes, Beliefs, and Conceptions of Students." The next chapter focuses on the level of preparation of students for post-high school education. The main data source is a written survey that was completed by graduates of Washington, Adams, and Jefferson high schools at midyear of the first academic year after graduation. These results are supplemented with ACT and SAT scores and registrars' data from two large universities.

APPENDIX

1. Descriptive Statistics on SBS Scales for all Students Completing the SBS at the Beginning and End of Course 1 and the End of Course 2 (α Reliabilities are From the Pre-Course 1 Administration)

Self Assessment (α = .68)

	Pre-Course 1			*Course 1*			*Course 2*		
Group	*N*	*Mean*	*SD*	*N*	*Mean*	*SD*	*N*	*Mean*	*SD*
Washington	77	3.64	.708	62	3.58	.706	82	3.62	.836
Adams	180	3.75	.626	179	3.84	.688	215	3.98	.618
Jefferson	350	3.78	.563	326	3.70	.716	365	3.67	.776
Females	334	3.72	.596	308	3.70	.672	360	3.75	.706
Males	273	3.79	.609	259	3.76	.752	302	3.79	.802
PAL 1	90[a]	4.21	.523	85	4.20	.612	108	4.33	.594
PAL 2	209	3.82	.584	213	3.86	.711	246	3.88	.705
PAL 3	198	3.66	.560	181	3.53	.642	215	3.57	.669
PAL 4	104	3.42	.511	87	3.37	.607	80	3.23	.687
TOTAL	607	3.75	.603	567	3.73	.710	662	3.76	.751

[a] A few students completed the belief scales but no achievement scale so, there is no basis to classify them in PAL groups. Thus the PAL N-counts total 601 for Pre-Course 1, 566 for Course 1, and 649 for Course 2.

Creativity (α = .79)

	Pre-Course 1			*Course 1*			*Course 2*		
Group	*N*	*Mean*	*SD*	*N*	*Mean*	*SD*	*N*	*Mean*	*SD*
Washington	77	3.78	.711	62	3.58	.837	82	3.42	.871
Adams	180	3.85	.637	179	3.87	.696	215	3.94	.723
Jefferson	350	3.82	.660	326	3.49	.773	365	3.41	.813
Females	334	3.82	.665	308	3.66	.741	360	3.65	.792
Males	273	3.84	.653	259	3.57	.813	302	3.50	.866
PAL 1	90	4.03	.619	85	3.77	.790	108	3.93	.682
PAL 2	209	3.88	.679	213	3.69	.803	246	3.65	.782
PAL 3	198	3.77	.638	181	3.53	.745	215	3.48	.843
PAL 4	104	3.65	.627	87	3.48	.715	80	3.27	.869
TOTAL	607	3.83	.659	567	3.62	.775	662	3.58	.829

Appendix continues on next page.

Cooperation (α = .64)									
	Pre-Course 1			Course 1			Course 2		
Group	N	Mean	SD	N	Mean	SD	N	Mean	SD
Washington	77	3.57	.700	62	3.38	.636	82	3.19	.669
Adams	180	3.61	.608	179	3.61	.608	215	3.63	.603
Jefferson	350	3.56	.641	326	3.33	.717	365	3.25	.705
Females	334	3.55	.619	308	3.45	.633	360	3.40	.637
Males	273	3.61	.662	259	3.40	.745	302	3.32	.755
PAL 1	90	3.52	.670	85	3.37	.733	108	3.36	.690
PAL 2	209	3.60	.628	213	3.45	.683	246	3.37	.690
PAL 3	198	3.60	.632	181	3.42	.668	215	3.39	.680
PAL 4	104	3.54	.626	87	3.43	.696	80	3.34	.741
TOTAL	607	3.58	.639	567	3.42	.686	662	3.37	.694

Genetic (α = .39)									
	Pre-Course 1			Course 1			Course 2		
Group	N	Mean	SD	N	Mean	SD	N	Mean	SD
Washington	77	3.26	.772	62	3.35	.713	82	3.40	.727
Adams	180	3.22	.762	179	3.15	.806	215	3.30	.792
Jefferson	350	3.31	.804	326	3.09	.970	365	3.06	.877
Females	334	3.49	.739	308	3.45	.825	360	3.40	.773
Males	273	3.02	.771	259	2.77	.842	302	2.91	.846
PAL 1	90	3.42	.828	85	3.05	.946	108	3.19	.837
PAL 2	209	3.33	.744	213	3.22	.893	246	3.24	.803
PAL 3	198	3.23	.794	181	3.13	.867	215	3.18	.869
PAL 4	104	3.16	.802	87	3.03	.920	80	2.96	.780
TOTAL	607	3.28	.788	567	3.14	.898	662	3.18	.843

Appendix continues on next page.

Challenge (α = .76)									
	Pre-Course 1			*Course 1*			*Course 2*		
Group	*N*	*Mean*	*SD*	*N*	*Mean*	*SD*	*N*	*Mean*	*SD*
Washington	77	3.03	.850	62	3.12	.923	82	3.05	.812
Adams	180	3.21	.823	179	3.20	.773	215	3.22	.796
Jefferson	350	3.16	.841	326	2.98	.842	365	2.97	.797
Females	334	3.18	.843	308	3.05	.826	360	3.07	.791
Males	273	3.13	.830	259	3.08	.846	302	3.05	.823
PAL 1	90	3.35	.837	85	3.15	.899	108	3.33	.860
PAL 2	209	3.19	.816	213	3.09	.888	246	3.09	.774
PAL 3	198	3.06	.817	181	2.99	.756	215	2.98	.792
PAL 4	104	3.15	.894	87	3.07	.789	80	2.94	.760
TOTAL	607	3.16	.837	567	3.06	.835	662	3.06	.805

Competition (α = .86)									
	Pre-Course 1			*Course 1*			*Course 2*		
Group	*N*	*Mean*	*SD*	*N*	*Mean*	*SD*	*N*	*Mean*	*SD*
Washington	77	2.90	.931	62	2.85	1.06	82	2.80	1.13
Adams	180	2.82	1.17	179	2.69	1.03	215	2.75	1.17
Jefferson	350	2.90	1.11	326	2.64	1.18	365	2.67	1.08
Females	334	3.02	1.09	308	2.81	1.09	360	2.75	1.10
Males	273	2.69	1.10	259	2.52	1.15	302	2.67	1.13
PAL 1	90	2.61	1.10	85	2.31	1.06	108	2.51	1.06
PAL 2	209	2.73	1.05	213	2.56	1.12	246	2.63	1.12
PAL 3	198	2.91	1.11	181	2.74	1.02	215	2.79	1.07
PAL 4	104	3.38	1.06	87	3.18	1.24	80	3.04	1.23
TOTAL	607	2.87	1.11	567	2.68	1.12	662	2.71	1.11

Appendix continues on next page.

2. Linear Regression Equations for Generalized Belief Scales Predicting Course Attitude

Coefficients (Dependent Variable – Course 1 Attitude)[a]					
	B	*SE B*	*β*	*t*	*Prob. Level*
Constant	.726	.133		5.450	.000
Creativity	.461	.045	.468	10.159	.000
Cooperation	.246	.052	.220	4.780	.000

[a] Adjusted R^2 = .410

Coefficients (Dependent Variable – Course 2 Attitude)[a]					
	B	*SE B*	*β*	*t*	*Prob. Level*
Constant	−.177	.157		−1.128	.260
Creativity	.294	.047	.301	6.249	.000
Cooperation	.370	.045	.318	8.168	.000
Self-Assessment	.245	.040	.228	6.063	.000
Competition	.006	.020	.081	2.892	.004

[a] Adjusted R^2 = .410

Appendix continues on next page.

3. Descriptive Statistics on CMI Scales for Students Completing the CMI at the End of Years 3 and 4. Year 4 Data is for Course 4 Students Unless Otherwise Indicated in the Table. α Reliabilities are From the Course 3 Administration

	N-Counts		*Usefulness of Mathematics* ($\alpha = .93$)				*Structure of Math Knowledge* ($\alpha = .72$)			
Group	*Co 3*	*Co 4*	*Mean 3*	*SD 3*	*Mean 4*	*SD 4*	*Mean 3*	*SD 3*	*Mean 4*	*SD*
Washington	46	18	4.84	1.10	4.92	1.17	4.33	.704	4.58	.427
Adams	134	64	4.57	1.08	4.55	1.12	4.66	.537	4.79	.648
Jefferson	270	63	4.35	1.16	4.03	1.18	4.28	.671	4.05	.639
Females	259	89	4.47	1.11	4.48	1.15	4.50	.647	4.55	.661
Males	191	56	4.45	1.18	4.19	1.15	4.26	.650	4.27	.759
PAL 1[a]	106	46	4.68	.982	4.58	1.04	4.61	.611	4.71	.743
PAL 2	196	72	4.60	1.09	4.30	1.29	4.43	.647	4.34	.640
PAL 3	134	27	4.10	1.20	4.21	1.16	4.20	.642	4.26	.724
AP Course		47			4.99	.812			4.61	.631
TOTAL	450	145	4.46	1.14	4.37	1.19	4.40	.658	4.44	.710

[a] A few students completed the CMI scales but no achievement scale so, there is no basis to classify them in PAL groups. Thus the PAL N-counts total 436 for Course 3 and 145 for Course 4.

Appendix continues on next page.

Group	*Doing Math* ($\alpha = .54$)				*Val Ideas in Math* ($\alpha = .64$)				*Status of Math Knowl* ($\alpha = .50$)			
	Mean 3	*SD 3*	*Mean 4*	*SD 4*	*Mean 3*	*SD 3*	*Mean 4*	*SD 4*	*Mean 3*	*SD 3*	*Mean 4*	*SD 4*
Washington	4.69	.580	4.44	.670	4.23	.706	3.94	.429	4.16	.677	4.17	.466
Adams	4.67	.503	4.71	.545	4.33	.595	4.24	.489	4.23	.499	4.24	.550
Jefferson	4.33	.587	3.94	.737	4.07	.658	3.68	.581	4.06	.527	3.88	.602
Females	4.54	.531	4.47	.671	4.19	.612	3.98	5.30	4.19	.501	4.13	.541
Males	4.37	.640	4.14	.810	4.13	.708	3.94	.666	4.03	.577	3.97	.644
PAL 1	4.52	.600	4.49	.718	4.36	.580	4.31	.635	4.06	.517	4.15	.588
PAL 2	4.52	.581	4.24	.814	4.25	.658	4.15	.689	4.14	.574	4.04	.602
PAL 3	4.34	.546	4.36	.532	3.90	.581	4.03	.595	4.16	.499	4.03	.546
AP Course			4.75	.613			4.58	.674			4.18	.553
TOTAL	4.47	.586	4.34	.742	4.16	.654	3.96	.584	4.12	.540	4.07	.586

Appendix continues on next page.

	Learning Mathematics ($\alpha = .56$)				*Composition of Math Knowl* ($\alpha = .43$)			
Group	*Mean 3*	*SD 3*	*Mean 4*	*SD 4*	*Mean 3*	*SD 3*	*Mean 4*	*SD 4*
Washington	3.99	.779	3.94	.429	3.83	.559	4.01	.400
Adams	4.09	.488	4.24	.489	3.74	.422	3.94	.449
Jefferson	3.84	.616	3.68	.581	3.59	.556	3.53	.509
Females	4.01	.547	3.98	.530	3.69	.517	3.77	.532
Males	3.83	.674	3.94	.666	3.61	.538	3.77	.514
PAL 1	4.10	.588	4.05	.717	3.80	.548	3.88	.530
PAL 2	3.96	.637	3.93	.518	3.71	.501	3.77	.547
PAL 3	3.75	.545	3.90	.496	3.48	.501	3.59	.402
AP Course			4.26	.686			4.01	.606
TOTAL	3.93	.609	3.96	.584	3.66	.527	3.77	.524

4. Linear Regression Equations for Generalized Belief and CMI Scales Predicting Course Achievement

Coefficients (Dependent Variable – Course 1 ITED-Q)[a]					
	B	*SE B*	β	*t*	*Prob. Level*
Constant	222.702	11.251		19.794	.000
Self-Assessment	26.778	2.345	.479	11.418	.000
Cooperation	−10.005	2.399	−.172	−4.170	.000
Competition	−.470	1.383	−.133	−3.397	.001

[a] Adjusted $R^2 = .233$

Coefficients (Dependent Variable – Course 2 EoC Examination)[a]					
	B	*SE B*	*b*	*t*	*Prob. Level*
Constant	10.241	3.977		2.575	.010
Self-Assessment	12.060	1.185	.502	10.177	.000
Cooperation	−7.393	1.324	−.283	−5.585	.000
Creativity	4.276	1.405	.192	3.043	.002

[a] Adjusted $R^2 = .314$

Appendix continues on next page.

Coefficients (Dependent Variable – Course 3 TIMSS-Based Mathematical Literacy)[a]					
	B	*SE B*	*β*	*t*	*Prob. Level*
Constant	30.196	8.668		3.476	.001
Structure of Math Knowledge	5.120	1.905	.180	2.687	.008
Validating Ideas in Math	5.013	1.871	.180	2.678	.008
Status of Math Knowledge	–3.963	1.794	–.118	–2.209	.028
Usefulness of Mathematics	2.168	1.000	.132	2.168	.031

[a] Adjusted R^2 = .143

Coefficients (Dependent Variable – Course 4 TIMSS-Based Advanced Mathematics)[a]					
	B	*SE B*	*β*	*t*	*Prob. Level*
Constant	1.902	2.267	.310	.839	.403
Learning Mathematics	2.164	.566		3.825	.000

[a] Adjusted R^2 = .089

Coefficients (Dependent Variable – Course 4 Reasoning Test)[a]					
	B	*SE B*	*β*	*t*	*Prob. Level*
Constant	–6.892	2.628		–2.622	.010
Structure of Math Knowledge	2.722	.633	.375	4.302	.000
Validating Ideas in Math	1.964	.685	.250	2.867	.005

[a] Adjusted R^2 = .302

PART IV

POST-HIGH SCHOOL SURVEY, INDIVIDUAL CASES, AND PERSPECTIVES

CHAPTER 11

PERFORMANCE IN POST-HIGH SCHOOL EDUCATIONAL INSTITUTIONS

The target students in this study graduated from high school in May or June of 2001. An important goal of the study was to gather evidence concerning how well students who completed the college preparatory material in the Core-Plus Mathematics curriculum (sometimes followed by AP Calculus or AP Statistics) performed in college mathematics courses. This goal was addressed by a written survey of 2001 graduates of Washington, Adams, and Jefferson high schools in January 2002 during the first academic year after graduation. Some comparative data from 2001–02 freshmen were also obtained from the registrars at two major universities, the University of Iowa (UI) and Western Michigan University (WMU).

In this chapter, the survey, its respondents, and its results are described, with reference to the UI and WMU data as appropriate. The chapter begins with a description of the survey instrument, the method of recruiting respondents, and the set of respondents. This is followed by a presentation of the results in which the focus is on the type of institution attended, mathematics courses taken, and grade earned. Information concerning mathematics-related college courses was also gathered and results are summarized here. Finally, the graduates' perceptions of their high school curriculum and how well it prepared them for college mathematics are summarized.

A Five-Year Study of the First Edition of the Core-Plus Mathematics Curriculum, pp. 269–299

PROCEDURES

Students were recruited for the survey in April or May of their senior year (2001). A project evaluator visited the college preparatory mathematics classes (Course 3 or higher, including AP Statistics and AP Calculus), explained the survey, and invited all seniors in the class to participate in the survey. It was explained that the survey would be conducted by mail or telephone in January 2002. Students were also told that they would receive a small stipend when they returned the completed survey. The name, home address, and home telephone number of each volunteer were then entered into a list.

The Survey Instrument

The survey consisted of three parts. The first part sought personal background information, including high courses and grades (to double check and complete any gaps in the records we already had). In the second part of the survey, students were asked what college or community college they were attending if any, whether they had completed a mathematics or statistics course in their first term, and if so, what grade they earned and what was the course like as compared to their high school preparation. They also were asked what other courses they had completed that used mathematics and what grade they earned in those courses. Finally, they were to indicate whether they were planning to enroll in a mathematics or statistics course in their second term (Winter or Spring of their freshman year).

The third part of the survey focused on the students' reactions to their experience in high school mathematics in light of their college experience to date. Respondents also listed what they considered to be the three greatest strengths of their high school mathematics experience, three changes they would like to see made in their high school curriculum, and how, if at all, their high school mathematics experience influenced what they chose in college and what they plan to do in the future.

The Survey Respondents

Of the 279[1] seniors enrolled in college preparatory mathematics classes (Core 3 or higher), 202 (72.4%) volunteered to complete the written survey during the following year. The written survey was sent to all volunteers, timed so it would arrive around the first of January 2002. This date was chosen for administration since it was after or very near the end of the students' first semester or quarter in postsecondary school, and near the beginning of their second term. Students would be able to reflect on their experiences during Fall term, and they would have already registered or at least given a good deal of thought to their second term class schedules. A secondary advantage of this timing was that many students, on holiday break from college, could be reached at their parents' or guardians' home (the address that was available for them). After allowing 2 weeks for returns, a second mailing went to those on our list who had not responded. Finally, after 4 weeks, we called all listed volunteers who had not yet responded to the written survey and administered the survey on the telephone to those we were able to reach. As a result of these mailings and telephone calls, 146 (72.3%) of the students who had volunteered eventually completed the survey. This total is 52.3% of the target population, that is, of seniors enrolled in college preparatory mathematics classes.

To what extent is the set of survey respondents representative of the target population of all graduates who were in college preparatory mathematics courses in their senior year? The percents of respondents within the target populations were similar by school (Washington, 51.9%; Adams, 59.5%; and Jefferson, 51.0%) and by ethnicity (95.2% and 92.2% Caucasian, respectively, among respondents and nonrespondents), but females (58.7%) responded to the survey at a higher rate than males (43.0%). Proportionally, the respondents' last high school mathematics courses were similar to those of the targeted nonrespondents. The respondents also had a somewhat higher pattern of ACT Mathematics scores on average than the nonrespondents, but none of the within-course mean differences are statistically significant (see Table 11.1). On the whole then, the sample of respondents contains disproportionately more females, but it is reasonably representative with respect to the three schools, to ethnicity makeup, to high school mathematics background, and to ACT Mathematics scores.

Response Validity

Students provided their own course and grade data on the written surveys. Funding limitations and privacy issues made it impossible to verify all student-reported information from all colleges and universities. However, as a check of the accuracy of the data, professors at three state universities in Michigan (Michigan State University, Western Michigan University, and Grand Valley State University) gained permission to verify the data for the 32 survey respondents who attended one of their schools. All 32 students' transcripts were located in the university records. For those 32 students, all transcript records agreed with the courses students

Table 11.1. Percents and ACT Mathematics Means (Standard Deviations) of Survey Respondents (*N* =146) and Targeted Nonrespondents (*N* =133) by Last High School Mathematics Course Taken by the Student

	Last High School Math (%)			*Last High School Math (ACT Math)*		
	No Course 4	*Course 4*	*AP Calculus*	*No Course 4*	*Course 4*	*AP Calculus*
Respondents	17.1%	54.8%	28.1%	21.4	21.7	25.8
Nonrespondents	18.0%	55.6%	26.3%	19.2	20.8	24.4

reported taking. In 31 cases, the grades reported by the students were either the same as those on their transcript or within a "+" or "–" of the reported letter grade. The survey allowed for students to report only letter grades with no "+" or "–" attached. The one remaining student reported a lower grade on the survey than actually earned, and the correct grade was entered into our data file. The overall average of the 32 reported grades was within one-tenth of a point of that of the grades on the students' transcripts. This reliability check is evidence that the information students reported on their surveys is very likely to be at a high level of agreement with official course and grade data.

RESULTS

Of the 146 respondents, 142 went on in Fall 2001 to a post-secondary educational institution. All 4 who did not attend a community college, 4-year college, or university completed Course 4 but no more advanced high school mathematics, and their mean high school mathematics grade point was about 3.2, slightly over a B average. The mean high school grade point average (4.0-scale) and the distribution of the 142 respondents who went immediately on to post-high school education across types of institutions are illustrated in Figure 11.1.[2] The "Community College" category includes several types of 2-year colleges, including private junior colleges, publicly supported community colleges, and technical or trade colleges. The "Liberal Arts College" category includes mainly private liberal arts colleges in addition to the less obvious inclusion of one school of music and one small 4-year technical college. The "Major University" category contains private and state-supported universities with enrollments of at least 10,000 students.

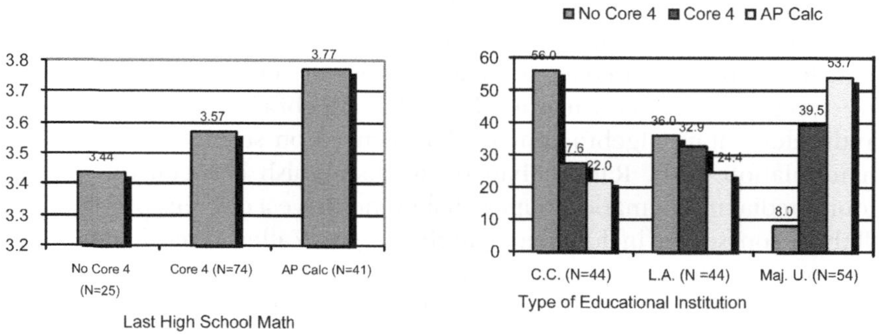

Figure 11.1. Mean High School Mathematics Grades and Percents of Students Attending Different Types of Postsecondary Educational Institutions by Students' Last High School Mathematics Course.

On average, the survey respondents (as well as the targeted non-respondents) had strong high school mathematics backgrounds as one would expect of students who are planning to attend college. It is also no surprise that students who took more high school mathematics had higher mean ACT scores and high school mathematics grades, and they were more likely to attend liberal arts colleges or major universities than community colleges.

Over 100 of the survey respondents indicated that they had chosen a college major either before or during their first term. Responses to the survey item about majors fell into four categories: Liberal Arts or undeclared (28.9%); Music, Art, Education, or Social Sciences (21.1%); Mathematics, Physical or Biological Sciences, Engineering, or Computer Science (20.4%); and Business, Economics, or Accounting (16.2%).

First College Mathematics Course

As discussed earlier, students reported their enrollments in mathematics course or a statistics course for Fall and Winter/Spring terms and their Fall mathematics or statistics course grades. Of the 142 students who attended an educational institution after high school, 114 (80.2%) enrolled in a mathematics or statistics course during their first or second semester, and 59 (41.5%) were enrolled in mathematics or statistics during both semesters. No doubt some of the students who did not take a mathematics or statistics course in their first two college terms will do so later. For example, in many universities most elementary education majors do not take their mathematics courses until their sophomore year.

Of the 142 respondents, 95 (66.9%) completed a mathematics or statistics course in Fall term and reported their grade. The courses that students reported as their first collegiate mathematics or statistics fell into one of five categories. Courses in the "Remedial Algebra" category were noncredit elementary algebra courses that focused on strengthening symbol manipulation skills. Rather than try to distinguish between the various nonremedial mathematics courses that do not have a calculus prerequisite, all these courses are included in a single category called "Precalculus." This category includes such courses as business calculus, intermediate algebra, college algebra, finite mathematics, algebra and trigonometry, as well as courses named Precalculus. "Calculus 1" and "Calculus 2" include only students in regular mathematics major calculus or engineering calculus courses. The "Statistics" category includes students in any statistics course. In the Winter term, four students enrolled in Linear Algebra, and one in both Multivariate Calculus and Differential Equations, but these were not the first college mathematics for these students as they had completed a Calculus course in the Fall. The percents of students in each of the last high school mathematics categories (no Core 4, Core 4, and AP Calculus) who enrolled in each of the five mathematics or statistics courses as their first college mathematics course are displayed in Figure 11.2.

Another variable that is associated with the college mathematics courses students took is the type of postsecondary educational institution that they attended. The percents of students in each type of post-secondary educational institution by their first college mathematics or statistics course are illustrated in Figure 11.3. A higher percent of community col-

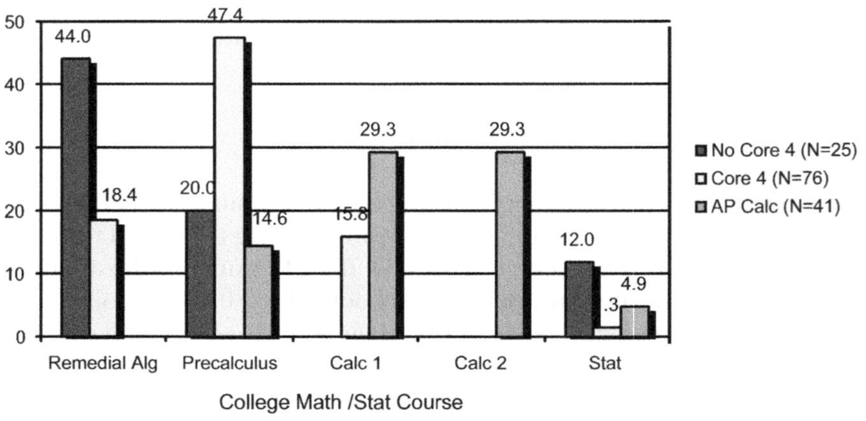

Figure 11.2. Percents of Students in Their First College Mathematics Course by Last High School Mathematics Course.

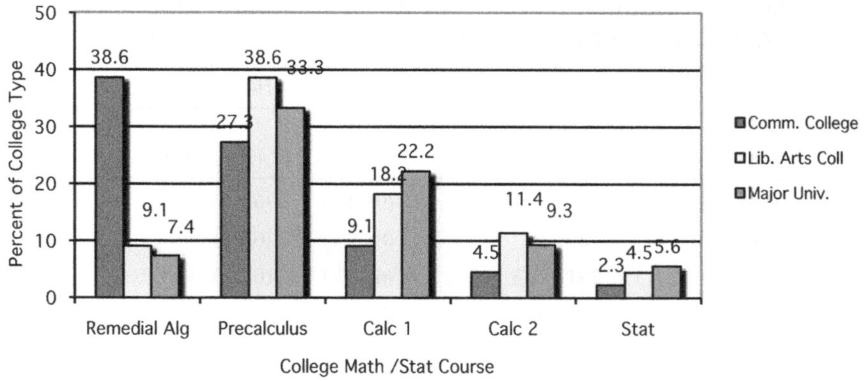

Figure 11.3. Percents of Students in Their First College Mathematics Course by Type of Post-Secondary Educational Institution.

lege students first enrolled in remedial algebra courses as would be expected, given their weaker high school mathematics background. However, the comparable percent of students in Calculus 1 and 2 in liberal arts colleges (29.6%) and in major universities (31.5%) may seem surprising in light of the fact that 33.7% of students who attended major universities completed AP Calculus in high school compared to 24.4% of those who attended liberal arts colleges (see the data displayed in Figure 11.1 and Figure 11.3).

One likely partial explanation is that major universities typically require students to complete very conventional placement examinations that are factors in determining their first mathematics course. Of the respondents to this survey who attended major universities, 94.4% reported taking a placement test, and 55.6% said it did not allow the use of a calculator. By comparison, only 34.1% of those attending a 4-year college took a placement test, and 15.9% indicated that it did not allow a calculator. Liberal arts colleges are more likely to base students' placements on their high school mathematics background than on a mathematics department placement test. The mismatch between the way these placement tests are often used and the strengths of Core-Plus Mathematics students is documented and discussed by Schoen and Hirsch (2003b).

Students' Perceptions of Their College Mathematics Courses

One important aspect of a course in today's technological world is the policy for the use of technology like graphing calculators. This policy var-

Table 11.2. Number (Percent) of Various Fall Term Mathematics Courses With Each of Four Graphing Calculator Policies

	Graphing Calculator Policy				
Math/Stat Course	*No Graphing Calculators*	*Homework, Not Tests*	*All Times*	*On Tests Only*	*Total*
Remedial Algebra		17 (94.4%)	1(5.6%)		18
Precalculus	2 (4.4%)	40 (88.9%)	3 (6.7%)		45
Calculus 1	2 (11.1%)	12 (66.7%)	3 (16.7%)	1 (5.6%)	18
Calculus 2	4 (40%)	6 (60%)			10
Statistics		3 (75.0%)	1 (25.0%)		4
Total	8 (8.4%)	78 (82.1%)	8 (8.4%)	1 (1.1%)	95

ied significantly ($p = .017$) by Fall mathematics or statistics courses, as can be seen in Table 11.2. Overall, the percent of courses in which no graphing calculator was allowed was the same as the percent in which the calculator was allowed at all times, including on tests (8.4%). The most common policy (82.1%) was to allow the use of a graphing calculator on homework, but not on tests. This may be a default policy since it would be difficult to enforce a policy of no calculator use on homework. A graphing calculator was not allowed in 40% of the Calculus 2 courses, but the policy was considerably more liberal in lower-level mathematics and statistics courses.

At a deeper descriptive level, the survey asked students to complete a checklist with the categories in Figure 11.4. The directions to the student were the following:

> For each "Process or Competence" in the table below, check (√) the **one** column under "Emphasis in this Course" that best describes what was or was not emphasized in the mathematics or statistics course you were in during Fall 2001.

Thus the data provide a view of the specific processes or competencies that were "emphasized," "required but not emphasized," or "not required" in the college course.

The two most heavily emphasized processes were "learning mathematics from lectures" and "paper-and-pencil algebra or calculus symbol manipulation skills," with "understanding the meaning of mathematical concepts" getting somewhat less emphasis. Processes receiving the least emphasis had to do with oral and written communication of mathematical reasoning and learning by working with other students. This pattern is certainly aligned more with conventional emphases than with goals

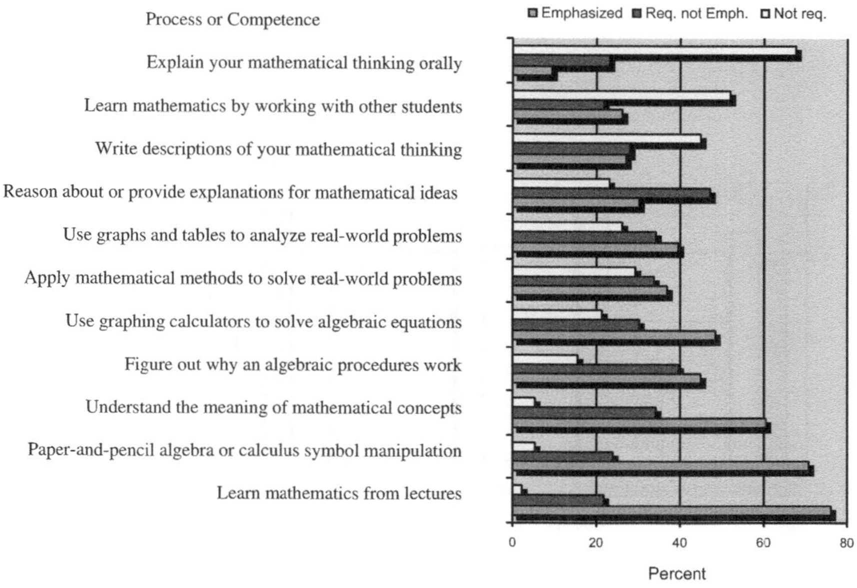

Figure 11.4. Percent of Respondents Indicating Each of Three Levels of Emphasis in Their Fall Mathematics Course Relative to 11 Processes.

recommended in progressive curriculum standards and appearing in reformed undergraduate curriculum materials.

Students' Grades in Their Fall Mathematics Courses

Mean grades in Fall mathematics and statistics courses by high school mathematics background category are displayed in Figure 11.5. Two observations of interest are the following. First, just four students completed a statistics course and all earned a grade of A, adding a bit to the consistent research evidence that this curriculum prepares students especially well in statistics. Second, four of the five students who completed AP Calculus in high school and who were nonetheless placed in a precalculus course earned grades of A, suggesting that perhaps these students were enrolled in a lower level course than they could have handled. After all, they had already successfully completed one or two courses at a higher level in high school. Furthermore, six other students who had completed a year less high school mathematics (through Core 4 only) passed Calculus 1 with a 3.1 average grade point.

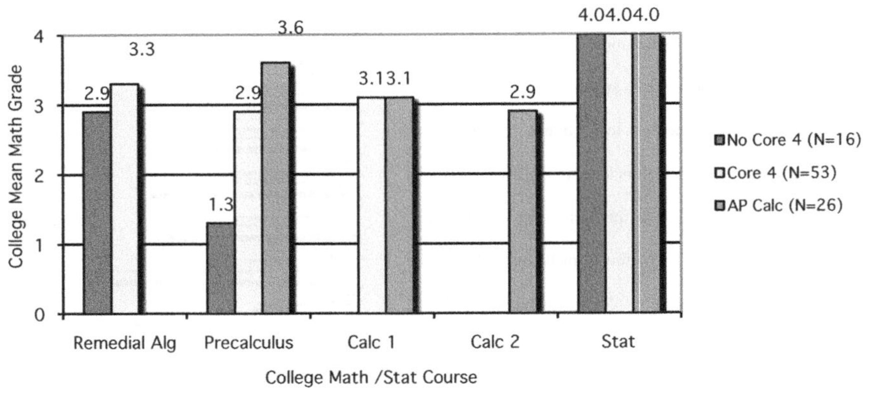

Figure 11.5. Mean Grades of Students in Their Fall College Mathematics Course by Last High School Mathematics Course.

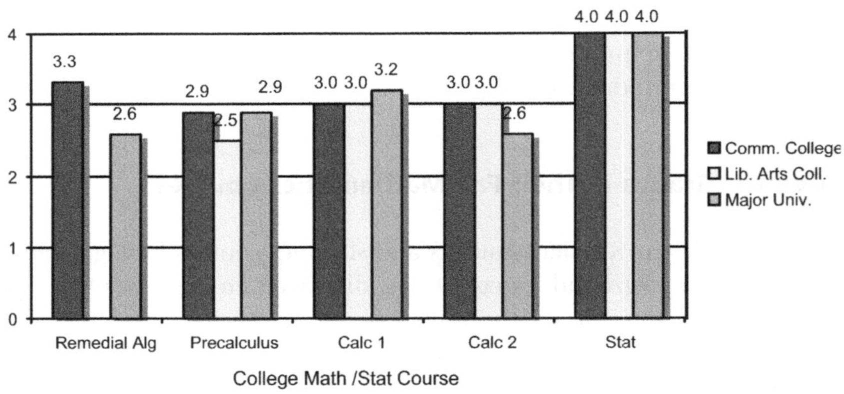

Figure 11.6. Mean Grades of Students in Their Fall College Mathematics Course by Type of Postsecondary Educational Institution.

Mean grades in Fall mathematics and statistics courses by type of post-secondary educational institution are shown in Figure 11.6. Grades in the Remedial Algebra category are considerably higher in community colleges than in the other two types of colleges, even though the community college students have a weaker high school mathematics background (see Figure 11.1). The Calculus 2 grades are based on only two to five students in each college type and so their variability should not be generalized. The 4.0 grade average in statistics courses is spread across the college types but, as mentioned earlier, it involves just four students.

Comparisons With Freshmen From Two Major Universities

A natural question at this point is, "How do course-taking patterns and grades of students in the previous section compare with similar students who complete a more conventional high school curriculum?" In this section, a partial answer to that question is provided. Data were drawn from the results of the survey described earlier, supplemented by data drawn from the records of two universities that many graduates of two of the three schools in this study attended (Western Michigan University and Grand Valley State University). The numbers of 2001 graduates for whom we have post-secondary data who reported attending a 4-year college/university or a community college in Fall 2001 are given in Table 11.3. The fact that nearly all respondents went directly into post-secondary education is partly due to the relative difficulty in contacting those who went into the work force.

This section focuses on the preparation of the graduates for college or university mathematics, a total of 145 students from the three schools. These graduates attended 39 different institutions all over the country. This sample consists of 95 students who completed the post-high school survey plus 50 more whose records were located in data from the registrar at one of the two colleges mentioned in the previous paragraph. Students

Table 11.3. Numbers of Graduates, Survey Respondents, and Postsecondary Activity by School

School	*2001 Graduates*	*Post-High Data*	*College or University*	*Community College*	*Work*
Washington	58	14	12	2	0
Adams	159	47	39	6	2
Jefferson	353	132	94	36	2
Total	570	193	145	44	4

attending community colleges were not included in the sample, since they differ in level of prior preparation, course selection, and often career goals from students attending 4-year (or more) institutions. To provide comparison data, we obtained records from two major universities, the University of Iowa (UI) for all freshmen in Fall 2002 and Western Michigan University (WMU) for all freshmen in Fall 2001. Since *Standards*-based curricula were used in only an estimated 3 to 5% of high schools in the country in 2001–02, it seems safe to assume that nearly all, at least well over 95%, of the UI and WMU students completed high school curricula that were more conventional than the Core-Plus Mathematics curriculum. Mean ACT Mathematics and ACT Composite scores for these three groups are given in Table 11.4. As shown, the means of both scores for graduates of schools in the present study were between the means of the two comparison groups, greater than WMU but less than UI. Seventeen of the present study graduates took the SAT rather than the ACT.

Comparison of All Freshmen. The percents of students in each group enrolling in various mathematics courses and the mean of their grades in each course are given in Table 11.5. The large difference between UI and WMU is mainly due to differing mathematics requirements, at least at the time that these data were collected. At UI, students were not required to take a mathematics course; rather, they had a quantitative literacy requirement that could be met with a number of courses other than mathematics. At WMU, a mathematics course was required of all students, and many took precalculus in their first semester.

Again, graduates in the present study tend to fall between UI and WMU in percent taking each course. Exceptions are Remedial Algebra, Calculus 1, and Calculus 2, each of which had a higher percentage of enrollees from the present study than either of the two university groups. The overall group differences, except for the one between UI and WMU, explained above, do not appear to be greater than one would expect by chance. (The large difference in cell size makes a chi-square statistical test impractical.)

Table 11.4. Numbers of Students and ACT Means and Standard Deviations by Group

		ACT Math		*ACT Composite*	
	N	*Mean*	*SD*	*Mean*	*SD*
Present Study	128	22.45	4.71	23.29	3.98
University of Iowa	3,998	24.32	4.33	24.58	3.71
Western Michigan	4,323	22.05	4.06	22.32	3.39

Table 11.5. Numbers and Percents of Students and Mean Grades by College Mathematics Course

	Present Study		*University of Iowa*		*Western Michigan*	
Math Course	*N (%)*	*Mean*	*N (%)*	*Mean*	*N (%)*	*Mean*
None	56 (38.6)	–	2,121 (50.9)	–	1,214 (28.2)	–
Rem. Algebra	10 (6.9)	2.12	203 (4.9)	2.74	243 (5.6)	2.54
Precalculus	52 (35.9)	2.64	1,170 (28.1)	2.71	2,406 (55.8)	2.44
Calculus 1	15 (10.3)	3.10	327 (7.8)	2.80	321 (7.4)	2.47
Calculus 2	8 (5.5)	2.81	117 (2.8)	3.33	9 (0.2)	2.83
Statistics	4 (2.8)	3.50	228 (5.5)	2.73	119 (2.8)	2.42
TOTAL	145	2.71	4,166	2.77	4,312	2.45

There is also not a clear pattern in mean grades with the present study graduates' remedial algebra grades being lower, but those in Calculus 1 and Statistics being higher than the two comparison groups. WMU grades are somewhat lower than the other two groups in most courses. That may be because WMU students are not as strong in entering mathematics achievement (see ACT Mathematics means), or it may just be institutional differences in grading practices.

Comparison by High School Mathematics Background. A perusal of the University of Iowa data makes it clear that college mathematics course-taking patterns and grades differ greatly by the number of high school mathematics courses students completed successfully. (Unfortunately, data on mathematics courses taken in high school by WMU students are not available.) Of the graduates of the three high schools in the present study for whom we have data, 4 completed just 2 years of college preparatory mathematics and 18 completed 3 years—in each case, too few students to provide reliable information. Therefore, we did separate analyses of course-taking patterns and grades for students who completed 4 years of high school mathematics (66) and for those who completed 5 years (57). The data for those taking 4 years of high school mathematics are given in Table 11.6.

A higher percent of students from the present study took a mathematics course in their first semester, and a higher percent of UI students completed a statistics course. These differences are probably due to the quantitative literacy requirement at UI, described above. A statistics course will satisfy that requirement. Present study graduates' grades in Remedial Algebra are lower than those of UI freshmen, but the reverse is true for grades in Calculus 1. Overall, there does not appear to be any strong pattern of differences.

Table 11.6. Course-Taking and Grade Data for UI Students and Those From the Present Study With 4 Years of High School Mathematics

	Present Study		*University of Iowa*	
Math Course	*N (%)*	*Mean*	*N (%)*	*Mean*
None	22 (33.3)	–	837 (48.7)	–
Remedial Algebra	5 (7.6)	2.53	73 (4.2)	3.13
Precalculus	31 (47.0)	2.59	591 (34.4)	2.59
Calculus 1	7 (10.6)	3.07	107 (6.2)	2.55
Calculus 2	0 (0.0)	–	22 (1.3)	3.45
Statistics	1 (1.5)	4.00	90 (5.2)	2.68
TOTAL	66	2.69	1,720	2.66

Table 11.7. Course-Taking and Grade Data UI Students and Those from the Present Study With 5 Years of High School Mathematics

	Present Study		*University of Iowa*	
Math Course	*N (%)*	*Mean*	*N (%)*	*Mean*
None	23 (40.4)	–	444 (37.7)	–
Remedial Algebra	1 (1.8)	1.50	9 (0.8)	2.67
Precalculus	14 (24.6)	3.14	378 (32.1)	3.04
Calculus 1	8 (14.0)	3.13	204 (17.3)	2.97
Calculus 2	8 (14.0)	2.81	93 (7.9)	3.30
Statistics	3 (5.3)	3.33	51 (4.3)	3.10
TOTAL	57	3.03	1,179	3.05

The data for students taking 5 years of high school mathematics are given in Table 11.7. In the Core-Plus Mathematics schools, students in this category completed the four Core-Plus Mathematics courses and either AP Statistics or AP Calculus, with the exception of nine students who completed both AP Statistics and AP Calculus. There do not seem to be notable differences between the results for the two groups of students.

In sum, these 145 graduates from Washington, Adams, and Jefferson High Schools entered college after completing as many as 7 years of *Standards*-based curricula. There are no patterns of deficiency overall or when high school mathematics background is kept constant. In their first college semester, graduates from the present study with similar high school mathematics backgrounds (and somewhat lower ACT scores) completed various college mathematics courses through Calculus 2 at similar frequencies and with similar success rates as students from more conventional high school mathematics programs.

Performance in Other Courses That Use Mathematics

An important goal of *Standards*-based mathematics curricula is to better prepare students to apply mathematical and statistical methods in mathematics-related fields. Relative to this goal, we asked students to report their Fall grades in such college courses. Of the 142 survey respondents who went on to postsecondary education, 101 (71.1%) reported their Fall term grade in a course that used mathematics or statistics. Some students reported grades in more than one course. These courses include the usual mathematics-related ones like the sciences, computer science, and engineering. In addition, students reported using statistics in business, economics, and psychology courses and geometric ideas in art/design courses.

The group of 101 students was strong academically with an average mathematics grade point average of 3.61 and average ACT Mathematics and Science Reasoning scores of 22.8 and 24.0, respectively. High school grades, ACT Mathematics scores, and college course grades for each of the categories of mathematics-related courses are summarized in Table 11.8. Mean grades across the different college courses ranged from 3.14 in geography classes to 3.78 in art and design classes. Clearly, these students met with a great deal of success in college courses that require mathematical or statistical concepts and methods.

Perceptions of Preparedness for College Mathematics and Math-Related Courses

Graduates' college course-taking patterns and class grades are important variables to consider when evaluating a high school curriculum, but students' perceptions of their preparedness can also be an important issue that is related but not identical to their performance. On the post-high school survey, the issue of preparedness for college mathematics or statistics was addressed in a somewhat general way with an item: "Do you think you were as well prepared as the other students in the [mathematics/statistics] course?" The preparedness issue was also addressed more specifically in another survey question, and those results will be presented later.

Table 11.8. High School Mathematics GPA, ACT Mathematics, and Course Grade Means (*SD*) of Survey Respondents Who Enrolled in a College Course That Required Mathematical or Statistical Thinking in Their First College Term

College Course	*N*	*HS Math GPA*	*ACT Math*	*College Course Grade*
Art/Design	9	3.59 (.57)	21.00 (4.14)	3.78 (.44)
Psychology	25	3.63 (.38)	19.92 (3.36)	3.76 (.44)
Economics	18	3.59 (.42)	20.27 (2.89)	3.67 (.59)
Computer Science	13	3.69 (.37)	24.40 (4.70)	3.62 (.65)
Business	14	3.53 (.50)	21.18 (2.44)	3.57 (.65)
Engineering	4	3.42 (.32)	29.33 (4.16)	3.50 (.58)
Physics	14	3.48 (.57)	21.46 (3.15)	3.36 (.74)
Biology	29	3.72 (.28)	21.75 (3.49)	3.31 (.76)
Chemistry	37	3.67 (.40)	23.74 (5.30)	3.30 (.74)
Anthropology	4	3.67 (.27)	22.50 (0.71)	3.25 (.50)
Geography	7	3.48 (.42)	21.17 (3.76)	3.14 (.38)

Table 11.9. Number (Percent) at Each Level of Perceived High School Preparation by Grade Earned in the College Course

	College Mathematics or Statistics Course Grade					
Level of Preparation	*A*	*B*	*C*	*D*	*E or F*	*Total*
Better prepared	14 (43.8)	8 (18.6)	2 (15.4)			24 (25.3)
About the same	17 (53.1)	28 (65.1)	7 (53.8)	1 (50.0)	4 (80.0)	57 (60.0)
Not as well prepared	1 (3.1)	7 (16.3)	4 (30.8)	1 (50.0)	1 (20.0)	14 (14.7)
Total	32	43	13	2	5	95

The number and percent of responses to the above items broken down by the student's college mathematics course grade are given in Table 11.9. The chi-square for this contingency table is significant at the .054 probability level. Other potential relationships between the preparedness item responses and gender, school, type of postsecondary educational institution, and college course were tested, but none of the resulting chi-squares was statistically significant. Overall, across the 96 students who responded to this item, 25.3% thought they were better prepared than other students in the course, 60.0% indicated that they were as well prepared, and 14.7% indicated they were not as well prepared. Not surprisingly, students who earned higher grades in their college mathematics or statistics course generally made a more positive assessment of their high school preparation than those with lower course grades.

Students were asked a similar question regarding the mathematics-related course they completed: "Do you think you were as well prepared as the other students for the mathematical material in this [mathematics-related] course?" On average, the 114 respondents who completed this item were slightly more positive about their high school preparation for the mathematics-related courses than for the mathematics courses. Overall, 28.1% indicated that they were better prepared than most students, 62.3% indicated a similar level of preparation, and 9.6% considered their high school preparation to be less than that of other students in the course.

Interestingly, there was not a significant difference across the three schools in the responses to the previous question concerning high school mathematical preparation for college mathematics or statistics courses. However, on the question of preparedness for mathematics-related courses, all 11 students who indicated that they were prepared less well than the other students were graduates of Jefferson High School. A closer look at the backgrounds of these 11 students shows that, as a group, they were placed in lower level college courses and had less success in some of those courses than was typical of the entire group of respondents. For 9 of the 11, their last high school mathematics course was Course 4; the other 2 completed AP Statistics without Course 4. In Fall semester, 3 of these students completed Remedial Algebra with a mean grade of 3.67, 5 completed precalculus with a mean grade of 2.34, and the other 3 did not take a mathematics course in the Fall term.

Lack of success in college mathematics was not always the explanation for a student's negative assessment of her high school mathematics program. One of the students who indicated she was not as well prepared as the other students for the mathematical material in these courses also wrote, "I never felt that I learned anything useful, and I also felt that I never really learned anything." In spite of this bleak assessment of her learning, this community college student earned grades of A in both Physics and Chemistry in her first college term. Such a negative assessment of preparation in the face of successful performance seems to appear nearly exclusively among the Jefferson graduates, perhaps suggesting that the local controversy sparked or intensified a negative mindset about their high school mathematics experience. For a description of the controversy, see Chapter 13.

Perceived Strengths of the High School Curriculum

The checklist of processes and competencies in Figure 11.4 was also presented to students with the following directions:

> Also check the **one** column under "High School Prep." that best describes how well your high school mathematics prepared you for that competence.

The data provide a view of the level of high school preparation—excellent, good, or weak—perceived by the students for each of those processes or competencies. As with much of the other data concerning high school preparation, Jefferson graduates were much more negative than graduates of the other two schools (see Table 11.10).

The processes or competencies are given in decreasing order of students' perceived level of preparation. In spite of the relatively negative ratings given by the Jefferson graduates, their percent of excellent or good ratings ranged from 68.6% to 98.6% across the 11 processes with a median of 75.7%. The percent of excellent or good ratings of the combined Washington and Adams graduates ranged from 68.0% to 96.0% across the processes with a median of 88.0%. Jefferson's relatively negative ratings will be discussed further in Chapter 13.

At least 70% of the students see their high school curriculum as providing good or excellent preparation in each of the individual processes. In a relative sense, the students definitely did not see their high school curriculum as conventional. Rather, their strongest ratings were for group work, using graphs and tables with graphing calculators, solving application problems using mathematical modeling, understanding mathematical concepts, and reasoning about mathematical ideas. Most of the processes in the lower half of Table 11.10 are typically associated with conventional curricula, such as paper-and-pencil symbol manipulation and learning from lectures. Exceptions to this pattern are that students rated their preparation for communicating mathematical ideas, orally and through writing, as relatively low. As was seen in the student attitude results in previous chapters, some students did not see themselves as proficient in either writing or speaking about mathematics, even though they were often expected to do both during their high school experience.

Further data concerning students' perceptions of their high school mathematics experience are provided by their open-ended responses to the following question: "What do you think are the three greatest strengths of your high school mathematics experience?"

This question asked students in the middle of their first school year after graduating to reflect and report on positive aspects of their high school experience. The 330 strengths listed by the 141 (96.6% of all respondents) students who responded to this question fit well into the categories in Table 11.11.

The vast majority of students who responded mentioned problem solving, conceptual understanding, reasoning, critical thinking, or logical thinking in at least one of the strengths they listed. Some students,

Table 11.10. Percent of Respondents Indicating Each of Three Levels of High School Preparation for Their Fall College Mathematics Course Relative to 11 Processes

	Jefferson Graduates (N = 70a)			*Washington & Adams (N = 25)*		
Process or Competence	*Excellent*	*Good*	*Weak*	*Excellent*	*Good*	*Weak*
Learn mathematics by working with other students	37 (52.9)	32 (45.7)	1 (1.4)	20 (80.0)	4 (16.0)	1 (4.0)
Use graphing calculators to solve algebraic equations or inequalities	41 (60.3)	23 (33.8)	4 (5.9)	22 (88.0)	2 (8.0)	1 (4.0)
Use graphs and tables to analyze mathematical and real-world problems	27 (39.1)	32 (46.4)	10 (14.5)	17 (68.0)	6 (24.0)	2 (8.0)
Apply mathematical methods to solve real-world problems	16 (23.5)	38 (55.9)	14 (20.6)	18 (72.0)	4 (16.0)	3 (12.0)
Understand the meaning of mathematical concepts and methods	15 (21.4)	38 (54.3)	17 (24.3)	12 (48.0)	11 (44.0)	2 (8.0)
Reason about or provide explanations for mathematical ideas or methods	15 (21.4)	38 (54.3)	17 (24.3)	12 (48.0)	10 (40.0)	3 (12.0)
Paper-and-pencil algebra or calculus symbol manipulation	20 (28.6)	33 (47.1)	17 (24.3)	11 (44.0)	11 (44.0)	3 (12.0)
Learn mathematics from lectures	16 (22.9)	41 (58.6)	13 (18.6)	6 (24.0)	11 (44.0)	8 (32.0)
Figure out why an algebraic procedure works	14 (20.0)	34 (48.6)	22 (31.4)	7 (28.0)	16 (64.0)	2 (8.0)
Write descriptions of your mathematical thinking	15 (21.7)	34 (49.3)	20 (29.0)	12 (48.0)	10 (40.0)	3 (12.0)
Explain your mathematical thinking orally	10 (14.5)	38 (55.1)	21 (30.4)	4 (16.7)	13 (54.2)	7 (29.2)

[a] One or two students left some processes blank, so the column numbers vary from 68 to 70 and from 24 to 25.

Table 11.11. Frequencies and Percents by Category of 330 Strengths of Their High School Mathematics Listed by Students in a Free-Response Format

Strength of High School Mathematics Experience	*Freq(%)*
Developed better problem solving, conceptual understanding, and reasoning	85 (25.8)
Worked in groups, communicated with other students about mathematics	64 (19.4)
Developed ability to apply mathematics, statistics, and probability	51 (15.5)
Learned to use the graphing calculator especially graph and table capabilities	47 (14.2)
Developed more confidence and/or interest in doing math and statistics	32 (9.7)
Developed a broad base of mathematical understanding	15 (4.5)
Learned algebraic equations and formulas	14 (4.2)
Developed calculus or statistics knowledge in AP courses	17 (5.2)
Learned geometry and trigonometry	5 (1.5)

especially majors in mathematics, science, engineering, or computer science, often mentioned the work ethic and discipline that they learned by trying to make sense of the mathematics, especially while collaborating with other students. As one student said, "The most important [strength] is the discipline it has taught me." One student said she learned to "love mathematics" and another student went so far as to say he had developed a "passion" for learning mathematics, but most were more pragmatic and focused on their mathematical preparation for college. Regarding group work, students made comments like, "I can explain math concepts clearly," "explaining my thought processes," or "I explain why better than just doing."

Students who took calculus and statistics in college were likely to identify the breadth of their knowledge from high school. As one student said, "I think I gained a greater knowledge of the study of calculus and had a good introduction to it in high school." Another student alluded to the strength of her background and the confidence it gave her when she said, "I had the opportunity to take AP Calc and AP Stat as well as the core math classes in high school. This allows me to feel that I can tackle nearly any problem I encounter." For another student, the applications of mathematics and statistics were "good news, bad news." According to her, "AP statistics was a very valuable experience. All of the information I learned seemed relevant to the real world, whereas what I learned in Core Math did not."

The reported advantages of using a calculator went beyond the ease of computation and graphing that is often the first to come to mind. Another perceived advantage is the prestige of having proficiency in the calculator's use in today's technological world. One student pointed out her advantage over other college students. "Being in college now, I see a lot of students who know nothing about [a graphing calculator]." The calculator also helps some students better understand mathematics, as a student noted, "I use the calculator to picture and figure out why things work or how to make something work better in my mind."

Some students who listed their knowledge of algebra as a strength of their high school experience saw algebra as a way to manipulate symbols, alluding to "balancing equations," "solving for *x*," or "solving equations." Others saw algebra as a mode of understanding. For example, one student referred as an example to "algebraic reasoning for the use of fairly simple equations in chemistry." She saw her knowledge of chemistry as dependent on her knowledge of algebra. Another student was not as concerned with skill at solving equations, as he was with "understanding working through an equation."

Students' Recommended Changes in Their High School Program

As this book makes clear in several places, students were not uniformly positive about their high school mathematics experience. To invite them to make critical but constructive recommendations from the perspective of their first year of college, they were asked the following question near the end of the survey: "If you could make three changes in your high school mathematics experience, what would the changes be?"

Interestingly, the changes recommended by 140 (95.9% of all respondents) were much more varied and individual than the strengths that students reported on the previous questions. The nature of the changes was also highly related to the students' high school background and their experience in college mathematics courses. Because of their relationship to the background of the students, it makes sense to report the recommended changes in terms of students rather than as a compilation of recommendations as was done in the previous section. The following discussion mentions some of the more frequently occurring recommendations, but notice that no single recommendation is made by more than a small percent of respondents.

Probably the closest to a general category that comes from the recommended changes is to move the curriculum more toward a conventional one, though each such recommendation has a specific intent that differs within the category. Some examples are the following. About 17% of respondents recommended a conventional alternative to their present curriculum, and about 7% recommended more lecture, direct instruction, or preparation for standardized tests. More often students with weaker mathematics achievement as measured by the ACT Mathematics test made these recommendations. One such response was, "Offer an alternative program of traditional math—traditional is taught in college, so those going to college need traditional." Another student went on to argue for the importance of traditional mathematics in later life. "I think that [Core] is not helpful in standardized tests or at the college level. I like the more traditional math. It is much more useful later on in life. It especially helps on placement exams and standardized tests." The latter comment illustrates a belief held by some students that has appeared often in this and our previous evaluation studies. When these students consider what is "useful for later life," they are thinking of their own life in the near future. Thus unlike most mathematics educators, these students considered preparation for standardized tests to be "useful for later life."

About 14% of respondents recommended less integration of content, and interestingly all but one of those making the recommendation were female. Perhaps girls have a greater need than boys for tightly specified rules and for conformity to what other college students had experienced in high school mathematics. As one female student said, "More emphasis on distinguishing between the different mathematical areas" was needed in her mathematics background. This same idea was emphasized by other female students, "Do not integrate different areas of mathematics (i.e., trigonometry, algebra, geometry) into one class—It's confusing" and "Less integration of ideas; we should receive the information in sequence so we consolidate skills rather than jumbling them up and never getting a clear picture."

About 8% of respondents recommended less use of a calculator. A sample comment on this change is, "Use the calculator a little less. We relied quite heavily on our calculators, although we also needed to know how to perform those calculations by hand. My college courses don't even require graphing calculators and neither do some of the other calculus classes offered here." Another respondent alluded to parents' difficulties with the calculator: "Maybe a handout for parents so they can help their children; or less of an emphasis on calculators parents have never seen."

As for recommended changes that are not necessarily favoring a more conventional experience, students who succeeded in AP Calculus in high school and Calculus 1 or Calculus 2 in college often suggested "more AP opportunities" in high school. About 3% of responses mentioned this. As one student said, "More emphasis (maybe even scholarship) to take AP exams—I wish I would have taken mine!" Related to this recommendation, about 3% of students, all with strong mathematical achievement, recommended tracking in the high school program, arguing for "more options for advanced and accelerated classes" and a "chance to work on my own at a faster pace." Another student wanted tracking as a way for the school to "offer more advanced math courses." The other two students wanted options based on mathematical ability, noting that schools need to "make sure students are in the right course for their ability. Some students were too advanced while others slowed everybody down," and schools should "Have more choices rather than just easy or hard classes."

Related to the issues of more AP opportunities and ability tracking, about 11% of students recommended more in-depth, harder, or more realistic mathematics. In recommending more depth, one student said, "Cover more material." Another student, on the topic of more realism, recommended that mathematics should be to "learn more useful things." Both of these students requested material that is, or can be, more applicable to their current lives, although it is not clear what they meant by this. These comments do not indicate why more topics or which extra topics should be covered, but the comments do suggest that these students perceived the covered material as inadequate in some way.

About 2% (3 students), all of lower mathematical achievement, suggested changes in the form of the curriculum materials from different perspectives. One student wanted worked examples; another wanted an advance organizer for each lesson and unit. A third recommended that "formulas that are used in the chapter [be given] in the beginning."

Perhaps surprisingly, about 5% of students recommended more hands-on experience, and all but one of these students was a major in mathematics, science, engineering, or computer science. Most such recommendations merely said "more hands-on" experience, but one student elaborated: "I took both [AP] statistics and calculus in high school. Sometimes, doing activities can get repetitive, but they are very helpful in understanding concepts. If we had done as many activities, or labs, in calculus as we did in statistics, maybe calculus would seem easier for some people."

About 17% of students, many with weaker mathematical achievement, recommended better teachers, or better teaching, in their mathematics classes. These recommendations were independent of the curriculum, such as, "[the] teacher moved on without making sure most students understood material," "I had poor teachers," or "it was taught to us poorly," and the typical recommendation was for "better teachers." It is interesting that more successful students rarely mentioned teachers, suggesting perhaps that they were more likely to take personal responsibility for their mathematics education and not blame external causes.

In fact, 4% of respondents, mostly those of higher achievement, indicated that they would not change a thing in their high school experience. All but one of these students made no further comment, but one of them said, "I really can't think of a thing! I enjoyed my high school math experience far more than my first semester of college and I often look back to my high school experience as a positive one."

There were several other recommendations for change, each made by no more than two students. These include more connections between topics, more motivational quizzes, provide study guides, less trigonometry, more trigonometry, more group homework, less vectors, teach use of the TI-92, less multiple-choice testing, and less homework.

Influence of High School Mathematics Experience on Choice of Major or Future Plans

The following two questions on the survey addressed the influence of the high school curriculum on choices of major and future plans.

- Did your high school mathematics experience influence your interests or choice of major?
- Did your high school mathematics experience influence or shape what you decided to do after high school or what you plan to do in the future? If yes, describe that influence and its result.

These questions prompted responses from just 17.8% and 26.0% of respondents, respectively. Not surprisingly, the tone of the responses varied by the mathematical achievement level of the student, with higher achieving students giving more consistently positive responses. Perhaps surprisingly, however, the responses differed dramatically across the three high schools in the study. In all, 11 graduates of Washington or Adams (about 30% of survey respondents from these two schools) indicated that their high school experience influenced their choice of major. Of these 9 (88.9%) indicated that the influence had been positive. Similarly, 13 graduates (about 35% of survey respondents) of Washington or Adams indicated that their high school mathematics experience influenced their future plans, and 10 of those indicated a positive influence, 1 indicated a neutral influence, and 2 (who had also given a negative response to the first question) indicated a negative influence. In contrast, a smaller percent of survey respondents who were Jefferson graduates (about 14% and 23% for the respective questions) indicated any influence of their high school experience. Of those who noted an influence on their choice of major, about 67% were positive and 33% were negative. Of those who cited an influence on their future plans, 68% were positive, 4% (1 student) were neutral, and 28% were negative. Because of this large school difference, mainly responses from Washington and Adams will be reported with some reference to related responses from Jefferson graduates. The full range of Jefferson responses, especially those pertaining to the story of their local controversy, will be discussed in Chapter 13.

Samples of the nine positive statements from Washington and Adams graduates concerning the influence of their high school mathematics experience on their choice of major are the following:

- I really enjoyed mathematics in high school. Enough to pursue a second year in calculus. Because math is a part of Physics, I believe choosing my major [Physics] was easier.
- I sincerely enjoyed my math experience and loved the subject so I decided to go into secondary education in math.
- I realized that math was a challenge, but it was my strong point. I noticed throughout H.S. that solving math problems, after thinking long and hard is satisfying. [engineering major]
- Because I did so well in math so I wanted to continue working with math. [accounting major]

The only two negative comments by Adams graduates (there were none by Washington graduates) were the following:

- I had such a hard time with math in high school that I never considered Physics or any math-related profession.
- They [my high school mathematics teachers] intimidated me enough to stay away from scientific and mathematical practices. I wanted to be in English Education from the start.

Concerning the influence of their high school mathematics experience on their future plans, many students' responses were similar to what they had said about the influence on their choice of major. Some exceptions are the following:

- I was confident in my high school math classes, therefore, I do not feel limited to what I can do, based on math skills.
- My high school math experience helped me to have confidence that I could do whatever I wanted in college. I also know that I will need math in many of the science courses I take and since I received a good math education in high school I know that I am well prepared for those courses.
- I enjoy math and everyday experiences so I want to work with it.

The one negative response by a graduate from Washington was,

> The Core Math Project helped me realize how much I dislike math. Oftentimes there was so much "story" in our story problems I was confused as to what was being asked of me. The approaches to teaching math at college I have found to be much more effective overall.

The neutral response of a Washington graduate was, "It [my high school mathematics experience] contributed to preparing me for college math, but didn't influence my decisions." The one negative response by an Adams graduate was, "I will not choose a career in which math is a crucial path because I didn't understand it and it frustrated me."

Anecdotes about High School Mathematics Preparation

Responses to the following survey item are discussed in this section: "If you have experienced a situation since high school in which you felt especially well prepared or especially poorly prepared by your high school mathematics background, please describe the situation."

This item prompted 95 responses, with a wide variety of themes. As with the questions discussed in the previous section, the responses varied by the mathematical achievement level of the student with higher achieving students giving more consistently positive responses, and the responses differed across the three high schools in the study. In all, 16 graduates of Washington or Adams wrote an anecdote, some very brief, of which 11 were quite positive, 3 had positive and negative elements, and 2 were entirely negative. In contrast, of the 79 respondents among Jefferson graduates, 34 were positive, 13 had positive and negative elements, and 32 were entirely negative. Responses from graduates of all three schools will be reported here to illustrate the general themes that emerge. The negative Jefferson responses will be reported and discussed mainly in the context of the story of Jefferson's local controversy in Chapter 13. In fact, some of the responses from Jefferson students referred specifically to their local controversy.

Some of the anecdotes help to clarify issues surrounding the transition from a *Standards*-based high school mathematics curriculum to a conventional college mathematics course. The two anecdotes that follow have similar elements. The first has a happy ending. A Washington graduate described his experience in Calculus 2 at a prestigious liberal arts college as follows:

> When I met with my mathematics professor to discuss my bad grade on my first test, she asked me to show her how I tried to solve one of the problems. I did not have the intermediate algebra skills necessary to solve it, but I drew a graph and showed exactly what I was trying to find and then

> explained a method on the calculator that would find a good estimate of the answer. My professor was very impressed with my grasp of graphical reasoning and understanding of the concepts. She encouraged me to keep moving in math as she said I would do really well once I practiced my algebra.

A Jefferson graduate related a somewhat similar anecdote concerning her experience in a precalculus class at a midsize state university. Unfortunately, this story did not have a happy ending, at least not at the time that it was written.

> In my math course during my first semester of college I felt very well prepared going into the class. The first two months I was doing very well until the Professor learned I was doing my work differently than the others in the class. He threatened me to learn math "his" way or fail me. I was very unaware of how to do traditional math, so I struggled learning his way. Now I have to repeat the course.

Several respondents describe examples of how what they view as their outstanding understanding of mathematical concepts served them well as they work with and help their classmates. The following anecdote is from a Jefferson graduate who attended a community college, even though he scored 28 on his ACT Mathematics test and had a perfect 4.0 in his high school mathematics courses. He is also the respondent referred to earlier as saying that he had developed a "passion" for mathematics.

> In general, I feel especially prepared for the classes I'm currently taking. I communicate with my classmates often, and we work well in study groups. I feel that I have knowledge to offer when we hit a stump in a math problem. I'm taking Calculus 3 and Differential Equations. There are about six others who are doing the same, and they came from a Core background as well. I enjoy challenging problems, which is very beneficial for me. Having the experience I had helped me to continue course work that may seem beyond my level of understanding.

Another Jefferson graduate indicated that he helped classmates in a mathematics-related class in a liberal arts college.

> In college [my] Biometrics course focuses on the interpretations of statistics with biological examples. I have helped other students with homework and have tutored one student in the class.

A Washington graduate in Calculus 1 at a large private university also reported helping classmates.

> I feel well prepared when explaining problems to those of less mathematical ability. I can articulate a lesson with such a good background.

A graduate of Jefferson High School who attended a community college did well on the mathematics placement tests and did not enroll in a mathematics course in her first term. Nevertheless, she reports helping other students in various mathematics and mathematics-related classes.

> I felt I was well prepared in math because I did very well on placement tests for college. I helped friends with their math homework often. I am able to explain a process to help them understand. I can show them a different way to do a problem that may be easier for them. In my chemistry and biology classes, I can understand the math in class because of my background. I feel I was very well prepared.

A third theme of the anecdotes reported by students speaks to good preparation for and remembering of particular mathematical content. A Washington student who attended an institute for art commented on his mathematical preparation in his precalculus class, "Well, in my math class, most people don't even remember how to do the basics, and I feel lucky that I can still remember most of what I learned in high school." An Adams graduate attending a liberal arts college indicated, "I felt well prepared for the math portion of the ACT test, it was my highest score of all the sections." A Jefferson graduate who completed Calculus 1 in her first term at a community college made the following comments:

> Whenever trigonometry was brought up, I always felt really prepared. My high school practiced it regularly. As I previously said, in my other non-mathematics courses I felt more advanced than most of my peers when math was brought up. Also, in college my teachers do not post our grades and many of the students didn't know how to calculate their grades, but I did. Overall, I feel that I was well prepared.

A Washington graduate related an anecdote from her Calculus 1 class at a large state university.

> I felt well prepared for working with parametric equations at the beginning of accelerated calculus because some of the class had never done them before. Also, the integrated math system prepared me to look at things more conceptually and to look at a full picture of a mathematical situation.

Graduates of Washington and Adams who were not all positive about their high school mathematics experience sometimes mentioned deficiencies in algebraic skills. As an Adams graduate attending a liberal arts college said, "In math 195 [precalculus] I knew much more about how to use the graphing calculators than others did. I really didn't have a grasp on algebra and had to learn it over again this fall." Another Adams graduate had similar views following a precalculus class at a large state university in which she earned an A.

> I have been prepared especially well in terms of the discipline and the need to do homework to understand the material, even though it is not required. My weakest point from high school is some of my basics, such as simple algebra rules. I had to learn all that as I was continuing the course in college.

Graduates of Jefferson High School were more inclined than graduates of the other two high schools to blame perceived hardships on poor preparation in high school mathematics. The following anecdote is illustrative. This Jefferson graduate was successful but not outstanding in mathematics in high school, completing high school mathematics through Course 4 with a B+ grade point average. Her ACT Mathematics score was 19, below the national average of 21 or 22. She enrolled in a precalculus course at a liberal arts college and had this to say about her experience.

> I had to study a lot more than other students for algebra—only to get a "B." Oftentimes I had to seek help and studied in the library excessively for the degree [sic] of the course. I had a tutor and stayed after class at least 3 days a week to talk to the teacher. I would often study after work till the library closed, it was a very tough and discouraging class and was only the lowest offered course for credit.

This mathematically average student worked hard to earn a B in her first college mathematics course. One might see this as a positive outcome, but like many Jefferson graduates, she tended to interpret her struggles as evidence of the weakness of her high school mathematics program. This phenomenon will be discussed in more detail in the story of Jefferson's local controversy in Chapter 13.

CHAPTER SUMMARY

A written survey of 2001 graduates of Washington, Adams, and Jefferson high schools was administered in January 2002 during the first academic year after high school graduation. The survey sought information concerning what the students did after high school with particular emphasis on any college mathematics or statistics course(s) they completed. The survey results with some comparative freshmen data obtained from the registrars at two major universities were presented in this chapter. A brief description of some of the main findings follows:

- About two-thirds of the respondents completed a mathematics or statistics course in their first college term and reported their grades. About 80% of respondents completed a mathematics or statistics course in their first year of college, and about 40% completed at least two such courses in their first year.
- Respondents perceived that their college mathematics or statistics courses were conventional with the main emphases being on "learning mathematics from lectures," "paper-and-pencil algebra or calculus symbol manipulation," and "understanding the meaning of mathematical concepts." There was little emphasis in these courses on explaining mathematical thinking or working with classmates.
- In their first college semester, graduates from the present study with similar high school mathematics backgrounds (and somewhat lower ACT scores) completed various college mathematics courses through Calculus 2 at similar frequencies and with similar success rates as University of Iowa freshmen from more conventional high school mathematics programs.
- About 90% of respondents believed that their high school preparation for college mathematics and mathematics-related courses was at least as good or better than most of their college classmates.
- When prompted, respondents identified many strengths of their high school mathematics experience with the most frequently mentioned ones having to do with the development of better conceptual understanding and of better problem-solving and reasoning abilities.
- When prompted, respondents recommended a wide variety of changes in their high school mathematics program. Generally, better students were more satisfied with the program as is or wanted more course options or hands-on activities, while less successful mathematics students recommended changes that would make the program more conventional.
- Respondents, especially Washington and Adams graduates, were quite positive about the impact of their high school mathematics programs. Jefferson students were generally positive, too, but there were notable exceptions, mainly among less successful students. Many of these exceptions appear to be related to the local controversy in that community which will be described in Chapter 13.

The next chapter, Chapter 12, reports longitudinal case studies of 5 years of mathematical achievement and affective outcomes for three students, one from each school.

NOTES

1. The three schools had a combined total of 595 graduates in 2001, so 279 seniors in mathematics classes comprise 46.9% of all graduates.
2. The last high school mathematics course category of "No Core 4" is used because the data indicated that having Course 4 was crucial to success in precalculus and calculus in college. On the other hand, students who completed AP Statistics after Course 3 performed in these college courses much like students who completed Course 3 only.

CHAPTER 12

LONGITUDINAL EXPERIENCES OF THREE STUDENTS

Quantitative and qualitative descriptions of large groups of students, like those in previous chapters, provide an important portrait of how these groups generally experienced mathematics during high school and 1 year after. By necessity, this picture describes group averages and variability, but it does not reveal detail about the experience of any individuals within the group. Yet such details can provide important and useful information for judging a curriculum's impact (Williams, 2007).

In this chapter, individual case studies of three students, one from each school, are reported. The chapter begins with a description of the process for selecting these students. Then a year-by-year story is written from data of each student's course taking, achievement, and beliefs across the 4 years of high school and into the following post-high school year. The final section of the chapter is a brief reflection on differences and similarities in the three case studies.

THE CASE STUDIES

The intent was to choose students for individual study from among those for whom data were essentially complete, including all achievement and affective instruments, problem interviews during courses, and the post-

A Five-Year Study of the First Edition of the Core-Plus Mathematics Curriculum, pp. 301–335

high school survey. In addition, the chosen students taken together should be interesting cases with variability in school, gender, and entering achievement level. In fact, there were no students for whom the data set was entirely complete. A small handful of students had been interviewed all 4 years, but nearly all of those had some other data source missing, often the post-high school survey.

As a practical necessity for providing a degree of closure to the students' stories, it was decided that the availability of post-high school survey data was crucial. Applying this criterion, a set of about 10 post-high survey participants was identified who had each been interviewed in at least 2 years and had no more than one score missing on achievement or affective measures administered during high school.

At first two students, one female and one male, from each school were selected. Drafts of case studies of all six students were prepared. However, space limitations made it necessary to limit the chapter to three students. The three students chosen for case studies can be viewed as somewhat representative of the group of all students in the study who went immediately on to higher education. Of course, they were more successful mathematically than the average of the entire study sample. The three case studies follow.

Washington High School Female

The first case is that of a Washington High School student (called Martie), who is a Caucasian female. As a baseline measure, Martie completed the *ITED-Q* at the beginning of Grade 9. Her score of 271 was at the 66th national student percentile and was very near the mean (270.1) of all students in the present study. On the Student Belief Survey (SBS) administered at the beginning of Course 1, Martie was at or near the most strongly positive score on all six mathematics belief scales. In spite of her average pretest score, she was confident of her mathematical ability, and she believed strongly that genetics or gender plays very little role in mathematical success. Martie indicated that she enjoyed a good mathematical challenge and very much enjoyed creativity and originality in mathematics. She got enjoyment from working with her peers, and she tended to dislike competing against them.

Mathematics Achievement in Year 1. In her freshman year, Martie enrolled in Course 1. Her teacher, *W, N, 1* in Chapter 4, was a female who was a novice at teaching the Core-Plus Mathematics curriculum and had a great deal of difficulty with classroom management. Brief descriptions of this teacher's beliefs about the curriculum and her implementation practices are given on pages 77 and 79. Martie was not interviewed during Course

1, but she completed the *ITED-Q* at the end of the year with a score of 317 at the 94th percentile, an impressive gain of 28 national percentile points over her *ITED-Q* score at the beginning of Course 1.

Martie completed Course 1 with a grade of A. At the end of the year, her total final examination score (92.3%) was considerably higher than the score (48.8%) predicted by her pretest *ITED-Q* score. To present a more descriptive profile of Martie's relative strengths in different mathematical areas, the score on each content subtest predicted (by linear regression) from her pre-*ITED-Q* score of 271 was subtracted from her mean subtest score and the difference, or residual, was divided by the standard error of measure. As Figure 12.1 shows, Martie scored higher than predicted on all of the final examination subtests. Her strongest relative performance (2.54 SEs more than predicted) was on the Geometry and Trigonometry subtest. Her relatively weakest area, although still nearly .5 SEs greater than predicted, was Algebra and Functions.

Mathematics Achievement in Year 2. As a sophomore, Martie completed Course 2 with a grade of A. Her teacher (*W, ES, 1*) was a man in the "Experienced Supporter" category in Chapter 4. While experienced at teaching the curriculum, the teaching approach of *W, ES, 1* was judged by observers to have some potentially important shortcomings. A brief description of some of his classroom practices can be found on page 75.

Martie was interviewed with a total of five problems, three in February and two at the end of May. In the first problem, Martie was asked to use a matrix representing a sports equipment order to answer a variety of follow-up questions (see Figure 6.8 for the complete interview problem). She was able to answer each of the questions correctly with the use of her calculator as well as with paper-and-pencil arithmetic, including one question in

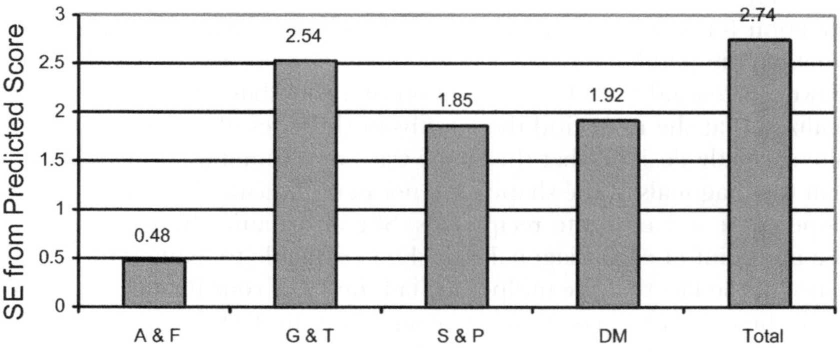

Figure 12.1. Martie's Difference From Predicted Scores on Course 1 Final Exam Subtests.

which she had to multiply two matrices. She often checked the calculations she performed on her calculator using paper-and-pencil arithmetic, because she did not want to become too reliant on her calculator.

On the second question, Martie was asked to solve a system of two linear equations using matrices and one other method of her choice. For the problem and a discussion of all student responses to it, see page 132. Initially, she could not remember how to solve this system of equations with matrices, but with a little prompting, she arrived at a correct solution. She substituted her solution into the equation to make sure it was correct. The second method she chose to use was cancellation. She noted that her answer was the same using both methods, and she also indicated without prompting that she loved math, especially equation solving.

On the third question, Martie was asked to analyze a situation involving a tournament of tennis players (the problem is given in Figure 6.9). She was able to draw a correct vertex-edge graph for the first part of the problem and to explain what the directions of the arrows meant in terms of the situation. She also constructed a matrix to model the situation, using 1s and 0s to represent wins and losses and dashes to represent when a player would be playing herself. Finally, she correctly ranked the players with the use of her matrix.

On the fourth question, Martie was asked to sketch a diagram of the route that a car traveled given the miles and directions driven (see Figure 6.5 for the problem statement). She correctly found the total distance driven but was only partially correct about how far a bird would fly from the starting point to the ending point of the car's journey. She incorrectly assumed that the bird's path crossed at the midpoint of the car's eastbound path. With prompting from the interviewer, she was able to correct her error and solve the problem.

On the fifth question, Martie was given a vertex matrix representation of a parallelogram (see the problem in Figure 6.7). She wrote a correct equation for a line containing two of the vertices. When asked to justify whether the parallelogram was a rhombus, she needed to ask the interviewer to remind her of the definition of a rhombus. With this help, she realized that she must find the lengths of the sides of the parallelogram. She correctly decided that the shape was not a rhombus, and she proved that the diagonals of the shape were not perpendicular by noting that the slopes were not opposite reciprocals. She also found the coordinates of the midpoint of each diagonal, but she was unable to explain the significance of the fact that the midpoints had the same coordinates.

At the end of Course 2, Martie completed the ETS *End-of-Course Algebra Examination*. Her total score of 81.5% was 3.05 standard errors higher than the 43.7% predicted by her *ITED-Q* pretest score. As Figure 12.2 shows, Martie scored higher than expected on all three subtests of the

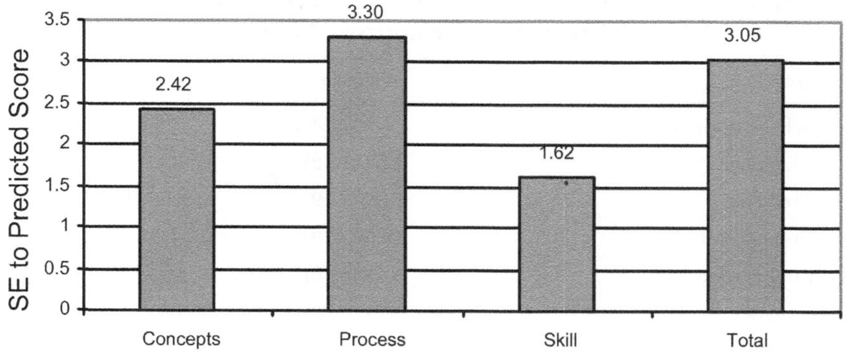

Figure 12.2. Martie's Difference From Predicted Scores on Subtests of ETS *End-Of-Year Algebra Examination* at End of Course 2.

ETS algebra test, and she scored particularly higher than predicted (3.30 standard errors) on the Process subtest. The Process subtest included problems involving multiple representations, deductive and inductive reasoning, analogical reasoning, and quantitative reasoning.

Beliefs and Attitudes About Mathematics—Years 1 and 2. At the end of both Courses 1 and 2, students completed the same survey of six scales of beliefs about mathematics that they had been administered at the beginning of Course 1. Martie's score for each scale where 1 is strongly negative and 5 is strongly positive is given in Table 12.1. The effect sizes of Martie's scores ([Martie's scale score—mean scale score for all students] / scale *SD*) within the entire set of subjects in the study are given in parentheses. With the exception of the Cooperation scale, Martie was considerably more positive than other students with effect sizes ranging from .49 to 1.58. She was the most positive (relative to her peers) about enjoying the challenge in doing and learning mathematics. In fact, she was more positive than about 90% of students about this aspect of mathematics.

Martie's beliefs about mathematics remained fairly consistent from Course 1 to Course 2. Her scores on the Self-Assessment scale indicate her confidence in her mathematical ability. In addition to enjoying the challenge of mathematics, she had high scores on the Creativity and Genetic scales. This indicates that she liked the creative and original aspects of mathematics and that she believed strongly that neither genetics nor gender contribute substantially to mathematical success.

Her lowest scores were on the Competition and Cooperation scales, but these were above neutral in both Courses 1 and 2. A higher score on the Competition scale indicates a lesser enjoyment of competitive characteristics such as finishing first or getting more problems correct. A higher

Table 12.1. Martie's Student Belief Survey Scale Scores and Effect Sizes for Courses 1 and 2

Scale	*Course 1*	*Course 2*
Self-Assessment	4.25 (.73)	4.50 (.99)
Challenge	4.33 (1.52)	4.33 (1.58)
Creativity	4.00 (.49)	4.63 (1.27)
Competition	3.50 (.73)	3.50 (.71)
Cooperation	3.38 (–.06)	3.33 (–.06)
Genetics	4.33 (1.33)	5.00 (2.16)

score on the Cooperation scale indicates a greater enjoyment of working with others to solve problems. Martie's scores on these scales indicate that she valued the cooperative aspects more than the competitive aspects of her mathematics experience. Cooperation was the only scale for which Martie's scores were below the mean of all students in the study. As positive as Martie's beliefs about mathematics were at the end of Courses 1 and 2, they were not as positive as they had been at the beginning of Course 1. At that time, her scale scores ranged from 4.0 to 5.0, inclusive.

As for Martie's specific attitudes about Courses 1 and 2, her mean in Course 1 was 3.55 or about .40 standard deviations higher than her study peers. However, her attitude about Course 2 was less positive with a mean of 2.91, about .36 standard deviations lower than her study peers. Martie agreed or strongly agreed at the end of both courses that she understood the mathematical ideas in the course and that the course helped her see that mathematical ideas make sense. Another area in which Martie's attitude was more positive in Course 2 than in Course 1 was that she found the textbook less difficult to read in Course 2. Her responses were at least neutral that she learned to reason mathematically, that the course helped her feel confident that she can solve mathematical problems, and that the course made her better at talking about mathematical ideas.

However, Martie was less positive at the end of Course 2 than at the end of Course 1 that the problems in the course were realistic, that group work was helpful or that it was enjoyable, that the course made her better at writing about mathematical ideas, and that she enjoyed using the calculator in the course. To summarize, Martie believed she was learning to understand and make sense of mathematical ideas in both courses, and by Course 2 she had little difficulty reading the textbook. However, her attitudes about how the course was taught (realistic problems, group work, writing mathematics, and using the calculator) were less positive at the end of Course 2 than they had been at the end of Course 1, both in terms of absolute response means and relative to the other students in this study.

Her open-ended descriptions of her experience in the courses provide no evidence as to why she was more negative about Course 2. At the end of Course 1, Martie wrote:

> My mathematics course this year was enjoyable. Although it was very confusing the first couple of weeks, because I was used to doing just Algebra, not stuff put together.

At the end of Course 2, Martie described her experience as follows:

> I guess it was pretty easy. I thought the way they put it in the book was pretty stupid. But other than that it was fine.

Mathematics Achievement in Junior Year. In her junior year, Martie decided to take advantage of the opportunity to accelerate in mathematics by completing a combined Course 3 and Course 4. She earned a grade of A. Her teacher (*W, ES, 2*) was a woman in the "Experienced Supporter" category. The general description of the practices of teachers in this category begins on page 66. A specific reference to *W, ES, 2* can be found on page 76.

Martie was interviewed with three different problems at the end of March. Recall that Course 3 interview problems were from the New Standards/Balanced Assessment project, and they focused on open-ended, non-routine problem solving. In the first problem, she was asked to analyze a table of data representing the handedness of a sample of people (this problem can be found in Figure 7.3). Martie was able to determine the number of people who are right-handed as well as find the percentage of people who are ambidextrous. She did, however, require a reminder that a decimal and a percent are not the same thing. She was also able to find the number of ambidextrous people in the sample's population, but she had some difficulty determining if her answer made sense and some trouble explaining why she was completing the steps she had chosen to complete.

In the second problem, Martie was asked to find the perimeter and area of a semicircle-topped rectangular window with variable dimensions found in Figure 7.4. She was able to determine both the perimeter and area of the window without any prompting or formula reminders. According to the interviewer, she seemed very confident and adept at applying formulas for perimeter and area.

For the third problem, Martie was given the dimensions of a piece of paper after it had been folded twice and was asked to first find the area of the paper (before it was folded) (the problem is given in Figure 7.6). She answered this part of the problem by doubling one of the dimensions twice and then finding the area of the resulting piece of paper. Next, she was asked to draw and describe two different possibilities for the shape of the original piece of paper. She found two possibilities by using the original example and unfolding twice one way and then unfolding twice the other way. She then solved the final part of the problem that asked her to find the original dimensions of the paper in terms of variables. After finding the solutions to the given questions, Martie independently explored what happens when the paper is folded on the diagonal. She realized that this exploration was problematic, because she could no longer identify the length and the width of the folded piece of paper.

At the end of junior year, Martie completed the written test of mathematical literacy compiled from items released by TIMSS. As Figure 12.3 shows, she scored higher than predicted on the Course 3 mathematical literacy test overall and on both the Number and Geometry scales. She did particularly well on the Geometry subtest, over two and a half SEs above the score predicted by her pretest score.

Mathematics Achievement in Senior Year. In her senior year, Martie enrolled in AP Calculus which was taught by her teacher in Courses 3 and 4 (*W*, *ES*, 2). Martie completed this course with a grade of A. Intending to go to college, Martie also completed the SAT reasoning test. Her scores were 630 in Mathematics and 610 in Verbal. These scores were .78 and .61 standard deviations above the respective subtest means in the distribution of all students in this study who completed the SAT.

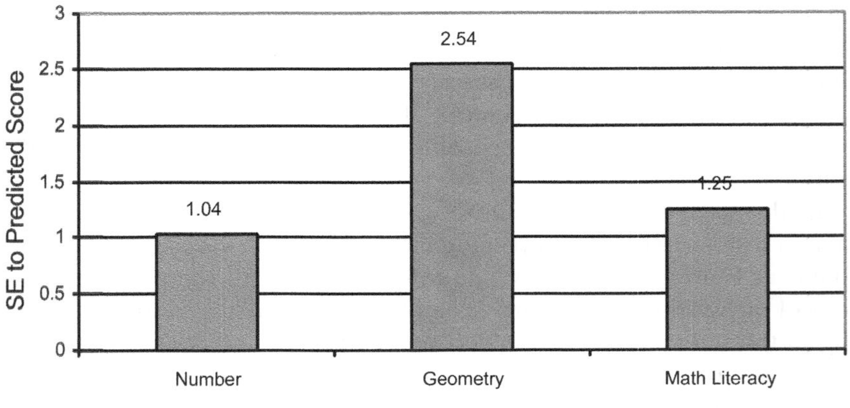

Figure 12.3. Martie's Difference From Predicted Scores on Subtests of the Course 3 TIMSS-Based Test at End of Year 3.

Martie was interviewed about two different problems in mid-April. The first problem (given in Figure 8.6) asked her to make a list of positive integers less than or equal to 70 such that the sum of the digits of the number could be divided by 7. She completed this list L and was immediately concerned with whether there were numbers on the list that she was missing. Then she was asked to determine whether a set of given conjectures about the list were correct. She correctly noted "If you start with 7 and keep adding 9s until the sum is 70 you **always** get a number in the list L." The second conjecture was "If you start with 7 and keep adding 9s until the sum is 70 you get **every** number in list L." At first, Martie indicated the second conjecture was also true, but she eventually thought of several counterexamples and realized that the conjecture could not be true. She concluded that the third conjecture, namely, that the first two conjectures say the same thing, must be incorrect. She noted that, "always and every are two totally separate things."

At the end of the school year, students in Course 4, AP Calculus, or AP Statistics, mainly seniors including Martie, completed two written mathematical achievement assessments. The first was a reasoning test composed of several content-specific subtests, and the second was a test compiled from released items from the TIMSS advanced mathematics test. These measures are described in more detail in Chapter 8, pages 170 through 172. As Figure 12.4 shows, Martie scored higher than predicted overall on the reasoning test and on the Number and Algebra and Geometry subtests, with Geometry being her relatively strongest area. Predicted scores were computed using the sample of students in the study who completed AP Calculus.

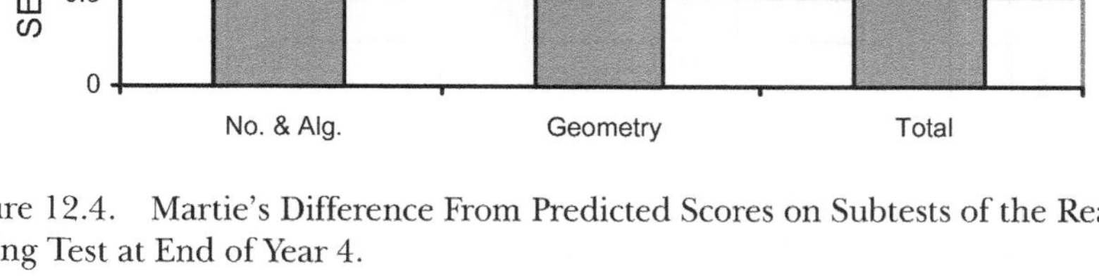

Figure 12.4. Martie's Difference From Predicted Scores on Subtests of the Reasoning Test at End of Year 4.

The advanced mathematics test consisted of four subtests based on the TIMSS content categories. As Figure 12.5 shows, Martie scored considerably higher than predicted on all of the subtests of the TIMSS-based exam. The differences between actual and predicted score on the subtests were between .79 standard errors for Probability and Statistics and 1.59 for Calculus.

Conceptions of Mathematics Inventory–Year 3 and Year 4. At the end of both junior year and senior year, Martie completed the *Conceptions of Mathematics Inventory* (CMI) described in detail in Chapter 10. Her mean score for each six-item scale is given in Table 12.2. A score of 3.5 is the center point of the 6-choice Likert scale that students responded to, with 6 being strongly positive and 1 strongly negative about an item statement. Table 12.2 also gives the effect size of each of Martie's scale scores in the distribution of all students who completed the CMI inventory at the end of Year 3. The effect size in Year 4 is relative to the distribution of all students in AP Calculus classes.

All of Martie's scores in both Year 3 and Year 4 were above the neutral score, and her effect sizes were all positive in Course 3. Compared to other AP Calculus students in Year 4, Martie was more positive on five of the seven CMI scales. Her highest scores were on scales 4 and 7. These scores were consistently strong and both grew over time. This indicates that Martie believed that it is more important to make sense of problems and understand why solution methods work than it is to know the correct formula to use. She also believed strongly that mathematics is a worthwhile subject to study and that it will be an important part of her adult life and work.

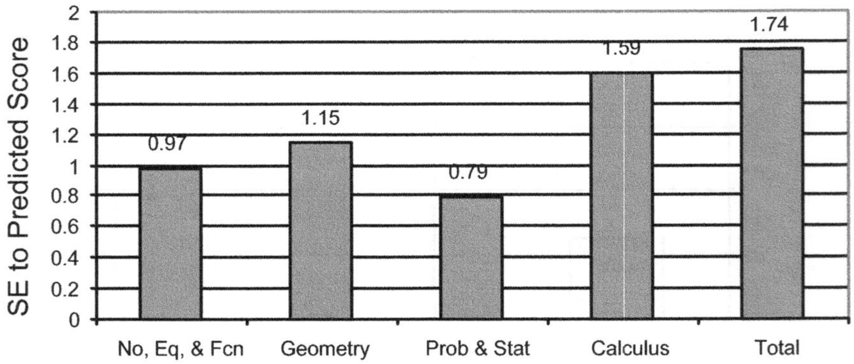

Figure 12.5. Martie's Difference from Predicted Scores on Subtests of the Advanced Mathematics Test at End of Year 4.

Table 12.2. Martie's Conceptions of Mathematics Scale Scores and Effect Sizes for Junior and Senior Years

Scale	*Year 3*	*Year 4*
1. Composition of Mathematical Knowledge	3.75 (.17)	4.00 (–.02)
2. Structure of Mathematical Knowledge	4.63 (.35)	4.63 (.19)
3. Status of Mathematical Knowledge	4.75 (1.17)	4.75 (1.03)
4. Doing Mathematics	5.00 (.90)	5.13 (.62)
5. Validating Ideas in Mathematics	4.63 (.72)	4.13 (–.67)
6. Learning Mathematics	4.50 (.94)	4.63 (.54)
7. Usefulness of Mathematics	5.13 (.59)	5.88 (1.19)

In both years, Martie's largest effect sizes were on scale 3, Status of Mathematical Knowledge, indicating that she felt much more strongly than other students in this study that mathematics is a growing and changing field in which students can come up with their own ideas and make their own mathematical discoveries. This finding is also consistent with her strong beliefs in Courses 1 and 2 concerning the creative and original aspects of mathematics.

On scales 1, 6, and 7, Martie's beliefs increased between the first and second testing period. These scores indicate that over time she felt more strongly that mathematical ideas, problem-solving skills, and conceptual understanding are more important than sets of procedures and facts. She also believed more strongly over time that important characteristics of working with mathematics include learning from one's mistakes, understanding how and why formulas work, and making connections between problems. In addition, Martie's belief that mathematics will be useful in her future career and in activities outside school grew stronger. By the end of Year 4, in fact, Martie's belief in the usefulness of mathematics was over one standard error greater than the mean of all AP Calculus students.

Martie's scale 2 scores were essentially the same each year. These scores reflect her belief that mathematics concepts and problems are all somewhat interconnected. The only scale for which Martie's scores decreased over time was scale 5. Despite the decrease and the negative effect size in Course 4, her beliefs on this scale were positive. This indicates that she believed at the end of both courses that it is important for her and others to justify solution methods and answers and that different solution methods can be correct. However, at the end of Year 4, her beliefs in this area were less strong than they had been at the end of Year 3 and less strong than the mean beliefs for all AP Calculus students in this study.

After High School. After graduating in the spring of 2001, Martie became a full-time student at a private liberal arts college in a Southeastern state the following autumn. In her first semester, she reported her major as Mathematics and French. In her second semester, she reported that she had switched her major to Physics. She believed that her high school mathematics experience influenced her choice of major, writing, "I really enjoyed mathematics in high school, enough to pursue a second year of Calculus. Because math is a part of Physics, I believe choosing my major was easier."

In the Fall 2001 semester, she took Introduction to Calculus, a course that dealt mainly with derivatives and their applications. In the course, a graphing calculator was allowed at any time, including on tests. Martie identified the following two areas as highly emphasized in this class: understanding the meaning of mathematical concepts and methods, and learning mathematics from a lecture by the teacher or instructor. She felt that much of the content of the class was review for her, and she remarked that she had been helping others in the class. She discovered that she was especially comfortable with matrices. Her final grade for the course was A.

Martie rated her mathematical preparation as better students in the class because the material came easier to her than most, and she was able to complete activities efficiently. On the 11 categories from the post-high school survey given in Table 11.10, she rated her preparation for her calculus course as "excellent" in all areas, except for "good" ratings of her preparation for learning mathematics from a lecture by the instructor and for explaining her mathematical thinking orally. In her second college semester, Spring 2002, Martie enrolled in Introduction to Calculus 2, which was a course that emphasized integrals and their applications.

After one semester of college, some of Martie's reflections on her high school mathematics program were the following:

- When asked to comment on the greatest strengths she gained from her high school mathematics experience, she wrote, "I am able to logically think in a step to step process. I find myself asking why and answering my questions through observation and experimentation. I appreciate math more than average."
- When asked what changes she would make in her high school mathematics program, she wrote, "I would change the wordiness of some of the questions. The wordiness made the questions hard to follow. I would try to throw more algebra emphasis in the course. Algebra throughout the entire course would be helpful. Maybe a handout for parents so they can help their children; or less of an emphasis on calculators parents have never seen."

Adams High School Female

The Adams High School case study student (called Abbie) is female and an Asian/Pacific Islander. Abbie scored well on the *ITED-Q* administered as a pretest at the beginning of Grade 9. Her score of 333 was at the 99th national student percentile. Unfortunately, she did not complete the SBS that was also administered at about that time.

Mathematics Achievement in Year 1. In her freshman year, Abbie enrolled in Course 1. Her teacher (*A,N,1*) was a female who was new to teaching the Core-Plus Mathematics curriculum, and she had no professional development to prepare her. Brief descriptions of this teacher's beliefs about the curriculum and her implementation practices are given on pages 77 and 78, respectively.

In an individual interview in the first week of February, Abbie attempted to solve two different problems. In the first problem, she was asked to solve for x in the linear equation $16x - 81 = 263$ and then check the solution. Abbie was able to solve for x using standard symbolic reasoning, explain what she did, and check her solution.

Her second interview problem was a four-part, verbally-stated application in which students were asked to consider a linear equation, $y = 18 - 2x$, for the number y of gallons of gasoline that are left in a boat after traveling x miles. The complete problem is given in Figure 5.3. In the first part of the problem, Abbie was asked to explain the meaning of the numerical coefficients in the given equation in terms of the number of gallons. She correctly interpreted the meaning of 18, the y-intercept, but she was unable to interpret the meaning of the slope (–2; the rate of fuel consumption). In the second part of the problem, Abbie correctly graphed the equation and explained the role that the numerical coefficients play in creating the graph. In the third part of the problem, Abbie determined the correct number of miles driven from fill-up until there were 10 gallons of gasoline remaining in the tank. Furthermore, she was able to explain how she found her answers in terms of both the equation and the graph. Finally, she correctly used the equation and symbolic reasoning to determine the number of gallons of gasoline that were left in the tank after driving 8 miles in the boat (when its tank was initially full).

Overall in the interview, Abbie seemed to have a good grasp of how the equation and graph relate to the problem situation. She realized that a negative number of gallons or miles did not make sense, so she ignored negative solutions. She was confident that she understood what the variables in the equation represented, and she was able to algebraically manipulate the linear equation as needed. Abbie noted at the end of the interview that, although she was struggling with learning how to work in groups and with having to explain her answers, she believed that such activities would be helpful to her in the future.

Abbie completed Course 1 with a grade point average of 3.67 or A–. At the end of the year, she completed the *ITED-Q* with a score of 335, a score that is at the 99th national student percentile and .25 standard errors greater than the score predicted by her pretest score. Her total final examination score (92.3%) was considerably higher than the score (80.7%) predicted by her pretest *ITED-Q* score. As Figure 12.6 shows, the one mathematical area on the final examination in which her achievement level was lower than expected was Geometry and Trigonometry. This result is not very meaningful, since there was just one geometry task on the form of the final exam completed by Abbie. She answered it incorrectly, accounting for the strongly negative effect size in this category. In her response, she erroneously indicated that a rotation of 180° about the center of a rhombus was not a symmetry of the rhombus, and that a reflection over the line containing the midpoints of two opposite sides was a symmetry.

Mathematics Achievement in Year 2. In her sophomore year, Abbie enrolled in Course 2, which she completed with a grade of A in each grading period. Her teacher was a man *(A, ES, 3)* in the "Experienced Supporter" category in Chapter 4. For brief descriptions of some of his classroom practices, see pages 68, 72, and 74. Abbie was not interviewed during Course 2, but she completed the ETS End-of Course Algebra Examination at the end of the course. Her total score of 81.5% was considerably higher than the 70.7% predicted by her *ITED-Q* pretest score. As Figure 12.7 shows, Abbie scored higher than expected on all three subtests of the EoC Algebra test. Her most outstanding area relative to predicted scores was Skills, a subtest that required students to solve, evaluate, simplify, and construct algebraic equations or expressions.

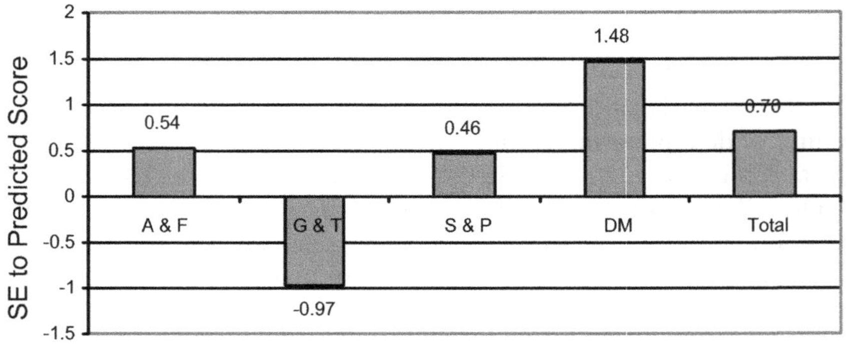

Figure 12.6. Abbie's Difference From Predicted Scores on Course 1 Final Exam Subtests.

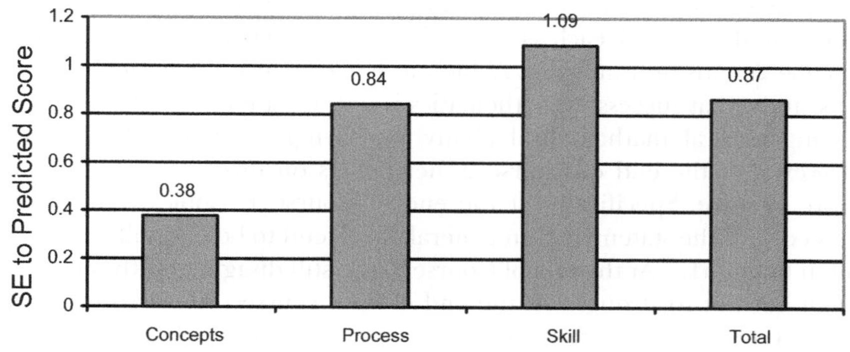

Figure 12.7. Abbie's Difference From Predicted Scores on Subtests of ETS *End-of-Year Algebra Examination* at End of Year 2.

Table 12.3. Abbie's Student Belief Survey Scale Scores and Effect Sizes for Courses 1 and 2

Scale	*Course 1*	*Course 2*
Self-Assessment	4.50 (1.08)	4.63 (1.16)
Challenge	3.83 (.92)	3.83 (.96)
Creativity	4.38 (.98)	4.37 (.95)
Competition	3.50 (.73)	2.25 (–.41)
Cooperation	4.33 (1.33)	4.00 (.91)
Genetics	2.67 (–.52)	3.33 (–.18)

Beliefs and Attitudes About Mathematics—Courses 1 and 2. At the end of each of Courses 1 and 2, Abbie completed the SBS. Abbie's average score for each of the six belief scales, where 1 is strongly negative and 5 is strongly positive, is given in Table 12.3 above. The effect sizes of Abbie's scores within the entire set of subjects in the study are given in parentheses.

Compared to her study peers, Abbie was very confident of her mathematical ability, and she valued cooperating with others when doing mathematics. She also enjoyed the creativity and, to a somewhat lesser extent, the challenge of mathematics. Abbie's scores and effect sizes on these scales (Self-Assessment, Challenge, Creativity, and Cooperation) were fairly consistent from Course 1 to Course 2. The largest change in beliefs for Abbie was on the Competition scale. She saw mathematics as considerably more competitive at the end of Course 2 than she had at the end of the previous year.

Abbie's score on the Genetics scale was lower than those of her study peers at the end of each course, although it increased by the end of Course 2. This indicates that Abbie was less convinced than her peers in this study, that success in mathematics is not just a matter of being male, having natural mathematical ability, or having a mathematical mind. However, at the end of Course 2, her beliefs on this scale had become more positive. Specifically, at the end of Course 1, Abbie strongly disagreed with the statement, "In general, boys tend to be naturally better at math than girls." At the end of Course 2, she still disagreed with the statement but not so strongly. At the end of both courses, Abbie agreed with the statement, "To be good at math, you need to have a kind of 'mathematical mind.' " The change in Abbie's beliefs on this scale is due mainly to her responses to the following statement: "Math is a subject in which natural ability matters more than effort." At the end of Course 1, she strongly agreed with this statement, but she disagreed at the end of Course 2. Assuming Abbie's responses were carefully considered, this result suggests that by the end of Course 2 she became more convinced of the importance of effort in mathematical success.

Abbie's specific attitudes about Courses 1 and 2 were quite positive overall with little difference between courses. Her respective Course 1 and Course 2 attitude scale scores with effect sizes were 3.82 (.76) and 3.64 (.54). She considered the problems in both courses to be realistic and the curriculum materials to be readable. She saw both courses as helping her to reason mathematically, to become more confident of her ability to solve mathematical problems, to see that mathematical ideas make sense, and to be better able to talk about and write about mathematical ideas. She also enjoyed using the calculator.

The one part of her experience in these courses that she was neutral about was working in groups. In her open-ended description of her experience in Course 1, Abbie wrote:

> In the beginning of the year, the Math was just different because the school I previously attended had algebra. At first most people worked in their groups, but then on their own. A disadvantage of group work is I had to wait until someone understood a problem. I did like that the problems were realistic and figure [sic] why you got an answer. I ended getting a good grade in math.

At the end of Course 2, Abbie described her experience as follows:

> This year in math was much easier than Core I. I found it tiresome however to always depend on the calculator even though I enjoyed the frequent use. I was glad group work was not enforced because I've found I like to figure

> out problems on my own and then consult others for help as a last resort. I liked the topics we covered also.

Mathematics Achievement in Year 3. In her junior year, Abbie completed Course 3 with straight A grades. Her teacher (*A, ES, 3*) was the same male Experienced Supporter she had for Course 2. Abbie was interviewed about two different problems in mid-October of her junior year.

In her first interview problem, she was given a diagram of the way a bandana is folded from a square of cloth (see the statement of the problem in Figure 7.5). The original dimensions of the cloth were also given, and Abbie was asked to calculate the length of the bandana. She was able to find the length of the bandana using the Pythagorean Theorem and algebraic methods.

In the second interview problem given in Figure 7.6, Abbie was able to find the original dimensions of a piece of paper when given the dimensions of the paper after it was folded in half twice. She determined the area of the original piece of paper by finding the area of the folded paper and multiplying it by four for the four folded sections. Next, Abbie was asked to draw and describe two different possibilities for the shape of the original piece of paper. She was able to do so; in fact, she drew and described three possibilities. Finally, this problem asked students to generalize this situation by finding the original dimensions of a piece of paper when they were given variables as dimensions for the paper after it was folded in half twice. However, Abbie ran out of time before she was able to complete the final part of the problem.

At the end of Course 3, students completed a written test of mathematical literacy compiled from items released by TIMSS. Unfortunately, Abbie did not complete this test.

Mathematics Achievement in Year 4. In her senior year, Abbie completed Course 4 with a grade-point average of 3.67 or A–. Her teacher was a male Experienced Supporter (*A,ES,1*). In fact, her teacher in Course 4 was "Mr. Schulte," whose implementation practices were described as a prototype of an "Experienced Supporter" on pages 69 through 72. Abbie was not interviewed during Course 4.

At the end of the school year, like other seniors in Course 4, AP Calculus, and AP Statistics, Abbie completed the reasoning test and the TIMSS-based advanced mathematics test. Her scores on both subtests of the reasoning test were well below the scores predicted by her high pre-*ITED-Q* score. Her predicted scores were estimated within the sample of students who completed these tests at the end of Course 4. The number of standard errors of the difference between Abbie's actual score and the score predicted by her *ITED-Q* pretest score for each of the reasoning test scales and the total is given in Figure 12.8.

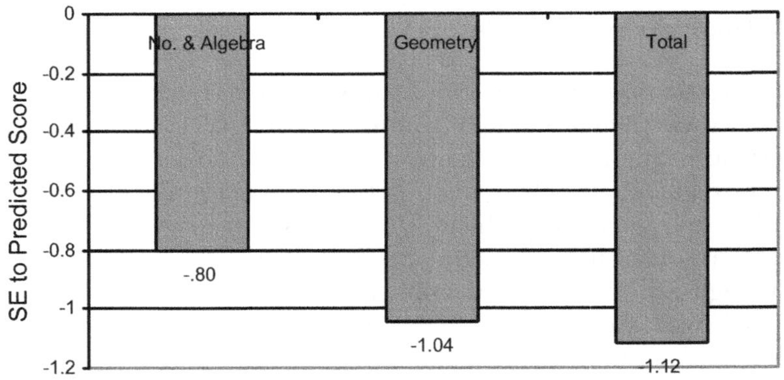

Figure 12.8. Abbie's Difference From Predicted Scores on Subtests of the Reasoning Test at End of Year 4.

Abbie scored much lower on the reasoning test and each of its subtests than predicted by her high pre-*ITED-Q* score. Her total score was over a full standard error below the score predicted by her *ITED-Q* pretest. Mathematical reasoning, whether in numerical, algebraic, or geometric settings, was relatively difficult for her. Nevertheless, it is important to keep in mind that the negative data in the figure is relative to scores predicted for students with a pretest score of 333, well above the 99th national percentile. Abbie's scores are somewhat above the means of Course 4 students on the Number and Algebra subtest (50.0% vs. 45.9%), the Geometry subtest (40.0% vs. 38.3%), and the total reasoning test (45.2% vs. 42.3%).

The second Year 4 test was composed of released advanced mathematics items from TIMSS and was divided into four subtests based on the TIMSS content categories. The number of standard errors of the difference between Abbie's actual score and the score predicted by her *ITED-Q* pretest score for each of the TIMSS scales and the total is given in Figure 12.9.

Abbie's total score was almost identical to the score predicted by her *ITED-Q* pretest score, but her subtest scores varied a great deal. She had perfect scores on the Numbers, Equations and Functions subtest and the Calculus subtest, both well over one standard error greater than her predicted scores. Abbie's relative weakness in Geometry was evident here as she answered correctly on just one of the seven Geometry items, a score that is nearly two standard errors below her predicted score. Abbie's TIMSS-Based Probability and Statistics score (50% correct) was also over one standard error below her predicted score.

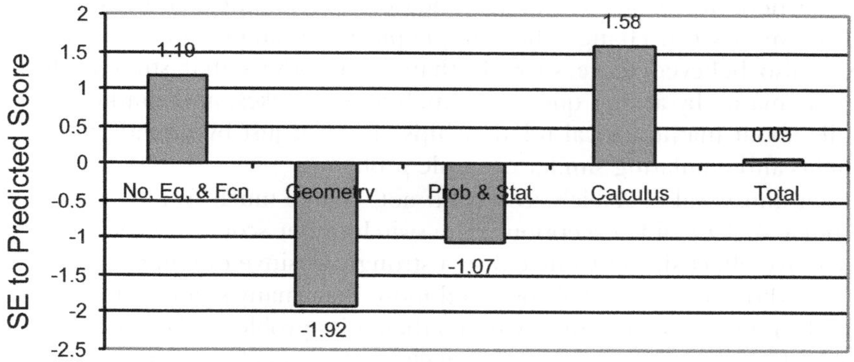

Figure 12.9. Abbie's Difference From Predicted Scores on Subtests of the Advanced Mathematics Test at End of Year 4.

Table 12.4. Abbie's Conceptions of Mathematics Scale Scores and Effect Sizes for Junior and Senior Years

Scale	*Year 3*	*Year 4*
1. Composition of Mathematical Knowledge	3.63 (–.06)	3.88 (.21)
2. Structure of Mathematical Knowledge	4.25 (–.23)	4.00 (–.62)
3. Status of Mathematical Knowledge	4.63 (.94)	3.88 (.32)
4. Doing Mathematics	4.38 (–.15)	4.88 (.73)
5. Validating Ideas in Mathematics	4.00 (–.25)	3.88 (–.14)
6. Learning Mathematics	4.25 (.52)	4.50 (.92)
7. Usefulness of Mathematics	3.88 (–.51)	4.25 (–.10)

Conceptions of Mathematics Inventory—Year 3 and Year 4. At the end of both Course 3 and Course 4, Abbie completed the CMI. Her mean score for each six-item scale is given in Table 12.4 above. A score of 3.5 is in the middle of the 6-choice Likert scale that students responded to, with 6 being strongly positive and 1 strongly negative about an item statement. Table 12.4 also gives the effect size of each of Abbie's scale scores in the distribution of all students who completed the CMI inventory at the end of Course 3 and at the end of Course 4. The Course 4 reference group does not include AP Calculus or AP Statistics students.

One thing to notice is that all of Abbie's scale scores are above neutral, but the effect sizes of her scores varied considerably. Her strongest scale scores relative to other students are on Scale 3 and Scale 6. Compared to other students in the study, Abbie believed strongly that mathematics is an area where people are still making new discoveries and that learning new mathematics can change the way people think about old mathematics. She also believed more strongly than many others that students learn mathematics by asking questions, analyzing mistakes, and thinking carefully about mathematical relationships, and not just by memorizing formulas and emulating similar example problems.

On most scales, Abbie's scores did not change much from Course 3 to Course 4. A notable exception is the switch in her score on scale 4 from a negative effect size in Course 3 to a strongly positive one in Course 4. At the end of Course 3, Abbie believed more than many students that knowing formulas is the key to solving mathematics problems. Her score at the end of Course 4 indicated a relatively strong belief that understanding concepts and ideas and relating different parts of mathematics is the key to solving mathematics problems. On Scale 1, Abbie was just slightly above the neutral score of 3.5 and near the mean of all students in the study each year. This indicates that Abbie, like the average student in this study, believed that, in mathematics, ideas and concepts are about equal in importance to procedures and facts.

On Scales 2, 5, and 7, Abbie's scores at the end of both courses were above neutral but were lower than the mean of all students. While she tended to believe that one concept can explain a variety of formulas, that ideas in one mathematics class can be used in other mathematics classes, and that most mathematical ideas are related, her beliefs in this regard were not as strong as those of the average student. Similarly, she believed that students can work individually or work collaboratively with other students to confirm the strength of a solution and that multiple solution methods are possible, but not so strongly as many other students. Finally, Abbie believed that mathematics will be useful in her future career and activities outside school, but not so strongly when compared to many other students in this study.

After High School. Intending to go to college Abbie completed the *ACT College Entrance Examination*. Her scores and effect sizes in the distribution of all students in this study for whom ACT scores are available were the following: 26 (1.46) in Mathematics, 26 (.78) in Science Reasoning, and an ACT Composite score of 27 (1.23).

After high school, Abbie became a full-time student at a major state-supported research university in the midwest. Her major was international business, and she said that her high school mathematics experiences were not an influence in her choice of a major. She completed a mathematics placement test to help place her in a mathematics course. The mathematics on the test included trigonometry, circles, exponential and linear functions, and other mathematics similar to that on the ACT test. Graphing calculators were allowed on the test. She rated her preparation for the test as about average and identified her algebra skills and ability to simplify equations as areas of weakness.

In the Fall 2001 semester she took Math 105—Data, Functions, and Graphs—which covered linear, exponential, and rational functions. In the course, a graphing calculator was allowed at any time, including on tests. Abbie identified the following areas as highly emphasized in this class: complete paper-and-pencil algebra or calculus symbol manipulation exercises, understand the meaning of mathematical concepts and methods, use graphs and tables to analyze mathematical and real-world problems, and learn mathematics by working with other students.

Abbie rated her mathematical preparation compared to other students in the course as about average. She indicated that she understood "most of the material pretty well," but it was "hard to keep up because topics are covered more quickly [than in high school] and this course includes exponential growth and the natural logarithm." She indicated that her high school mathematics prepared her very well in the following areas: use graphing calculators to solve algebraic equations and inequalities and/or to approximate derivative and integrals, understand the meaning of mathematical concepts and methods, apply mathematical methods to solve real-world problems, reason about or provide explanations for mathematical ideas or methods, learn mathematics from a lecture by the teacher or instructor, and write descriptions of your mathematical thinking. Abbie felt that she was not as well prepared to complete paper-and-pencil algebra or calculus symbol manipulation exercises or to figure out why a procedure or an algebraic symbol manipulation technique works. Her final grade for the course was B.

In a biopsychology course that used mathematics, Abbie also earned a course grade of B. She considered her preparation compared to other students in the class to be about average, because "it [the course content] was fairly understandable." In the next semester, Spring 2002, Abbie enrolled in Math 115—Calculus—a course that covered derivatives and an introduction to integrals. She also took an economics course that used mathematics.

After one semester of college, some of Abbie's reflections on her high school mathematics program were the following:

- Three greatest strengths gained from her high school mathematics experience: explaining her answers concisely, working in groups, and using a graphing calculator to solve problems.
- Three changes she would make to her high school mathematics program: more group homework, more algebraic work, and more problems that are not story problems.

- Areas in which she felt especially well prepared: explaining her answers, doing story problems, and using different calculator methods.
- Areas in which she felt especially poorly prepared: use of *e* in continuous growth rates and her algebra skills.

Jefferson High School Male

The Jefferson High School case study student (called Tom) is a Caucasian male. Tom scored very well on the *ITED-Q* administered as a pretest at the beginning of Grade 9. His score of 323 was at the 98th national student percentile. On the SBS administered at the beginning of Course 1, Tom was at or near the most strongly positive score on four of the six mathematics belief scales. He was very confident of his mathematical ability, and he valued the creative, challenging, and cooperative aspects of mathematics. On the Competition and Genetic scales, Tom's scores were above the neutral score of 3 but less than 4. This indicates that he tended to dislike competing with his peers in mathematics, and he believed that genetics and gender were not major factors in determining success in mathematics. However, his beliefs in these two areas were not as strongly held as those measured by the other four scales described earlier in this paragraph.

Mathematics Achievement in Year 1. In his freshman year, Tom enrolled in Course 1. His teacher (*J, ES, 3*) was a female Experienced Supporter whose teaching style was an especially good example of the use of small groups. A brief description of this teacher's implementation practices is on page 74.

In an individual interview in mid-March, Tom attempted to solve three different problems. In the first interview problem, he was asked to describe the distribution that is represented by a given box plot (the box plot is given in Figure 5.13). He was able to correctly identify and describe many different statistics represented by the given box plot, including the interquartile range and the median. He then was asked to determine which of two histograms could possibly describe the same distribution as the previously given box plot and why. He had some trouble giving sufficient explanations relating the histograms to the given box plot. He tried to choose the histogram with the closest matching range, but he struggled with making sense of the scale and median. He seemed confident in interpreting each representation individually, but he had trouble when he tried to compare two different representations.

In the second interview problem, Tom was asked to describe all of the symmetries (line, rotational, and/or translational) of the plane shape given in Figure 5.10 and for a strip pattern. He was asked to make sketches and give descriptions of each of the symmetries he could find. For the given plane shape, he was able to correctly find and describe the rotational symmetry and line symmetry. With the strip pattern, he was able to identify the line symmetry, but he did not identify the translational symmetry. He was confused about which symmetry was which and was not sure how to apply them to the given shapes. With some help from the interviewer, he was able to find more of the symmetries than he did on his own, but he was still confused about applying the transformation definitions to the shapes.

In the third interview problem, Tom was asked to indicate what type of graph model (Euler circuits and paths, graph coloring, or critical paths) he would use to represent three different situations. Once he chose a graph model, he was asked to describe what the vertices and edges represented as well as provide an explanation for why he chose that particular graph model. In the first given situation (see Figure 5.18), he correctly identified the type of graph model to use (Euler circuits and paths), but he was unable to identify what the vertices and edges would represent in the problem situation. In the second situation, given in Figure 5.20, he again identified the type of graph model to use (critical paths), and he also identified what the vertices and edges would represent with respect to the situation. Although he ran out of time on the third situation (see Figure 5.21), he was able to identify graph coloring as the appropriate model and begin to explain what such a model would look like.

Tom completed Course 1 with a grade of A. He also completed the *ITED-Q* at the end of the year earning a score of 332, which is at the 99th national percentile and .45 standard errors higher than the score predicted by his already high pretest score. His total Course 1 final examination score (82.1%) was higher than the score (77.4%) predicted by his pretest *ITED-Q* score. As Figure 12.10 shows, the two mathematical areas on the final examination in which his achievement level was lower than expected were Geometry and Trigonometry and Statistics and Probability.

Mathematics Achievement in Year 2. In his sophomore year, Tom completed accelerated Course 2 (which included two or three units of the beginning of Course 3) with a grade of A. His teacher (*J*, *ES*, 7) was a woman in the "Experienced Supporter" category who, like his Course 1 teacher, was judged to be especially effective in her use of small-group work. A brief discussion of this teacher's implementation practices begins on page 73. Tom was not interviewed during Course 2, but he completed the EoC exam at the end of the course. His total score of 91.5% was considerably higher than his predicted score of 66.3%. In fact, as Figure 12.10 shows, he scored much higher than predicted on all three subtests of the EoC exam, with scores that ranged from nearly one and one-half to

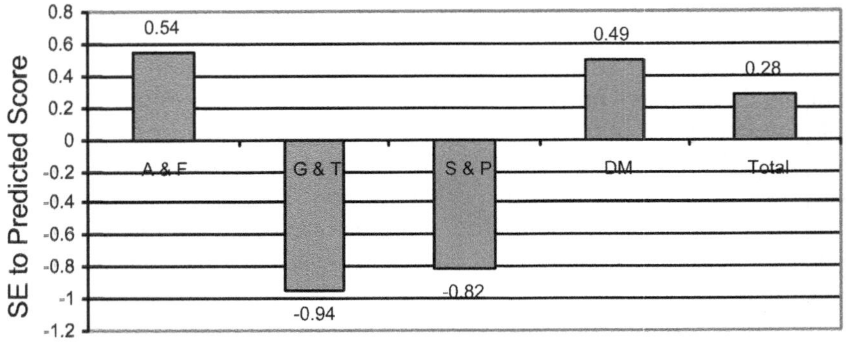

Figure 12.10. Tom's Difference From Predicted Scores on Course 1 Final Exam Subtests.

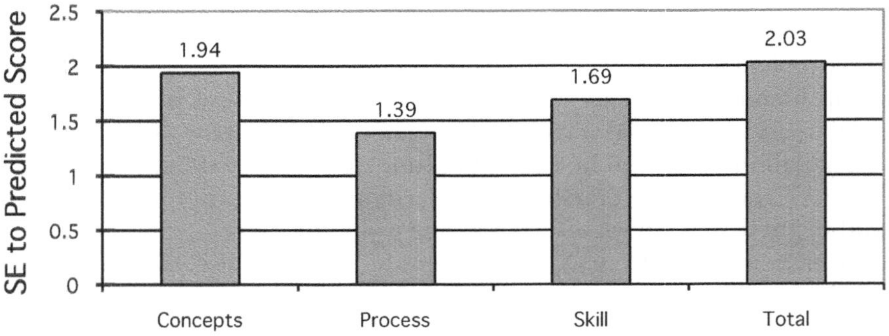

Figure 12.11. Tom's Difference From Predicted Scores on Subtests of ETS *End-Of-Year Algebra Examination* at End of Course 2.

two standard errors above his predicted score. In fact, Tom was one of three students in this study who score a perfect 100% on the EoC Concepts subtest.

Beliefs and Attitudes About Mathematics—Years 1 and 2. At the end of each of Courses 1 and 2, Tom completed the belief survey. Tom's average score for each of the six belief scales where 1 is strongly negative and 5 is strongly positive is given in Table 12.5. The effect sizes of his scores within the entire set of subjects in the study are in parentheses.

Tom's Self-Assessment score remained consistently high across the testing periods indicating that he was very confident about his mathematical ability. His scores on the Challenge scale were also above

Table 12.5. Tom's Student Belief Survey Scale Scores and Effect Sizes for Courses 1 and 2

Scale	*Course 1*	*Course 2*
Self-Assessment	4.63 (1.27)	4.75 (1.32)
Challenge	3.83 (.92)	4.00 (1.17)
Creativity	3.25 (–.48)	4.88 (1.57)
Competition	1.00 (–1.50)	3.50 (.26)
Cooperation	2.17 (–1.82)	3.83 (.66)
Genetic	4.00 (.96)	3.00 (–.21)

neutral and consistent, indicating that he enjoyed the challenging aspects of his mathematics experience.

His other scale scores, however, differed considerably from Course 1 to Course 2. While Tom indicated that he strongly valued the competition with his mathematics classmates at the end of Course 1, he disliked the competition more than most of his study peers at the end of Course 2. Similarly, his beliefs about cooperating with his mathematics classmates and his valuing of the creative aspects of mathematics went from being much more negative than the average Course 1 student in this study to being considerably more positive in Course 2.

The one scale on which Tom's score declined from Course 1 to Course 2 was Genetics. Specifically, at the end of Course 1, Tom was neutral about the statement "In general, boys tend to be naturally better at math than girls." At the end of Course 2, he strongly agreed with this statement. At the end of both courses, Tom strongly disagreed with the statement, "Math is a subject in which natural ability matters more than effort." He evidently believed that effort was the more important factor in mathematical success. Interestingly, Tom was less certain about the statement "To be good at math, you need to have a kind of 'mathematical mind.'" At the end of Course 1, he disagreed with this statement, but he was neutral about it at the end of Course 2. Assuming Tom responded seriously, the main source of his decline on the Genetic scale was a deepening of his belief that boys are naturally better at mathematics than girls.

The pattern of his improvement in beliefs, with the exception of the Genetic scale, suggests that Tom may have had a better overall experience in Course 2 than in Course 1. Alternatively, perhaps the improvement in beliefs could be a sign of his general maturing about mathematics or about school. The latter hypothesis is supported by the fact that Jefferson ninth-grade students were in a junior high school building. Moving to a high school building with more mature peers may have had a maturing effect.

Like his general beliefs about mathematics, Tom's specific attitudes about each course differed markedly, providing further evidence of an overall improvement in his disposition toward mathematics. In Course 1, Tom's course attitude score was 2.64, below the neutral level of 3.00 and .78 standard deviations below the mean attitude of all Course 1 students in the study. At the end of Course 2, his course attitude score was 3.91, well above neutral and .88 standard deviations above the mean attitude of all Course 2 students in the study. Clearly, Tom liked Course 2 much better than Course 1.

Specifically, at the end of Course 2, Tom agreed or strongly agreed with statements dealing with confidence in his ability, understanding the ideas in the course, learning to reason, and seeing that mathematical ideas make sense. He also agreed that the problems in the course were realistic and that the group work helped him learn and was enjoyable. At the end of Course 2, Tom was neutral about whether he learned to read or write mathematics better, about the readability of the textbook, and about his enjoying use of the calculator. The major sources of improvement in his attitude score from Course 1 to Course 2 were relative to learning to reason, seeing that mathematical ideas make sense, enjoying and learning from group work, and the readability of the curriculum materials. In each of these areas, Tom's levels of agreement from Course 1 to Course 2 increased by at least 2 score points, that is, either from strongly negative to neutral, from negative to positive, or from neutral to strongly positive.

On the SBS, students were invited to write in an open-ended format about their experience in the course that they just completed. In his open-ended description of his experience in Course 1, Tom wrote:

> Personally, I do not appreciate being a guinea pig with this struggling system of collegiate workbooks. We have many problems interpreting the smushed slop that is confusing. The work is over-redundant and boring. Although it's applied with life and tries to tie in various maths, I want solid, competent work to do. If these math systems continue to be tested, those responsible must revise more of the material.

The main issue for Tom seems, arguably, to be resentment of what he perceived as being used as a "guinea pig."

At the end of Course 2, Tom described his experience as follows:

> This year has brought me many challenges in the mathematical world. I have learned a considerable amount, but I have been particularly plagued by the aspect of written explanations. Our discussions in group and as a class have been extremely valuable for me, but writing pages of explanations

> over the year for homework has been exhausting. I do know that it is important to understand the concepts, but I have suffered from having to write out the same idea various times just to get credit for my work. Discussions and interactions are very good to explore concepts.

By the end of Course 2, Tom no longer mentioned being a guinea pig. He seemed to believe that he was learning quite a lot and that discussion with others was very helpful, but he disliked what he saw as an overemphasis on writing explanations.

Mathematics Achievement in Course 3. In his junior year, Tom accelerated by enrolling in a combined Course 3 and Course 4 class. His teacher (*J, ES, 6*) was a woman in the "Experienced Supporter" category who was very conscientious about continuing to improve her teaching. A brief discussion of this teacher's practices can be found on pages 69 and 72. Tom was not interviewed during Year 3, but he completed the mathematical literacy test compiled from items released by TIMSS.

Tom was one of 11 students in this study to earn a perfect score on all subtests of the mathematical literacy test. Of course, his perfect scores were much better than predicted by his pretest score, as seen in Figure 12.12. His perfect score in Geometry was particularly impressive, since the Geometry mean of all students in the study was just 56.4% with a standard deviation of 22.3. In addition to his stellar mathematical literacy scores, Tom completed the combined Course 3 and 4 with a grade of A.

Mathematics Achievement in Year 4. In his senior year, Tom enrolled in both AP Calculus and AP Statistics. Both his AP Calculus teacher (*J,ES,5*) and his AP Statistics teacher (*J,ES,6*) were women in the "Experienced

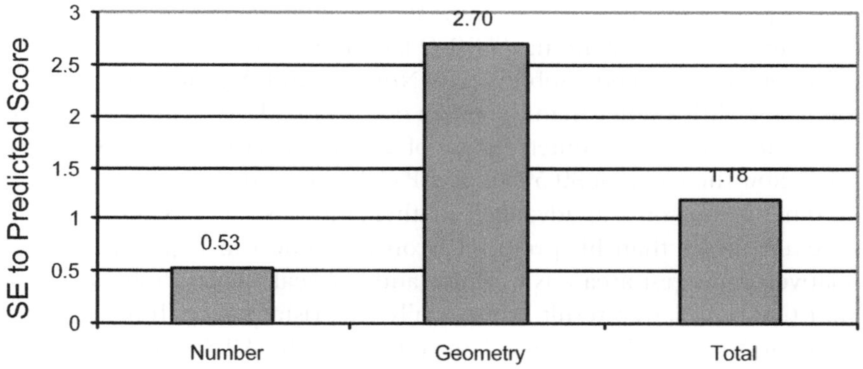

Figure 12.12. Tom's Difference From Predicted Scores on Subtests of the Mathematical Literacy Test at the End of Year 3.

Supporter" category. Brief discussions of the teaching beliefs and practices of *J,ES,5* can be found on pages 68 and 72.

Tom was interviewed with two different problems at the beginning of December. The first asked him to make a list of positive integers less than or equal to 70 such that the sum of the digits of the number could be divided evenly by 7, a list that he was easily able to create. Then he was asked to determine whether each of a set of three given conjectures about this list was true (see Figure 8.6 for the complete statement of the problem). Initially, Tom believed that all of the conjectures about the formation of the list were correct statements. With a little prompting from the interviewer, he tried a few examples and found that the second conjecture, "If you start with 7 and keep adding 9s until the sum is 70, you **always** get a number in the list **L,**" was not correct. He then reasoned that the third conjecture, "If you start with 7 and keep adding 9s until the sum is 70, you get **every** number in list **L,**" must also be incorrect. After realizing his initial mistake, he gave a convincing argument about why the last two conjectures were false.

In the second interview problem, Tom was asked to determine whether dividing the coefficient of x by the coefficient of y and reversing the sign in a linear equation of the form $ax + by = c$, $a \neq 0$ always gives the slope of the line (see the problem statement in Figure 8.7). He was able to correctly and convincingly explain why the given pattern was correct. He first explained how he would find the slope for a specific example, and he then explained that in order to be convincing he should generalize his equation. He then found the slope of the generalized equation and showed that the general form for slope is consistent with his result.

At the end of Year 4, Tom completed the reasoning test and the TIMSS-based advanced mathematics test. As Figure 12.13 shows, Tom scored poorly on the Number and Algebra subtest relative to the score predicted by his outstanding *ITED-Q* baseline score, and he scored even worse on the Geometry subtest. His Number and Algebra score of 60% was just slightly higher than the mean of 57% for all AP Calculus students in the study, but his Geometry score of 25% was over one standard deviation below the mean of 39.5% of all AP Calculus students.

Tom's scores on the advanced mathematics test and its four subtests were also lower than his predicted scores as shown in Figure 12.14. His relatively strongest area was Calculus and his weakest was Probability and Statistics. The latter result is especially surprising since Tom earned a grade of A in his AP Statistics class and a 5 on the AP Statistics examination. Tom's subtest scores were mainly at or below the means of all AP Calculus students in the study with respective effect sizes as follows: –.70, –.39, –1.72, and .03.

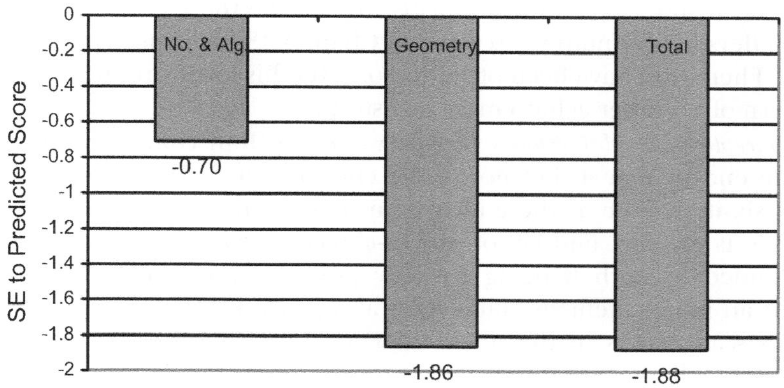

Figure 12.13. Tom's Difference From Predicted Scores on Subtests of the Reasoning Test at the End of Year 4.

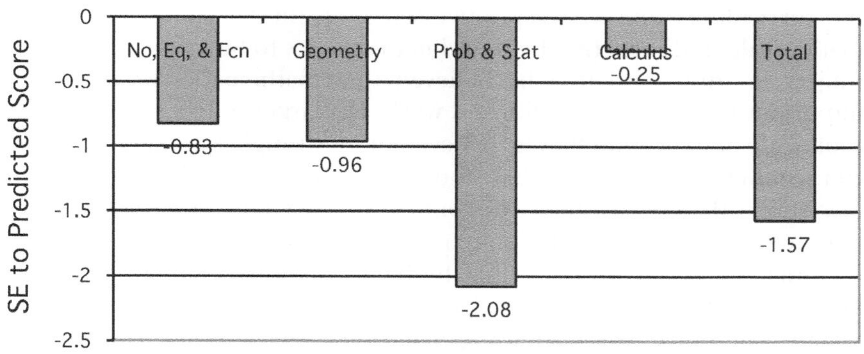

Figure 12.14. Tom's Difference From Predicted Scores on Subtests of the Advanced Mathematics Test at End of Year 4.

Following truly outstanding scores on the EoC Algebra test at the end of Course 2 and the TIMSS-based mathematical literacy test at the end of Course 3, Tom's relatively weak scores on the two tests at the end of Year 4 are surprising. His relatively low scores notwithstanding, he earned grades of A in both his AP Calculus and his AP Statistics class, scored a 5 on both the AP Calculus exam (AB) and the AP Statistics exam, and scored 28 on the ACT Mathematics test, 31 on the ACT Science Reasoning test, and had a composite ACT score of 28. His three ACT scores are 1.49, 1.98, and 1.46 standard deviations higher than the respective means of all students in this study for whom ACT are available. Perhaps Tom had low motivation to do well on the Year 4 tests for some reason. He may have been suffering from "senioritis," or maybe the local controversy in the Jefferson community discussed in Chapter 13 had a negative effect on him. There may have been other reasons, but his low scores do not fit the pattern of his other achievement measures.

Conceptions of Mathematics Inventory—Year 4 Tom completed the CMI at the end of Year 4, but not at the end of Year 3. His mean score for each six-item scale at the end of Year 4 is given in Table 12.6. A score of 3.5 is in the middle of the 6-choice Likert scale that students responded to, with 6 being strongly positive and 1 strongly negative about an item statement. Table 12.6 also gives the effect size of each of Tom's scale scores in the distribution of all AP Calculus students who completed the CMI that year.

It is interesting to note that all of Tom's scores are quite positive, indicating that his conceptions of mathematics were well aligned with those underlying a *Standards*-based curriculum. Clearly, his relatively low scores on the two tests at the end of Year 4 cannot be attributed to disagreement with the view of mathematics and mathematical teaching and learning in the curriculum. Tom's most positive score, on the Usefulness of Mathematics scale, indicates that he found mathematics to be a very worthwhile subject to study, and that he believed that mathematics would be an important part of his adult life and work. His largest effect size, however, is on scale 5, indicating that he believed more strongly than other AP Calculus students in this study that students can work individually or collaboratively with other students to confirm the strength of a solution and that multiple solution methods are possible.

Tom's scores also indicate that he believed more strongly than most other AP Calculus students that learning occurs from one's mistakes and asking questions, understanding concepts and making connections between problems is the key to solving mathematics problems, and under-

Table 12.6. Tom's Conceptions of Mathematics Scale Scores and Effect Sizes for Senior Year

Scale	*Year 4*
1. Composition of Mathematical Knowledge	4.00 (–.02)
2. Structure of Mathematical Knowledge	5.00 (.62)
3. Status of Mathematical Knowledge	4.38 (.34)
4. Doing Mathematics	5.00 (.41)
5. Validating Ideas in Mathematics	5.25 (.99)
6. Learning Mathematics	4.75 (.71)
7. Usefulness of Mathematics	5.38 (.48)

standing formulas is more important than gathering and memorizing information. He also agreed that mathematics is an area where people are still making new discoveries and that learning new mathematics can change the way people think about old mathematics.

Tom believed that mathematics concepts and problems are interconnected and that making sense of problems and understanding why problems work are more important than memorizing the correct formula. He also believed strongly that justifying one's solution and problem-solving method is important and that different solution methods can be correct. He disagreed with the notion that teachers are the sole keepers of mathematical knowledge.

The only scale for which Tom's score was near the mean of all AP Calculus students was Composition of Mathematical Knowledge. This scale measures the extent to which the student believes that mathematics is more about problem solving than computation and that although formulas are important, the ideas behind the formula are more important. His beliefs in this area were quite positive, but about average among the AP Calculus students in the study. Overall, there does not seem to be anything in his CMI data to suggest that Tom was lacking in mathematical motivation at the end of Year 4, making his weak achievement test results at this time even more puzzling.

After High School. After high school, Tom became a full-time student at the local community college. His reported major was secondary mathematics education. He believed that his high school mathematics experience was a positive influence on his interests and his choice of major, writing, "Math became a passion for me. I enjoyed solving difficult questions, and chose to pursue teaching math."

In the Fall 2001 semester, he enrolled in Calculus 2, a course that covered such topics as the applications of derivatives and integrals, arc length, surface area, centers of mass, and infinite series. Tom identified the following areas as highly emphasized in this class: completing paper-and-pencil algebra or calculus symbol manipulation exercises, using graphing calculators to solve algebraic equations and inequalities and/or approximate derivatives and integrals, understanding the meaning of mathematical concepts and methods, and learning mathematics by working with other students. In this course, a graphing calculator was allowed at any time, including on tests.

Tom felt that his mathematics preparation compared to that of other students in the course was better than most. He wrote, "I followed an advanced track in math through high school, and continued my education without a long break from it. Math was a high priority for me, and I made room in my schedule to study." He rated his overall high school preparation for this course as excellent, except that he rated his preparation for learning mathematics from a lecture by a teacher or instructor and writing descriptions of his mathematical thinking as good. His final grade for the course was A.

In the next semester, Spring 2002, Tom enrolled in Calculus 3, a course that covered three-dimensional applications, multivariable functions, partial derivatives, and iterated integrals. He also enrolled in a differential equations course that covered systems of differential equations and linear algebra. In addition, he registered in the Spring for a sociology class that required the use of mathematics.

After one semester of college, some of Tom's reflections on his high school mathematics program were the following:

- The greatest strengths that he gained from his high school mathematics experiences were the following: "Comprehension—being able to work my way through problems using what I know. Confidence—trusting my own abilities, using what I know to help a discussion. Passion—anything can be fun if I want it to be."
- He suggested the following changes to his high school mathematics program: more hands-on applications/labs, periodic check-ups on previously learned skills/concepts that connect to current material, and more encouragement for all students to offer their thoughts/ideas or questions.
- He felt that his high school mathematics experience had a positive influence on what he decided to do after high school, writing, "My high school math experience solidified my interest in pursuing math further. I want to continue learning higher and higher levels of math. For me, math knowledge is a prize, earned through study and practice. Teaching would be a profession that harbors this prize for others. Many people fear math, and I think that I could inspire some of my future students. I want to help make math fun."
- He believed that he was especially well-prepared for college mathematics, writing, "In general, I feel especially prepared for the classes I'm currently taking. I communicate with my classmates often, and we work well in study groups. I feel that I have knowledge to offer when we hit a stump in a math problem. I'm taking Calc III and Differential Equations. There are about six others who are doing the same, and they come from a Core background as well. I enjoy challenging problems, which is very beneficial for me. Having the experience had helped me to continue coursework that may seem beyond my level of understanding." (This quote, like one or two others in this chapter, also appears in Chapter 11.)

CHAPTER SUMMARY AND DISCUSSION

The three case study students display some interesting commonalities and differences. The baseline measure of mathematical achievement at the beginning of Grade 9 indicates that Martie was near the average of all students in this study. By contrast, both Abbie and Tom were near the very top in national student percentile (99 and 98, respectively) at the beginning of Grade 9, suggesting that they could be expected to do well in high school mathematics. Although all three students were successful in high school mathematics, their mathematics course-taking and their performance on common achievement tests did not align especially well with expectations, and the alignment became weaker with the passage of time. A snapshot comparison of the mathematical course-taking and achievement patterns of the three students is given in Table 12.7.

All three students earned A or A– grades in all their high school mathematics courses. Interestingly, Abbie, who had the highest pretest score, was the only one of the three students not to accelerate in high school mathematics and the only one to earn high school mathematics course grades below A. On mathematics achievement tests, Martie was somewhat

Table 12.7. Courses, Grades, and Achievement Test Scores of the Three Case Study Students

		Martie	*Abbie*	*Tom*
Year 1	Course (Grade)	Course 1 (A)	Course 1 (A–)	Course 1 (A)
	Pre-*ITED-Q*	271 (66%-tile)	333 (99%-tile)	323 (98%-tile)
	ITED-Q	317 (94%-tile)	335 (99%-tile)	332 (99%-tile)
Year 2	Course (Grade)	Course 2 (A)	Course 2 (A)	Course 2-3 (A)
	EoC Exam	81.50	81.50	91.50
Year 3	Course (Grade)	Course 3-4 (A)	Course 3 (A)	Course 3-4 (A)
	Math Literacy	78.57	---	100.00
Year 4	Course	AP Calc (A)	Course 4 (A–)	AP Calc (A) AP Stat (A)
	Math Reasoning	48.39	45.16	41.94
	Advanced Math	57.69	53.85	42.31
	Coll. Ent. Exam	SAT Math (630)	ACT Math (26)	ACT Math (28)
Post-High	College Type	Liberal Arts	Major U.	Comm. College
	Major	Math/French	Intern. Business	Math Education
	Fall Math Co.	Calculus 1 (A)	Precalculus (B)	Calculus 2 (A)

lower than the other two students in Year 1, but her performance caught up to Abbie's in Year 2 and surpassed her in Years 3, 4, and post-high school. Tom's EoC examination and mathematical literacy test scores were outstanding, but Martie and Abbie both scored higher than Tom on the two Year 4 tests. Tom's surprisingly poor performance on those two tests was discussed earlier. Both Martie and Tom majored in mathematics or a related field in college, but Abbie did not. Martie earned an A in Calculus 1 and Tom earned the same grade in Calculus 2 in their first college semester, while Abbie earned a B in a precalculus course.

As for attitudes and beliefs in Courses 1 and 2, there was some fluctuation for each student but in different directions and for different apparent reasons. Martie held very positive beliefs in both courses except for average beliefs about cooperating with other students. Martie was positively disposed about her experience in Course 1, but she had much lower attitudes about Course 2. She did not indicate why, but it may be a factor that her teacher in Course 2 was somewhat rigid and not popular with the students, although her teacher in Course 1 was also not strong. Abbie had strong beliefs on all scales except Genetics, as she believed that natural ability and a "math gene" were important factors in mathematics learning. She was quite positively disposed toward both courses. Tom's beliefs and attitudes were very negative in Course 1, but they became much more positive in Course 2. He indicated that he strongly resented being treated as a "guinea pig" in Course 1, an attitude that was not evident at the end of Course 2 and did not resurface again during this study.

On the CMI administered at the end of Years 3 and 4, Abbie's scale scores were somewhat variable and generally lower than those of the other two students who had strongly positive scores on nearly all scales. This difference may be partially due to, or perhaps just associated with, the fact that Abbie did not accelerate in mathematics, and the other two students did. As is evident in the data from all students in this study, having completed more mathematics is associated with higher scores on the CMI. Thus Abbie's CMI data was obtained at the end of Course 3 in Year 3 and at the end of Course 4 in Year 4, whereas Martie's CMI data were obtained at the end of Course 4 in Year 3 and at the end of AP Calculus in Year 4. Tom did not complete the CMI in Year 3, but he had just completed both AP Calculus and AP Statistics when the CMI was administered at the end of Year 4.

If three different students had been chosen for this chapter, the picture that is painted would clearly not be exactly the same. However, any three case studies would likely show, as these do, that within the large group distributions whose means and variabilities were summarized in previous chapters, there are individual students whose personal experiences differer markedly from those of other students. In fact, a single student's experiences sometimes differ a great deal from year to year.

In the next chapter, the local controversy in the Jefferson community and its effects on students and teachers are described and interpreted.

CHAPTER 13

DESCRIPTION AND EFFECTS OF A LOCAL CONTROVERSY

Many small educational changes are implemented within school systems on a regular basis with little, if any, notice from those outside the buildings in which they occur. Small alterations in class length, hiring of school personnel, addition of new resources, upgrades in technology, and introduction of new courses that meet the needs of particular groups of students are common changes that are generally welcomed in the community and likely viewed by all as needed improvements that keep the local schools on par with neighboring school districts. Larger changes, especially those initiated at the state level (e.g., state graduation and testing requirements, number of instructional days, and sports schedules), are sometimes met with resistance within districts, but such mandates eventually work their way into the system and are accepted. Larger district-initiated changes, such as those in recent decades associated with block scheduling or reconfiguration to a middle school structure, take much convincing of local stakeholders but are eventually adopted in some format (cf. Fullan, 1991). Even adoption changes involving most K–12 school curricula often go into effect with little controversy. It is against such a backdrop of change that the Core-Plus Mathematics curriculum was implemented in the Jefferson School District during the 1990s and took an interesting turn during the 5 years of this study. In many ways, the controversy that developed in this district mirrors what happened

A Five-Year Study of the First Edition of the Core-Plus Mathematics Curriculum, pp. 337–367

with *Standards*-based curricula in school districts across the country during this same time period.

This chapter takes a different methodological approach from the previous ones because of greater reliance on data of a qualitative nature. As a result, the interpretations are perhaps more subjective, linking together diverse pieces of qualitative information into a coherent picture of what transpired in one of this study's school districts. The chapter begins with organizational notes intended to better define the district environment and the major stakeholders involved in the controversy over the district's high school mathematics curriculum. The next section briefly outlines the major events of the controversy in chronological order, ending with the current status as of this writing. The following four sections then present perspectives on the controversy from key stakeholder groups involved: teachers, administrators, students, and parents. These sections fill in important details of the controversy as it unfolded and illustrate how complicated and frustrating the situation became, especially for teachers supporting the Core-Plus Mathematics curriculum. After an attempt to understand some of the motivations of the various groups, the chapter concludes with some general observations regarding the aftermath of the curriculum controversy.

Data for this chapter were drawn from extensive interviews of teachers, key administrators, and students throughout the study. Teachers and curriculum coordinators at the Jefferson schools were interviewed, and teachers were observed multiple times during each year of this study. Students were questioned about the controversy in conjunction with problem-solving interviews and through open-ended survey items, described in earlier chapters. No parents were interviewed, but their views were expressed through various local media outlets, and all relevant articles and district information packets were included in the data collection. Activities related to the curriculum committee and school board meetings including actions taken by parents were reported through teachers and administrators who were in attendance. Reporting of the mathematics curriculum controversy followed an approach similar to that of other researchers who have studied the micropolitics of school reform in K–12 schools (Hargreaves, 1991).

THE JEFFERSON SCHOOL DISTRICT AND COMMUNITY

As noted in Chapter 3, the Jefferson community has two high schools, each comprised of students in Grades 10–12, and the designated focus of this study was one of the high schools, called Jefferson High School. However, by the beginning of this study, both high schools were using the

Core-Plus Mathematics curriculum with all students. For purposes of this chapter, it is sometimes necessary to refer to each of the two high schools, so the designation Jefferson High School A (or HS-A) was used to represent the focus school and Jefferson High School B (or HS-B) was used to refer to the sister school. As noted in Chapter 3, ninth graders were housed in two feeder middle schools, but students from either middle school could attend either of the high schools. Despite this flexibility, there is a proximal link between each high school and one of the two middle schools that strongly influenced the high school of choice for many students. Because this proximal connection played a role in the events that occurred, the middle schools are designated as Jefferson MS-A or MS-B where needed.

Events are generally described at the district level, because many decisions (and compromises), those related to curriculum matters in particular, were made at the district level and ultimately affected actions at both high schools. For example, the district-wide mathematics curriculum committee consisted of educators associated with each of the schools (see note 1). Important recommendations from this committee were made to the school board and, if approved, implemented in all schools (elementary, middle, and high) where they applied.

Educators and researchers who often visit schools and talk to teachers quickly develop a feel for how teachers assess themselves. In mathematics education, there is a range of teaching practices and beliefs about how students learn, but in simplest form the current tendency is to categorize teachers as more inclined toward conventional teaching practices (e.g., lecturer and procedure-oriented, authoritarian classroom structures) or more *Standards*-based (e.g., facilitator, conceptual-oriented, investigative, or group-oriented classrooms). In Chapter 4, these beliefs and practices were used to classify teachers as either Experienced Supporters or Experienced Critics, with a category of Novices for teachers whose emerging teaching practices had yet to be solidified.

The categorization of the Jefferson High School teachers was consistent with teachers' self-assessments and school-level group assessments collected during interviews and classroom observations. By and large, individual Jefferson High School teachers describe both groups of Jefferson middle school teachers to be generally supportive of *Standards*-based practices and of their *Standards*-based curriculum, although Jefferson MS-A (the main feeder middle school for the focus high school) seemed to have a number of teachers who struggled with implementation both of the ninth-grade Core-Plus Mathematics materials and of the Connected Mathematics materials in the lower middle grades in the same building. A major issue, in addition to the new pedagogical demands, was the middle school teachers' unfamiliarity with some of the content ideas (e.g., discrete mathematics) they encountered. Visits to these classrooms and discussions with the teachers confirmed these problems. At the high schools, teachers consistently described Jefferson HS-A to be the more *Standards*-based (despite having at least two Experienced Critics) and Jefferson HS-B to be almost the mirror opposite with at most two teachers identified to be ardent supporters of the new curriculum. The struggles of these two teachers to help their departmental colleagues with implementation issues were noted frequently in interviews and were a source of constant frustration for the teachers themselves.

In addition to teachers' assessments of the situations at their schools, interviews revealed differing perceptions regarding the socioeconomic make-up of the two school populations: Jefferson HS-A, the newer school, served more students of lower socioeconomic status within the community than Jefferson HS-B. The middle school characterizations were more complicated, but Jefferson MS-B was another newer building in the district at the time. The main point of these characterizations is to acknowledge that issues of perceptions about each school—its place and reputation in the community, expectations for students past and present, and where people of position and power were situated within the community and their connections within the school system—emerged as important variables in the events that transpired before and during the curriculum controversy. One teacher who worked in two of the buildings (first MS-B, then Jefferson HS-A) during this study summed up the above issues during one of the first interviews at the middle school. Her summary foreshadowed many of the problems that eventually ensued:

> I know that problems exist. I hear about them. And when it comes to our high school [Jefferson HS-A] and right now both high schools, they both exist but they are existing at the old high school, so on one end of campus [town] we have the new high school and on the other end we have the old high school. They're both there. One will soon leave at Christmas time and go to their new building with their new facility and their beautiful everything. They're very gung ho on change and what's new and reform, where the people there at the old high school are the chalkboards and the apple tree [computer] lab. They want to do things the way they have always been done. They want to factor, they want to solve, they want to evaluate, they want to number crunch. They see the old system as being very effective, so this is not something new to our district; we just went through that when we opened the new junior high [Jefferson MS-B]; the junior high is four years old and it used to be at the old junior high. Same thing the high school is [now] going through, growing pains that we will be going through. What's happening right now is one school leads the way for the others. When you're effective and you have results, the other school has to change and they know they have to. Eventually when we go to two separate systems, our junior high will feed our old high school and the old junior high will feed

> the new high school. It is interesting because there are a lot of issues: one is that most of the wealthy people in the community go to this junior high and they go to the old high school. That is how it's broken down. The poorer students go to the old junior high, but the new high school. I think it was great planning. Because of this there is a lot of change that will happen. But, what I am afraid is going to happen is that there will be no communication between the two programs. We'll be just on our own and they'll be on their own, east against west, we won't have the dialogue that has been real healthy in the past. *(J, N, 2)*

At the time, many teachers in both middle schools provided similar characterizations of the Jefferson district environment.

A BRIEF HISTORY OF THE CONTROVERSY

Teachers in the Jefferson School District prided themselves as being progressive: quick to adopt new technology innovations, thorough in their research on K–12 teaching and learning innovations, and often on the "cutting edge" of trying new curricula in their schools.[1] It is not surprising that of the 36 schools that participated in the pilot and field testing of first edition Core-Plus Mathematics (see Chapter 3), this district would emerge as a prime candidate and then be chosen for inclusion in the present study. Most teachers and administrators were enthusiastic about the opportunity to continue their association with the project and build on the professional development links that would continue to improve the mathematics teaching and learning of students within the district. One teacher noted the benefits while also hinting at the difficulties some teachers faced:

> As we implemented the Core Math Project, we required an in-service for staff. You people at Western helped a fair amount with that. But as we implemented it we worked to improve it, to improve practice. We had great success with it, we felt, early on. As we implemented it as the only curriculum, math curriculum, in the district, I think ... we brought staff along who were not either willing or able to deliver the curriculum the way it was set up. *(J, A, 1)*

Thus at the beginning of this study, a number of potentially positive and negative factors were already in place that continued to develop over time. Jefferson HS had a reputation for innovation and a number of teachers and administrators had already invested significant time and effort in implementing the curriculum—5 years to be exact. Most of these teachers embraced the *Standards*-based pedagogical changes, inquiry-based learning, and new content. At the same time, some teachers were finding it too different and too difficult to implement despite a district-wide mandate for professional development designed to smooth the transition. In addition, although the new mathematics curriculum had been in place for several years, parents naturally had questions about the program. Those whose son or daughter was nearing graduation wondered how well the curriculum would prepare students for the SAT, ACT, and for AP Calculus. More generally, since the program was quite different from what they had experienced in school, parents were anxious about whether their children would learn everything needed to get into college and succeed there. Some parents wanted a list of colleges that would accept reform mathematics programs, and colleges were only then beginning to deal with this issue; integrated, *Standards*-based mathematics programs were new to them as well. Parents of "gifted" students were concerned that their children were not challenged enough, and the district was only starting to pilot ways to deal with this group.

An important set of connections seems to link together the above teacher and parent factors. Parents were beginning to ask questions related to the "new" mathematics curriculum required of all students. These questions were legitimate, consistent, and persistent across the years of this study. Teachers were the natural contact points for answering these questions, and they did so with varying effectiveness. Teachers comfortable with the program, and usually those with the most experience teaching it, found this a matter of routine. Teachers who struggled, for a number of the reasons described above, including not fully understanding the program and its scope and sequence, found defense of the program difficult. Some teachers simply could not reconcile their own beliefs about mathematics and its teaching and learning with those of the program and chose not to defend it, believing what and how they had always taught was still best for students. Some emerged as vocal critics. Many teachers noted the problem of effective communication regarding all of these issues within the district as a major problem developing within the first 2 years of this study. Communication among the four schools became strained and in many ways adversarial.

The above issues notwithstanding, all evidence collected for this study indicated that, while many parents asked many questions, it was a *small* group of parents (emphasized again and again in interviews) and eventually some teachers, who were not satisfied with the answers and initiated many of the actions that followed. For example, when teachers' and administrators' answers were considered to be inadequate, the group of parents began to bring their concerns to the attention of the school board. They bypassed the district mathematics curriculum committee, a body supposedly in place to deal with all curriculum decisions.[2]

As the school board became a point of attack, its first response was to work with the curriculum committee to ask teachers to address problems by attending more to the issues within their own buildings and classrooms. For example, parents who argued that their children needed more repetition, more skill problems, and more examples to practice could be accommodated with various kinds of supplementing. The Core-Plus Mathematics *Reference and Practice* (RAP) books became available about this time (1999–2000) and their use seemed to help temporarily. Suggestions about how to accommodate advanced students with extra work and, eventually, extra credit also had some limited appeal.[3] But some parents still wanted to see more examples and routine work for their children, and some did not appreciate the investigative nature of the curriculum. There also was a persistent undercurrent of not wanting "advanced" students in the same classroom with "stragglers" or those less academically motivated; as one teacher noted, "the main concern of some parents is they don't think their 'gifted' kids should be in classes with everyone else" (*J, ES, 1*). This issue will be revisited at the end of the chapter.

During the first year of this study, vocal parents heightened their rhetoric regarding what they perceived to be inadequacies with the curriculum. In addition to regular venting at school board meetings, opponents of the curriculum made their views known through letters to the administrators and local radio and newspaper outlets. Newspaper articles consisted of anecdotes from some students who reported having difficulty with their first college mathematics course (although some of these did quite well when particular cases were further examined by some of the high school teachers—see examples discussed below). "Surveys" and "studies" posted on the Internet (with virtually no details related to methodology) about the use of Standards-based curriculum in other districts were also cited.

The Internet played a significant role in disseminating such information, and the opposition parents were quick to latch on to anything that supported their position. The data they cited as evidence of weaknesses of the *Standards*-based curriculum seldom related to the Jefferson district itself.

Other factors fed the controversy as well. During the media campaign, a staunchly conventional teacher from Jefferson HS-B emerged as a very vocal supporter of moving the district back to a more conventional track. This teacher had participated, though minimally, in professional development in preparation for teaching the *Standards*-based curriculum and had voiced opposition to the program since its inception 5 years earlier. He was joined by others at the same high school, but also by one of the teacher critics at Jefferson HS-A, who voiced his own critique of the program in the school newspaper, while arguing for "choice" of curricula. This move came as a surprise to the mathematics department at Jefferson HS-A, which until then had presented a fairly united front in resisting any changes back to a conventional curriculum. This new tactic of framing the opposition to the *Standards*-based curriculum as support of "choice" for students and parents proved to resonate well with many people in the community. By the second year (1999) of this study, the group of vocal parents was pushing for an alternative conventional curriculum track. Despite a vote of "26 to nothing" by the district mathematics curriculum committee to maintain Core-Plus Mathematics as the single curriculum option, the school board voted otherwise and sided with the opposition parents. By fall of that year, a plan to introduce a second mathematics curriculum option was approved by the school board for the 2000–01 freshman class. The two curriculum options were implemented in the middle and high schools, solidified in the succeeding years, and they continue at the time of this writing.

Before concluding this section, it should be noted that only a handful of students in this study were directly affected by these events in the sense that a special section of conventional geometry was approved and offered to them ahead of the more wholesale two-track option that eventually emerged in the Jefferson middle and high schools. However, the controversy was well publicized and clearly affected the dialogue among the teachers, their students at Jefferson HS-A, and the community at large. It may be an understatement to say that for at least 2 full years, this controversy was one of the dominant issues of discussion within the Jefferson community. As the dust settled at the end of this study, an exhausted district administrator commented:

> Personally, *I* couldn't go through it again. I could not face that much angst over that period of time. I can't walk into—everywhere I walk in [Jefferson], or walk into a Chamber of Commerce breakfast, or even a social gathering, the conversation is about math, you know. In fact, just the other night we were playing in a basketball game ... a league game here in town, and the referee had been at one of the parent meetings. She was a real nice gal and real funny. She miss-set the score on the scoreboard, and I said, "I think that score is wrong." She goes, "It is wrong. Oh, I must have been in your math program." It is just everywhere we go. (*J, A, 1*)

During the controversy, the mathematics program was called into serious question, and it was often difficult for those involved to separate fact from fiction. Teachers at Jefferson HS-A worried about the future of the program, but most were adamant about not returning to a conventional curriculum, as voiced by one teacher: "I'm worried we'll be back to exactly where we were in the 70s and 80s. And it didn't work then and now it's not going to work again. And I don't know when this insanity is going to stop" (*J, ES, 7*). And some teachers worried that their judgment was being called into question. As one of them noted before the change was approved, "If choice is available, and I think it will be, then parents will wonder why we're changing and the assumption will be that there's something wrong with what we have and that there will be a mass exodus" (*J, N, 2*).

Students could not help but be aware of the controversy because of the media coverage, and it carried over into their classroom conversations. Perhaps most frustrating for many involved was the lack of coordinated vocal support for the program outside the walls of Jefferson HS-A. Some teachers felt a handful of influential parents imposed their own agenda on the majority, as one teacher noted: "Unfortunately, those in the community who were displeased with the program were the most vocal, and those who liked Core-Plus were not outspoken about it" (*J, ES, 5*). Some of the issues involving four major stakeholder groups in this drama are examined further in the sections below.

In the following sections, readers should keep in mind that the controversy described *was not the focus of this study*. It simply developed coincident with, or on the heels of, our following of one cohort of students longitudinally. And, it became of interest because of the many ways in which it seemed to filter into the culture of the schools and classrooms in this study. Therefore, we openly acknowledge two obvious selection biases in the reporting. First, since we were not studying the controversy as a phenomenon, we did not seek to deeply investigate both sides of the issue by interviewing all parties involved or to investigate the legitimacy of every issue and grievance regarding the curriculum. Our resources allowed for us to gather information only from teachers at the Jefferson middle schools and at Jefferson HS-A, although these did include some critics, as we indicated above. There was limited contact and discussion with a few teachers at Jefferson HS-B. Additional information included reports on other district activities in which the Jefferson HS-A teachers were involved, such as school board and mathematics curriculum committee meetings. The second selection bias was our commitment to limit our attention to teachers who were implementing the curriculum during each year of interest for this study. Thus teachers who taught multiple years of the curriculum were generally interviewed more often than those who taught only Course 1, for example, or those new to the district toward the end of the study. We also did not revisit, in any systematic fashion, the middle school teachers once our cohort of students moved on to the high school. Thus it is possible that opinions and situations changed in different directions over time as events unfolded, and our data did not detect the change.

TEACHER PERSPECTIVES

Teachers played a key role in this local controversy, both supporting and opposing the Core-Plus Mathematics curriculum. Despite their beliefs one way or the other regarding its design and efficacy, they represented the front line of communication between the school policies and how those were articulated to the students and, in many cases, the parents. Interviews with teachers were generally semistructured with consistent talking points focused on pacing and other classroom issues related to the curriculum itself. However, when asked to comment on the curriculum controversy, teachers were given free rein to explain what they felt was happening in the district and with their students. After this study was completed, the transcripts were analyzed by looking for common themes and points of corroboration among the teachers' accounts of what occurred and their perceptions of the motivations for various actions. In the limited available space, three of the more interesting and consistent themes regarding the teachers are discussed.

A Sense of Pride and Professionalism

Mathematics educators have noted that one of the purposes and outcomes of the NCTM's 1989 *Curriculum and Evaluation Standards for School Mathematics* was to raise the level of professionalism of mathematics teachers (Peressini, 1998; Romberg, 1992). This was intended to occur in at least two ways: (1) by creating a set of established national standards for which mathematics teachers could become more recognized as a profession (similar to those in the medical and legal professions), and (2) by serving as a catalyst for improving practice through professional development associated with learning to teach new curricula aligned with the NCTM *Standards* documents. For Jefferson HS-A teachers and their middle school colleagues, one consistent theme was their sense of professionalism and pride in their work.

One important aspect of professionalism is being seen by other stakeholder groups as experts in their field of school mathematics teaching and learning and having their decisions and opinions valued on related matters of importance. In the Jefferson district, administrators largely left it up to the teachers to decide the direction of curriculum changes through actions of the district's mathematics curriculum committee. Teachers commented that they regarded membership on the committee to be an important professional task and noted that decisions were planned with great thought and deliberation. Members were expected to know current mathematics education research, and several teachers pointed to how they incorporated "the latest brain research" into their curriculum choices. Teachers at all experience levels emphasized the importance of professional development as a way to improve their teaching practices and strongly linked this to the Core-Plus Mathematics workshops completed during the field testing of the curriculum and continuing during the present study. Several teachers were enlisted by the Core-Plus Mathematics Project to speak at professional meetings and serve as workshop leaders, and these activities added to their sense of professionalism.

Through their workshop and classroom experiences, teachers also saw professional growth in terms of their own understanding of mathematics teaching and learning. Many of the veteran teachers had substantial histories of teaching conventional mathematics before experiencing the Core-Plus Mathematics curriculum. This experience often transformed their views of what students were capable of learning. One experienced teacher contrasted his experiences this way:

> When I taught traditional [mathematics], I didn't know how bad it was. And now I look back and I think how did my kids learn anything, how did they retain anything? They had no sense of it, and I think part of that is because there were so many things I had no sense of myself and when all of a sudden you have to make sense of it, it's like a light bulb goes on. And so I know we're doing what's right and what's best for kids. I can see that now. And our site here [Jefferson HS-A] has been really involved in brain research, and I'm on a group that meets once a month to look at brain research, and all of that points to Core-Plus math. *(J, ES, 6)*

A second teacher supported this point and focused on the broad spectrum of students the curriculum was trying to reach:

> It's a plus to the curriculum in that the curriculum is understandable for all student abilities and they can stretch themselves. No matter what their background is— and so [student 1] in the corner could ask the question about data and he knew his group knew the answer but they hadn't put it on paper yet, and so they could all contribute something special to the discussion. [Student 2] in the warm-up, he had an excellent idea and he is a Special Ed student. So it's the strength of the curriculum. I would like to think it's because we are pushing the pace quickly that we are also keeping the strong students excited as well. *(J, ES, 3)*

And one teacher, a transfer from another school using the Core-Plus Mathematics curriculum, added comments concerning both the students and working with her new peers at Jefferson HS-A:

> It is just, so, a thousand times better here than at [my previous school]. The fact that we have people willing to work together, that know what they are doing, that have really looked at how to make some major changes in their approach [to teaching]. It is not so much—you don't even have to have a specific, I think personally, textbook. It is just the whole idea behind it, in flushing out what students really know, and making sure they discover it for themselves, rather than me standing up there and lecturing them. It is so wonderful to have such a trained knowledgeable staff to work with; that has been a huge asset. (*J, N, 4*)

Despite the linking of their sense of professionalism to the implementation of the Core-Plus Mathematics curriculum amongst most of the mathematics teachers at Jefferson HS-A, there were teachers who exhibited less enthusiasm. One Experienced Critic (*J, EC, 1*) during interviews actually expressed support for the investigative approach and context-focus of the materials, but classroom observations revealed that he had major struggles with classroom management issues (resulting in individual and some pair work as the norm in his class) and a penchant for working his own examples on the board, both of which circumvented the investigative nature of the materials. The second Experienced Critic (*J, EC, 2*) reported participation in "all of the WMU workshops" (at least C1–C3), but still was convinced that a focus on skills and procedures was the basis for a good understanding of mathematics "and success in Calculus," and observations of his classrooms revealed his use of a very conventional pedagogy to teach the *Standards*-based materials. Surprisingly, once the alternative track was introduced near the end of this study, this teacher voiced somewhat greater enthusiasm for the *Standards*-based approach.

Because it was difficult to clearly delineate the root problems these critics had with the curriculum, it is even more difficult to conjecture what motivated the larger group of critic teachers at Jefferson HS-B to want to revert back to a more conventional approach. In addition to the several issues catalogued thus far (e.g., classroom management, pacing, unfamiliar content, and demands on pedagogical skills), another reason may stem from challenges to teachers' sense of efficacy associated with their teaching—the sense that many of the conventional measures for which they were judged as good teachers, such as teaching as telling students what they need to know to do well on largely skill-based achievement measures, were now being called into question (cf. Smith, 1996). There is also some indication that teaching for understanding was simply too much work for some critics; they wanted "something that will be easy for people to teach" (*J, ES, 7*). This motivation may relate closely to the anxiety that some teachers expressed over "keeping up the pace" associated with investigative learning.

A Sense of Frustration

A second, related theme emerged from the interview data in the form of frustration among the *Standards*-based curriculum's supporters, particularly the large group at Jefferson HS-A. Frustration manifested itself in a variety of forms. For example, there seems to be an important link between the teachers' sense of professionalism described in the previous section and the quote by *J, N, 2* (see above) that parents would perceive a change to alternative mathematics curriculum tracks as a possible mistake in judgment by the supporters of *Standards*-based curricula, thus an attack on one aspect of their professionalism. The parent opposition group needed only a few teachers to question the *Standards*-based approach to legitimize their argument, and they got the support they needed. Curiously, support came from other teachers as well, some even outside of mathematics, as with the case of the [Fine Arts] teacher who assigned high school students the task of creating cartoons around the theme of "problems with Core-Plus Mathematics." Some teachers of science weighed in with their displeasure as well, tracing problems of manipulation skills needed in their classes to the new mathematics approach.

And, problems were not confined to the high school, as the entire K–12 mathematics curriculum was under attack from the parent critics, supported by enough teachers to make the arguments seem legitimate. Concurrently, criticism of curriculum choices extended to a highly touted social studies program as well (see note 1). All of these incidents occurred over a period of a couple of years, and the most important result was arguably that both sides of the controversy now had teacher advocates to support their cases; they all could claim that they had professional "expertise" on their side. Who were parents to trust? As one teacher noted,

> If you had teachers convinced, you wouldn't have the parents having this problem ... general studies have shown that people trust their child's teacher, so if they're going to trust you, and you have accepted the idea that you have to access [the NCTM] process standards too, then they're going to buy into what you're doing also. (*J, ES, 5*)

A second source of frustration for Jefferson HS-A supporters stemmed from the use of data (or lack thereof) by opponents to argue their position. Two examples illustrate this frustration, one at the elementary and another at the secondary level. Criticism of the elementary mathematics curriculum focused on many issues, among them the perceived notion that younger children could no longer perform basic skills at a proficiency level that parents thought they once had attained. The Jefferson curriculum coordinator describes one situation:

> At our elementary level, parents have kept saying what our kids can't do. They are talking about they can't do long division, they can't do division of fractions, and they've picked on a couple of other issues. I have spoken at a lot of elementary schools about this. One in particular, last year parents were just in an uproar about it and it is a good school. Our 4th-grade [state assessment] scores, I believe, last year were 82% of our district performed satisfactory on the [state] test. That is a huge score. It is one of the top scores. And, the school that parents were having the most difficult time with that I met with four times last year to talk to them about math curriculum issues, they got a $50,000 Apple Award because they were in the top ten in the state on the [state assessment] scores. $50,000 for a small elementary school after they had said the kids didn't know anything! *(J, A, 1)*

At the high school, a similar frustration appeared, but here in connection with alleged historically poorer SAT, ACT, and AP Calculus scores. The above quote continued: "The AP is another interesting thing, because our district's results in AP Calculus were abysmal for years when our kids were coming through traditional math and a traditional calculus course. They are now better than ever." Special informational meetings were one mechanism used by the district to get information about the mathematics program to parents. Some parents remained skeptical despite the evidence to the contrary: "They were not convinced when [the two curriculum coordinators] gave them all kinds of statistics that back up the importance of CPMP and the tests results we have already" *(J, ES, 3)*. A visit from the state mathematics coordinator that showed parents the link between their K–12 mathematics curricula and state standards had little effect either.

Parents who supported the curriculum echoed the frustration of the Jefferson HS-A teachers in trying to fathom the opposition's argument about test scores. Several teachers described what occurred after some of the parent information meetings:

> Parents in each session would ask a question like, "Now let me get this right: Our ACT scores are fine, our SAT scores are fine, we have 93 percent of our juniors passing the [state assessment], and they're going to college and doing fine. So, let me get this right again, why are we switching to traditional math?" *(J, ES, 5)*

Perhaps the height of this frustration came near the end of the controversy when no data generated by the district were acceptable and the opposition parents simply argued that all data, district-generated or Core-Plus Mathematics project results, were just part of "one big conspiracy." The parent group would settle for nothing less than alternative mathematics curriculum tracks at all grade levels and, furthermore, a track to accommodate accelerated students.

A Sense of Apprehension and Resignation

In early 2000, the district reluctantly capitulated to the parent opposition group as the school system decided to go with two curricula for the following school year, each with an accelerated track. As one teacher supporter described the decision, "the school board doesn't want to deal with these irate parents, they just want to fix [the problem]" (*J, ES, 6*). A number of the most ardent supporters of the *Standards*-based curriculum at Jefferson HS-A declared that they wanted to continue to teach "reform math," and the school agreed to accommodate them to the extent possible. A first iteration of this declaration came at a meeting in which the mathematics department voted "100%" (*J, ES, 6*) to stay with a single track at Jefferson HS-A, even if Jefferson HS-B went to the two-curriculum option. But for the district, this was not an option; the two "choices" were to be implemented at both middle and high schools.

For the most experienced teachers, this was a bitter pill to swallow. Shortly after the decision, a number of the teachers flatly stated that they would "quit before teaching the alternative curriculum." By the next set of interviews, tempers had mollified somewhat, and the most vocal supporters were resigned to see how the "numbers would play out." At that point, they were unsure of what was going to happen the next year or what they would have to teach. One teacher described the situation in the following way:

> There were several of us that already said we want to stay with the reform math, I want to continue teaching Core, [*J, ES, 7*] wants to, [*J, ES, 5*] wants to. We aren't sure how that will play out. It's going to all come down to the numbers. So they will try to accommodate us as best as possible, but it may be possible that I teach some traditional; I may not have a choice. So we've made it known what our feelings are, but it's going to be driven by the number of students that sign up for each type. We have the first parent meeting for them to decide next Thursday night. It's a meeting that I will be running; an informational meeting. It's for tenth- and eleventh-grade students only as to what they will choose to do next year. And again, it is purely an informational meeting; it is not an open forum for debate. It is, if your student has felt successful in this program, has had a good experience and likes the program, etc., then they may want to continue with it next year. If your student tends to be that type of student where they want teacher direction, where the teacher tells them how to do it, and then they do less work with the calculator, less group work. If you feel your student is that type of a student, you may want to consider the traditional program. There is a brochure that is being made and will be out Tuesday. (*J, ES, 6*)

Even the more inexperienced teachers were now wondering what their future might hold. When one novice teacher was asked what she would do if she were assigned some "traditional" courses the following year, we recorded the following exchange:

(*J, N, 3*):	I don't know. If I end up teaching traditional next year and our numbers are growing in traditional because the 8th-grade teachers are sending them that way, and if we start going more and more traditional, I don't know. My husband and I joke that maybe it's time to …
I:	… move to the other side of town?
(*J, N, 3*):	… have kids and stay home. Give it a few years for Core to come back. I'll be very frustrated if I have to teach traditional.

Not surprisingly, the Experienced Critics at Jefferson HS-A offered to teach traditional courses as needed.

The brochure referred to at the end of the previous quotation represents yet another source of frustration for the teachers. It was supposed to represent a "side by side" comparison of the two programs, but with a twist. In this case, the brochure

> had to downplay the benefits of Core because it looked too good. So it's going to come down to parents making a choice; they have to decide. It will come down to a lot of other things after that because it will come down to the teachers who are teaching it. (*J, ES, 6*).

To the supporters of *Standards*-based curricula, the brochure represented another attempt by the vocal opposition to "control" information relating to the efficacy of the curriculum already in place, including achievement data.

To end this section, the following comment provides another perspective on the important role that teachers' opinions and beliefs played in influencing the future direction of their students and, likely, their emerging beliefs about mathematics. After students signed up for classes for the 2000–01 school year, *J, ES, 5* commented:

> I'm upset that we had so many students go from 9th [grade CPMP] into 10th [grade] geometry. My concern is that, it's not the program that is pushing kids out, it's the teachers. If we look at where the kids came from in those five sections—there are three ninth-grade teachers currently teaching Core 2—about five kids came from one teacher, about ten kids came from another teacher, and about 130 kids came from the other teacher. The problem was not the curriculum; the problem was the teacher.

ADMINISTRATOR PERSPECTIVES

Given the list of frustrations presented in the previous section, the reader may infer that administrators, other than the two curriculum coordinators, were neutral participants in the drama that unfolded. Our data suggest that this was not the case however, as they emerged as generally strong supporters of keeping *Standards*-based curricula, including Core-Plus Mathematics at the secondary level, as the sole option in the Jefferson school district. Administrators included the elementary and secondary mathematics coordinators, the principals in the various school buildings, and the district superintendent(s).[4]

The school board was the ultimate decision maker regarding implementation of a second K–12 mathematics curriculum. Some of the actions taken by the board, as reported by teacher supporters, were interesting. For example, it was not clear to what extent the board sided with the "conspiracy theory" promoted by the parent opposition group regarding the unreliability of all data collected by the Core-Plus Mathematics Project. Some board members even eventually appeared to doubt the reliability of the district's own data collection and monitoring of various kinds of achievement. The board seemed to make every effort to maintain a balancing of data supporting both sides of the controversy, which in effect placed the district's own data collection system on a par with that of uncritically accepted Internet-based anti-reform sentiments and agendas far removed from the Jefferson community.

One outcome of this position by the board was to devalue the years of hard work of the administrators and many teachers within the district. In addition to this position, the school board also appointed the main teacher critic at Jefferson HS-A to the position of co-coordinator of secondary curriculum in charge of examining textbooks for the conventional track. This board action came on the heels of a unanimous vote by the teachers not to support such an appointment; in effect, the board created a new position while sending a message that the opinions of supporter teachers in this matter were viewed as suspect. As noted above, it may be the case that, in the end, the school board was content with simply taking actions that would quickly put the controversy to rest, an outcome that was rapidly achieved at the high school once the two-curriculum decision was final. One teacher commented: "We [the teachers] are still fighting some battles, but [our superintendent] told me last week when he was here that he has not received one complaint about mathematics since this other option has been in place" (*J, ES, 6*).

The relationship between principals and teachers can be an uneasy one, since principals are the chief negotiators who must strike a delicate balance between being lead teachers of their building and chief communicators to parents whose wishes concerning their children and their taxes must be heard.[5] Anderson (1991) describes principals as

> knowing instinctively that schools are loosely coupled, that bureaucratic and coercive forms of control are seldom effective, that the relationship between principals and teachers is an essentially political one, and that the control versus autonomy is fought out in subtle and not-so-subtle ways daily among principals, teachers, parents, and students in schools. (p. xxx)

In the Jefferson controversy, the principals of both high schools and the majority of teachers were on the same political side, but control was ultimately in the hands of the school board.

Well before this study began, teachers reported the support and involvement of administrators in implementing the Core-Plus Mathematics curriculum. A ninth-grade teacher at Jefferson MS-B at the beginning of this study (1997) reported:

> Administrators are totally supportive [of Core-Plus Mathematics]. Our head principal ... works pretty closely with us. He knows the program real well. I wouldn't know if he would say he knows all the units, but he knows what we do, he knows what we expect. He stays real close to that. Our special ed teachers are real involved too. Our [vice] principals are probably up to speed, you know, maybe 50%, but our principal I would say he's real on top of that because of parent issues. (*J, ES, 1*)

A teacher at Jefferson HS-A described similar support 2 years later in the following way:

> Our principal has been great! [He] has been wonderful at supporting the program. [Jefferson HS-A] is not having a lot of problems; you're not hearing kids in class saying, "I don't like this program." As you walked around today, you probably weren't hearing that. (*J, ES, 5*)

At Jefferson HS-B, where much of the controversy originated, the administrators generally supported the program, but the situation was much more of a challenge because the majority of teachers were not supportive. In an interview yet another 2 years later (2001) after the two-track system was in place, the same teacher quoted above contrasted the current situation with the situation 2 years before in the following way:

> [Jefferson HS-B] has been disastrous. There is no other way to describe it. Teachers that were teaching Core that really didn't want it at the beginning

> of this year were telling their kids that they should really go into traditional math, even though these kids signed up [for Core-Plus]. The kids over there come through an absolutely fantastic program at the junior high level. But, [the main enthusiastic supporter at Jefferson HS-B] is now going to take a year off from teaching and he was the one holding things together there. I just don't know what is going to happen over there. They forced the principal out again. That is seven principals in, like, nine years. (*J, ES, 5*)

As we noted above, the district mathematics coordinators were active supporters of the curriculum and, in addition to meeting with parents to apprise them of district test score trends, they were actively involved in providing information to both the teachers and parents of elementary school children:

> What we have to do at the elementary [level], we've done two things; one is, I've worked with the 5th-grade teachers to make sure that we are assessing multiplication and division so that the kids can do that. I also took our assessment that we wrote and put it up on an overhead in front of the parents and said, "Here is the assessment. Does this tell us whether our students know how to multiply and divide?" And the parents had to admit that it did. (*J, A, 1*)

As with the curriculum coordinators, throughout the controversy the two superintendents (successively) were also supportive of keeping the single-track, *Standards*-based mathematics program by meeting with parents, supporting the mathematics teachers at all levels, and responding in the media to inaccuracies related to Core-Plus Mathematics and defending the actions of the district in keeping the program. At the end of the present study, the current superintendent was described by one teacher as

> willing to accept responsibility. He is pretty much no nonsense. If you show him results, or if he sees results, he will support what is happening. If he doesn't see results, then there is going to be a price to pay. He has said that in public. He said our [district] scores are good and doesn't want anything to change those scores. If he sees we've made a change and our scores are impacted, he said he'll deal with that. And I believe he will. (*J, ES, 5*)

Given the actions of the Jefferson school board described above, one may legitimately wonder about the limits of data-based decisions, even at the superintendent level, especially when the decisions may be unpopular with some of the more vocal parents. To close this section, district- and school-level administrators were surprised that the controversy turned so ugly, so quickly, and that they were unable to reason with the upset parents. The whole thing "just really blew up on us" (*J, A, 1*).

STUDENT PERSPECTIVES

Previous chapters have dealt extensively with the student achievement and attitudes of Jefferson students (at MS-A, MS-B, and HS-A) separately and together with the other two schools in this study. In doing so, it was noted that there was some depression of results for Jefferson HS-A students relative to Washington and Adams, the other two schools in the study. For example, Jefferson HS-A students did not score as well as the other two schools, on average, on the End of Course Algebra Examination (EoC) at the end of Course 2. However, they scored much higher than the national group of first-year algebra students who took the EoC on Concepts (E.S. = .47) and Processes (E.S. = .25) and almost the same on Skills (E.S. = .04). Their mathematical literacy means at the end of Course 3 did not differ significantly from the other two schools, and they were near the scores of the Netherlands, the highest scoring country in the world on the 1995 TIMSS. Graduates of Jefferson HS-A in this study also met with about the same level of success in college mathematics as the other students in this study and the comparison students who had conventional mathematics in high school. Whatever depression there may have been in achievement scores was mainly at the end of the fourth year, and the local controversy that was near its peak in Years 3 and 4 of this study may have been a contributing factor.

It was also clear in the belief, attitude, and conceptions data, that many Jefferson HS-A students were affected negatively on these variables by the local controversy. A good example is the case study student, Tom, who had a very negative attitude about Course 1, complaining bitterly about being a "guinea pig" in an experimental curriculum (see Chapter 12). Tom's attitude improved after that, and he became a strong supporter of *Standards*-based curricula. He earned an A in Calculus 2, his first college mathematics course, and he credited his high school mathematics program as a major factor in his success. Overall, students at Jefferson HS-A had positive attitudes about the curriculum, but a higher percent of students made negative comments than was the case at either Washington or Adams. Some comments, like the following by a graduate in the year after high school, mentioned the local controversy:

> I don't feel well prepared. In fact, I feel extremely poorly prepared. I have no foundation and no basics. I have to take summer courses to catch up. This program is not designed for students going to college. My parents and

> I are involved in a petition back in [Jefferson] to get an alternative program offered at [Jefferson HS-A].

The student comments reported in earlier chapters were taken from open-ended prompts on the Student Belief Surveys administered at the end of each of the first 2 years of this study or from the written post-high school survey. Such forums allow students to comment without interaction from an interviewer who may press them to further explain their points of view, perhaps yielding less candid information. Unless otherwise stated, student data and quotes in this chapter were drawn from problem-solving interviews in which the main purpose was the problem-solving activity and, at most, a brief time was devoted to other issues, such as their perspectives on the local controversy. It is therefore not surprising that across all of the interviews, there was little additional data that added new insights to the picture of students' perceptions of the controversy outlined previously. In this section, our previous data were combined with further teacher comments (1) to see what they add to our treatment of the controversy, (2) to provide some data regarding opposition claims related to the decline of Jefferson student achievement scores over time, and (3) to briefly illustrate one problem of using or misusing student anecdotes in a politically charged environment such as the one described.

Some Additional Student Comments

Of the nearly 100 interviews conducted with students at Jefferson HS (A) during the course of this study, slightly more than 20 yielded comments that were in some way connected to the controversy over the mathematics curriculum. In many cases, students simply used the interview opportunity to weigh in on the pros and cons of the curriculum with no direct link to the controversy per se. A content analysis of these comments showed the general categories to be ones already identified in the analysis of strengths and recommended changes on the post-high school survey in Chapter 11. Most of these perceived strengths and weaknesses seem unlikely to have had much bearing on the local controversy, with two possible exceptions. Some students expressed anxiety about their preparation for college, a common feeling for high school students in any mathematics curriculum, but a feeling that likely would be blamed on the *Standards*-based curriculum in the charged environment at Jefferson in those years. Some students also noted that their parents couldn't help them with their homework in this curriculum. Both of these issues are discussed from the parent perspective in a later section.

One student comment may well represent the most common relationship between students, their parents, and mathematics class:

Interviewer: "Have you ever talked to your parents about this [Core-Plus Mathematics] program? Do they know the sort of math you're taking or doesn't that ever come up?"
Student: "Oh, never."
I: "Do you ever talk to your parents about the program?"
S: "Not really."
I: "OK, do they know what you are studying now?"
S: "Not really."

Such interchanges are not meant to trivialize how parents and students interact about their educational experiences, but rather to note an important factor that seems to dominate hundreds of interviews with students conducted during this and other studies: most students are rather "low key" when describing their mathematics class experiences to others. They often take much of what goes on in class, including expectations about their learning, in stride as part of the process in which they are immersed. And some negative comments may not have really been a true reflection of what students feel, as noted in the following interchange with a teacher:

I: "The other school seems to get a lot of press related to how Core-Plus is not working. Have you seen any of that resonate with the kids here [at Jefferson HS-A]?"
J, ES, 4: "There's a little bit. I mean you hear particularly before you had choice, a kid would say, oh, I don't like da-da-da. I think a lot of the things I heard kids saying was just a repeat of what you hear the parents saying."

For many students, all they had experienced in both their middle school and high school mathematics programs were *Standards*-based curricula, so it was difficult to find a point of comparison for students contemplating choices between *Standards*-based and conventional mathematics. For example, one high school junior said she did not like conventional mathematics because it was too "boring and repetitious." When asked to elaborate on her comparison, she said she thought that conventional mathematics was exactly what she did in sixth grade with no deepening of the mathematical content. Another example came from a junior who "transferred in from Saxon Math" and liked its format better, but was adjusting to the "Core-Plus way." Many students, however, simply wanted to continue with the mathematics they already were used to, as noted in this exchange with a junior:

> I: "Next year it looks like you will have a choice of traditional algebra, or pre-calc Core 4, or AP Stats. Have you decided what you will take yet?"
>
> S: "Yes. Next year I'm going to keep taking Core because (*J,EC,1*) told me it was going to go back to regular math. Since I have grown up with this for the past five years, I might as well stay with it and finish doing that. I mean I got used to it after five years of doing it. Why not stick with it?"

Another student added,

> The first couple of years I didn't even want to accept the system because it was different. And it is a fact that people aren't very acceptable of any kind of change, but now I believe the Core-Plus system has helped me in a lot of ways because I have learned a lot of math and I understand a lot of it and I can apply it.

The student went on to note that he received a "28 overall on his ACT and 29 in the math. From our admittedly limited data concerning students' perceptions of the controversy, it does not seem likely that many of them had strong investment on either side. Most seemed comfortable with what they were doing in the *Standards*-based curriculum, but they would adjust to whatever the school offered.

Claims About Student Achievement Data

Throughout the Jefferson controversy, one of the persistent claims by those opposed to a single *Standards*-based mathematics curriculum was that students would not perform as well on high stakes tests. As noted earlier, achievement test scores at Jefferson HS-A were lower than at the other two schools in this study in some cases, but they were still strong as compared to groups outside the study. However, the claims of the opposition were about state assessments, the SAT, and the ACT. Several earlier comments by teachers suggested that there was little substance to these claims at either the elementary or at the high school level. The state assessment scores were some of the highest in elementary schools where the parent group complained the most, and some of the highest statewide—winning a substantial monetary reward for performance. The state assessment scores for the high school students were equally impressive with 93% of students passing. One teacher commented further:

> I looked at all the subject tests on our site for the [state] test, which we just finished, and math scored the highest. We had ninety-some percent of our kids pass the [state] math [test]. That is huge! And it's not that they are scoring 3's and just passing, they are scoring 1's and 2's and passing and those are all kids who have come through a reform curriculum! (*J, ES, 7*)

Another teacher added that "70% of our students are getting the [state assessment] scholarship here" (*J, ES, 6*). Equally impressive for Jefferson HS-A were increased enrollment in AP Calculus and AP Statistics and better performance on their exams. The teachers with primary responsibility for teaching those courses reported, "If you look at our AP scores, our AP scores are better than they've ever been" (*J, ES, 5*).

According to data provided by the Jefferson district, in 1994–95 just 12 students took the AP Calculus AB level examination and 4 (33%) passed. In 2000–01, the senior year of the target students in this study, 114 students took the examination and 95 (83%) passed. This incredible increase in both numbers and passing rates occurred fairly steadily over the intervening 6 years. Until 1997–98, all seniors had completed conventional mathematics courses. The first year that some seniors completed the Core-Plus Mathematics curriculum was 1997–98, and by 1999–2000 all graduates had done so.

Another concern involved performance on ACT and SAT exams for students, tests generally used for admission to college. While some claims were made that Jefferson HS students were not doing well on these exams, the Jefferson HS teachers reported "no drop in ACT scores." We investigated this claim over time. From 1994–95 through 1999–2000, according to the annual school reports directly from the ACT company, Jefferson HS's ACT Mathematics means never varied by more than 1 point. They were either 21 or 22 each year. In 2000–01, the ACT Mathematics mean of the 221 students in this study who took the ACT at Jefferson HS-A was 21.2. The report of the Jefferson teachers, mentioned above, was right on target; there was no drop in ACT Mathematics scores. No trend data were available for SAT scores at Jefferson HS-A, but in 2000–01 the Mathematics mean of the 37 students who took the SAT was 559.5 and their Verbal mean was 553.5. The SAT used a standardized score scale with mean of 500 and standard deviation of 100, so Jefferson HS-As means were over .5 standard deviations above the national mean.

Anecdotal Evidence

One of the common tactics of opponents of *Standards*-based mathematics programs is to present testimony from a student whose performance in college mathematics was less than hoped for and to let the reader then infer that this is the general case. This strategy has the powerful effect of inflaming parents' fears of such programs and has been effective in sowing seeds of doubt in school systems regarding their mathematics programs. The Internet has become an incredibly efficient way to disseminate such stories. Once in the hands of local opposition groups, these anecdotes, true or not, can play a pivotal role in quickly marshalling support to abandon a *Standards*-based mathematics program despite supportive student achievement data.

Parents and newspaper reporters are also notorious for ignoring typical experiences of students regardless of their high school mathematics background in first mathematics courses taken in college when they read or write about the negative experiences of one or two individual students who completed a *Standards*-based curriculum. For example, a check of the Fall 2007 freshman mathematics enrollments at Western Michigan University showed offerings of only 15 sections of Calculus I taken by 579 students compared to 56 sections of lower mathematics courses taken by 2,677 students (these numbers reflect only students enrolled in freshman mathematics courses). Most of the courses below calculus would be considered typical high school material taught in traditional styles with conventional textbooks. A 2007 study by ACT shows that only 28% of students who took that test were prepared for college algebra. Yet a negative anecdote about a student from a *Standards*-based high school curriculum who had difficulty in a college mathematics course can have a devastating effect on the stability of the local high school program. Seemingly well-established programs can be dismantled in a matter of months by a few disgruntled parents.

The Jefferson controversy was a case in point. As the controversy began to heat up, an inflammatory article appeared in the local newspaper reporting parts of an angry letter from a parent to the school district, blaming the *Standards*-based mathematics program for problems her son encountered in his first year of college mathematics. According to this parent, her son completed Core-Plus Mathematics with straight As, but when he attended a nearby university, he flunked the first mathematics course in a premedical program. According to the article, he was apparently unprepared because of his inadequate high school mathematics curriculum. The curriculum coordinator finished the story in this way:

> My supervisor came to me and said we need to deal with this [the angry parent letter], we need to deal with this now. We need to write her back. I said, "The first thing you need to do is investigate that it is true, because often what you find when you investigate further, is that some of the things people say aren't true." He went back and investigated and sure enough, he was a BC student. He was not in any of the accelerated courses and he had an

> [IEP] plan for some learning impairments. Well, that is a long way from being a straight A student at Jefferson and going and flunking math at the university there, and yet that's what has happened to us here. (*J, A, 1*)

Some of the issues associated with this kind of complaint and other parent issues are discussed in the next section.

PARENT PERSPECTIVES AND OTHER FACTORS

In this final section, a theoretical framework proposed by Peressini (1998) is presented that may help to explain the controversy that developed in the Jefferson school district. An attempt is then made to draw together several threads in the comments and other evidence presented in the previous sections to help explain the actions of the various stakeholders. In doing so, two points are examined that shed additional light on possible motives of the small parent group opposed to the *Standards*-based curriculum. A brief discussion follows of some contributing factors that aided this parent group to achieve their goal of a second mathematics curriculum option in the Jefferson school district.

In his 1998 survey of state and national education and mathematics reform documents produced during the previous two decades, including the 1989 NCTM *Standards,* Peressini examined the explicit and implicit roles of parents relative to the changes being advocated. He concluded that "undeniably, parents have taken on various roles from spectator to partner, advanced multiple agendas, and functioned as deterrent and catalyst. They have been portrayed as both friend and foe in the course of educational reforms" (Peressini, 1998, p. 577). As part of his argument, he noted that parents and teachers each work under "regimes of truth" that position them in various ways with respect to power and authority. For example, in some standards documents the primary change agents are seen as teachers and little mention is made of parents' understanding of education and the system in which their children participate; parents are at the margins or not mentioned as important players in the decisions that are to be made. This is, at least in part, because of the standards writers' respect for teachers' specialized knowledge of mathematics content and pedagogy and their perspective from within the system. The perspectives of standards writers and some teachers may differ from one another, as this study has clearly shown. Perhaps even more often, the perspectives of either of these professional groups may be at odds with the beliefs of most American adults, beliefs generally based on their own often negative experiences with school mathematics.

Thus members of the educational establishment like mathematics educators and K–12 teachers may have very different views than parents about what changes are important for improving teaching and learning of school mathematics, assuming that changes are even warranted. Educators and parents may be operating under quite different regimes of truth when they are faced with educational change. Peressini (1998) argued that many educational reforms fail because educators marginalize parents in their plans for educational change, and they act as if parents already share, or can be easily convinced of, their own view of "truth" about the reform effort. Peressini cautioned educators to recognize that contradictory regimes of truth may exist simultaneously and to seek effective ways to understand them. Including parents' views as part of the change process may be crucial for achieving changes that are long-lasting and beneficial to all involved parties.

It seems clear that several regimes of truth were at work in the drama that unfolded in the Jefferson district. For most of the experienced supporter teachers, their regime of truth led them to value the "teacher professionalization" as outlined in the NCTM *Standards* documents and the curriculum they adopted and implemented based on those documents. The Jefferson administrators for the most part shared this regime of truth. Teacher critics operated under a different regime of truth, one largely rooted in conventional teaching practices and procedural learning outcomes. They at times paid lip service to the *Standards*-based curriculum, but their actions in the classroom and public statements indicated their beliefs were tied to past practices and experiences. Their regime of truth led them to value traditional notions of "efficacy" that have historically defined mathematics curriculum and teaching. This value resonated with the opposition parent group.

Characterizing the regimes of truth within the parent groups is more speculative. For the vast majority of supportive parents, perhaps they shared the regime of truth of the supportive teachers, or perhaps they simply did not see a conflict between their interests and what the district was trying to do with their *Standards*-based mathematics programs. Like most parents, they likely trusted the "professionals" and agreed that improvements can be made in teaching and learning, just as they can in most other fields. If this is the case, the evidence lies in the silence of this majority (to the noted frustration of some of the teacher supporters).

It is more difficult to fathom the regime of truth under which the opposition parents operated. On the surface it seems simple and well aligned with those of the teacher critics. Certainly the more vocal and public statements made by members of those two groups during the controversy meshed, although it is not certain if there was strong agreement on all points of what "traditional" or "conventional" entails for mathematics curriculum and teaching. But if the "regime of truth" framework is to be useful for including parents in conversations about reform, as Peressini suggested, a good starting point would be to find some common understanding or agreement about some obvious points of truth. How does one go about looking for common ground when a small group of parents totally rejects any and all data that run counter to their point of view? Likely fueled by questionable information from the Internet, they rejected all district and outside data, even state-level reports, as a conspiracy; in their view, it was all manufactured. Teacher supporters were also baffled when they met with parents to explain why their choice of curriculum track was important for their children. A teacher illustrated with the following comment:

> We are learning a lot of new things about how kids learn and I tell people, when they say "I want my kid in traditional math," I always ask them how they did in traditional math. And the majority of them say, "I hated it" or "I did poorly" or "I dropped out after the second year." It's like, "So why do you want to subject your child to that?" And some of them say, "To make them stronger." They truly believe that the pain is what makes their students good; they don't understand that it's the understanding and the problem solving. *(J, ES, 6)*

Such a tenet within the regime of truth of parents may be impossible for teachers to change with evidence-based argument. This belief may be related to issues students noted above as a negative aspect of the curriculum—that parents can't help them with their homework, because it looks so different from what they experienced in school. Teachers of *Standards*-based curricula may correctly see this situation as evidence of gaps in parents' understandings of mathematics, but this problem is one that may have a solution. Teachers and curriculum developers have begun to recognize the importance of finding ways to make *Standards*-based curricula accessible to parents.

Another tenet within the regime of truth of the opposition parents may be a serious candidate for what ultimately lay at the root of the Jefferson controversy. As noted several times above, there was an undercurrent that pervaded the controversy from the very beginning of this study. Observations at the middle schools in the first year found teachers trying to deal with the heterogeneous grouping of students advocated by the *Standards*-based curriculum. Teachers noted at that time that one of the complaints of some parents was wanting their children to be more challenged with the material and receive recognition for their extra work and effort. They did not understand or appreciate mixed abilities in the same classroom.

In effect, the teachers at that time were trying to accommodate "accelerated students" within the heterogeneous classrooms.

Two years into the study, the arguments were dominated by the question of whether students and parents should have a "choice" of *Standards*-based or traditional curriculum. Advance 2 more years to the decision to accommodate choice and the issue of two tracks emerged as a central issue. At first, there would be an accelerated track for those choosing the conventional curriculum, but no such option for the *Standards*-based students. According to one teacher supporter, "they want an honors track; they don't feel that one size fits all works." Teacher supporters were now caught in a bind. Once a "designated" accelerated traditional track was in place, every parent with a "gifted" child would want that track and the *Standards*-based curriculum would de facto be one for the average or lower students. It would be the lower track. In the end, two tracks were offered in both curricula, and teachers noted the difference in dynamics of *Standards*-based classrooms. Perhaps implementing a two-track system of Core-Plus Mathematics in the Jefferson school district at the outset would have avoided one of the problems at the root of the controversy. But perhaps not, as the opposition agenda all along may have been much bigger. As one teacher remarked after the decision was final,

> There's already the parent group out there, the same group. They've said, now we have to go after the junior high and elementary. At least at the high school you can give a choice and that can be successful, but at the elementary school? (*J, ES, 5*)

Another issue that may have resonated most with parents was the transition to college: How well does the *Standards*-based curriculum prepare students for college? As illustrated above, the Jefferson district data related to ACT, SAT, and AP Calculus were very strong. Reports from their former students, albeit anecdotal, were largely positive. Yet, all those data were set aside in favor of the anecdote of the student who did not do well in college, and it was agreed that the *Standards*-based curriculum must be to blame.

Another regime of truth about *Standards*-based curricula appears to have had an impact on the Jefferson controversy. Apparently, some (few, we hope) professors have decided that *Standards*-based school curricula are so inadequate that their use in schools must be fought by whatever means available. It seems that this regime of truth leads them to reject, or more likely ignore, the growing body of research showing many positive benefits of these programs for students and teachers (cf. the review by Stein, Remillard, & Smith, 2007). This group seems particularly adamant that *Standards*-based high school curricula cannot possibly prepare students as well for college mathematics as conventional curricula do, no matter what the empirical evidence might be. For this group, it appears to be acceptable to post and maintain on the Internet negative anecdotes, comments, and results of long outdated "studies" and "surveys" that were strongly criticized on methodological grounds when they were originally posted. Opposition parents at Jefferson drew on these Internet studies to solidify their case. In one Jefferson newspaper article, studies posted on the Internet comprised the entire opposition case against the *Standards*-based curriculum.

THE AFTERMATH OF THE CONTROVERSY

Jefferson now has a choice of Core-Plus Mathematics or a conventional curriculum in Grades 9–12. In the junior high schools (Grades 6–8), they use Connected Mathematics, but parents or students can choose an approach that is traditional or investigative or a combination of the two, that is, the main curriculum will be supported by "traditionally" styled worksheets, "investigative" type worksheets, or both. While the main issues of the Jefferson controversy were resolved enough to satisfy the most vocal opposition parents, the teachers since then must confront another set of problems, including producing and distributing appropriate worksheets and dealing with students switching from one curricular path to the other. For example, students switching from one curriculum to another make it difficult for teachers to easily access students' prior knowledge based on a common experience. This is a critical issue in a *Standards*-based curriculum because of the spiral approach to topics as well as the knowledge based in contextualized situations. This switching also makes creating classrooms of learning communities more difficult, since expectations are not consistent for students when they switch between programs. In addition, Jefferson has a reform AP Calculus program that may leave students in the conventional track at a disadvantage as they progress along that path.

Finally, perhaps the most predictable outcomes were shown in student and teacher reactions once the second option was in place and students had made their course selections. One teacher summarized:

> Kids that are good at symbol manipulation are going to do well [in the conventional curriculum] and kids that can retain it are doing just fine. But the push to go back to an accelerated path has been by one particular teacher here again. That teacher has had to teach those Geometry courses by request and now is saying it is really hard, so I think the teacher wants to have a group of only good kids. Get rid of the bad kids, you know; they don't belong in math. We did have several students this semester that went

> back into Core Math. We didn't have any that went from Core into traditional at semester, but we did have students that went from traditional back to Core and said they needed something that makes sense. But we did have a lot at the beginning of the year switch back to Core. And then again, I think I told you last fall about the high drop-out rate from traditional as opposed to the Core; many more students leaving traditional math, especially at the beginning of the year. They were just struggling when they went into whatever class they did and many just dropped math all together. So they are not even taking a math class any more, which is pretty scary. Hopefully, they will pick back up on one next year. (*J, ES, 5*)

The Jefferson story is a good example of how resolving one controversy may lead to many unintended consequences. What satisfied the few opposition parents and teachers, in the end, had a questionable impact on many students at Jefferson. In the next and final chapter of this volume, results across the study are summarized and discussed, including some final comments about local curriculum controversies.

NOTES

1. Jefferson HS-A was also implementing a reform social studies program "with great success on the state test" at the same time as the mathematics controversy took place. Teachers describe the unfolding of events surrounding social studies and the results to be identical on many points to those described here.
2. The committee consisted of representative mathematics teachers from each school, special ed teachers, counselors, two mathematics curriculum coordinators (elementary and secondary), and lead building administrators.
3. The district's implementation strategy was to use heterogeneous ability grouping of students as the curriculum suggested and avoided "tracking of students."
4. The district replaced several principals and superintendents during the course of this study as noted in a number of comments in this chapter.
5. See, for example, Fullan (1991) for relationships between principals, teachers, and other stakeholders.

CHAPTER 14

SUMMARY AND INTERPRETATIONS

The report of this 5-year study describes achievement and affective outcomes in three high schools that implemented the first edition of the Core-Plus Mathematics curriculum with all their students. These high schools had used the field-test version of the curriculum for at least 3 years prior to the present study. Thus many of the teachers had participated in professional development workshops designed to prepare them for teaching the program and had 1 to 3 years experience teaching preliminary versions prior to this study. The target students entered high school from a *Standards*-based middle school program, either Connected Mathematics or MATH Thematics. By the end of high school most students in the study had completed 7 years of *Standards*-based curricula, and some had completed Advanced Placement Calculus or Statistics. For 4 years of high school and 1 year after, the study monitored the mathematics courses students completed and their achievement, beliefs, and attitudes at the end of each course. During each of the 4 years of high school, evaluators visited each site to observe classes and interview teachers and students. Overall, the implementations of Core-Plus Mathematics curriculum were fairly stable with the exception of a local controversy that developed in one of the communities during the study.

Outcomes relative to each of the seven goals of the study, given at the beginning of Chapter 2, were reported year by year in earlier chapters. In

A Five-Year Study of the First Edition of the Core-Plus Mathematics Curriculum, pp. 369–400

the first section of this chapter, after a discussion of the study's limitations, the main outcomes of the study are summarized from a longitudinal perspective. In the second main section, the evidence that this study provides concerning academic tracking is presented in the context of differential teacher effects on student achievement and affective outcomes. Finally, the implications of this study for revision of the first edition are discussed, including a description of relevant changes in the second edition of the Core-Plus Mathematics curriculum.

LIMITATIONS OF THE STUDY

As described in the Preface to this volume, the investigators were members of the Core-Plus Mathematics Project team. The longitudinal evaluation of the first edition was under the codirection of the first and second authors with the assistance of the fourth author and of an outside advisory group. The third author is the principal investigator of the Core-Plus Mathematics Project. Beginning in 2002, the second author directed the formative evaluation of the second edition of the curriculum, copyrighted 2008, 2009, and 2010, which the results of the reported study helped to inform in ways that are discussed later in this chapter. Readers should take this information into account as they read and interpret the study's findings and implications.

Another type of limitation relates to the three schools in the study. Although there was some variation in the demographics across the schools, the percentage of minority and lower socioeconomic students was not large and no school was in an urban setting. The findings may not be valid in other schools, especially in those in very different socioeconomic settings.

By design, this study was a description of what transpired over 4 years in the mathematics classrooms of three high schools including the self-reported educational activities of the schools' graduates in their first year after high school. Thus the level of scientific "control" is not the same as with smaller scale, focused experiments. For example, teachers were depended on to fairly administer project-supplied written tests and attitude scales in their own classrooms albeit with careful written guidance from the evaluators. Teachers' and students' self-reports in oral interviews and written surveys are treated as valid data (with some cross-checking where feasible as described in earlier chapters), although again there are potential difficulties with such data. Even classroom visits by members of the evaluation team may sometimes result in teachers changing their usual behavior to more align with what they think the observer would like to see.

This was intended to be a careful descriptive, longitudinal study, not a comparative quasi-experimental one. Yet, as available, comparisons between achievement data of students in this study and that of other groups of students on the same measures are reported—for example, data from national norm groups, students nationally who completed particular tests, or samples of students in the 1995 TIMSS from the United States or other countries. These comparisons are reported to provide information that may be of interest to readers. Any individual comparisons of this type may be invalid because of preexisting group differences and/or differences in test administration conditions. However, the investigators believe that consistent patterns across several measures and several such "comparisons" are informative, and, in this study, they strengthen the case for the efficacy of a *Standards*-based curriculum.

SUMMARY OF OUTCOMES FROM A LONGITUDINAL PERSPECTIVE

All three schools were located in small town communities, although the Jefferson community was considerably larger than either Washington or Adams. The students were predominantly Caucasian. Washington High School had by far the largest underrepresented minority population (27.9%), compared to less than 5% at both Adams High School and Jefferson High School. Entering mathematics achievement levels of students were somewhat above the national average (55th to 65th national student percentile on a standardized test at the beginning of Year 1).

Teachers

All teachers in the study held a bachelor's degree or higher, and 23.3% had a master's degree in mathematics education. The set of teachers was almost evenly split by gender with a median of 8 years of teaching experience. Of 21 teachers for whom sufficient data were available, 16 had completed at least one workshop designed to prepare participants to implement the curriculum. Of the 16 teachers who were experienced with this curriculum, all but 2 expressed generally positive beliefs about the curriculum and the problem-based teaching approach that it was designed to support. The other 5 teachers were novices in the use of the curriculum, but they, too, had mainly positive impressions and beliefs.

Many of the supportive teachers believed that the curriculum had a positive impact on students' understanding and problem-solving abilities and, in some cases, on other variables such as social skills, writing and reading mathematical content, and a better understanding of more applications of mathematics. Some teachers were less sure that the curriculum provided sufficient emphasis on developing students' paper-and-pencil algebraic skills. The two experienced teachers who were critical of the curriculum believed that a *Standards*-based curriculum and teaching approach were less efficient than direct instruction typically associated with a conventional curriculum.

In general, the experienced supporters implemented the curriculum in ways that were consistent with the intent of the developers, although there were some potentially important differences in teaching practices. The novices were less sure of themselves and some of them had management problems that contributed to weaknesses in their implementations. The two experienced critical teachers mainly used direct teaching focusing on an answer-oriented approach to the *Standards*-based curriculum with little of the intended involvement of the students in making sense of the mathematical ideas or sometimes taught from a substitute conventional textbook.

Mathematical Achievement Each Year of High School

On the standardized test *ITED-Q* administered in alternate forms at the beginning and end of Year 1, students in this study grew about the same in 1 year as the nationally representative norm group. On a written test of curriculum-specific goals and interview-based problems, students generally did better on algebra tasks (especially on algebraic operations and algebraic modeling) than on tasks that assessed the other three content strands, a finding that also reflects the relative levels of emphasis of content in the course. Students averaged over 40% correct on tasks in each of Geometry, Statistics, and Discrete Mathematics. Their learning of this content was far from mastery level. Students in conventional first-year algebra classes could not be expected to learn any of the content of these three strands as it is not included in their syllabi, although some algebra topics that are in Course 2 of this curriculum would be included in most conventional first-year algebra courses.

At the end of Year 2, students in this study scored higher overall on the ETS End of Course Algebra Examination than the group of all first-year algebra students in the country who completed the test that year. Consistent with other research (cf. the review by Stein, Remillard, & Smith, 2007), students in the *Standards*-based curriculum scored especially well on the Concepts subtest and better than the comparison group on the Processes subtest, but about the same on the Skills subtest. On interview-based algebra problems, students demonstrated strength in use of the Pythagorean Theorem and in determining the equation of a line given two points, but they struggled with some purely symbolic algebra like solving a system of two linear equations in two variables. In geometry, students demonstrated a solid understanding of the coordinate plane and of reflections and size transformations, but some had difficulty drawing an image of a figure under a rotation and analyzing properties of a rhombus. In discrete mathematics, students showed proficiency with matrices both in performing matrix operations and in using matrices as representations of information in contexts described verbally. They also were able to apply and interpret vertex-edge graphs in a contextual situation, but few were able to use matrices to solve a system of two linear equations in two variables.

At the end of Year 3, students in this study had nearly the same mean on 12 released TIMSS mathematical literacy tasks as the Netherlands, the top-scoring country in the 1995 TIMSS. Course 3 students scored much higher than the U.S. TIMSS sample on both the Geometry and Numbers subtests, with the Numbers mean being relatively higher than the Geometry mean. Selected Course 3 students were interviewed with problems from the Balanced Assessment Project that were either numerical or geometric in content and required use of a wide range of problem-solving strategies. Interviewed students were able to read information from a table, compute percents, find percentages of numbers, find perimeters and areas of complex figures, and visualize figures transformed by folding. They also were comfortable with many problem-solving strategies, including guess-and-check, checking the reasonableness of an intermediate answer and adjusting if needed, working backwards, and computation. The most difficult problem (53% success rate compared to near 90% or more on other problems) involved a logo covered by different colored square tiles in which a great deal of information was given to describe all the problem's parameters. Interviewed students sometimes got bogged down trying to process the complex information provided in the problem.

At the end of Year 4, students completed a test composed of 20 released TIMSS advanced mathematics tasks. Students in this study scored better than the U.S. sample on three of the four subtests—Geometry, Probability and Statistics, and Calculus—and about the same on the fourth, namely, Numbers, Equations, and Functions. On the Probability and Statistics subtest, students in this study scored much higher than both the U.S. and the international TIMSS samples. On both the advanced mathematics and the reasoning test given at the end of Year 4, the adjusted mean of Course 4 students was significantly higher than that of a conventional precalculus comparison group.

Interview problems in Year 4 focused on reasoning and proof. About three-fourths of interviewed Course 4 students were able to recognize and generalize patterns and represent the patterns using algebraic symbols.

Most students were able to reason correctly about a fairly complex method for generating a number pattern, but some students were confused about the connection of the slope of a line to the implicit symbolic form of a linear function, that is, $ax + by = c$. The geometric reasoning problem involved checking a method for making a kite that was purported to guarantee pairs of equal sides. About 70% of students understood the method and most of them produced a counterexample to disprove it. The students who had difficulty made the mistake of assuming the equality of some segments based on their appearance in the given figure. About half of the interviewed students were able to solve a statistical reasoning problem that involved transforming the mean of a distribution by multiplying each value by the same number.

Overall, the students in this study scored well on achievement tests each year compared to data from the comparison groups of students described above. Areas of particular strength appear to be conceptual understanding in algebra, mathematical literacy, and probability and statistics.

Attitudes, Beliefs, and Conceptions of Students

Students' attitudes and beliefs at the end of Years 1 and 2 and their conceptions of mathematics at the end of Years 3 and 4 were virtually all more positive than the neutral position on the various scales. Without a comparison group, however, it is difficult to judge how positively to interpret these results. Results on the belief scales at the end of Years 1 and 2 indicate that students, on average, had positive assessments of their mathematical abilities and were positively disposed toward the creative and challenging aspects of mathematics and toward cooperating with peers to learn mathematics.

Students' specific attitudes about both Courses 1 and 2 were positive, particularly about the value and enjoyment of group work and of using calculators. (Interestingly, students in this study had generally positive attitudes about the curriculum and teaching approach, but not as positive as field test students 3 years earlier when the curriculum was completely novel to them.) The only scale on which mean responses were negative was the Competition scale in Years 1 and 2. Since a negative response on this scale was defined to mean the student liked to compete with and do well in comparison to his or her peers in mathematics class, this result means that students tended to be more positive than negative about such competition with classmates. This finding is consistent with the research reported by Boaler (2002) and Boaler and Staples (2008).

Positive results on the Conceptions of Mathematics Inventory (CMI) scales at the end of Years 3 and 4 are evidence that students' conceptions of mathematics, on average, were more aligned with the conceptions implicit in a *Standards*-based curriculum than in opposition to them.

In general, students had positive assessments of their mathematical abilities, valued group work and calculator use, and were positively disposed toward the creative, competitive, and challenging aspects of mathematics and toward cooperating with peers to learn mathematics. By the last 2 years of high school, their conceptions of mathematics tended to be aligned with those implicit in a *Standards*-based curriculum.

Outcomes by School, Gender, and Preachievement Level

Achievement results are presented year by year in Chapters 5–8, and attitude, belief, and conceptions results are the focus in Chapters 9 and 10. From a more longitudinal perspective, significant pairwise school, gender, and preachievement level comparisons on all achievement tests across the 4 years of high school are given in Table 14.1. Summaries of outcomes by school, gender, and preachievement level (PAL) follow.

Outcomes by School. At the end of Year 1 and of Year 3, adjusted achievement means did not differ significantly by school, but at the end of both Year 2 and Year 4, the means of Jefferson High School on all achievement tests and nearly all subtests were significantly lower than at least one of the other schools. At the end of Year 2, the descending order of the school means was Washington High School, Adams High School, and Jefferson High School. On both tests at the end of Year 4, the ordering of means was Adams High School, Washington High School, and Jefferson High School. The tests at the end of Year 2 (EoC) and at the end of Year 4 (advanced mathematics and reasoning) measured mathematical outcomes that students would be expected to learn in a college preparatory mathematics curriculum. By contrast, the *ITED-Q* and mathematics literacy tests were more general tests of mathematical thinking and applications

Table 14.1. Statistically Significant Pairwise Comparisons of School Gender, and PAL Means on Achievement Measures Adjusted for Variance in *ITED-Q* Pretest Scores Over the 4 Years of High School

	Test or Subtest	*School*	*Gender*	*PAL*
Year 1	ITED-Q	NSD	G > B	NSD
Year 2	EoC Concepts	W > J	NSD	1 > 3
	EoC Processes	W > J	G > B	1 > 2, 1 > 3, 4 > 3
	EoC Skills	NSD	G > B	1 > 2, 4 > 2, 4 > 3
Year 3	MaLit Number	NSD	NSD	NSD
	MaLit Geometry	NSD	NSD	1 > 2, 1 > 3, 2 > 3
Year 4	Advanced Math	A > W, A > J, W > J	B > G	NSD
	Reasoning Test	A > W, A > J, W > J	NSD	1 > 2

that are important for mathematically literate citizens. Jefferson High School students did as well on the latter two more general tests, but they lagged behind students in the other two schools on tests of college preparatory mathematics.

Significant pairwise school, gender, and preachievement level comparisons on the Student Belief Survey scales at the end of Courses 1 and 2 and on the Conceptions of Mathematics Inventory at the end of Courses 3 and 4 are given in Table 14.2. At the end of Years 1 and 2, beliefs and attitudes toward courses were consistently and significantly more positive for students at Adams High School than for students from the other two schools. In addition, specific attitudes toward the two courses were significantly more positive at Jefferson High School than at Washington High School. At Washington High School, the lower attitudes may be due to a teacher effect. The two teachers who taught both Course 1 and Course 2 at Washington High School were not well liked by the students, and they both had difficulties implementing the curriculum.

At the end of Years 3 and 4, CMI scale means of students at Washington and Adams high schools were (in most cases significantly) higher than those of students at Jefferson High School at each administration and on nearly all scales. This result indicates that the conceptions of mathematics of Jefferson High School students compared to students in the other two schools were less well aligned with the conceptions of mathematics implicit in a *Standards*-based curriculum. With the exception of the two experienced critic teachers, there did not seem to be a general teacher issue at Jefferson High School as there was in the first two courses at Washington High School, but the local controversy in Jefferson is probably a partial explanation of their results. The role that the controversy

Table 14.2. Statistically Significant Pairwise Comparisons of School, Gender, and PAL Means on Affective Scales Over the 4 Years of High School

Scale	*Year*	*School*	*Gender*	*PAL*
Self Assessment	First	A > W, A > J	NSD	1 > 2 > 3 > 4
	Second	A > W, A > J	NSD	1 > 2 > 3 > 4
Creativity	First	A > W, A > J	NSD	1 > 3, 1 > 4
	Second	A > W, A > J	NSD	1 > 2, 1 > 3, 1 > 4, 2 > 4, 3 > 4
Cooperation	First	A > W, A > J	NSD	NSD
	Second	A > W, A > J	NSD	NSD
Genetic	First	W > A, W > J	G > B	NSD
	Second	W > J, A > J	G > B	NSD
Challenge	First	A > J	NSD	NSD
	Second	A > J	NSD	1 > 2, 1 > 3, 1 > 4
Competition	First	NSD	G > B	1 < 2 < 3 < 4
	Second	NSD	NSD	1 < 2 < 3 < 4
Course Attitude	First	A > W, A > J	NSD	NSD
	Second	A > J > W	NSD	1 > 3, 1 > 4, 2 > 4, 3 > 4
Usefulness of Mathematics	Third	W > J, A > J	NSD	1 > 3, 2 > 3
	Fourth	W > J, A > J	NSD	NSD
Structure of Math Know.	Third	A > W, A > J	B > G	1 > 2 > 3
	Fourth	W > J, A > J	NSD	NSD
Doing Mathematics	Third	W > J, A > J	G > B	1 > 3, 2 > 3
	Fourth	W > J, A > J	NSD	NSD
Validating Math Ideas	Third	A > J	NSD	1 > 3, 2 > 3
	Fourth	A > W > J	NSD	NSD
Status of Mathematics	Third	A > J	NSD	NSD
	Fourth	W > J, A > J	NSD	NSD
Learning Mathematics	Third	W > J, A > J	G > B	1 > 3, 2 > 3
	Fourth	A > W, A > J	NSD	NSD
Composition of Math Know.	Third	W > J, A > J	G > B	1 > 3, 2 > 3
	Fourth	W > J, A > J	NSD	NSD

may have played in Jefferson's relatively weak achievement and CMI results was discussed in Chapter 13.

Overall, students at Jefferson High School, which experienced a local controversy about the program, did not achieve as well and had less positive attitudes and conceptions about mathematics compared to students at the other two schools.

Outcomes by Gender. Consistent with findings in earlier research that reported higher achievement for boys, in the present study boys scored significantly higher than girls on the *ITED-Q* pretest at the beginning of Year 1. To summarize the 4 years of achievement evidence adjusted for variance in the pretest, girls did better than boys on quantitative thinking, algebraic processes, and algebraic skills, and they did as well on algebraic concepts, mathematical literacy, and mathematical reasoning. Boys did better than girls on just one achievement measure, advanced mathematics, and the difference was due mainly to boys' higher scores on less conventional and more advanced content (statistics and calculus). There were no significant interactions between gender and preachievement level on any of these tests, so the above differences cut across students at all levels of mathematical aptitude. A plausible explanation for these results is that, with regard to achievement outcomes, girls profit from the *Standards*-based curriculum more than boys, in general. However, as the mathematics becomes more advanced and less standard and the pool of students becomes more academically elite, boys do better than girls, as was often the case in earlier gender research (cf. the review by Leder, 1992).

On specific attitudes toward courses, the gender effect was not statistically significant in either Year 1 or Year 2. However, among students in the 90th national percentile pretest group, at the end of Year 1 boys had more positive course attitudes and valued the competitive and challenging aspects of mathematics more as compared to girls in the same group. Among this group of top students, boys had higher assessments of their own mathematical abilities at the end of both years. Among students below the 33rd national percentile on the pretest, girls were more positive about the competitive aspects of mathematics than boys at the end of Year 1, but no Competition scale differences involving gender were significant in the second year. At the end of both years, girls, especially high-achieving ones, believed much more strongly than boys that gender is not a factor in mathematical ability.

In the third year, gender results on the CMI scales were mixed. Girls agreed more strongly that solving mathematics problems is a process that can be reasoned through and made sense of, that learning mathematics involves asking questions, analyzing mistakes, and thinking carefully about mathematical relationships, and that mathematical knowledge is more about the connections between ideas and concepts than about knowing procedures and facts. Boys agreed more strongly than girls that mathematics consists of connected topics and relationships between ideas. At the end of the fourth year, there were no significant gender differences on the CMI scales.

Some of the affective outcomes align well with earlier research findings in which brighter boys had stronger assessments of their own mathematical ability and greater enjoyment of the challenge and competition of mathematics than brighter girls (Leder, 1992). The relative competitiveness of boys may also explain the finding that among students at the lowest preachievement level, boys are more negative than girls about competition in mathematics learning. Less able boys may have a stronger desire than less able girls to avoid a competitive situation in which they realize that they are not likely to do well. However, the finding that girls, especially more able ones, believe very strongly that boys are not naturally better at mathematics than girls may be evidence of the recent emergence of girls from the mathematical shadows of boys, at least when the referent is "all girls" rather than "self." Girls' conceptions of mathematics were somewhat better aligned than boys' with those conceptions that underlie a *Standards*-based curriculum, although not on every scale and only at the end of Year 3.

In general, girls had higher achievement than boys on many measures, although among students in fourth-year high school mathematics courses boys had higher achievement on advanced topics than girls. Boys and girls differed little in their overall attitudes and beliefs, but girls' conceptions of mathematics in the last 2 high school years were somewhat better aligned than boys' with the conceptions that underlie a *Standards*-based curriculum.

Outcomes by Preachievement Level. Briefly, on some, but not all, achievement measures (notably the EoC in Year 2 and the reasoning test in Year 4), students with better entering mathematical achievement had higher adjusted achievement scores. These results may be partially due to a tracking effect since higher proportions of students with better preachievement scores were in accelerated classes. Affective outcomes by preachievement levels were somewhat mixed. At the end of Course 2, but not at the end of Course 1, students' attitudes and beliefs on most scales were in the same order as their entering achievement levels. Exceptions were that the higher achieving students were more positive about competition in mathematics than other students, a belief that was indicated by negative scores on the Competition scale, and the Cooperation and Genetic scale scores did not differ significantly by preachievement level. Students in all preachievement level groups were generally positive about cooperating with other students and believed that genetics and gender were not important predictors of success in mathematics.

Students' conceptions of mathematics, as measured by the CMI scales, differed in the same order as the preachievement level groups on most scales at the end of the third year, but there were no significant differences by preachievement group at the end of the fourth year. This result suggests that students' conceptions of mathematics across all preachievement levels were fairly well aligned with the conceptions implicit in a *Standards*-based curriculum. The different patterns in CMI results in Year 3 and Year 4 are probably attributable, at least in part, to the greater homogeneity of the students in mathematics courses in the fourth year.

In sum, students at all levels of mathematical aptitude scored well compared to comparison groups of students in conventional programs, but posttest scores of students at higher aptitude levels tended to be stronger than predicted by their pretest scores. Attitudes and beliefs were positively correlated with entering mathematical achievement levels, although students at all levels of mathematical aptitude had positive attitudes and beliefs about mathematics.

First Year After High School

A written survey of 2001 graduates of Washington, Adams, and Jefferson high schools was administered in January (2002) during the first academic year after high school graduation. Complete results are presented in Chapter 11. All but a few respondents attended a college or community college, and they completed mainly conventional college mathematics or statistics courses at about the same rate and with same degree of success as freshmen students who attended the University of Iowa or Western Michigan University. About 85% of respondents indicated that their high school preparation for college mathematics and mathematics-related courses was at least as good as or better than (over 25%) most of their college classmates.

The most frequently mentioned strengths that students indicated they gained from their high school mathematics were good conceptual understanding and strong problem-solving and reasoning skills. When asked about changes they would recommend in their high school mathematics program, better students tended to be satisfied with the program as is or to ask for more course options or hands-on activities, while less successful mathematics students tended to recommend changes that would make the program more conventional. Graduates of all three schools were quite positive about the impact that their high school mathematics program had on their decisions after high school such as choice of major in college. Notable exceptions among Jefferson High School graduates appear to have been negatively influenced by the local controversy that developed there.

TEACHER AND CLASS COMPOSITION EFFECTS

This study sheds new light on the effects of teachers and academic tracking on achievement and attitudes of students. Previous research indicated that teachers differ in terms of how they implement a curriculum, and there is some evidence that what teachers do in a *Standards*-based classroom is associated with their students' achievement (cf. Schoen, Cebulla, Finn, & Fi, 2003). Students were linked to teachers in the data set in the present study, so exploratory tests of achievement and affective differences by teacher group in each school each year were conducted. Since this study's data on teacher beliefs and practices were not fine-grained enough to say much about reasons for the results that were found, these results were not reported with the study's main findings in earlier chapters. They may be useful, though, for generating hypotheses for future research on teacher beliefs and practices.

In the process of analyzing the data for teacher effects, it became clear that how the classes were grouped academically also made a consistent and significant difference. The three schools in this study all used the Core-Plus Mathematics curriculum both in heterogeneous classes and in tracked classes for better students who wanted to accelerate. In an initial analysis of teacher groups within each school, it became clear that both the achievement and the affective data of students in accelerated classes were nearly always better than those of students in regular classes even after using analysis of covariance to adjust for variance in baseline achievement (i.e., the *ITED-Q* pretest). Since accelerated classes used the same *Standards*-based curriculum as the regular classes, the achievement differences that remained after adjusting for baseline achievement as well as the affective differences were not due to a curriculum effect. A more likely explanation is that differences were at least partially due to an academic tracking effect. Research on tracking has consistently shown that, compared to regular college preparatory classes, classes considered by teachers and students to be in the higher academic track have higher expectations and content coverage, richer student-student and teacher-student interactions, and higher mathematical achievement (cf. reviews by Kulik & Kulik, 1982; Slavin, 1990). In this study, there were little direct data concerning expectations and student-student and teacher-student interactions in particular classes, but certainly the intent of the accelerated classes was to cover more content in more depth each year.

For each year, a one-way teacher group ANCOVA was run within each school with the achievement test administered that year as the dependent variable. It is important to note the analyses were based on the entire group of students taught by a teacher that year. Sometimes that was one class, but often it was more than one. A summary of the statistically significant pairwise differences is given in Table 14.3. Using the identification scheme in Chapter 4, the teachers in each school year are listed in the table in the order of their students' adjusted achievement mean that year. The analysis in the fourth year was restricted to Course 4 students' scores on the TIMSS-based advanced mathematics test.

Scanning the table suggests some interesting patterns. First, there are many more statistically significant teacher differences than would be expected by chance, suggesting that teacher differences were associated with differences in student achievement. The mathematical literacy test at the end of Course 3 is an exception. A possible explanation is that this test was not as closely tied to the goals of the course that students had just completed as the other achievement measures, therefore making mathematical literacy scores less dependent on teacher differences.

A natural question is whether the classification of teachers as experienced supporters, novices, or experienced critics was in any way associated with student achievement. Focusing on statistically significant pairwise differences, by the classification of the teacher, all but one involved students of an experienced supporter doing better than students of a novice or experienced critic. The exception was at Washington High School in Course 2, in which a novice teacher (*W, N, 1*) prevailed over *W, ES, 1*. However, as reported in Chapter 6, both of these Washington

Table 14.3. Statistically Significant Pairwise Comparisons of Teacher Group Means Within School on Annual Achievement Measures

	Course 1 ITED-Q		*Course 2 EoC*		*Course 3 Math Lit*		*Course 4 Adv. Math*	
School	*Teachers*	*Sig. Diffs.*	*Teachers*	*Sig. Diffs.*	*Teachers*	*Sig. Diffs.*	*Teachers*	*Sig. Diffs.*
Washington	W, N, 1 W,E S, 1	NSD	W, N, 1 W, ES, 1	W, N, 1 > W, ES, 1	W, ES, 2[a] W, ES, 1 W, ES, 3	NSD	W, N, 1	–
Adams	A, ES, 1 A, U, 1[b] A, ES, 3 A, N, 1	A, ES, 1 > A, N, 1	A, ES, 3[a] A, ES, 4	A, ES, 3 > A, ES ,4	A, ES, 1 A, ES, 3[a]	NSD	A, ES, 1[a] A, ES, 1	Acc. > Regular
Jefferson	J, ES, 3 J, ES,1 J, ES, 2 J, N, 2	All diffs. signif. except last pair	J, ES, 7[a] J, N, 3 J, U, 1 J, U, 2 J, U, 3 J, ES, 4 J, EC, 2	J, ES, 7 > each of last 6	J, EC, 1 J, ES, 5	NSD	J, EC, 1 J, ES, 7 J, ES, 4	NSD

[a] Accelerated group
[b] "U" means there was not sufficient data to classify the teacher.

teachers had some implementation problems. In particular, *W, ES, 1* was considered by class observers and his students to be rigid and to have difficulty facilitating student exploration. In general, the students of novice and experienced critic teachers did not fare as well as those of experienced supporters.

The student achievement means of the two experienced critics at Jefferson High School differed from one another in ways that seem predictable from the available information about them. Both of these teachers (*J, EC, 1* and *J, EC, 2*) had serious doubts about the *Standards*-based curriculum and teaching approach and both made adjustments to make their classes more conventional. However, *J, EC, 1* was more cooperative, and he did not work against the curriculum. *J, EC, 2* was vocally negative about the curriculum, actively trying to convince his students and teacher colleagues of its inadequacy. *J, EC, 1* taught Course 3 and Course 4, and the adjusted means of his students did not differ significantly from those of his colleagues in the experienced supporter category. However, *J, EC, 2* was at the bottom of the list of seven Course 2 teachers, and each pairwise difference was statistically significant.

As for affective teacher effects, for each year a MANOVA by teacher group within school was run with the seven SBS or CMI scales administered that year as dependent variables. A summary similar to the one for achievement is given in Table 14.4. Using the identification scheme in Chapter 4, the teachers in each school year are listed in the table in the order of their students' affective scale means that year. (The ordering was not always the same on all scales, but there was always a clearly prevailing order across scales.) Differences listed as statistically significant reached significance beyond the .05 level on at least four of the seven scales. The analysis in the fourth year was restricted to Course 4 students.

There were more statistically significant differences than would be expected by chance, indicating that the teacher variable was associated with students' attitudes, beliefs, and conceptions. Most of the above discussion about student achievement for teachers in different categories also applies to the affective outcomes of their students. Within the limits of the data, the results suggest that teaching practices that align better with a problem-based approach were associated with both higher achievement and stronger beliefs and attitudes of students.

The achievement and affective data reported in the tables also elucidated a pattern of a different kind. Briefly, there were five accelerated groups all taught by strong teachers in the experienced supporter category. At Adams High School, there were accelerated groups in each of the last 3 years. At Jefferson High School, there was an accelerated group in Course 2. (In Course 3, Jefferson High School had an accelerated group, but its teacher also taught some regular classes that were

Table 14.4. Statistically Significant Pairwise Comparisons of Teacher Group Means Within School on Annual Affective Measures

	Course 1 SBS		*Course 2 SBS*		*Course 3 CMI*		*Course 4 CMI*	
School	*Teachers*	*Sig. Diffs.*	*Teachers*	*Sig. Diffs.*	*Teachers*	*Sig. Diffs.*	*Teachers*	*Sig. Diffs.*
Washington	W, ES, 1 W, N, 1	NSD	W, ES, 1 W, N, 1	NSD	W, ES, 2[a] W, ES, 1 W, ES, 3	All diffs. signif,	W, N, 1	–
Adams	A, ES, 3 A, N, 1 A, U, 1[b] A, ES, 1	Self Assess: A, ES, 3 > each of last 3	A, ES, 3[a] A, ES, 2 A, ES, 4	NSD	A, ES, 3[a] A, ES, 1 A, ES, 2	A, ES, 3 > each of last 2	A, ES, 1[a] A, ES, 1	NSD
Jefferson	J, ES,3 J, ES, 2 J, ES, 1 J, N, 2	Top 3 each > J, N, 2	J, ES, 7[a] J, N, 3 J, U, 1 J, ES, 4 J, U, 3 J, U, 2 J, EC, 2	J, ES, 7 > each of others; Top 6 each > J, EC, 2	J, ES, 5 J, EC, 1	NSD	J, ES, 7 J, ES, 4 J, EC, 1	NSD

[a] Accelerated group

[b] "U" means there was not sufficient data to classify the teacher.

not distinguishable in the data set.) At Washington High School, there was an accelerated group in Course 3. (By Course 4, there was just one class.) On the EoC at the end of Course 2, the adjusted mean of the accelerated group was highest among all teacher groups within each school and significantly higher than every other teacher group in the school. In Course 4 at Adams High School, the same teacher taught the accelerated group and the regular group. The accelerated group's adjusted mean was significantly higher on the advanced mathematics test. On the mathematical literacy test in Course 3, the adjusted means of the accelerated groups were higher, but not significantly higher, than regular groups in the same school. The nonsignificant results in Course 3 may be partially explained by the fact that the tests administered at the end of Course 2 and Course 4 measured topics that were specific goals of the course each year, whereas the mathematical literacy test measured more general mathematical concepts and methods useful in daily life. Means of accelerated students on affective measures were also generally higher than those of students in regular classes, although the pattern of significance was a little different.

How can the dominance of the accelerated students be explained? All students and teachers used the same curriculum, whether in accelerated or regular classes, so these differences cannot be attributed to the curriculum. The teachers of the accelerated students were strong, all in the experienced supporter category, but so were many teachers of the regular classes. In fact, in Course 4 at Adams High School, the same teacher taught the accelerated and regular classes, so the differences are not a teacher effect. Students in the accelerated classes had higher scores on the *ITED-Q* pretest, and they also had higher scores on achievement posttests. Using analysis of covariance, the variance in the *ITED-Q* pretest was removed statistically from the variance in the posttest scores. This statistical technique is intended to "equate" the groups in terms of their entering achievement, but the accelerated classes still scored significantly higher than the regular classes on almost all posttest measures. The consistently stronger results for the accelerated classes seem to be a classic example of the tracking effect, discussed earlier.

The tracking effect seems to be an extremely important consideration for any quasi-experimental comparison of two or more curricula in which the researcher intends to attribute differences in student outcomes to a curriculum effect. A common approach is to use analysis of covariance or hierarchical linear modeling to remove variance due to one or more baseline variables, usually student variables like entering achievement, minority group status, and socioeconomic background. That approach may work well if the two curricula have essentially equal status in the view of students and teachers in the school. However, the existence of two curriculum options in a school suggests the likelihood that one curriculum is viewed as the rigorous college preparatory program and the other is not. If that is the case, the tracking effect is introduced as a confounding variable.

For example, Davis and Shih (2007) noted that the tracking effect may have been an issue in their comparison of college algebra grades and calculus readiness test scores of students from the same school district who completed the Core-Plus Mathematics curriculum and those who completed more conventional curriculum. After statistically accounting for differences in several student baseline measures, Davis and Shih found that the results were better for students from the conventional curricula. Because the conventional curriculum was considered by teachers and students to be *the* college preparatory curriculum in the district and the Core-Plus Mathematics was seen as the curriculum for less capable and less serious mathematics students, the results cannot necessarily be attributed to a curriculum effect.

IMPLICATIONS FOR THE SECOND EDITION OF THE CURRICULUM

At the end of the present study, in 2002, the Core-Plus Mathematics Project received a 5-year award (ESI-0137718) from the National Science Foundation to prepare a major revision of the 4-year curriculum. Since the researchers were members of the Core-Plus Mathematics Project team, the revision was informed by the results of the present study as well as by extensive feedback from teachers using the first edition. The revision also took into account recent changes in middle school mathematics programs, particularly in the area of algebra, proposals for change in undergraduate mathematics (CUPM, 2004; Ganter & Barker, 2002), and advances in technology. Second editions of Courses 1–4 are now published under the title *Core-Plus Mathematics* (Hirsch, Fey, Hart, Schoen, & Watkins, with Ritsema, Walker, Keller, Marcus, Coxford, & Burrill 2008a, 2008b, 2009, 2010).

Results of the present study suggest that the published first edition of the curriculum was more effective than the unpublished, field-test material. The possible deficit in algebraic manipulative skills of students who used the field-test version of the curriculum seems to have been eliminated or greatly reduced, as evidenced by, for example, the finding that students at the end of Course 2 scored better on an algebra test than comparison students who had just completed first-year algebra. Furthermore, in a quasi-experimental comparison at the end of Course 4, students scored significantly higher than students in conventional precalculus comparison groups on tests of advanced mathematics and reasoning.

Nevertheless, students and teachers in this study often mentioned the need for more algebraic manipulative skill practice. Some students were critical of what they perceived as repetitive questions in some of the investigations and expressed the need for more explicit questions and information, especially at the beginning of an investigation. In addition, students and teachers of the first edition noted that in the cases of selected algebra and geometry units there was perhaps a too sharp increase in abstraction and difficulty in the transition from Course 2 to Course 3. On the positive side, teachers and students were almost uniformly positive about the way graphing calculators were incorporated into the curriculum as a tool for learning and problem solving.

Content Revisions

Drawing on all the above sources of guidance, the revision work resulted in some shifts in priorities and positioning of mathematical content in the 4-year curriculum, most notably in the algebra and functions strand and in the geometry and trigonometry strand. Second edition changes in the treatment of algebra and functions included:

- an accelerated introduction of symbol-based reasoning—including symbol manipulation and proof
- more explicit development of symbol sense—connecting algebraic forms to numeric, graphic, and context interpretations and implications
- earlier introduction of inverse functions and logarithms
- greater use of computer algebra systems (CAS) to enhance concept development and support problem solving

Far more than skill supplements, these changes in algebra involve an earlier and more cohesive incorporation of symbolic procedures as a meaningful and important part of mathematics.

In the case of the geometry and trigonometry strand, major second edition content changes resulted in:

- a reorganized development of key geometric ideas—congruence, properties of circles, and trigonometric ratios and functions
- earlier and more careful development of geometric reasoning and proof

- increased use of coordinate representations and algebra to support geometric reasoning and problem solving
- use of interactive geometry software to support discovery and application of properties of shape and geometric transformations

The assumption that most students would be entering second edition Course 1 after completion of a revised *Standards*-based middle school curriculum like Connected Mathematics helped to make the earlier work with symbolic manipulation and reasoning feasible. Conventional middle school curricula, too, include more work with algebra than was the case 10 or 15 years ago. The above changes in both strands were also intended to smooth the transitions in complexity and formality of content from one course to the next. Major shifts in content emphases and placement can be seen by comparing the unit titles in Table 14.5 with those in Tables 1.1 and 1.2 the revision of Course 4 strengthens students' preparation for calculus.

Table 14.5. Core-Plus Mathematics 2nd Edition Units

Unit	*Course 1*	*Unit*	*Course 2*
1	Patterns of Change	1	Functions, Equations, and Systems
2	Patterns in Data	2	Matrix Methods
3	Linear Functions	3	Coordinate Methods
4	Vertex-Edge Graphs	4	Regression and Correlation
5	Exponential Functions	5	Nonlinear Functions and Equations
6	Patterns in Shape	6	Network Optimization
7	Quadratic Functions	7	Trigonometric Methods
8	Patterns in Chance	8	Probability Distributions
Unit	*Course 3*	*Unit*	*Course 4*
1	Reasoning and Proof	1	Families of Functions
2	Inequalities and Linear Programming	2	Vectors and Motion
3	Similarity and Congruence	3	Algebraic Functions and Equations
4	Samples and Variation	4	Trigonometric Functions and Equations
5	Polynomial and Rational Functions	5	Exponential Functions, Logarithms, and Data Modeling
6	Circles and Circular Functions	6	Surfaces and Cross Sections
7	Recursion and Iteration	7	Concepts of Calculus
8	Inverse Functions	8	Counting Methods and Induction

Descriptions of the key mathematical ideas in these units can be found in the Chapter 14 Appendix.

Refined Lesson Structure

The instructional materials reflect the same design principles that guided development of the first edition as described in Chapter 1, albeit with some refinements based on reports from first edition users and comments from both participants in the present study and second edition field-test teachers. Refinements include the development of focusing questions at the beginning of each lesson investigation to provide an advance organizer for the mathematics to be discovered or developed. For example, in a new Course 1 unit, *Quadratic Functions*, the introduction to an investigation in the third lesson includes:

> As you work on the problems in this investigation, make notes of answers to these questions:
>
> *What calculations in the quadratic formula give information on the number of solutions of the related quadratic equation?*
>
> *What calculations provide information on the x-intercepts and maximum or minimum point of the graph of the related quadratic function?*

A second refinement involved streamlining investigations by removing or rewriting questions that were perceived as repetitive by students. In some investigations, there also was reduction in the amount of scaffolding and step-by-step instructions.

In addition to sharpening the focus of investigations and the updating of data and problem situations, new *Summarize the Mathematics* checkpoints at the end of investigations were developed to better prompt student articulation of important mathematics and strategies. An example from an investigation in the Course 1 unit *Patterns in Shape* is given in Figure 14.1. This pedagogical feature also provided a way for the project to respond to questions from parents and critics of the first edition as to "Where is the mathematics?"

A fourth refinement that was made in response to findings of this study and corroborated by many users of the first edition is the inclusion of Review exercises in each homework set. These exercises are designed to build proficiency with concepts and skills through distributed practice, to provide just-in-time review, or to address possible prerequisite gaps due to the more robust assumption about middle school preparation of students.

Summarize the Mathematics

In this investigation, you examined applications of the Pythagorean Theorem and its converse. You also used careful reasoning to provide arguments for why these statements are true.

a) Describe the general idea behind your argument that the Pythagorean Theorem is true for all right triangles.

b) Describe the general idea behind your argument that the converse of the Pythagorean Theorem is true.

c) Give two examples, one mathematical and one not involving mathematics, to illustrate that if a statement is true, its converse may not be true.

d) What is the smallest number of side lengths you need to compare in order to test if two right triangles are congruent? Does it make a difference which side lengths you use? Explain.

Be prepared to share ideas and examples with the class.

Figure 14.1. Articulating Important Mathematics and Strategies

Expanded Role of Technology

Because of concerns for access and equity, the first edition curriculum materials were based on a modest technology assumption—students would have access to graphing calculator technology in class and outside of school. As noted earlier, teachers and students, including those in this study, were very positive about the curriculum-embedded use of graphing calculators in the first edition. As work began on the second edition, the contextual and mathematical problems that the curriculum was being organized around and the learning expectations for students were such that it was decided to augment graphing calculator technology with computer tools. To meet this challenge and maintain the project's commitment to access and equity, the project systematically explored development of Java-based software that eventually evolved into *CPMP-Tools* (www.wmich.edu/cpmp/CPMP-Tools/). The software includes a computer algebra system (CAS), a spreadsheet, and interactive geometry, data analysis, and discrete mathematics tools. The suite of tools and their functionality are organized by course to focus on the intended mathematics and to reduce the steepness of the learning curve for using the tools. Tools share similar menu screens and interface, thereby promoting learning transfer from one tool to another. Further features of *CPMP-Tools* and their curriculum applications can be found in Hart, Hirsch, and Keller (2007).

The decision to move in the direction of Java-based software was supported by a report of the *Teens and Technology* survey by the Pew Internet and American Life Project that suggested 87% of U.S. teens aged 12–17 use the Internet and of those, 87% have Internet access at home. Among survey respondents, 89% of Hispanic youth, 87% of White youth, and 77% of African American youth indicated going online (Lenhart, Madden, & Hitlin, 2005). Additionally, Java WebStart permits safe, easy, and reliable distribution of the software and software updates across different types of computers. We believe this evolving public domain software holds promise for democratizing access to powerful mathematical tools for students and teachers independent of their use of the Core-Plus Mathematics curriculum.

The development process for the second edition remained similar to that used in the first edition, as described in Chapter 1. Each revised course textbook was the product of a 3-year cycle of research and development, pilot testing and refinement, and field testing and further refinement prior to publication. In addition, mathematicians Deborah Hughes-Hallett (University of Arizona/Harvard University), Stephen B. Maurer (Swarthmore College), William McCallum (University of Arizona), Doris Schattschneider (Moravian College), and statistician Richard Scheaffer (University of Florida) reviewed and commented on units as they were developed, tested, and refined. This collaboration proved to be beneficial and rewarding for both developers and consultants (Maurer & McCallum, 2006). Preliminary field-test results indicate better achievement for students using the second edition curriculum materials as compared to that of students using the first edition materials in the present study, which in turn was better than the achievement of students using field-test materials as this study shows. As intended, this curriculum development process has resulted in improvement in the effectiveness of successive iterations of the written curriculum as measured by student achievement.

A FINAL NOTE

This study provides a longitudinal description of the beliefs and implementation practices of teachers and the mathematics course-taking patterns, achievement, beliefs, and conceptions of students, many of whom had completed 7 years of *Standards*-based mathematics by the last year of this study. A variety of cognitive and affective measures were used during the study in order to distinguish areas of strength and weakness in the impact of the curriculum. In order to enrich the description, statistical comparisons were made and interpreted between schools, gender groups, and students grouped by entering mathematical achievement. Some comparisons between test scores of students in this study and outside groups of students were presented and discussed. These comparisons were also meant to enrich the description of what happened in the three target schools during the study.

As reported in Chapter 13, during the study a local controversy developed in one school district. The controversy was not a planned focus of the study, but the data provided sufficiently rich background for a description and interpretation of the controversy from the perspective of teachers and students in Jefferson High School. The controversy was originally centered in a less stable implementation of the curriculum in a second high school in the Jefferson district, but fueled by questionable information from the Internet it soon encompassed the entire district. For the supporters of the *Standards*-based curriculum in Jefferson, the controversy was painful and difficult. Unfortunately, there have been a number of similar controversies in other communities when *Standards*-based curricula are adopted, especially at the high school level. Some of the consequences for students and teacher supporters of the *Standards*-based curriculum at Jefferson High School were described in Chapter 13. The school board's resolution, providing parents and students with a choice of a conventional curriculum, quieted the controversy but had some undesirable consequences as well.

The situation nationally that helped inflame the controversy has probably not changed much since 2001 despite a growing body of quite positive scholarly evidence concerning the effects of *Standards*-based curricula (cf. the review by Stein et al., 2007). In an analysis of the "math wars," of which Jefferson's skirmish was one local battle, Schoenfeld (2004) concluded that the main underlying issue is an old one in the history of education, namely, the (*Standards*-based) view that "schools should serve the needs of democracy by promoting equality and providing training for citizenship" versus the (conventional) view that "schools should serve the needs of individuals by providing the means of gaining advantage in competitions for social mobility" (p. 281). The centrality of the issues of academic tracking and preparation for college in the Jefferson controversy was consistent with Schoenfeld's analysis of the national "math wars."

In fact, it seems evident that, by public demand, some sort of acceleration option must be available in U.S. comprehensive high schools, whether or not the accelerated students are grouped together. Perhaps the most important remaining question is whether a *Standards*-based curriculum with its concrete entry points and problem-based teaching approach pressing toward sophisticated understanding of formal mathematical ideas and methods can serve the needs of all high school students, regardless of how they may be grouped. Relative to this question, all students in the three schools in the present study used the *Standards*-based curriculum, and the data on a wide range of student achievement outcomes are quite positive. At one end of the spectrum of mathematical outcomes, on a test of mathematical literacy constructed from tasks used in the 1995 TIMSS, students at the end of Course 3 scored at about the same level as students in the top-scoring country, the Netherlands. At the other end of the spectrum of outcomes, graduates of the three target schools, after 7 years in *Standards*-based curricula, were at least as successful in college mathematics courses as freshmen at two major universities who completed conventional high school curricula.

This study also shows clearly that the curriculum is not the only variable that affects student outcomes, as there were significant school effects, teacher effects, and academic grouping effects. The school effect may be most positive when the *Standards*-based curriculum is used with all students as the developers originally intended. When that is not the case, the academic grouping or tracking effect becomes a concern. At any rate, all three variables must be taken into account in experimental or quasi-experimental comparative curriculum evaluation studies, and that is no easy task. In particular, evaluators who try to isolate a curriculum effect using statistical techniques for equating curriculum groups need to somehow account for the tracking effect. No matter how sophisticated the statistical model, the tracking effect cannot be accounted for by adjusting for student baseline variables since tracking is not a student effect. Once tracking with different curricula occurs in a school, it becomes virtually impossible to isolate a curriculum effect in a comparative study of students in the high-track curriculum versus those in the low-track curriculum.

As mentioned in the Preface, item data and all unpublished testing instruments from this study are available at http://www.wmich.edu/cpmp/evaluation.html as a baseline of instruments and data for future curriculum evaluators or users who may wish to compare results of new groups of students to those in this study on common tests or surveys. Taken together, this volume, the supplement at the CPMP Web site, and the first edition Core-Plus Mathematics curriculum materials (samples of which are also available at the Web site) serve as a fairly complete description of the nature and impact of an exemplar of first edition *Standards*-based high school mathematics curricula as it existed and was implemented with all students in three schools around the turn of the twenty-first century.

APPENDIX

Core-Plus Mathematics 2nd Edition

Course 1 Units	
Unit 1	**Patterns of Change** develops student ability to recognize and describe important patterns that relate quantitative variables, to use data tables, graphs, words, and symbols to represent the relationships, and to use reasoning and calculating tools to answer questions and solve problems. *Topics include* variables and functions, algebraic expressions and recurrence relations, coordinate graphs, data tables and spreadsheets, and equations and inequalities.
Unit 2	**Patterns in Data** develops student ability to make sense of real-world data through use of graphical displays, measures of center, and measures of variability. *Topics include* distributions of data and their shapes, as displayed in dot plots, histograms, and box plots; measures of center including mean and median, and their properties; measures of variability including interquartile range and standard deviation, and their properties; and percentiles and outliers.
Unit 3	**Linear Functions** develops student ability to recognize and represent linear relationships between variables and to use tables, graphs, and algebraic expressions for linear functions to solve problems in situations that involve constant rate of change or slope. *Topics include* linear functions, slope of a line, rate of change, modeling linear data patterns, solving linear equations and inequalities, equivalent linear expressions.
Unit 4	**Vertex-Edge Graphs** develops student understanding of vertex-edge graphs and ability to use these graphs to represent and solve problems involving paths, networks, and relationships among a finite number of elements, including finding efficient routes and avoiding conflicts. *Topics include* vertex-edge graphs, mathematical modeling, optimization, algorithmic problem solving, Euler circuits and paths, matrix representation of graphs, vertex coloring and chromatic number.
Unit 5	**Exponential Functions** develops student ability to recognize and represent exponential growth and decay patterns, to express those patterns in symbolic forms, to solve problems that involve exponential change, and to use properties of exponents to write expressions in equivalent forms. *Topics include* exponential growth and decay functions, data modeling, growth and decay rates, half-life and doubling time, compound interest, and properties of exponents.

Appendix continues on next page.

Unit 6	**Patterns in Shape** develops student ability to visualize and describe two- and three-dimensional shapes, to represent them with drawings, to examine shape properties through both experimentation and careful reasoning, and to use those properties to solve problems. *Topics include* Triangle Inequality, congruence conditions for triangles, special quadrilaterals and quadrilateral linkages, Pythagorean Theorem, properties of polygons, tilings of the plane, properties of polyhedra, and the Platonic solids.
Unit 7	**Quadratic Functions** develops student ability to recognize and represent quadratic relations between variables using data tables, graphs, and symbolic formulas, to solve problems involving quadratic functions, and to express quadratic polynomials in equivalent factored and expanded forms. *Topics include* quadratic functions and their graphs, applications to projectile motion and economic problems, expanding and factoring quadratic expressions, and solving quadratic equations by the quadratic formula and calculator approximation.
Unit 8	**Patterns in Chance** develops student ability to solve problems involving chance by constructing sample spaces of equally-likely outcomes or geometric models and to approximate solutions to more complex probability problems by using simulation. *Topics include* sample spaces, equally-likely outcomes, probability distributions, mutually exclusive (disjoint) events, Addition Rule, simulation, random digits, discrete and continuous random variables, Law of Large Numbers, and geometric probability.

Core-Plus Mathematics 2nd Edition

Course 2 Units	
Unit 1	**Functions, Equations, and Systems** reviews and extends student ability to recognize, describe, and use functional relationships among quantitative variables, with special emphasis on relationships that involve two or more independent variables. *Topics include* direct and inverse variation and joint variation; power functions; linear equations in standard form; and systems of two linear equations with two variables, including solution by graphing, substitution, and elimination.
Unit 2	**Matrix Methods** develops student understanding of matrices and ability to use matrices to represent and solve problems in a variety of real-world and mathematical settings. *Topics include* constructing and interpreting matrices, row and column sums, matrix addition, scalar multiplication, matrix multiplication, powers of matrices, inverse matrices, properties of matrices, and using matrices to solve systems of linear equations.
Unit 3	**Coordinate Methods** develops student understanding of coordinate methods for representing and analyzing properties of geometric shapes, for describing geometric change, and for producing animations.

Appendix continues on next page.

Topics include representing two-dimensional figures and modeling situations with coordinates, including computer-generated graphics; distance in the coordinate plane, midpoint of a segment, and slope; coordinate and matrix models of rigid transformations (translations, rotations, and line reflections), of size transformations, and of similarity transformations; animation effects.

Unit 4 **Regression and Correlation** develops student understanding of the characteristics and interpretation of the least squares regression equation and of the use of correlation to measure the strength of the linear association between two variables.

Topics include interpreting scatterplots; least squares regression, residuals and errors in prediction, sum of squared errors, influential points; Pearson's correlation coefficient and its properties, lurking variables, and cause and effect.

Unit 5 **Nonlinear Functions and Equations** introduces function notation, reviews and extends student ability to construct and reason with functions that model parabolic shapes and other quadratic relationships in science and economics, with special emphasis on formal symbolic reasoning methods, and introduces common logarithms and algebraic methods for solving exponential equations.

Topics include formalization of function concept, notation, domain and range; factoring and expanding quadratic expressions, solving quadratic equations by factoring and the quadratic formula, applications to supply and demand, break-even analysis; common logarithms and solving exponential equations using base 10 logarithms.

Unit 6 **Network Optimization** develops student understanding of vertex-edge graphs and ability to use these graphs to solve network optimization problems.

Topics include optimization, mathematical modeling, algorithmic problem solving, digraphs, trees, minimum spanning trees, distance matrices, Hamilton circuits and paths, the Traveling Salesperson Problem, critical paths, and the PERT technique.

Unit 7 **Trigonometric Methods** develops student understanding of trigonometric functions and the ability to use trigonometric methods to solve triangulation and indirect measurement problems.

Topics include sine, cosine, and tangent functions of measures of angles in standard position in a coordinate plane and in a right triangle; indirect measurement; analysis of variable-sided triangle mechanisms; Law of Sines and Law of Cosines.

Unit 8 **Probability Distributions** further develops student ability to understand and visualize situations involving chance by using simulation and mathematical analysis to construct probability distributions.

Topics include Multiplication Rule, independent and dependent events, conditional probability, probability distributions and their graphs, waiting-time (or geometric) distributions, expected value, and rare events.

Appendix continues on next page.

Core-Plus Mathematics 2nd Edition

Course 3 Units	
Unit 1	**Reasoning and Proof** develops student understanding of formal reasoning in geometric, algebraic, and statistical contexts and of basic principles that underlie those reasoning strategies. *Topics include* inductive and deductive reasoning strategies; principles of logical reasoning—Affirming the Hypothesis and Chaining Implications; relation among angles formed by two intersecting lines or by two parallel lines and a transversal; rules for transforming algebraic expressions and equations; design of experiments including the role of randomization, control groups, and blinding; sampling distribution, randomization test, and statistical significance.
Unit 2	**Inequalities and Linear Programming** develops student ability to reason both algebraically and graphically to solve inequalities in one and two variables, introduces systems of inequalities in two variables, and develops a strategy for optimizing a linear function in two variables within a system of linear constraints on those variables. *Topics include* inequalities in one and two variables, number line graphs, interval notation, systems of linear inequalities, and linear programming.
Unit 3	**Similarity and Congruence** extends student understanding of similarity and congruence and their ability to use those relations to solve problems and to prove geometric assertions with and without the use of coordinates. *Topics include* connections between Law of Cosines, Law of Sines, and sufficient conditions for similarity and congruence of triangles, centers of triangles, applications of similarity and congruence in real-world contexts, necessary and sufficient conditions for parallelograms, sufficient conditions for congruence of parallelograms, and midpoint connector theorems.
Unit 4	**Samples and Variation** extends student understanding of the measurement of variability, develops student ability to use the normal distribution as a model of variation, introduces students to the binomial distribution and its use in decision making, and introduces students to the probability and statistical inference involved in control charts used in industry for statistical process control. *Topics include* normal distribution, standardized scores, binomial distributions (shape, expected value, standard deviation), normal approximation to a binomial distribution, odds, statistical process control, control charts, and the Central Limit Theorem.
Unit 5	**Polynomial and Rational Functions** extends student ability to represent and draw inferences about polynomial and rational functions using symbolic expressions and manipulations. *Topics include* definition and properties of polynomials, operations on polynomials; completing the square, proof of the quadratic formula, solving quadratic equations (including complex number solutions), vertex form of quadratic functions; definition and properties of rational functions, operations on rational expressions.

Appendix continues on next page.

Unit 6 **Circles and Circular Functions** develops student understanding of relationships among special lines, segments, and angles in circles and the ability to use properties of circles to solve problems; develops student understanding of circular functions and the ability to use these functions to model periodic change; and extends student ability to reason deductively in geometric settings.

Topics include properties of chords, tangent lines, and central and inscribed angles of circles; linear and angular velocity; radian measure of angles; and circular functions as models of periodic change.

Unit 7 **Recursion and Iteration** extends student ability to represent, analyze, and solve problems in situations involving sequential and recursive change.

Topics include iteration and recursion as tools to model and analyze sequential change in real-world contexts, including compound interest and population growth; arithmetic, geometric, and other sequences; arithmetic and geometric series; finite differences; linear and nonlinear recurrence relations; and function iteration, including graphical iteration and fixed points.

Unit 8 **Inverse Functions** develops student understanding of inverses of functions with a focus on logarithmic functions and their use in modeling and analyzing problem situations and data patterns.

Topics include inverses of functions; logarithmic functions and their relation to exponential functions, properties of logarithms, equation solving with logarithms; and inverse trigonometric functions and their applications to solving trigonometric equations.

Core-Plus Mathematics 2nd Edition

Course 4 Units

Unit 1 **Families of Functions** extends student understanding of linear, exponential, quadratic, power, and trigonometric functions to model data patterns whose graphs are transformations of basic patterns; and develops understanding of operations on functions useful in representing and reasoning about quantitative relationships.

Topics include linear, exponential, quadratic, power, and trigonometric functions; data modeling; translation, reflection, and stretching of graphs; and addition, subtraction, multiplication, division, and composition of functions.

Unit 2 **Vectors and Motion** develops student understanding of two-dimensional vectors and their use in modeling linear, circular, and other nonlinear motion.

Topics include concept of vector as a mathematical object used to model situations defined by magnitude and direction; equality of vectors, scalar multiples, opposite vectors, sum and difference vectors, dot product of two vectors, position vectors and coordinates; and parametric equations for motion along a line and for motion of projectiles and objects in circular and elliptical orbits.

Unit 3 **Algebraic Functions and Equations** reviews and extends student understanding of properties of polynomial and rational functions and skills in manipulating algebraic expressions and solving polynomial and rational equations, and develops student understanding of complex number representations and operations.

Appendix continues on next page.

Topics include polynomials, polynomial division, factor and remainder theorems, operations on complex numbers, representation of complex numbers as vectors, solution of polynomial equations, rational function graphs and asymptotes, and solution of rational equations and equations involving radical expressions.

Unit 4 **Trigonometric Functions and Equations** extends student understanding of, and ability to reason with, trigonometric functions to prove or disprove trigonometric identities and to solve trigonometric equations; to geometrically represent complex numbers and complex number operations and to find powers and roots of complex numbers expressed in trigonometric form.

Topics include fundamental trigonometric identities, sum and difference identities, double-angle identities; solving trigonometric equations and expression of periodic solutions; secant, cosecant, and cotangent functions; absolute value and trigonometric form of complex numbers, De Moivre's Theorem, and roots of complex numbers.

Unit 5 **Exponential Functions, Logarithms, and Data Modeling** extends student understanding of exponential and logarithmic functions to the case of natural exponential and logarithmic functions, solution of exponential growth and decay problems, and use of logarithms for linearization and modeling of data patterns.

Topics include exponential functions with rules in the form $f(x) = Ae^{kx}$, natural logarithm function, linearizing bivariate data and fitting models using log and log-log transformations.

Unit 6 **Surfaces and Cross Sections** extends student ability to visualize and represent three-dimensional shapes using contours, cross sections, and reliefs, and to visualize and represent surfaces and conic sections defined by algebraic equations.

Topics include using contours to represent three-dimensional surfaces and developing contour maps from data; sketching surfaces from sets of cross sections; conics as planar sections of right circular cones and as loci of points in a plane; three-dimensional rectangular coordinate system; sketching surfaces using traces, intercepts and cross sections derived from algebraically-defined surfaces; and surfaces of revolution and cylindrical surfaces.

Unit 7 **Concepts of Calculus** develops student understanding of fundamental calculus ideas through explorations in a variety of applied problem contexts and their representations in function tables and graphs.

Topics include instantaneous rates of change, linear approximation, area under a curve, and applications to problems in physics, business, and other disciplines.

Unit 8 **Counting Methods and Induction** extends student ability to count systematically and solve enumeration problems, and develops understanding of, and ability to write, proofs by mathematical induction.

Topics include systematic listing and counting, counting trees, the Multiplication Principle of Counting, Addition Principle of Counting, combinations, permutations, selections with repetition; the binomial theorem, Pascal's triangle, combinatorial reasoning; the general multiplication rule for probability; and the Principle of Mathematical Induction.

REFERENCES

Anderson, G. L. (1991). Cognitive politics of principals and teachers: Ideological control in an elementary school. In J. Blase (Ed.), *The politics of life in schools: Power, conflict, and cooperation* (pp. 120–138). Newbury Park, CA: Sage.

Arbaugh, F., Lannin, J., Jones, D. L., & Park-Rogers, M. (2006). Examining instructional practices in Core-Plus lessons: Implication for professional development. *Journal of Mathematics Teacher Education, 9*, 517–550.

Armstrong, G. M., & Hendrix, L. J. (1999). Does traditional or reformed calculus prepare students better for subsequent courses? A preliminary study. *The Journal of Computers in Mathematics and Science Teaching, 18*(2), 95–103.

Balanced Assessment. (2007). *High school balanced packets*. Boston: The Concord Consortium. Retrieved June 22, 2009 from http://balancedassessment.concord.org/packeths1.html

Bay, J. M., Beem, J. K., Reys, R. E., Papick, I., & Barnes, D. E. (1999). Student reactions to standards-based mathematics curricula: The interplay between curriculum, teachers, and students [Electronic version]. *School Science and Mathematics, 99*(4), 182–188.

Baxter, J. L., Majumdar, D., & Smith, S. D. (1998). Subsequent-grades assessment of traditional reform calculus. *PRIMUS, 8*, 317–330.

Ben-Chaim, D., Fey, J. T., Fitzgerald, W. M., Benedetto, C., & Miller, J. (1998). Proportional reasoning among 7th grade students with different curricular experiences [Electronic version]. *Educational Studies in Mathematics, 36*(3), 247–273.

Bishop, A. J., & Forgasz, H. J. (2007). Issues in access and equity in mathematics education. In F. K. Lester (Ed.), *Second handbook of research on mathematics teaching and learning*, (pp. 1145–1167). Charlotte, NC: Information Age.

Boaler, J. (2002). *Experiencing school mathematics: Traditional and reform approaches to teaching and their impact on student learning* (revised and expanded ed.). Mahwah, NJ: Lawrence Erlbaum.

Boaler, J., & Staples, M. (2008). Creating mathematical futures through an equitable taching approach: The case of Railside School. *Teachers' College Record, 110*(3), 608–645.

Brown, A. L. (1992). Design experiments: Theoretical and methodological challenges in creating complex interventions in classroom settings. *Journal of the Learning Sciences, 2*(2), 141–178.

Burkhardt, H., & Schoenfeld, A. H. (2003). Improving educational research: Toward a more useful, more influential, and better-funded enterprise. *Educational Researcher, 32*(9), 3–14.

Cain, J. S. (2002). An evaluation of the Connected Mathematics project. *The Journal of Educational Research, 95*(4), 224–233.

Cobb, P. (1995). Where is the mind? Constructivist and sociocultural perspectives on mathematical development. *Educational Researcher, 23*(7), 13–20.

Collins, A. (1992). Toward a design science of education. In E. Scanlon & T. O'Shea (Eds.), *New directions in educational technology* (pp. 15–22). New York: Springer-Verlag.

Coxford, A. F., Fey, J. T., Hirsch, C. R., Schoen, H. L., Burrill, G., Hart, E. W., & Watkins, A. E. (with Messenger, M. J., & Ritsema, B.). (1998a). *Contemporary mathematics in context: A unified approach.* (Courses 1). Chicago: Everyday Learning Corporation.

Coxford, A. F., Fey, J. T., Hirsch, C. R., Schoen, H. L., Burrill, G., Hart, E. W., & Watkins, A. E. (with Messenger, M. J., & Ritsema, B.). (1998b). *Contemporary mathematics in context: A unified approach* (Course 2). Columbus, OH: Glencoe/ McGraw-Hill.

Coxford, A. F., Fey, J. T., Hirsch, C. R., Schoen, H. L., Burrill, G., Hart, E. W., & Watkins, A. E. (with Messenger, M. J., & Ritsema, B.). (1999). *Contemporary mathematics in context: A unified approach* (Course 3). Columbus, OH: Glencoe/ McGraw-Hill.

Coxford, A. F., Fey, J. T., Hirsch, C. R., Schoen, H. L., Hart, E. W., Keller, B. A., & Watkins, A. E. (with Ritsema, B., & Walker, R. K.). (2001). *Contemporary mathematics in context: A unified approach* (Course 4). Columbus, OH: Glencoe/ McGraw-Hill.

Cuoco, A., Goldenberg, E. P., & Mark, J. (1996). Habits of mind: An organizing principle for mathematics curricula. *Journal of Mathematical Behavior, 15,* 375–402.

CUPM Curriculum Guide 2004. (2004). Retrieved March 24, 2008, from www.maa.org/cupm/curr_guide.html

Darken, B., Wynegar, R., & Kuhn, S. (2000). Evaluating calculus reform: A review and a longitudinal study. In A. H. Schoenfeld, E. Dubinsky, & J. J. Kaput (Eds.), *Research in Collegiate Mathematics Education IV* (pp. 16–41). Providence, RI: American Mathematical Society.

Davidson, N., & Kroll, D. L. (1991). An overview of research on cooperative learning related to mathematics. *Journal for Research in Mathematics Education, 22,* 362–365.

Davis, J. D., & Shih, J. C. (2007). Secondary options and post-secondary expectations: Standards-based mathematics programs and student achievement on college mathematics placement exams. *School Science and Mathematics, 107*(8), 336–355.

Design-Based Research Collective. (2003). Design-based research: An emerging paradigm for educational inquiry. *Educational Researcher, 32*(1), 5–8.

Douglas, R. (1987). *Toward a lean and lively calculus*. Report of the Tulane Conference on Calculus. Washington, DC: Mathematical Association of America.

Feldt, L. S., Forsyth, R. A., Ansley, T. N., & Alnot, S. D. (1993). *Iowa Tests of Educational Development* (Forms K & L). Chicago: Riverside.

Fey, J., & Hirsch, C. (2007). The case of Core-Plus Mathematics. In C. Hirsch (Ed.), *Perspectives on the design and development of school mathematics curricula* (pp. 129–142). Reston, VA: National Council of Teachers of Mathematics.

Fey, J., Hart, E., Hirsch, E., Schoen, H., & Watkins, A. (2007). Editor's endnotes. *American Mathematical Monthly, 114*(7), 654–655.

Freudenthal, H. (1983). *Didactical phenomenology of mathematical structures*. Dordrecht, The Netherlands: D. Reidel.

Fullan, M. G. (1991). *The new meaning of educational change* (2nd ed.). New York: Teachers College Press.

Ganter, S. L. (2001). *Changing calculus: A report on evaluation efforts and national impact from 1988—1998*. Washington, DC: Mathematical Association of America.

Ganter, S. L., & Barker, W. (2002). A collective vision: Voices of the partner disciplines. In *Curriculum Reform and the First Two Years: The Curriculum Foundation Project*. Retrieved March 24, 2008, from www.maa.org/CUPM/crafty/cf_project.html

Gravemeijer, K. (1990). Context problems and realistic mathematics instruction. In K. Gravemeijer, M. van den Heuvel-Panhuizen, & L. Streefland (Eds.), *Context, free productions, tests, and geometry in realistic mathematics education* (pp. 10–32). Utrecht, The Netherlands: Vakgroep Onderzoek Wiskundeonderwijs en Onderwijscomputercentrum, Rijksuniversiteit.

Gravemeijer, K. (1994). Educational development and developmental research in mathematics education. *Journal for Research in Mathematics Education, 25*, 443–471.

Grouws, D. (Ed.). (1992). *Handbook of research on mathematics teaching and learning*. Indianapolis, IN: Macmillan.

Grouws, D., Howald, C., & Colangelo, N. (1996, April). *Student conceptions of mathematics: A comparison of mathematically talented students and typical high school algebra students*. Paper presented at the American Educational Research Association, New York.

Hargreaves, A. (1991). Contrived collegiality: The micropolitics of teacher collaboration. In J. Blase (Ed.), *The politics of life in schools: Power, conflict, and cooperation* (pp. 46–72). Newbury Park, CA: SAGE.

Hart, E., Hirsch, C. R., & Keller, S. A. (2007). Amplifying students' learning in mathematics using curriculum-embedded, Java-based software. In W. G. Martin & M. E. Strutchens (Eds.), *The learning of mathematics: Sixty-ninth yearbook of the National Council of Teachers of Mathematics* (pp. 175–202). Reston, VA: National Council of Teachers of Mathematics.

Harwell, M. R., Post, T. R., Maeda, Y., Davis, J. D., Cutler, A. L., Andersen, E., & Kahan, J. A. (2007). Standards-based mathematics curricula and secondary students' standardized achievement tests. *Journal for Research in Mathematics Education, 38*(1), 71–101.

Harwell, M. R., & Post, T. R. (2009, April). *High school mathematics curricula and college mathematics achievement and course taking.* Paper presented at the annual meeting of the National Council of Teachers of Mathematics, Washington, DC.

Hiebert, J., Carpenter, T. P., Fennema, E., Fuson, K., Human, P., Murray, H., Olivier, A., & Wearne, D. (1996). Problem solving as a basis for reform in curriculum and instruction: The case of mathematics. *Educational Research, 25*(4), 12–21.

Hill, R. O., & Parker, T. H. (2006, December). A study of Core-Plus students attending Michigan State University. *American Mathematical Monthly,* 109–123.

Hirsch, C. (Ed.). (2007). *Perspectives on the design and development of school mathematics curricula.* Reston, VA: National Council of Teachers of Mathematics.

Hirsch, C., Fey, J. T., Hart, E. W., Schoen, H. L., & Watkins, A. E. (with Ritsema, B. E., Walker, R. K., Keller, S., Marcus, R., Coxford, A. F., & Burrill, G.). (2008a). *Core-Plus Mathematics,* Course 1 (2nd ed.). Columbus, OH: Glencoe/McGraw-Hill.

Hirsch, C., Fey, J. T., Hart, E. W., Schoen, H. L., & Watkins, A. E. (with Ritsema, B. E., Walker, R. K., Keller, S., Marcus, R., Coxford, A. F., & Burrill, G.). (2008b). *Core-Plus Mathematics,* Course 2 (2nd ed.). Columbus, OH: Glencoe/McGraw-Hill.

Hirsch, C., Fey, J. T., Hart, E. W., Schoen, H. L., & Watkins, A. E. (with Ritsema, B. E., Walker, R. K., Keller, S., Marcus, R., Coxford, A. F., & Burrill, G.). (2009). *Core-Plus Mathematics,* Course 3 (2nd ed.). Columbus, OH: Glencoe/McGraw-Hill.

Hirsch, C., Fey, J. T., Hart, E. W., Schoen, H. L., & Watkins, A. E. (with Ritsema, B. E., Walker, R. K., Keller, S., Marcus, R., Coxford, A. F., & Burrill, G.). (2010). *Core-Plus Mathematics,* Course 4 (2nd ed.). Columbus, OH: Glencoe/McGraw-Hill.

Hirsch, C. R., & Coxford, A. F. (1997). Mathematics for all: Perspectives and promising practices. *School Science and Mathematics, 97*(5), 232–241.

Huntley, M. A., Rasmussen, C. L., Villarubi, R. S., Sangtong, J., & Fey, J. T. (2000). Effects of Standards-based mathematics education: A study of the Core-Plus Mathematics Project algebra and functions strand. *Journal for Research in Mathematics Education, 31*(3), 328–361.

Hurley, J. F., Koehn, U., & Ganter, S. L. (1999). Effects of calculus reform: Local and national. *American Mathematical Monthly, 106,* 800–811.

IEA TIMSS. (1998). *TIMSS released item set for the final year of secondary school: Mathematics and science literacy, advanced mathematics, physics.* Boston: Boston College.

Kahan, J. A. (1999). *Relationships among mathematical proof, high-school students, and a reform curriculum.* Unpublished doctoral dissertation, University of Maryland.

Kieran, C. (2007). Learning and teaching algebra at the middle school through college levels: Building meaning for symbols and their manipulation. In F. K. Lester (Ed.), *Second handbook of research on mathematics teaching and learning* (pp. 707–762). Charlotte, NC: Information Age.

Kulik, J. A., & Kulik, C.-L. (1982). Effects of ability grouping on secondary school students: A meta-analysis of evaluation findings. *American Educational Research Journal, 19*, 415–428.

Leder, G. C. (1992). Mathematics and gender: Changing perspectives. In D. A. Grouws (Ed.), *Handbook of research on mathematics teaching and learning* (pp. 597–622). New York: Macmillan.

Lenhart, A., Madden, M., & Hitlin, P. (2005). *Teens and technology: Youth are leading the transition to a fully wired and mobile nation.* Washington, DC: Pew Internet and American Life Project.

Lester, F. K. (Ed.). (2007). *Second handbook for research on mathematics teaching and learning*. Charlotte, NC: Information Age.

Lewis, G., Lazarovici, V., & Smith, J. (2001). *Meeting the demands of calculus and college life: The mathematics experiences of graduates of some reform-based high school programs*. Paper presented at the annual meeting of the American Educational Research Association, Seattle, WA.

Lloyd, G. M. (1999). Two teachers' conceptions of a reform-oriented curriculum: Implications for mathematics teacher development. *Journal of Mathematics Teacher Education, 2,* 227–252.

Lloyd, G. M. (2002). Mathematics teachers' beliefs and experiences with innovative curriculum materials: The role of curriculum in teacher development. In G. C. Leder, E. Pehkonen, & G. Torner (Eds.), *Beliefs: A hidden variable in mathematics education* (pp. 149–159). Dordrecht, The Netherlands: Kluwer.

Lloyd, G. M., & Wilson, M. S. (1998). Supporting innovation: The impact of a teacher's conceptions of functions on his implementation of a reform curriculum. *Journal for Research in Mathematics Education, 29*, 248–274.

Maurer, S. B., & McCallum, W. (2006). Advising a precollege curriculum project. *Notices of the AMS, 53*(9), 1018–1020.

McLeod, D. B. (1992). Research on affect in mathematics education: A reconceptualization. *Handbook for research on mathematics teaching and learning* (pp. 575–596). New York: Macmillan.

Nathan, M. J., & Koedinger, K. R. (2000a). An investigation of teachers' beliefs of students' algebra development. *Cognition and Instruction, 18*, 209–237.

Nathan, M. J., & Koedinger, K. R. (2000b). Teachers' and researchers' beliefs about the development of students' algebraic reasoning. *Journal for Research in Mathematics Education, 31*, 168–190.

National Council of Teachers of Mathematics. (1989). *Curriculum and evaluation standards for school mathematics*. Reston, VA: Author.

National Council of Teachers of Mathematics. (1991). *Professional standards for teaching mathematics*. Reston, VA: Author.

National Council of Teachers of Mathematics. (2000). *Principles and standards for school mathematics*. Reston, VA: Author.

National Research Council. (1989). *Everybody counts: A report to the nation on the future of mathematics education.* Washington, DC: National Academy Press.

National Research Council. (2004). *On evaluating curricular effectiveness: Judging the quality of K–12 mathematics evaluations.* Washington, DC: National Academies Press.

Nelson, R. (2006). *A matched study of Washington state 10th grade assessment scores of students in schools using the Core-Plus Mathematics program* [Electronic version]. Retrieved June 10, 2009, from http://www.wmich.edu/cpmp/districtreports.html

Oakes, J. (1990). Opportunities, achievement, and choice: Women and minority students in science and mathematics. In C. B. Cozden (Ed.), *Review of research in education* (Vol. 16; pp. 153–222). Washington, DC: American Educational Research Association.

Peressini, D. D. (1998). The portrayal of parents in the school mathematics reform literature: Locating the context for parental involvement. *Journal for Research in Mathematics Education, 29*(5), 555–582.

Philipp, R. A. (2007). Mathematics teachers' beliefs and affect. In F. K. Lester (Ed.), *Second handbook of research on mathematics teaching and learning* (pp. 257–315). Charlotte, NC: Information Age.

Post, T. R., Harwell, M. R., Davis, J. D., Maeda, Y., Cutler, A., Andersen, E., Kahan, J. A., & Norman, K. W. (2008). Standards-based mathematics curricula and middle-grades students' performance on standardized achievement tests. *Journal for Research in Mathematics Education, 39*, 184–212.

Price, G. (1997). Quantitative literacy across the curriculum. In L. A. Steen (Ed.), *Why numbers count* (pp. 155–160). New York: College Entrance Examination Board.

Remillard, J. T., Herbel-Eisenmann, B. A., & Lloyd, G. M. (Eds.). (2009). *Mathematics teachers at work: Connecting curriculum materials and classroom instruction.* New York: Routledge.

Reys, R., Reys, B., Lapan, R., Holliday, G., & Wasman, D. (2003). Assessing the impact of *Standards*-based middle grades mathematics curriculum material on student achievement. *Journal for Research in Mathematics Education, 34*, 74–95.

Riordan, J., & Noyce, P. (2001). The impact of two standards-based mathematics curricula on student achievement in Massachusetts. *Journal for Research in Mathematics Education, 32*(4), 368–398.

Romberg, T. A. (1992). Further thoughts on the standards: A reaction to Apple. *Journal for Research in Mathematics Education, 23*, 432–437.

Ross, J. A., McDougall, D., & Hogaboam-Gray, A. (2002). Research on reform in mathematics education, 1993–2000. *Alberta Journal of Educational Research, 48*, 122–138.

Schmidt, W. H., McKnight, C. C., Cogan, L. S., Jakwerth, P. M. , & Houang, R. T. (1999). *Facing the consequences: Using TIMSS for a closer look at U.S. mathematics and science education.* Dordrecht, The Netherlands: Kluwer.

Schoen, H. L., & Pritchett, J. (1998). *Students' perceptions and attitudes in a standards-based high school mathematics curriculum.* Paper presented at the annual meeting of the American Educational Research Association, San Diego, CA. (ERIC Document Reproduction No. ED 420 518)

Schoen, H. L., Cebulla, K. J., Finn, K. F., & Fi, C. (2003). Teacher variables that relate to student achievement when using a standards-based curriculum. *Journal for Research in Mathematics Education, 34*(3), 228–259.

Schoen, H. L., & Charles, R. I. (Eds). (2003). *Teaching mathematics through problem solving grades 6–12*. Reston, VA: National Council of Teachers of Mathematics.

Schoen, H. L., & Hirsch, C. R. (2003a). The Core-Plus Mathematics Project: Perspectives and student achievement. In S. L. Senk & D. R. Thompson (Eds.), *Standards-based school mathematics curricula: What are they? What do students learn?* (pp. 311–343). Mahwah, NJ: Lawrence Erlbaum.

Schoen, H. L., & Hirsch, C. R. (2003b, February). Responding to calls for change in high school mathematics: Implications for collegiate mathematics. *American Mathematical Monthly*, 109–123.

Schoenfeld, A. H. (2004). The math wars. *Educational Policy, 181*, 253–286.

Senk, S. L. (1983). *Proof-writing achievement and Van Hiele levels among secondary school geometry students*. Unpublished doctoral dissertation, University of Maryland.

Senk, S. L., & Thompson, D. R. (Eds.). (2003). *Standards-based school mathematics curricula: What are they? What do students learn?* Mahwah, NJ: Lawrence Erlbaum.

Skemp, R. R. (1987). *The psychology of learning mathematics*. Hillsdale, NJ: Lawrence Erlbaum.

Slavin, R. E. (1990). Achievement effects of ability grouping in secondary schools: A best-evidence synthesis. *Review of Educational Research, 60*(3) 471–499.

Slavin, R. E., Lake, C., & Groff, C. (2008). *Effective programs in middle and high school mathematics: A best evidence synthesis*. Baltimore, MD: Johns Hopkins University. Retrieved June 6, 2009, from http://www.bestevidence.org/

Smith, J. P. (1996). Efficacy and teaching mathematics by telling: A challenge for reform. *Journal for Research in Mathematics Education, 27*(4), 387–402.

Smith, J. P., & Star, J. R. (2007). Expanding the notion of Standards-based curricula. *Journal for Research in Mathematics Education, 38*(1), 3–34.

Steen, L. A. (Ed.). (1990). *On the shoulders of giants: New approaches to numeracy.* Washington, DC: National Academy Press.

Steen, L. A. (Ed.). (2001). *Mathematics and democracy: The case for quantitative literacy.* Washington, DC: The National Council on Education and the Disciplines.

Steen, L. A. (2007). Facing facts: Achieving balance in high school mathematics. *Mathematics Teacher, 100*, 86–95.

Stein, M. K., Remillard, J., & Smith, M. S. (2007). How curriculum influences student learning. In F. K. Lester (Ed.), *Second handbook of research on mathematics teaching and learning* (pp. 257–315). Charlotte, NC: Information Age.

Superfine, A. C. (2008). Planning for mathematics instruction: A model of experienced teachersí planning processes in the context of a reform mathematics curriculum. *The Mathematics Educator, 18*(2), 11–22.

Suurtamm, C., Lawson, A., & Koch, M. (2008). The challenge of maintaining the integrity of reform mathematics in large-scale assessment. *Studies in Educational Evaluation, 34*, 31–43.

Third International Mathematics and Science Study (TIMSS). (1997). TIMSS *mathematics and science items for the final year of secondary school*. Boston: TIMSS International Study Center.

Tall, D. (Ed.). (1991). *Advanced mathematical thinking.* Dordrecht, The Netherlands: Kluwer Academic.

U.S. Department of Education. National Center for Educational Statistics. (1998). *Pursuing excellence: A study of U.S. twelfth-grade mathematics and science achievement in international context*, NCES 98-049. Washington, DC: U.S. Government Printing Office.

Walker, R. (2006). Student voices and the transition from reform high school mathematics to college mathematics: Rethinking the courses below calculus. In N. B. Hastings (Ed.), A fresh start for collegiate mathematics (pp. 193–209). Washington, DC: The Mathematical Association of America.

Williams, S. (2007). The story's the thing. *Journal for Research in Mathematics Education, 38*(4), 342–343.

Printed and bound by CPI Group (UK) Ltd, Croydon, CR0 4YY
15/09/2026
14962373-0004